South Flows the Pearl

China and the West in the Modern World

William Christie, Series Editor

China and the West in the Modern World publishes original, peer-reviewed research on relations between China and the West from the accession of the Manchu Qing dynasty in 1644 to the present. The series brings into play different national and disciplinary perspectives to achieve a more thorough and cross-culturally nuanced understanding of the political, economic, and cultural background to the negotiations and realignments currently underway between China and Western nations.

The Poison of Polygamy
Wong Shee Ping, translated by Ely Finch

South Flows the Pearl: Chinese Australian Voices
Mavis Gock Yen, edited by Siaoman Yen and Richard Horsburgh

Tribute and Trade: China and Global Modernity, 1784–1935
Edited by William Christie, Angela Dunstan and Q.S. Tong

South Flows the Pearl

Chinese Australian Voices

Mavis Gock Yen

Edited by Siaoman Yen and Richard Horsburgh

SYDNEY UNIVERSITY PRESS

First published by Sydney University Press
© Mavis Yen, Siaoman Yen and Richard Horsburgh 2022
© Sydney University Press 2022

Reproduction and communication for other purposes
Except as permitted under the Act, no part of this edition may be reproduced, stored in a retrieval system, or communicated in any form or by any means without prior written permission. All requests for reproduction or communication should be made to Sydney University Press at the address below:

Sydney University Press
Fisher Library F03
University of Sydney NSW 2006
Australia
sup.info@sydney.edu.au
sydneyuniversitypress.com.au

This project is supported by the Heritage Council of NSW's Small Grants Program, administered by the Royal Australian Historical Society on behalf of the NSW Government.

 A catalogue record for this book is available from the National Library of Australia.

ISBN 9781743327241 paperback
ISBN 9781743327234 epub
ISBN 9781743328392 pdf

Cover image: Evelyn Yin Lo (nee Parkee) and her brother Cecil Parkee departing Sydney for Hong Kong, 1939 (Yin Lo family).
Backcover image: Peter Chung Fung, his wife Isa Ken You, and their children Charlie, Aubrey and Leslie, c. 1912. (Ken Chang)
Cover design by Diana Chamma

Contents

About the Author: Mavis Gock Yen   vii
Foreword   xiii

Introduction   1
Preface   19
Maps   29
A Note on the Text: Names, Places, Facts and Figures   37
1 'In a Nutshell'   39
2 Memories of Sydney's Chinatown   51
3 Third-Generation Migrant   67
4 A Childhood in North Queensland   77
5 Chung Shan County   87
6 Two Worlds   97
7 The Great Adventure   117
8 'There's No Gold'   135
9 The Ancestral Home   145
10 'Unite to Fight the Japanese'   165
11 The Fortune Teller   179
12 Return to Australia   193
13 Wartime   207
14 The Lineage   219
15 Postwar   229
16 Pioneers in Western Australia   243
17 Don and the Family   255

18	Gold Rush Heritage	273
19	'We Grew Up in the Bush'	297
20	From a Chinese Garden	313
21	The Northern Territory Story	333
22	'I Was the Lucky One'	343

Conclusion	355
Epilogue	357
Acknowledgements	359
Bibliography	361
Glossary	363
Index	381

About the Author: Mavis Gock Yen

Richard Horsburgh and Siaoman Yen (顏小曼)

Mavis Yen (1916–2008) would have loved to have held this book in her hands. From the time she commenced school, she loved reading and she loved books; in primary school, she would read her older brother's books as well as her own. Never a great fiction reader, she devoured history books, particularly those about China and its people. But she never had a chance to leaf through a book she had written herself. She published some newspaper articles and a few short stories in Australian compendiums of Australian women writers. Her most prominent work was the English translation of *Shanghai Princess* (上海的金枝玉葉), written by Chinese author Chen Danyan (陳丹燕), a biography of Mavis' distant Sydney-born relative Daisy Kwok (郭婉瑩). That book was published posthumously. So, holding this book would have meant a tremendous amount to her.

The inspiration for *South Flows the Pearl* came from one of the darkest times of Mavis' life. When Mao Zedong (毛澤東) unleashed the Cultural Revolution (文化大革命) on all sectors of Chinese society, she, along with other staff and students, were required to live on the campus of the Beijing Second Foreign Languages Institute (北京第二外國語學院), where she taught English to mature-aged students. Later, the entire institute was relocated to a small village in Henan (河南) province where it set up its May Seven Cadre School (五七幹校) and helped the local villagers with farm work. One ordeal endured by those targeted during the Cultural Revolution was the constant requirement to engage in self-criticism – to account for their lives, confess their class crimes, and aspire to reeducation.

Having been born in Australia, Mavis now for the first time began to critically analyse how people of Chinese heritage like herself were treated and discriminated against by the dominant Anglo-Saxon population. Balancing this was the treatment she endured during the Cultural Revolution as a suspected foreign counter-revolutionary, despite her belief that she had been conscientiously helping to build a new nation during the previous twenty years. Where did she fit in? How was it that she was considered a foreigner in both the countries she called home? Readers will recognise many variations on this theme in *South Flows the Pearl*.

Mavis Yen lived an adventurous life that could easily sit alongside the oral history stories she recorded for this book. As you will read in her brother Harry Gock Ming's stories, she was born Mavis Gock Ming in 1916 in Perth, Western Australia, to a successful immigrant Chinese shopkeeper, William Gock Ming, and Bendigo-born Australian woman Mabel Jenkins. When William and Mabel married in 1910, so-called mixed marriages were looked down upon by mainstream Australians, who generally supported the federal government's recently legislated White Australia policy.

From the ages of nine to nineteen, Mavis lived in China with her parents and three siblings; two of those years were spent in her father's ancestral village in the Pearl River Delta, before she finished high school in Shanghai. In the mid-1930s, she returned to Sydney and obtained a teaching certificate in physical education before moving to Hong Kong in 1939 to run a physical education school. Following the occupation of Hong Kong by the Japanese Army in December 1941, Mavis staged a remarkable escape in March 1942 when she and a group of others walked through Japanese lines into China then embarked on a 3,000 kilometre journey by river boat, truck and train all the way to the city of Chongqing (重慶), which was the allied wartime capital. There she worked for the British embassy for the duration of the war, looking after refugees from Hong Kong.

After the war, Mavis went to live in Shanghai and worked for the Chinese Industrial Cooperatives (中國工業合作協會) movement supporting the revival of Chinese manufacturing and industry. Following the declaration of the People's Republic of China, she moved to Beijing in 1950 and worked for the Xinhua News Agency (新華通訊社), first as a subeditor before teaching English to the agency's journalists. During this time, Mavis married and had a daughter. The Xinhua school evolved into the Beijing Second Foreign Languages Institute, where Mavis taught English to mature-aged students prior to the Cultural Revolution.

Mavis' hardships during the Cultural Revolution convinced her that she should return permanently to Australia and bring her daughter so she could complete her education, as high schools in Beijing had been closed for several years during that turbulent period. Both arrived and settled in Canberra in 1981. At the age of sixty-five, Mavis could have enjoyed a comfortable retirement but instead she enrolled at the Canberra College of Advanced Education (now the University of Canberra) where within five years she completed a Bachelor of Arts degree in Professional Writing followed by a Graduate Diploma in Applied Economics.

Reflecting on her Cultural Revolution experiences, Mavis drew a connection between her life in China and Australia and a growing interest during the 1980s in the importance of oral history. Now in her seventies, her desire to record the lived experience of Chinese Australians like herself, to look beyond the dry contents of archival documents and legislation, led her to record interviews with a diverse

About the Author: Mavis Gock Yen

Figure 0.1. Mavis Yen on her wedding day in Beijing, 1 May 1950. (Yen family)

range of Chinese Australian people from across Australia between 1987 and 1995. In all, approximately forty-five hours of invaluable Chinese Australian history was recorded on some forty-one cassette tapes. While there was a contemporaneous interest among academics and history researchers in oral history, Mavis was not active within that movement. She had no professional or academic support. This was a project she conceived and completed on her own. As she was from the same generation as her interviewees, and had similar life experiences, she was able to draw out information that may have eluded someone from outside the Chinese community or of a more academic bent. Some of her interviews were even recorded

Figure 0.2. Mavis Yen in Beijing, c. 1951. (Yen family)

over yum cha (飲茶) in Sydney's Chinatown with the clatter of plates and trolleys audible in the background.

Mavis haunted the National Library of Australia and the Australian National University Library in Canberra, as well as the State Library of New South Wales, with their vast collections of Australian, Chinese and Southeast Asian materials, to delve into the complex relationship between the two nations and its peoples stretching back over 150 years. She was not a professional historian and the scope of academic research on China–Australia relations at that time was not as wide or as deep as it is today, but Mavis had a keen intellect that allowed her to put each story into its historical context. Armed, at first, only with her manual typewriter,

About the Author: Mavis Gock Yen

Figure 0.3. Mavis Yen (left) and Evelyn Yin Lo. (Yin Lo family)

she meticulously transcribed her tapes in question-and-answer format, stopping and starting her tape recorder endlessly as she typed the verbatim conversation. She then took the interviewees' responses and edited them into first-person narratives. Again, a laborious task which took tremendous application. With the purchase of her first personal computer, she quickly mastered the new technology and polished and refined her manuscript over a number of years to create this unique work by the time she was in her early eighties.

Mavis was a humble person. She had returned to Australia with little money and lived on the age pension and in government housing. But she was generous with her time and what little money she had, and asked for nothing in return. When living in Canberra during the 1980s, many a recently arrived Chinese student was pointed in her direction for advice, a chat and some home-style Chinese food. She made friends and acquaintances easily, as evidenced by her overflowing address book.

Sadly, Mavis Yen passed away in 2008 before she could see her work in print, but her manuscript stands as both legacy and testament to a pioneering achievement by a remarkable woman who, though largely self-educated, had the foresight to see the lasting value in recording the soon-to-be-passed lives of everyday people from the Australian Chinese community. This was the generation who, like herself, had direct links, via parents and grandparents, to the first mass wave of Chinese immigration to Australia in the mid-1800s. They were hard-working people who suffered blatant state-endorsed discrimination but carried on regardless to create fulfilling lives for themselves, their children and grandchildren so they could take their rightful place in the fabric of today's multicultural Australian society.

Foreword

Kam Louie (雷金慶)

Former Dean of Arts, Hong Kong University

In recent years, books and articles about China and the Chinese diaspora have mushroomed. In Australia, interest in Australia–China relations and the Australian Chinese has gathered so much momentum that the media is saturated with reports about things Chinese, including the impact of Chinese international students, the political situation in Hong Kong and the fluctuations of trade with China. There are also numerous accounts about the Chinese diaspora from journalists, academics and Australian Chinese themselves. Novelists and other creative writers have also produced an abundance of work about Australian Chinese life. The growing knowledge about things Chinese is enabled, too, by the sheer number of ethnic Chinese in Australia. The 2016 census tallies some 1.2 million people in Australia as having Chinese ancestry, and the average Australian would most likely know a Chinese person as friend, neighbour, colleague or family member. Yet, while Chinese matters are a mundane phenomenon in Australia now, actual documentation of what the people thought or felt prior to and during the White Australia policy days is almost non-existent. Given this backdrop, a book subtitled 'Chinese Australian Voices' is timely and poignant.

The voices captured so touchingly and compellingly in this book by Mavis Yen are special. They belong to 'everyday people from the Australian Chinese community' in the days under the White Australia policy, when the Chinese population dropped from 30,000 at Federation to as low as 10,000 after the Second World War. The Chinese people presented here belong to a different category to those the average Australian would now encounter. Whereas ethnic Chinese are highly visible in the current Australian landscape, the Chinese presence then was confined mainly in vegetable market gardens, restaurants or Chinatowns in Sydney or Melbourne. The people recorded here do not see themselves as exceptional. Indeed, their refrain, when recalling their experiences in their amazing lives, is along the lines of Elizabeth Lee's remark: 'I just heard a little bit of this and a little bit of that. Myself, I'm just an ordinary person.' It is precisely this insistence on being ordinary in what were extraordinary circumstances that makes *South Flows the Pearl* a riveting read.

The book is a collection of twelve interview transcriptions of Australian Chinese speaking about themselves and their families and it is augmented with an informative introduction by Sophie Loy-Wilson and additional notes by the editors Siaoman Yen and Richard Horsburgh. Apart from Lee Sing and Leung Pui, the interviewees all spoke in English. While they had all spent most of their lives in Australia, they were not wordsmiths. Their language is neither ornate nor complex. They spoke simply, eagerly recalling as much as they could about conditions in Australia and China and how they and their families reacted to those conditions. The majority were very elderly by the time of the interviews in the 1980s or 1990s, and most have since passed away. They were happy to have their reminiscences documented so their descendants could know something of their lives and times.

And some of those times were tough. To cite Elizabeth Lee again: 'In the early days, a lot of Australian people ill-treated the Chinese people … When my father was young, he had a pigtail. The Australian boys in Darwin would tie their pigtails together, you know, they were so cruel. That's why the Chinese people hated Australians.' The shocking revelation of this statement is not so much that the 'Australians' were cruel or that the Chinese hated them. Rather, it is shocking because notwithstanding both she and her father were born in Australia, the term 'Australian' clearly was not one they applied to themselves. The same sentiment is expressed by many of the participants, even those whose father or mother were European or Indigenous. Sadly, 'Australian = White People' was taken for granted in the White Australia policy days.

The constant name-calling was something several of the interviewees hark back to, often with bitterness but also bemusement. As Hoy Lee recalls, 'We were all of course "Ching Chong Chinaman"… They called you things, but you sort of turned a deaf ear to them, to a certain extent. We got used to it, see'. Interestingly, the converse situation also occurred. Thus, in the case of Evelyn Yin Lo, who was born in Australia but who like many of her contemporaries was sent to Hong Kong as a child to learn Chinese, she would encounter people in the streets calling her a *gwai paw* (barbarian woman) because she dressed and behaved like a Westerner. Her response? 'I knew what they were saying, but I didn't care.' Having a white mother did not shield one from this constant taunting, as Harry Gock Ming remembers. He also learned to react in the same nonchalant way, 'It was very upsetting when I was young but later I got used to ignoring it.' This defence mechanism of consciously disregarding insults and hurtful remarks may have helped them to continue to live peaceably and productively in a hostile environment, but it came at a price. And the price was to wilfully block out mainstream white society, resulting in social and psychological isolation.

These early Chinese Australians were also highly mobile. Although they spent most of their lives in Australia many also lived for considerable periods in China. Similarly, Albert Lee On proudly declared that he 'grew up in the bush' and Doris

Fong Lim hailed from the Northern Territory, even though the majority circulated between Sydney's Chinatown and Chung Shan, Hong Kong and Shanghai. They tended to have some connection to the famed Wing On Company, the banana wholesalers in Haymarket (Chinatown) which evolved into the first modern department store in China, modelling itself after the Anthony Hordern store in Sydney. Leslie Chang for example points to his father as one of the first investors in the company. Moreover, they identified with their Chung Shan origins, and take pride in speaking 'the purest Chung Shan dialect.' Many also remembered places that served as their community centres. The Chinese Youth League for example featured prominently in their memories, with Evelyn Yin Lo unreservedly declaring she was the first female member and Peter Wong describing how and why he joined and later became president. While the interviewees might have moved between Shanghai and Sydney by way of Chung Shan, Hong Kong, Darwin, Perth and Melbourne, their social circles tended to converge.

There was no shortage of adventures. China was in great tumult for most of their lives and Australia too was undergoing dramatic transformations. The interviewees speak of wars, banditry, poverty and opulence in China; they also speak of the hardships of the previous generation in Australia, a land that was thought to yield untold riches, as reflected in the name New Gold Mountain. This was a myth, and money was only made through physical labour. 'There's no gold,' as Leung Pui's father insisted to a disbelieving family back in the village, 'it's all muscle power.' There is no question that the lives of these early Australian Chinese seemed as unreal to outsiders then as they are alien to people now. But they tell their life stories simply and straightforwardly, with no hyperboles and artifice. Mostly it was about family: who got sent back to China, who married whom, and, most significantly, what they ate when. There are numerous fond recollections of food from their childhood and festivals that they savoured. As Lee Sing says, 'the Chinese, no matter how hard they work, they must eat well.' Surviving racism and hardship was an achievement, but satisfying hunger was an everyday concern. As luck would have it, most were employed for some time in restaurants.

Though caught between Chinese and Australian cultures, the interviewees are quite comfortable in themselves. They speak with passion about their experiences in Australia and China, but they are not sentimental about life here and there, and they certainly do not play a victim role nor try to pull heartstrings. I can attest to their authenticity because as well as knowing some of the people involved, their stories resonate with my own, even though I am almost a generation behind them. I left my village in Chung Shan when I was a child and sojourned in Shekki and Hong Kong for a few years before joining my father in Sydney in 1959. He himself came as a young man to join his father, who spent most of his life here. I then lived in the Wing On warehouse in Haymarket for several years before moving to the suburbs. I was also an active committee member of the Chinese Youth League in the early 1970s. And, like so many of the interviewees, I moved between Australia and Hong Kong and China for education and work before retiring back in Sydney. Most importantly, like most Australian Chinese then and now, I cherish the opportunity to travel back and forth between Australia and China.

The desire among the Australian Chinese to be conversant in both countries will only continue to grow as the million odd Chinese in Australia seek to make sense of their place in this lucky country. Many enjoy the career and personal opportunities that having two world outlooks bring. And their linguistic and cultural capabilities afford them much advantage in dealing with the world. But as in earlier times, unpleasant behaviour such as racist name-calling is still noticeable at times of economic and social stress. The memories recorded in this book are a timely reminder that even during the xenophobic days of White Australia and political chaos in the anti-Japanese and civil wars in China, basic humanity prevailed. No matter how demanding a situation they find themselves in, people mostly just want good food, harmonious family life and safe social networks in which to live. Australia is now a country of migrants, and migrants tend to travel between their home and host countries, in the process enriching both materially and spiritually. Today, when it is comparatively easy to cross national and cultural boundaries, the voices in this book are acutely relevant and compelling.

Introduction
Sophie Loy-Wilson

The overseas Chinese diaspora has a familiar migration history. The expansion of the British Empire into Asia after 1815 provided the conditions for Chinese migrants who 'moved on the fringes of the great European migrations' to the USA, Canada, Hawai'i, Australia and New Zealand.[1] These migrations were both forced and voluntary: the Chinese came as indentured labourers and free settlers, gold miners and prospectors. By the twentieth century their descendants were subjected to a series of exclusion laws which worked to bar further Asian migration and deny existing communities their political and legal rights. In Australia this legislation became known as the White Australia Policy. As these global events and forces indicate, the exodus of Chinese migrants from their ancestral homelands and their occupation of the colonial frontier were shaped by both British settler colonialism and imperial contests for control in Asia.

Over two million Chinese left South China between 1842 and 1949 to migrate to the West.[2] This was a profound movement of people on par with European migration to the Americas in the same period. Some 40,000 Chinese migrants arrived in Australia, making them the most significant non-Indigenous ethnic group after Europeans. Few first-hand accounts remain to document their lives. This is because most Chinese migrants were workers, many were illiterate and few left writings behind.

The impact of these early migrants is still around us: in the farmland they cleared and cultivated, in the remnants of Chinese market gardens marking the old boundaries of towns and cities, in irrigation lines and river systems, in buildings and temples, graves and memorials. As Mavis Yen writes in her preface:

---

1 Walton Look Lai, 'Asian Diasporas and Tropical Migration in the Age of Empire: A Comparative Overview', *Journal of Chinese Overseas* 5 (2009), pp. 28, 32; Adam McKeown, *Melancholy Order: Asian Migration and the Globalization of Borders* (New York: Columbia University Press, 2011), pp. 1–19.
2 Adam McKeown, *Melancholy Order*, pp. 1–19.

They worked on stations, on the goldfields, in the tin mines. They cleared the land for cultivation. They served as the nation's market gardeners for more than a century. The names of their descendants who fell in two world wars are inscribed on rolls of honour.

But first-hand accounts telling their stories are rare. Wang Gungwu (王賡武), a preeminent scholar of the overseas Chinese, blamed the destruction of old Chinatowns and rapid urban development. Wang, who travelled the world in the 1980s and 1990s documenting the overseas Chinese past, felt that most of these personal documents – what he called 'expressive documents', capturing 'the wide range of human desires [of Chinese migrants]' – had been lost: 'How does one begin to understand the nature of these desires if they are not documented in any way?'[3]

Mavis Yen used oral history to capture her community in all its complexity. Recording more than forty hours of interviews between 1987 and 1995, she was among the first Chinese Australian historians to use such a method; she was a pioneer.[4] She wanted to 'account [for] the legacy left by 19th century Chinese pioneers [and] bring to life a segment of Australian history that is fast disappearing.' Today there are thousands of oral histories of migrants in Australian libraries, archives and museums, usually commissioned by government organisations or migrant groups.[5] But Mavis' collection is in a class of its own; this was no polite exercise, no simple history project, this was a call for justice. Mavis describes the collection in the following way:

> Told by descendants, it is about discrimination, ostracism, denial of cultural identity and denial of human rights. Mainly in their seventies and eighties when interviewed, they included Australian-born sons and daughters of Chinese parents, those of mixed Australian-Chinese origin, and the China-born sons of commuters who were not allowed by Australian law to bring their wives or families with them. Others, who spoke equally willingly and freely, decided not to perpetuate their still fresh memories in print. But they also contributed because they confirmed what the others said.

Mavis didn't live to see this book in print as she died in 2008. Her work had been consistently rejected by publishers for being too academic and therefore

---

3   Wang Gungwu, 'Mixing Memory and Desire: Tracking the Migrant Cycles', in Tan Chee-Beng, Colin Storey and Julia Zimmerman (eds), *Chinese Overseas: Migration, Research and Documentation* (Hong Kong: The Chinese University Press, 2007), pp. 3–20.
4   Morag Loh recorded interviews with Chinese Australian war veterans from 1976 to 1983. See Morag Loh, *Dinky-Di: The Contributions of Chinese Immigrants and Australians of Chinese Descent to Australia's Defence Forces and War Efforts, 1899–1988* (Canberra: Office of Multicultural Affairs, 1989).
5   'Introduction', Kate Darian-Smith and Paul Hamilton (eds), *Remembering Migration: Oral Histories and Heritage in Australia* (Cham, Switzerland: Palgrave Macmillan, 2020).

not commercially viable. Her daughter, Siaoman, has found rejection letters from publishers such as Allen & Unwin in her papers. We know that Mavis laboured over her manuscript, taking 'the taped reminiscences of many older Australians of Chinese descent, including her own brother Harry, and refining the stories and re-writing them many times, over many years.' As her son-in-law Richard explained in her eulogy, her preface to the work 'is very revealing of what motivated Mavis to embark on this work and what also perhaps motivated her to make some of the choices she made in her life.'[6] My aim in this introduction to her book is to honour Mavis' intent. I reflect on her legacy. This is a book that offers a new way to be Australian in this country, and it casts Chinese Australians as the protagonists in their own stories.

She knew the people

In 2020, at the height of the first wave of the Covid-19 pandemic in Sydney, Siaoman and Richard began listening to the oral history interviews Mavis conducted for this book over twenty-five years earlier. Working in the 1980s, Mavis had used cassette tapes and a tape recorder, sometimes recording over old radio broadcasts or law lectures taped by her son-in-law Richard. Reviving these recordings for new technological formats, Richard and Siaoman listened to Mavis' voice, travelling across time and space to hear her as she sat opposite her interview subjects, accompanied by the hiss and crackle of TV and radio sets left on in the background, the clattering of plates in yum cha restaurants, the hum of cars and planes, the shifting of bodies in seats and settees. Some were conducted in Cantonese, which Mavis had learned as a nine-year-old when her family travelled from Perth to live in China; she learned Cantonese from her stepmother in Shanghai after her mother died of smallpox in 1925. Having spent a year in her own family's Cantonese village, Chuk Sau Yuen (竹秀園), in China, Mavis was then exposed to the local dialects. The voice of frail ninety-five-year-old Lee Sing (李成) rose and fell on the tapes, speaking what Mavis called the 'purest Chung Shan (中山) dialect, only using English to drive a point home.' As he told her about life in Australia since his arrival in 1909 at the age of thirteen, he reflected, 'It's the language that's the obstacle. It doesn't flow. I can't communicate so well.'

Lee would die months after his interview, but he left much behind for us – Mavis made sure of that. In the tapes, and the written stories Mavis crafted from them, his voice joined that of a generation of Chinese Australians now passed on. *South Flows the Pearl* allows us to meet them once again and ponder the radical new version of Australian history they lay before us. This is what people do when

---

6   Eulogy for Mavis Gock Yen, in the possession of Siaoman Yen and Richard Horsburgh.

they agree to tell their story: they speak to the future and they impart a faith in its possibilities, in our ability to hear them. Whether or not we listen is up to us.

South Flows the Pearl is made up of twenty-two chapters charting the lives of twelve Chinese Australian families with diverse ties to regional and metropolitan Australia. Importantly, the book does not simply focus on the eastern states or Australia's big cities. Instead, through the lives of Mavis' subjects, regional Australian towns such as Babinda, Mossman and Camooweal in Queensland, Moree, Tamworth and Wellington in New South Wales, Bendigo in Victoria, and Broome in Western Australia are connected to port cities such as Sydney and Hong Kong and finally to the lush flood plains of the Pearl River Delta, where the city of Shekki (石岐) sat at the crossroads of regions such as Heung Shan (香山), with their villages dotting the landscape, fringed by lychee orchards. Words such as 'China' and 'Australia' become less important in these stories, as the ties between Australian towns and Chinese villages become clearer, ties that were built and maintained for over a hundred years, and across generations.

South Flows the Pearl represents a community whose desire to preserve something of their Chinese Australian lives had been consistently thwarted by hostile forces: European colonialism, Australian nationalism and the White Australia policy, the Chinese revolution, two world wars, communism, capitalism, the Cold War. But by far the biggest challenge was a more insidious one. Decades of White Australia, compounded by Cold War anxieties, meant that for many Australians, 'China was at best an exotic mystery and at worst a threatening source of communism, compounding a sense that Chinese immigrants and their descendants were outsiders.'[7]

This book is unique because it was researched and written by an insider, by someone who not only spoke the languages of her subjects but had lived her life, in a cultural sense, in parallel to them. She too had travelled between China and Australia, as a 'commuter' in her words. She too had suffered discrimination for her Chinese Australian roots, both in Australia and China. She too had lived through wars and revolutions.[8] She too had seen her family divided after 1949 as politics rendered travel between China and Australia all but impossible. Most importantly, she shared a sense of being absent from the national story, having also come of age at a time when Australian history writing ignored her family's deep roots in the country.

In the late 1990s when Mavis undertook her interviews this was changing, but the storytellers were largely still non-Chinese, still outsiders looking in, albeit more benevolent ones. In Darwin, Diana Giese was recording the lives of the Northern

---

7 Sophie Couchman and Kate Bagnall, 'Memory and Meaning in the Search for Chinese Australian Families' in Darian-Smith and Hamilton (eds), *Remembering Migration*, p. 335.
8 Sophie Loy-Wilson, 'Daisy Kwok's Shanghai: Life in China Before and After 1949', in K. Bagnall and J.T. Martínez (eds), *Locating Chinese Women: Historical Mobility between China and Australia* (Hong Kong: Hong Kong University Press, 2021), pp. 230–54.

Introduction

Territory Chinese[9] and in New South Wales the farmer turned historian Eric Rolls was compiling *Sojourners*, his chronicle of Chinese–Australian relations since early colonial times.[10] Melbourne-based historian Paul Macgregor recorded interviews as part of the *Postwar Chinese Australian Oral History Partnership* (1992-2002) and the *Australia–China Oral History Project* (1993-94).[11] And in Sydney Shirley Fitzgerald would later interview some of Mavis' own subjects, such as Evelyn Yin Lo (黎鑽好), for her book on Sydney's Chinese, *Red Tape, Golden Scissors*.[12] Across the seas in Hong Kong, Michael Williams was in the midst of formulating his 'village centred' approach to these histories, interviewing Cantonese communities about their family ties to Australia, finding that just as Chinese Australians had left their mark in Australia, so too in China: the Chinese names for Australian towns and cities etched onto community halls, honouring the names and locations of those who sent money home, and long-lost Australian relatives who had never returned, alive in the minds of those he talked to.[13]

But Mavis was one of the first historians, and the only Chinese Australian, to record *her own* community on *their own* terms.[14] She was one of them, and they spoke more openly with her, 'because she [knew] the people'. Each subject recognised themselves in Mavis and she in them. In one of her first interviews, recorded with Thelma and Leslie Chang in 1988 around their Sydney kitchen table, the cassette tapes captured the following exchange:

> *Mavis:* And the Hawai'ian Chinese have written a lot about them [Chinese immigrants]. Here, nothing much has been written. The Australian academics have studies, they have used all the documents, there is a man, a station owner, you know a retired man [Eric Rolls], he's been writing something and he goes to all the different places and interviews people. But the stories that you tell and Harry [Gock Ming] tells and so on, these are the real human-interest stories.

---

9   Diane Giese, 'All the Flavour of the Time Returns': Using Oral History to Record the Top End's Chinese Heritage', Occasional Paper No. 45, State Library of NSW, Darwin 1994; *Beyond Chinatown* (Canberra: National Library of Australia, 1995); Diana Giese, *Astronauts, Lost Souls and Dragons: Voices of Today's Chinese Australians in Conversation with Diane Giese* (Brisbane: University of Queensland Press, 1997).

10 Eric Rolls, *Sojourners: The Epic Story of China's Centuries-old Relationship with Australia* (Brisbane: University of Queensland Press, 1992).

11 Paul Macgregor, 'Crossing Between Cultures: The Australia–China Oral History Project', *National Library of Australia New* 5.1 (October 1994).

12 'Interview with Evelyn Yin-lo', Shirley Fitzgerald Papers, City of Sydney Council Archives (CoSA) 2014/441808 Box SFO444; Shirley Fitzgerald, *Red Tape, Golden Scissors: The Story of Sydney's Chinese* (Sydney: State Library of NSW Press, 1996).

13 Michael Williams, 'Chinese Australia: The View from the Village', *Locality* (Autumn 2003), pp. 17–22.

14 Morag Loh was completing oral histories with Chinese Australian war veterans around the same time as Mavis began her work. Morag Loh, *Dinky-Di: The Contributions of Chinese Immigrants and Australians of Chinese Descent to Australia's Defence Forces and War Efforts, 1899–1988* (Canberra: Office of Multicultural Affairs, 1989).

Thelma: Because you know the people.

Mavis: Well, you know the people and you know what it was really like. You know how difficult it is for white people to write about the Aborigines, because they can only write superficially.

Leslie: They can't penetrate and they won't get inside the information.[15]

Beyond White Australia

Mavis began her work after multiculturalism became government policy in the 1970s. Here was an acknowledgment at a political level that many Australians came from diverse cultural backgrounds and had a right to express these cultural differences. 'Multiculturalism' presented Australia as an ethnically diverse nation, ushering in a new inclusive era as the racially restrictive White Australia policy was wound back. This policy had been in place for over seventy years.[16] Much good came from funding linked to multicultural initiatives. In Canberra, Morag Loh was hired by the newly established Office of Multicultural Affairs to interview Chinese Australian war veterans. The introduction to her book, however, hinted that beneath the multicultural rhetoric, racism persisted, and was often directed at Chinese Australians:

> With continuing controversy about the scale of migration from Asia and the role of Australians of Asian descent in the country's economic, cultural and social life, the Office felt that it was perhaps timely to draw attention to the contributions of Australia's defence members of our country's largest group with Asian ancestry – Australians of Chinese descent.[17]

The marginal place of Chinese Australians in the Australian community was confirmed when academic Geoffrey Blainey argued in a public speech in 1984 that in effect multiculturalism encouraged the arrival of poor Asians to compete with unprepared poorer Australians in a contracting job market.[18]

This was not an easy time to force a reckoning with Australia's Chinese past. Working to document her community, Mavis' scholarship did not court controversy, nor did she insert herself into this ugly debate over Asian migration. But she did want justice: through her work she wanted Chinese Australians to reclaim a history that had been taken from them. Sophie Couchman and Kate Bagnall have written of families so intent on erasing their Chinese heritage that they vandalised photographs and destroyed records: 'in the face of racist sentiments

---

15   Private collection of Siaoman Yen and Richard Horsburgh.
16   Gwenda Tavan, *The Long, Slow Death of White Australia* (Melbourne: Scribe Publishing, 2005).
17   Loh, *Dinky-Di*.
18   Andrew Markus and M.C. Ricklefs (eds), *Surrender Australia? Essays in the Studies and Uses of History: Geoffrey Blainey and Asian Immigration* (Sydney: Allen & Unwin, 1985).

Introduction

and policies they changed their names, moved to places where their heritage was unknown, discarded family papers and invented stories to explain "foreign" colouring or to hide gaps in the family story.'[19] I think that Mavis wanted to repair the effects of this silence and loss. As she writes in her preface:

> Before the spread of multiculturalism many Australian-born Chinese knew little about China and its rich cultural heritage. Often the strongest association which remained with them was their food. The Euro-centricity of the Australian education system had deprived them of any glimpse into the cultural history of China and Asia. The whipped-up scares about yellow hordes threatening Australia had made them feel inferior and even ashamed.

But there were limitations on what this new multicultural history could offer Chinese Australians. The rise of 'ethnic studies' in the 1990s – such as Asian American history or Asian Australia history – recounted shared histories of oppression and victimisation promoting Asian inclusion in the civic life of the state, 'erecting a multicultural ethnic studies framework.'[20] But these histories often privileged the perspectives of white observers over Chinese Australian experience. They documented a surveillance archive of Chinese Australia: anti-Chinese immigration laws, labour laws, anti-Chinese cartoons, and print journalism. Focusing on racism and discrimination, they told the story of Asian oppression under white supremacy as part of a contemporary struggle to bolster Asian rights in Western democratic states. Historians learned much about White Australia, and less about the Chinese migrants forced to live within its constraints.

The ethnic-studies framework led to another problem as well. Using the word 'Chinese' at a time when many Australians had little China-literacy was misleading. For most Australians, 'China' was associated with the Han Chinese culture of the north, as opposed to the eclectic Cantonese culture of the south. It is hard to emphasise enough how different these two groups were. South China in the nineteenth century was more akin to Europe, with each province and district divided not only by geographic boundaries, such as the many tributaries of the massive Pearl River Delta, but also by dialect and ancestry. Mandarin Chinese was as foreign in these villages as French or German would be in an English village. Anglo-Australians were not expected to homogenise their Scottish, Irish or Welsh roots, but widespread ignorance in Australia about China led many to homogenise the complex backgrounds of Chinese Australians.

Each village in the Pearl River Delta has an origin story. These stories are about ancestors, migration, discovery, settlement. They honour the first arrivals in the area who left behind clan names and clan loyalties; the Gock clan, for example,

---

19 Sophie Couchman and Kate Bagnall, 'Memory and Meaning in the Search for Chinese Australian Families', in Darian-Smith and Hamilton (eds), *Remembering Migration*, p. 357.
20 Williams, 'Chinese Australia', pp. 17–22.

or the Ma clan. In Heung Shan, a pair of brothers and their descendants were divided into 'Blues' and 'Whites' depending on which family line they came from. Mavis' daughter, Siaoman, can still relate the importance of these 'Blue' and 'White' distinctions; her grandfather was a 'White'. As Harry told Mavis: 'One of these two brothers became known as the "Blue Sky" ancestor and his progeny the Blues. The other was styled "hundred years" ancestor and his descendants the Whites, because the character for white has the same pronunciation as that for hundred.' In Mavis' interviews, her subjects spoke of these distinctions because they mattered and because they knew she would understand. Leung Pui (梁社培) told her of his Leung clan ties, while Lee Sing explained, 'In our village of Hei Fung Waan (起鳳環), in Lung Du (隆都) district, the second district of Chung Shan county, we are all Lees.' Harry recalled that his father told him never to marry an 'outsider' to the Gock clan – ideally he would choose a 'white' not a 'blue' Gock descendant. Others spoke of Bendigo being populated by See Yup (四邑) or Four Counties people (the four counties of Sun Wooey 新會, En Ping 恩平, Hoy Ping 開平 and Toishan 台山) and that Tamworth was full of 'Tung Koon (東莞)' people. This ethnic complexity did not end once Cantonese migrants arrived in Australia. John Fong (鄺寶贊) was just one of a number of Mavis' interview subjects who spoke of Indigenous ancestry: 'Quite a few Chinese married Aboriginal or part Aboriginal women. I had a cousin who was married to a Chinese woman. They got divorced and then he married a part-Aboriginal woman whose first husband was a Japanese diver.' These are all stories which expose the inadequacy of an ethnic label such as 'Chinese'; how can such a label capture the differences between Cantonese peoples and the depth of their interconnection to Australian places and peoples?

Australian public memory-making around Chinese migration remains heavily weighted towards the gold rushes of the 1850s and tends to represent the Chinese in Australia as victims of white racial violence rather than as active historical subjects shaping their own lives in the colonies.[21] Such an approach allows for a distancing between 'then and now', a type of redemption narrative that paints multicultural Australia in a positive light in comparison to the brutal gold rush era of rampant anti-Chinese nationalism on the part of white Australian miners. The afterlife of Chinese migration to the Australian colonies in the twentieth century, those who stayed and made lives as settlers, can sometimes be forgotten.

So where are the Chinese in Australian history? In her 1995 interview with famed Stuart Town shopkeeper Hoy Lee (黃沛均), whose life is recounted in chapter eighteen of this book, Mavis expressed her own thoughts on this question.

---

21 Sophie Loy-Wilson, 'Peanuts and Publicists: "Letting Australian Friends Know the Chinese Side of the Story" in Interwar Sydney', *History Australia* 6.1 (2009), pp. 1–20. An important exception is Sophie Couchman, John Fitzgerald and Paul Macgregor (eds), *After the Rush: Regulation, Participation and Chinese Communities in Australia, 1860–1940*, special edition of *Otherland* 9 (December 2004).

Introduction

> *Mavis*: Some history of the gold mining areas has been documented by Australian history teachers and they've written fairly extensively about the Chinese. But whenever Australians write about Chinese it's always from the outside. They can't get inside. They aren't 'in', you see, they aren't Chinese. It happens to be they aren't Chinese, but if they lived with Chinese and mixed with them then they might get a better insight, but they can't get inside them.

South Flows the Pearl is a powerful reclamation of a way of being Australian on this land that is far richer, far more multifaceted than we had thought. It is an Australian story so far removed from any other Australian story I've encountered before because it shows how and why our varied Australian pasts cross, intersect, break apart and come back together. Chinese-Indigenous family ties are as common in this world as are Chinese-Irish grandmothers and, in the case of Frank Lee Gee (李植良), an Italian mother he never knew.[22] Family ties stretch across vast distances, from Broome to Perth to Sydney to Hong Kong, and deep into the Pearl River Delta. Sometimes these ties stretch and hold under pressure and at other times they snap.

What we learn is that words such as 'multiculturalism' cannot but scratch the surface of this story. In the hands of these storytellers we feel the soil in our hands, roasted pork on our lips, incense in our eyes:

> In the old days, when you wanted to ripen bananas you had to pack the incense with the bananas in a circular drum and cover the drum up well, so that the fumes from the burning incense would circulate. The bananas were ripened by the fumes.

In Tamworth at the turn of the century, hundreds of Chinese farmers gambled with tobacco crops that could disappear in a night if the frost came too early: 'All you'd see was tobacco, high, beautiful, waiting for harvesting.' On the Atherton tablelands the soil was black and rich. The Chinese had cleared the land, selling the good timber and burning the rest, 'The ashes made the soil very rich and they grew bananas, especially around Cairns. After the bananas were cut the suckers would come up, what they call the next generation.' All across Australia on special nights, pig ovens built into the ground (and often mistaken for termite mounds today) would glow and spark: 'When the pig got to a certain heat, they brought it up and used a fork to make the skin crackle.'

We are taken to the heart of a new Australian history of community. Hoy Lee worrying over his Australian customers in the 1930s, their nerves shot by war, their breath smelling of alcohol, buying tins of salmon off him to eat on the road as they searched for work or to resell to pay for their next drink. Frank Lee Gee's young foster mother, the daughter of the second wife of the famous Darwin and Cairns Chinese merchant Kwong Sue Duk (鄺仕德), running away from her new,

---

22 Frank's parentage remains unclear to this day. We are unsure if his father or mother was Italian.

much older Chinese husband, his foster father, and finally bringing Frank along after his distress became apparent: 'I was very attached to her.' Evelyn Yin Lo's husband, a quietly spoken Chinese sailor, arriving back in Sydney's Chinatown after years away, sitting down for a meal, and instinctively rising to put an apron on when he was told the restaurant was short on waiting staff. Peter Wong's (黃寶榮) shock upon arriving in Sydney from Macao at fourteen to work in his grandfather's market garden, only to see the old man, who seemed so strong in his letters home to the family, stooped and frail, bent double from years of carrying drums of water on a shoulder pole to water the garden. These were the stories that mattered to Mavis. In 1988, while she was interviewing John Wong, she explained why:

> *Mavis:* We know why the Chinese came to Australia, in the hope of bettering their lives and the lives of their families. How they came is one [thing], but who they are …? Several books have been written about how the Chinese came in the gold rush. Nothing has been written about Western Australia. I'm looking for human interest stories. I want to show the Chinese people as they really are. Most people are good, some are bad in extremes in limited cases. Because of the gold rush all kinds of people came – doctors, even scholars.

Between worlds

Mavis identified herself and her interviewees as Chinese Australians, but this is not the term the Australian state typically used for them. Over their lives they had been variously designated as aliens, Asiatics, illegals, naturalised Chinese. White Australians often fell back on the denigrating nineteenth-century terminology 'Chow' or 'John Chinaman'. In China they were known as *gum shan haak* (金山客) or gold mountain guests. Frank Lee Gee's foster father was called a *choy gee lo* (財主佬, rich fellow), in his village, but he wasn't all that *choy gee* (財主, wealthy). Back in Australia, their parents worried they would *bin gwei la* (變鬼啦, turn into barbarians), so many were sent back to China for an education.

Harry Gock Ming, Mavis' charismatic older brother, admitted that being born the first son had turned him into a *tai jee jay* (太子仔), a crown prince or wastrel son or grandson, 'who bludged on the labours of their gold mountain fathers'. Frank Lee Gee, the son of mixed Chinese and Italian parentage, was told that he was *loi lek bat ming* (來歷不明, of unknown provenance): 'That's what I told some Chinese in a Sydney barber shop when they asked me where I came from. I've got no idea where I come from.' Frank was one of many Eurasian children in this generation. Hoy Lee's shop served this population in Stuart Town: 'I would say the Eurasians were tolerated. We called them *sap jat dim* (十一點), "not quite 12 o'clock, not quite the full dozen".' Evelyn Yin Lo met a fellow Chinese Australian in Hong Kong in the 1930s, the son of an Aboriginal mother and a Chinese father: 'He was very dark for a Chinese and they called him *haak gwai jaai* (黑鬼仔, black barbarian boy). I don't know whether he minded. I always called him Wesley.' In Hong Kong, Evelyn herself was known as a *gwai paw* (鬼婆, barbarian woman).

Rules, rights and restrictions

The Chinese Australians documented in this book lived their lives in the shadow of various anti-Chinese immigration laws introduced by governments in the colonial era (1850–1901) and after federation, beginning in Victoria in 1855 with 'An Act to make provisions for certain immigrants'. These laws were complex, discriminatory and ever changing.[23] At various times they precluded Chinese migrants from bringing their wives to Australia, from travelling, from working in certain professions or at certain hours of the day, from owning land, and from voting in elections or accessing welfare.[24] White Australia was dismantled between 1966 and 1975. Historians have only begun to understand the social consequences of such a policy.

In her preface, Mavis paints a picture of life in this 'White Australia'. Her family was like many Chinese Australian families – mixed race, battling, ostracised – and encountering an Australian society that reserved its egalitarianism for whites only:

> From the goldfield days onwards, independent-minded Australian women who chose to marry Chinese were ostracised and their families turned against them. The children of mixed marriages as well as those of Chinese parents were taunted, bullied and insulted by their peers. Educated in Australian schools in the values of common decency and a fair go, they were made to feel ashamed of their origin. While some learned to fight back, most suffered in silence and resentment. Extreme cases suicided.

Life wasn't necessarily easier for Chinese wives left behind in the Pearl River Delta. While transnational ties were successfully maintained by many families despite White Australia, punitive anti-Chinese laws made return travel harder for husbands, fathers, brothers – and therefore less frequent.[25] Leung Pui's father was determined his daughter would never marry an overseas Chinese or gold mountain traveller: 'To do so, he said, was as good as to condemn her to the life of a widow.'

Many of the individuals interviewed in *South Flows the Pearl* refer to the so-called colonial era before federation in 1901, recalling family stories from the

---

23 Myra Willard, *History of the White Australia Policy to 1920* (Melbourne: University of Melbourne Press, 1923).
24 Kate Bagnall, 'Rewriting the History of Chinese Families in Nineteenth-Century Australia,' *Australian Historical Studies* 42.1 (March 2011), pp. 62–77.
25 For more on the phenomenon of the so-called 'left-behind wives', see Huifen Shen, *China's Left Behind Wives: Families of Migrants from Fujian to Southeast Asia, 1930–1950* (Honolulu: University of Hawai'i Press, 2012).

pre-federation decades. Colonial anti-Chinese immigration laws were in place before 1901 and these differed between each Australian colony. These laws were amended, repealed, and then re-introduced many times across different colonies before 1901. The application of these laws also differed between colonies. At their most basic, anti-Chinese immigration laws acted as a colour bar, blocking Asian migrants from entering Australia unless they paid steep taxes.[26] There were some exemptions. If Chinese migrants were born in Australia or Hong Kong (British territories), they were natural-born British subjects, and this status allowed some Chinese migrants a degree of stability and inclusion in colonial Australian society. Others were granted special certificates or letters of exemption. After the introduction of the White Australia policy, Chinese Australians travelled between 1901 and 1905 using Certificates of Domicile. After 1905 they used Certificates of Exemption from the Dictation Test. Naturalisation documents and birth certificates were vital and there is evidence of a black market in these documents, a practice common in America as well.[27]

Kate Bagnall has drawn attention to the importance of birth certificates in Chinese Australian families.[28] Frank Lee Gee's return to Australia from China in 1937 was dependent on his Australian birth certificate, although it didn't guarantee him re-entry into the country. His foster father, Lee Gee, returned before him, travelling on a CEDT (Certificate of Exemption from the Dictation Test). While Frank had been granted one of these in 1923, he had been out of Australia for fourteen years, so had to wait for new paperwork. The Australian government would occasionally grant requests to extend CEDTs for an added three years, but eventually these certificates expired. Frank's foster father left his wife behind:

> You couldn't bring your wife in those days, not like today. Not even Australian-born Chinese could marry a girl in Hong Kong or China and bring her over. You had to be in business to bring a wife out, and even then, only for six months. A worker or a gardener couldn't.

White Australia made sourcing labour for Chinese businesses challenging, leaving many vulnerable to foreclosure and placing a burden on business owners and their family members to do a large share of the work. Harry Gock Ming remembered the Chinese workers from his dad's shop very fondly, as if they were family. When they left, his father couldn't replace them: 'Now Dad had to take on men not from our district, with different customs and even speaking a different dialect.' Evelyn

---

26 Kate Bagnall, 'Anglo-Chinese and the Politics of Travel from New South Wales, 1898–1925', in Sophie Couchman and Kate Bagnall (eds), *Chinese Australians: Politics, Engagement and Resistance* (Leiden: Brill, 2015), pp. 203–38.
27 Beth Lew Williams, 'Paper Lives of Chinese Migrants and the History of the Undocumented', *Modern American History* (2021) pp. 1–22.
28 Kate Bagnall, 'Anglo-Chinese and the Politics of Travel from New South Wales, 1898–1925.'

Introduction

Yin Lo worked long hours in her parents' restaurants, toiling alongside them, partly because it was so difficult to get Chinese chefs:

> Dad didn't want me to work in the restaurant because it was hard work for a girl. He was trying to get another cook from China. So I said to him: 'Listen, Dad, you're not well and we need the money, so I'm going to help. It doesn't matter what you think.' As for Dad's friend, who was arranging for another cook to come, he kept saying: 'The papers are coming through.'

The promised workers from China never did turn up, a disastrous outcome for the family, who eventually lost their business.

Mavis remembered the Second World War as a turning point in Australian attitudes towards immigration. This was an era she knew well as it was recent history in the 1980s, and everyone she spoke to would have been affected by this postwar and Cold War era in some way. In her preface she writes that by 1947 'the controversial 1903 ban on Chinese wives and dependants entering Australia' was finally overturned, and 'the pressure for more liberalisation continued to lead to even greater reforms.' In 1957 the right of naturalisation was given to non-Europeans who had lived in Australia for fifteen years or more and in 1958 a new *Migration Act* replaced the 1901 *Immigration Restriction Act* and abolished the dictation test. In 1972 Australia recognised the People's Republic of China after an historic visit by Prime Minister Gough Whitlam, and by the late 1970s ' multiculturalism' was introduced as official government policy.

Mavis' view of these changes was qualified by a sense of loss. She writes of a generation cut off from their Chinese roots:

> Then suddenly at the end of 1972 Australia turned its old immigration policy on its head by recognising the People's Republic of China and introducing multiculturalism and non-discriminatory immigration. The Australian Chinese were ready for this. They had already contributed much to the land and its prosperity. They were part of it ... The early Chinese wanted their children in Australia to know the Chinese language and understand Chinese culture, and those who could afford to would send their sons and sometimes daughters to China for this purpose. Today many in their fifties, sixties and even seventies, do not speak Chinese and know little about China. They have lost all touch with their roots there.

Mavis wrote these words decades ago, but they remain true today in anxious and COVID-critical times. Chinese Australians still struggle to claim their heritage, still being asked to choose between Australia and China.[29] But the meaning of 'China' in these debates is not the southern Pearl River region featured in this book, but

---

29   David Brophy, *China Panic: Australia's Alternative to Paranoia and Pandering* (Melbourne: Black Inc., 2021).

a 'communist' China, synonymous for some Australians with military and cultural threat, with espionage and corruption. As before, Chinese Australians are being asked to prove they belong in Australia, even when many of their families arrived with the Australians of predominantly European heritage who now govern here.[30]

South flows the Pearl

From the air, the Pearl River Delta looks like melted silver thrown across the sea. Three rivers meet here, flowing south, swirling around islands of land, forming countless arteries of water, always prone to flooding. In 1557 the Ming dynasty (明朝, 1368–1664) allowed the Portuguese Empire a foothold here, in Macao, at the mouth of the delta. The English East India Company followed in 1637, and with them centuries of opium trade. And from the 1840s onwards, Cantonese migrants from the delta region left from here to join the gold rushes. In 1928 Mavis' brother, Harry Gock Ming, travelled through the delta, a journey he recounted vividly to Mavis in her interview with him. They passed islands, his family telling him that it was here, in the opium-running days, that ships loaded their cargo:

> As we crossed the sea from Hong Kong to the mouth of the Pearl River, the junk was propelled by a tug tied alongside it. But once we reached the delta the tug went forward and took the junk in tow because of the narrowness of the river. This was necessary to fit in with the tides. We came up the estuary of the river, then turned left and came around the Shekki River. Everywhere I saw green mountains with silvery water flowing down their sides. Heung Shan looked truly beautiful … After a twelve-hour trip, our junk tied up on the east bank of the Shekki River, almost opposite Dai Ma Loo (大馬路, Big Horse Street), in other words, Shekki's main street. We made a brief visit to the Wing On (永安) Bank in the main street, had a good dinner in a restaurant and spent the night in a hotel on the waterfront. The very next day, Dad had all our luggage and paraphernalia transferred to a paddle-wheel junk to take us to Chuk Sau Yuen (竹秀園).

This was a journey so familiar to most Chinese Australians of Harry Gock Ming's generation that I suspect that in their memories of these trips they could feel the lurch of the boat as it came into dock, smell the lychees ripening in the trees. They would know that once they completed the long journey – Hong Kong to Shekki to the village – gifts would be distributed to relatives. Leung Pui remembered one such return from his childhood:

---

30 Natasha Kassam and Jennifer Hsu, *Being Chinese in Australia: Public Opinion in Chinese Communities*, Lowy Institute Report, 2021.

Introduction

> That evening, all the neighbours and everybody else around gathered in our house. *Gum Shan Haak* (金山客), travellers from the golden mountain, always brought one or two crates of things we didn't have in the village. There would be golden mountain biscuits, golden mountain, or Sydney soap. We didn't have soap in those days. We used berries from the tea trees. Dad used to bring other things like clothing, woollen material, woollen singlets. We were all very excited. We wanted to see what was in the boxes. There was bound to be something tasty and most probably we'd be given presents.

Mavis knew these stories were part of a larger global tapestry, with threads reaching out from the Pearl River Delta to California, British Columbia, New York, Otago, Hawai'i and all over Australia. She records her interpretation of this Pearl River Delta migration story in her preface:

> The participation of Chinese in the gold rushes to both California and Australia shared a similar history. During the mid-nineteenth century, China was plagued with official corruption, overpopulation, floods, famine and drought, civil war and uprisings … So when news of gold discoveries in California in 1848 arrived, emigration was welcomed by the See Yup people as a way out of their plight. But ancestor worship is the dominant feature of traditional Chinese religion. To avoid being regarded as unfilial for deserting the graves of their ancestors and leaving their spirits without sacrificial offerings, the See Yup miners decided to go but with the intention of returning to China. They would become sojourners, make enough money to improve the life of their families and then return home for good.

Departures

In July 2020 I joined Richard and Siaoman at Rookwood Cemetery in Sydney to look for graves. Rookwood is so large that it is called Sydney's 'sleeping city'. We are like tiny ants moving through a million graves. Frank Lee Gee is buried here, as is Hoy Lee, and Evelyn and Don Yin Lo (羅順忠). Lee Sing is here as well, and Leung Pui. Richard navigates for us using the digital grave finder provided on the Rookwood website: 'Plot 218, Plot 219'.

We are in the 'new' Chinese section. The new section is tightly packed and orderly. Family surnames such as 'Lee' or 'Choy' are etched in gold, on large, gleaming red marble head stones. The old section is sandstone only, and erosion hasn't left much behind. Only a few sandstone gravestones bearing Chinese characters are still legible, and long stretches of open grass indicate that other graves have simply crumbled into the ground or were never marked to begin with; many graves never bore headstones. One sandstone structure has survived, though: the towering Quong Sing Ting monument, built in 1877 by the Quong Sing Ting society. It is used during Chinese ancestral festivals such as Ching Ming (清明),

when descendants arrive to sweep the graves of the dead, to remember them, and to bring respect. The monument plays another role as well. It bears the names of the many migrants whose bones were returned to China. Before 1950 Chinese migrants paid to have their bodies exhumed and re-buried in their local village with their parents, guaranteeing a resting place for their souls. This was in accordance with community beliefs and practices.

Cemetery days were pork days. A whole pig was slow-roasted and the meat divided between families who would travel to Rookwood or other cemeteries to place the meat on the graves of their ancestors, before eating it themselves. In Bendigo, Thelma Chang's grandfather, Louey Fong Goon, and his Irish wife, 'supplied all the pork when the Chinese went to the cemetery … Grandfather supplied the pork to quite a few outlying places around Bendigo too. He and grandmother would arrange for people to do the slaughtering.' Hoy Lee would have attended Ching Ming at the cemetery near Stuart Town, and the Parkee family in Tamworth, against the backdrop of tobacco plantations. Archaeologists have found Chinese pig ovens all over Australia, dug into the ground, reinforced with brick.[31] In Wellington, New South Wales, close to Stuart Town, a pig oven sits on the land of Tim Sing Lee in an old market garden, heaped with scrap metal. I got to see it in person in 2019 when Tim pointed it out to us.[32]

At Rookwood we find the grave of Lee Sing. It is well maintained, with photos of the deceased, information in Chinese. Family names and village locations transport us back to the Pearl River Delta. Lee, of course, came from the delta region, from a village in Lung Du, a district of Chung Shan. He died in 1989, the year a whole new generation of Chinese migrants – the Tiananmen generation – would depart China for Australia. There are three photographs on his headstone. Lee's photo has been placed beside his two wives. His second wife, Lam Tim Yuk (林添玉), who died in 1996, and his first wife, Siu Gim Hee (蕭金喜), who died in 1930. Richard, Siaoman and I are touched. Siu Him Hee died in the village, the year after the Wall Street crash, and a year before the Japanese invasion of Manchuria, far from Rookwood, far from Australia. She died so young, so long ago, but presumably on Lee Sing's instructions his family included her photograph on the headstone, despite the absence of her body. Mavis, of course, recorded Lee's story – so we have far more than this headstone. We have his voice to guide us:

> It took me seven years to save up enough money to go home the first time. After that, I went back every few years, whenever I had enough money. The first time I went back to get married. My first wife, Siu Gim Hee, and I had three children. Unfortunately, she died when she was only thirty-two. I remarried, a girl named

---

31 Gordon Grimwade, 'Crispy Roast Pork: Using Chinese Australasian Pig Ovens', *Australian Historical Archaeology* 26 (2008), pp. 21–28.
32 Juanita Kwok, 'Wonderful Wellington: The Longevity of the Chinese Community in Wellington NSW', *Chinese Southern Diaspora Studies* 8 (2019), pp. 1–25.

Introduction

Lam Tim Yuk in the next village, and we had another three children. The present Mrs Lee is my second wife.

Mavis is not buried at Rookwood. She rests with her brother Harry and her two sisters, Edna and Sheila, in the Northern Suburbs Crematorium on Sydney's North Shore. At the end of her preface to this book, she wrote the following words. They are hopeful. They are proud. They stake a claim for Chinese Australians in this country's history:

> The history of the Chinese in Australia is almost as long as Australia's colonial history. Their descendants can now look back with pride at the contribution made by their forefathers, which today is finally being made known.

Preface

Mavis Gock Yen (郭美華)

This preface was written by Mavis Yen between 1995 and 2000.

This account of the legacy left by nineteenth-century Chinese pioneers brings to life a segment of Australian history that is fast disappearing. Told by descendants, it is about discrimination, ostracism, denial of cultural identity and denial of human rights. Mainly in their seventies and eighties when interviewed, they included Australian-born sons and daughters of Chinese parents, those of mixed Australian-Chinese origin, and the China-born sons of commuters who were not allowed by Australian law to bring their wives or families with them. Others, who spoke equally willingly and freely, decided not to perpetuate their still fresh memories in print. But they also contributed because they confirmed what the others said.

During the colonial days the Chinese were actively recruited and sought after for what Europeans viewed as their hard-working ethic and docile attitude. They worked on stations, on the goldfields, in the tin mines. They cleared the land for cultivation. They served as the nation's market gardeners for more than a century. The names of their descendants who fell in two world wars are inscribed on rolls of honour. Why did the early Chinese come to Australia? What motivated them? In order to understand the early Chinese presence, it is necessary to know a little about Chinese history.

The Portuguese were the first Europeans to set up trading relations by sea with China, arriving early in the 16th century. In 1557 they were allowed by the Ming dynasty (明朝, 1368–1664) to settle in Macao at the mouth of the Pearl River Delta. The earliest English ships did not reach Canton (廣州) until 1637 but by 1715 the English East India Company had the monopoly over the eastern trade. Officially all trade was then confined to the port of Canton. During the 1770s however, opium was grown in India under the auspices of the English East India Company for export to China. This was done in order to balance the silver required to pay for the tea and silk purchased. More than half the cargoes carried by English ships consisted of opium grown for this purpose. While the sale and smoking of opium was prohibited in China, a great deal of opium smuggling was being carried on.

When China tried to suppress the smuggling, the First Opium War (1840–42) broke out. China lost the war and had to cede Hong Kong to Britain as well as open five other treaty ports to Western trade. After China lost the Second Opium War (1856–60) the legalisation of overseas emigration was enforced as well as the importation of opium. Eleven more treaty ports were opened. Kowloon (九龍) peninsula was added to Hong Kong and China's customs were placed under foreign control.

The movement of Chinese migrant labour into Southeast Asia pre-dated the establishment of the first European colony on Chinese soil by many centuries. This continued following the arrival of the European powers but intensified in the nineteenth century for many complex reasons. The abolition of the African slave trade to the American colonies and, in the case of Australia, the winding back of the convict transportation system, saw an increase in the Chinese indentured labour trade in the nineteenth century, otherwise known as the 'coolie'[1] trade. Western merchants, mainly English sea captains, in collusion with Chinese merchants, initially settled on the new treaty port of Amoy (廈門) as their base because the local officials there were obliging and Amoy had a centuries' old junk trade with Southeast Asia which was still continuing illegally. Singapore was later made the point of trans-shipment for Southeast Asia and Australia. Thus, all the early indentured labourers in Australia prior to the gold rushes came from Amoy or Singapore. However, from 1851 onwards the indentured labourers and gold miners overwhelmingly came from the Pearl River Delta and spoke Cantonese.

The participation of Chinese in the gold rushes to both California and Australia shared a similar history. During the mid-19th century, China was plagued with official corruption, overpopulation, floods, famine and drought, civil war and uprisings which gave further impetus for the movement away of villagers from the delta region. Twenty million lost their lives in the Taiping rebellion (太平天國)[2] which broke out in 1850 and lasted till 1864. In 1854 the fourteen-year Hakka War

---

1   The word 'coolie' was first used in the sixteenth century to refer to Indian indentured labourers and derives from the Hindustani word 'quli' and also appeared in the Tamil language as 'kuli'. It gained greater currency in the nineteenth century when the systemic Asian migrant labour trade increased.
2   The Taiping rebellion or civil war was a conflict waged by a theocratic movement known as the Taiping Heavenly Kingdom against the Qing dynasty beginning in Guangxi province and reaching as far north as the outskirts of Shanghai before it was finally put down. Led by Hong Xiuquan, a Hakka from Guangdong, the movement was a messianic mixture of Christianity and traditional Chinese beliefs and was religious, nationalist and political in nature.

(土客械鬥)³ exploded in See Yup (四邑, Four Counties)⁴ in the western part of the Pearl River Delta, as tension escalated between the local and Hakka (客家) people.

The Hakka were a distinct branch of the Han Chinese people who progressively moved over many centuries from northern China to the southern provinces including Kwangtung (廣東). They are the only Han branch not associated with a particular geographical region. They spoke their own dialect and retained their own customs. The earliest movement south can be dated to the 4th century (307–313). The name Hakka was a later attribution given to them during the Ching dynasty because they were not native to the southern parts of China and so they were dubbed *hak ka* (客家), or guest people.

The main battleground during the Hakka War was in Toishan county which was devastated. So when news of gold discoveries in California in 1848 arrived, emigration was welcomed by the See Yup people as a way out of their plight. But ancestor worship is the dominant feature of traditional Chinese religion. To avoid being regarded as unfilial for deserting the graves of their ancestors and leaving their spirits without sacrificial offerings, the See Yup miners decided to go but with the intention of returning to China. They would become sojourners, make enough money to improve the life of their families left behind and then return home for good. Over time, some who could save enough money would visit their homes in China every few or more years and return, the so-called commuter system.

The majority of Chinese who joined the rush to California where gold was discovered in 1848, were from See Yup, half of them from Toishan county. By the time gold was found in New South Wales and Victoria in 1851, gold supplies in California were diminishing and Hong Kong emigration agents directed the miners to Victoria. As in California, the largest number of Chinese arrivals in Victoria also came from See Yup, with half also estimated to be from Toishan.

The gold miners from the Pearl River Delta came to Australia under the credit ticket system nominally as free emigrants, with relatives, clan businesses or agents advancing their passage money. In fact, they came under invisible agreements, usually with clan businesses, to work and live under strict conditions imposed on them until the debt had been repaid. Like the indentured labourers, they came under the supervision of overseers or headmen. They mainly embarked from Hong Kong and some from Macao. Very few of the early Chinese came to Australia independently.

The entire process was highly organised. Hong Kong immigration agents set up branches at the main ports of arrival to cater to the needs of the indentured labourers and gold diggers. Sydney's first Chinatown was located at The Rocks shipping area where the 'pigs'⁵ landed. Successful Chinese migrants, usually the

---

3   The Hakka War resulted from the simmering tensions, more so over land, between the Hakka and local people in southern provinces. It is estimated that more than one million people died in the conflict, with Hakka losses more extensive, and thousands of villages destroyed or sacked. There was fierce fighting in particular in the See Yup counties of the Pearl River Delta region.
4   The four counties are Toishan (台山), Sun Wooey (新會), En Ping (恩平) and Hoy Ping (開平).

businessmen who came as headmen with the indentured labourers, were quick to establish their own similar import-export businesses or *gum shan jong* (金山莊, golden mountain shops). Their businesses were the first to engage in Australia–China trade.

The early Chinese arrivals came from villages with only one or two surnames. As much as half a village's rice fields were owned by the local clan. The clans also ran businesses. Law and order were maintained by the village elders, who came from the better-off families. It was a paternalistic clan-tied relationship that stressed loyalty to the family and clan over all other obligations.

As they were recruited by clan-related businesses, the early Chinese arrivals depended on their clans for support. They set up societies based on places of origin to care for their fellow clansmen. These societies played a leading role among the Chinese immigrants in the 19th century. Usually the district societies were housed in the premises of a clan business which served as a meeting place. Over time they established an all-embracing social system for their members. They provided accommodation, arranged jobs, were de facto banks and post offices, arranged for savings to be remitted to families in China, provided scribe services for the illiterate and managed the shipment of bones of the deceased to their home villages for re-burial.

The early arrivals also set up temples or joss houses wherever there were major concentrations of Chinese settlers. The See Yup Society (四邑會館) was established in Melbourne in 1854 to take care of immigrants from the four counties of Toishan, Sun Wooey, En Ping and Hoy Ping. The Kong Chew Society (岡山同鄉會) for immigrants from Sun Wooey county was set up even earlier. The See Yup Temple (四邑關帝廟) in Melbourne was built in 1856 and the Chinese temple in Bendigo in the 1860s.

By contrast with Melbourne, sixteen different district societies were established in Sydney by 1891, representing a far wider mix of county origins. The largest numbers of these later Chinese arrivals in New South Wales are believed to have come from Tung Koon (東莞) and Heung Shan (香山) counties. The Goon Yee Tong (公義堂) was set up in 1875 by Tung Koon immigrants and the Heung Shan Society (香山同鄉會), the forerunner of today's Chung Shan Society (中山同鄉會), by about 1880. There are two Chinese temples still functioning in Sydney today. The See Yup Temple (四邑關聖帝廟) in the inner-city area of Glebe, once noted for its market gardens, was set up in 1898 by See Yup immigrants. The second is the Hong Shing Temple (洪聖宮) in the suburb of Waterloo, once another area of Chinese concentration, particularly market gardens and furniture workshops. This

---

5   This epithet is a reference to the inhumane living conditions under which Chinese coolies in the nineteenth century and earlier were forced to live and work.

smaller temple was set up by settlers from Kou Yiu (高要) and Kou Ming (高明) counties in 1904. But Chinese temples are open to all.

When gold was discovered in New South Wales and Victoria in 1851, historians estimate that no less than 3,000 Chinese indentured agricultural labourers were already working in eastern Australia. They were the first Chinese to reach the goldfields. But while the colonial governments and squatters welcomed the Chinese arrivals, the European miners did not. The first Victorian census in 1854 counted only 2,341 Chinese, but by mid-1855 the number reached 17,000. Agitation and riots followed on the goldfields and in 1855 Victoria passed legislation restricting one Chinese arrival to every ten tons of shipping, as well as a poll tax of ten pounds. To avoid this regulation ship captains landed their Chinese passengers in nearby South Australia and left them to walk to the Victorian diggings. The most serious riot in Victoria took place in 1857 when between 1,000 and 3,000 Chinese miners at Buckland River were driven from their camps to the bush. Several died. Although South Australia passed similar restrictive legislation in 1857, the arrival of Chinese miners continued in New South Wales where Chinese labour was still wanted and there were no restrictions. Some walked to the Victorian goldfields from there. There were at least 42,000 Chinese in Victoria by 1859, according to the 1891 Victoria Census Report estimates.

As more gold was found in New South Wales, census figures revealed a jump in that colony's Chinese population from 1,806 in 1856 to just under 13,000 in 1861. These included many who had crossed the border from Victoria as well as new arrivals heading for Victoria. In 1861 a brutal riot took place at Lambing Flat when a mining population of 3,000 razed the Chinese camps, cutting off the queues of the Chinese diggers. Only then did New South Wales pass an Act similar to the Victorian one of 1855.

As a result, the numbers of Chinese arrivals fell heavily. Consequently, the legislative restrictions were repealed, by South Australia in 1861, by Victoria in 1865 and finally by New South Wales in 1867. Until 1877, no further restrictions were imposed on Chinese arrivals.

Although gold was discovered along the Palmer River inland from Cooktown in 1873, by 1877 Queensland was still officially exploring the possibility of recruiting more Chinese when the colony's Chinese population suddenly reached an estimated 17,000. Queensland quickly passed its first restrictive Act in 1877, similar to the one already withdrawn in New South Wales, and urged the other colonies to do the same. Furthermore, Queensland excluded Chinese from any new goldfields found by Europeans for three years. Thousands of Chinese were then building the Darwin-Pine Creek railway in the neighbouring Northern Territory and Queensland actively sought to stem an overflow of Chinese across the border. No restrictions were raised against Chinese arrivals in the Northern Territory before 1888.

The Palmer River gold rush marked a turning point in the attitude towards Chinese migration. Until then Queensland, Western Australia, the Northern

Territory and Tasmania had refrained from imposing any restrictions. But now the Chinese were no longer welcome and stricter entry rules were introduced. In 1886 Western Australia passed its first immigration restriction legislation, following the discovery of gold in the Kimberley, but exempted indentured labourers brought in by Australian station owners and pearlers. An overall consensus was finally reached by the colonies in 1888 to end Chinese migration, with the introduction of the highest tonnage limit of 500 tons by Victoria, Western Australia, Queensland, South Australia and the Northern Territory. New South Wales had already raised its tonnage limit to 300 tons and made no further change. Tasmania also made no change to its introduction in 1887 of a limit of 100 tons for every Chinese arrival.

But even before the gold rushes ended during the 1880s, the Chinese had started leaving the goldfields. The successful older ones were returning to China while others sought new outlets. Shifting to the country towns, those remaining found employment as ring barkers, land clearers, scrub-cutters, shearers and tobacco growers. They became storekeepers, hawkers, cooks and servants. Gradually their major occupation became market gardening and Chinese vendors of vegetables were a familiar sight in country towns. Increasing numbers of those with carpentry skills joined the furniture making trade in the capital cities.

In contrast to the movement of Chinese to country towns and the capital cities in Victoria and New South Wales, in north Queensland the Chinese retreating from the Palmer River goldfields achieved spectacular results in agriculture in the new coastal settlements. At one time they were the main growers of sugar cane and produced the first sugar in Cairns. When the sugar industry declined in a depression, they created the banana industry, and in so doing cleared north Queensland for its prosperous sugar industry today. The profits from the banana trade later provided the capital for the banana merchants from Australia to branch out into commercial activities in Hong Kong and Shanghai.

In 1901 the six Australian colonies united to form a new nation – the Commonwealth of Australia. Despite the Chinese population having dropped to 30,000, one of the first major pieces of legislation passed by the new Federal Parliament was the Commonwealth *Immigration Restriction Act 1901*. It was the culmination of the increased stringent entry regulations operating in the colonies over the previous twenty years, trade union agitation against Chinese competition in certain industries like furniture manufacturing and a strident nationalism that wanted the new nation to be exclusively European.

The 1901 Act introduced a dictation test of fifty words in any language, later modified to any European language, directed at excluding non-European immigrants. This was the cornerstone of the White Australia policy which operated for the next seventy years. The 1903 *Naturalization Act* cancelled the right of naturalisation for non-Europeans which had been taking place during the 19th century. Also, in 1903 the clause in the Act permitting the entry of wives and dependants of already domiciled non-Europeans was cancelled. For non-citizens already resident in Australia before 1901, a Certificate Exempting from Dictation

Test (CEDT) could be issued to enable them to temporarily leave the country and then return, thus perpetuating the commuter system. Further exemptions were permitted for import-export merchants of good standing for the entry of their assistants and to students. The wives of such import-export merchants could be allowed to visit for periods up to six months.

During the 1930s these exemptions were extended to permit the sponsored immigration of assistants and substitutes for local traders, as well as for chefs and market gardeners. This was the only way the China-born son of a commuter could join his father's shop or garden. But no such concession was offered to wives and other dependants. Meanwhile the exodus of older Chinese continued and by 1947 the Chinese population had declined from 30,000 in 1901 to its lowest figure of some 9,000, or 12,000 including the Australian-born. The White Australia policy confined the Chinese to non-competitive occupational areas, chiefly market gardening, the fruit and vegetable trade, and a diminishing carpentry trade by virtue of the position won by Chinese craftsmanship. A small minority engaged in the import-export trade.

Almost all the early Chinese migrants were males. The 1861 census reports listed just eight Chinese women in Victoria and one in New South Wales and the numbers remained low for the remainder of the century. As the emigration of Chinese men slowed after 1901, Australian-born females steadily increased the proportion of women within the Chinese population. From the goldfield days onwards, independent-minded Australian women who chose to marry Chinese were often ostracised and their families turned against them. The children of mixed marriages as well as those of Chinese parents were taunted, bullied and insulted by their peers. Educated in Australian schools in the values of common decency and a fair go, they were made to feel ashamed of their origin. While some learned to fight back, most suffered in silence and resentment. Extreme cases suicided.

Excluded from mainstream Australian life, the Chinese longed for a stronger China to protect their interests and closely followed the revolutionary nationalist struggle in China. After the young emperor Kuang Hsu (光緒) tried to introduce reforms in 1898 and was deposed, the Chinese community became divided into two factions. The royalists, the older conservative merchants, supported the monarchy, while the revolutionaries, some merchants, market gardeners, carpenters and others supported Sun Yat-sen (孫逸仙) who wanted to overthrow the monarchy. Ultimately, Sun Yat-sen's nationalist party, the Kuomintang (國民黨), won the support of the community and a new expression of unity was reached during the Second World War years. However, this wartime unity became fragmented during the Cold War period.

Following the outbreak of the Pacific war in 1941, there was some relaxation of the restrictions on non-Europeans. All arrivals, mainly wartime refugees, were issued with certificates of exemption from the dictation test and allowed to work. Some former closed occupations were opened to them.

Then came the end of the war and Australians began to see the Chinese in a new light. The Chinese were wartime allies, they had fought the Japanese and suffered heavy losses. The descendants of the Chinese pioneers had installed themselves as Australian. They had prospered and educated their children. Some of their children had joined the professions. Their way of life was Australian. They were accepted as Australians with a Chinese ethnic background. Increasingly a growing number of church leaders, intellectuals and individual politicians began demanding changes to the immigration laws.

One of the earliest reforms in 1947 was the lifting of the controversial 1903 ban on wives and dependants entering Australia. It also became easier for students and assistants, chefs and cafe workers to enter the country. But the White Australia policy was still in place. Although Australia had embarked on a massive postwar migration program, non-Europeans who had entered Australia during the war as refugees were asked to leave. Many went voluntarily, but some Chinese seamen wanted to stay. Among them were those who had married Australian women, started businesses or found jobs. In 1949 the *Wartime Refugees Removal Act* was introduced to hasten their departure.

With the end of the war, the changing perceptions saw a wide range of previously closed occupations open their doors to non-Europeans. Increasing numbers of young people joined the professions and trades. Although the Chinese furniture industry had virtually disappeared and market gardening was slowly declining, the cafe and restaurant industry took their place as a more secure form of employment for Chinese.

The pressure for more liberalisation continued to lead to even greater reforms. In 1957 the right of naturalisation was restored to non-Europeans with 15 years' residence. Ten years later, in 1966, this was reduced to five years as against three years for British migrants. Then in 1958 a new *Migration Act* replaced the 1901 *Immigration Restriction Act* and abolished the dictation test.

The reforms continued. By 1959 Australian citizens were permitted to bring in non-European spouses and unmarried minor children, to be immediately eligible for citizenship, while distinguished and highly qualified non-Europeans were admitted for permanent residence. This reform was later extended to include professionals and semi-professionals. In 1960 non-European spouses were allowed to accompany British subjects with permanent residence. In 1964 conditions for the entry of Eurasians were further relaxed. In 1965 both the Australian Labor Party and the Liberal Party removed the White Australia policy from their platforms. Thus by 1971 the Chinese population had risen to 26,000.

Then suddenly at the end of 1972 Australia turned its old immigration policy on its head by recognising the People's Republic of China and introducing multiculturalism and non-discriminatory immigration. The Australian Chinese were ready for this. They had already contributed much to the land and its prosperity. They were part of it.

Preface

Before the spread of multiculturalism many Australian-born Chinese knew little about China and its rich cultural heritage. Often the strongest association which remained with them was their food. The Euro-centricity of the Australian education system had deprived them of any glimpse into the cultural history of China and Asia. The whipped-up scares about yellow hordes threatening Australia had made them feel inferior and even ashamed.

The early Chinese wanted their children in Australia to know the Chinese language and understand Chinese culture, and those who could afford to would send their sons and sometimes daughters to China for this purpose. Today many in their fifties, sixties and even seventies, do not speak Chinese and know little about China. They have lost all touch with their roots there.

This situation has now been reversed. Apart from Chinese language courses offered by primary and high schools and tertiary institutions, Chinese classes run by numerous community organisations throughout Australia are being attended by thousands. Cultural activities have been revived while popular events are reaching other sections of Australian society.

The history of the Chinese in Australia is almost as long as Australia's colonial history. Their descendants can now look back with pride at the contribution made by their forefathers which today is finally being made known.

Maps

Figure 0.4 Australia, showing key locations mentioned in the book.

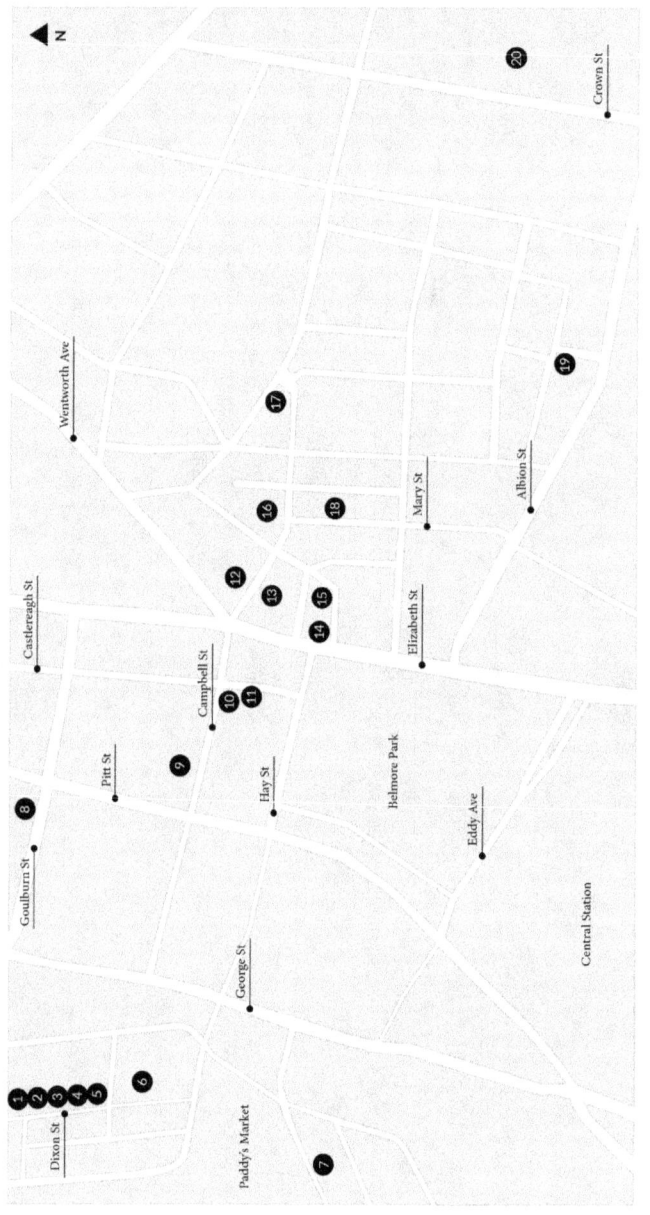

1. Eastern Restaurant (52 Dixon Street)
2. Lean Sun Low Café (54 Dixon Street)
3. Say Tin Fong & Co. (56–58 Dixon Street)
4. Green Jade Café (60 Dixon Street)
5. Chinese Youth League (66 Dixon Street)
6. Kwar Wah Chong (82–84 Dixon Street)
7. Wing On & Co. (37 Ultimo Road)
8. Anthony Hordern's Department Store
9. Nanking Café (44 Campbell Street)
10. Canton Café (Campbell Street)
11. Tivoli Theatre (329 Castlereagh Street)
12. Tientsin Café (74 Campbell Street)
13. Shanghai Café (65–67 Campbell Street)
14. Nga Gee Goong Restaurant (224 Elizabeth Street)
15. Lai Parkee house (49 Foster Street)
16. Lai Parkee house (92 Campbell Street)
17. Chinese Presbyterian Church (108 Campbell Street)
18. Gee Gong Tong Chinese Masonic Hall (18 Mary Street)
19. St Francis Convent School (96 Albion Street)
20. Crown Street Public School (356 Crown Street)

Figure 0.5 Sydney's Chinatown during the period described in the book.

Maps

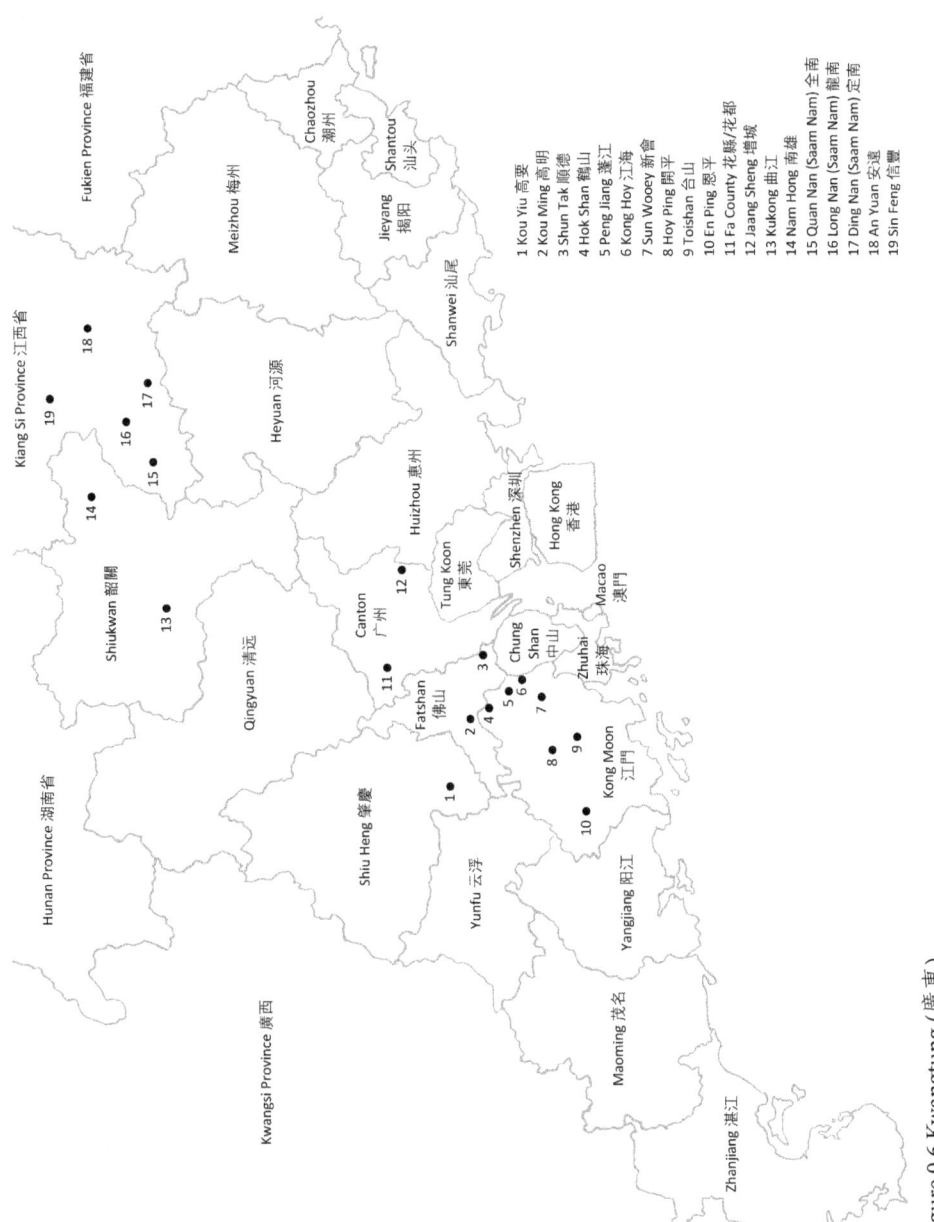

Figure 0.6 Kwangtung (廣東).

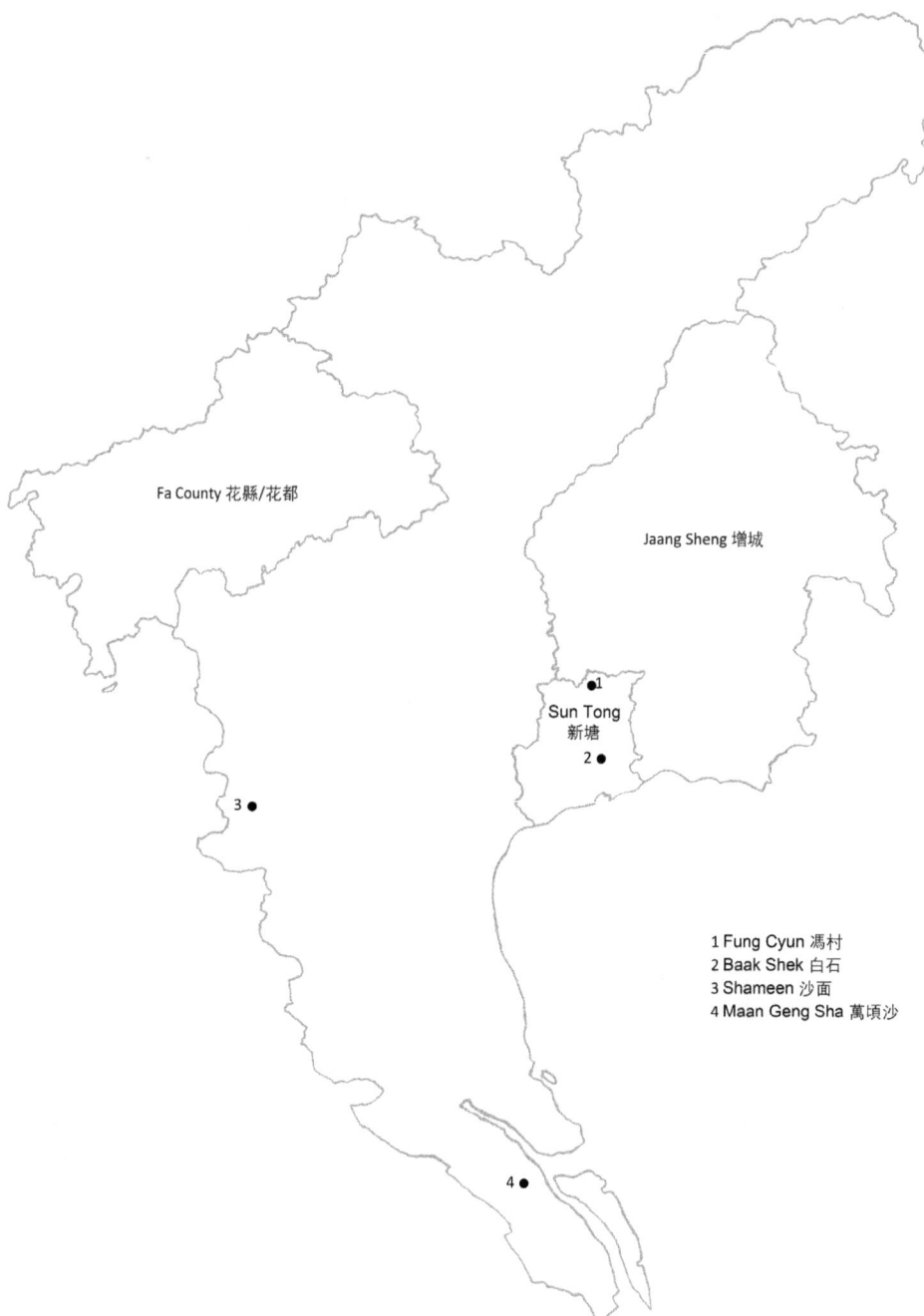

Figure 0.7 Canton (廣州).

Maps

Figure 0.8 Tung Koon (東莞).

South Flows the Pearl

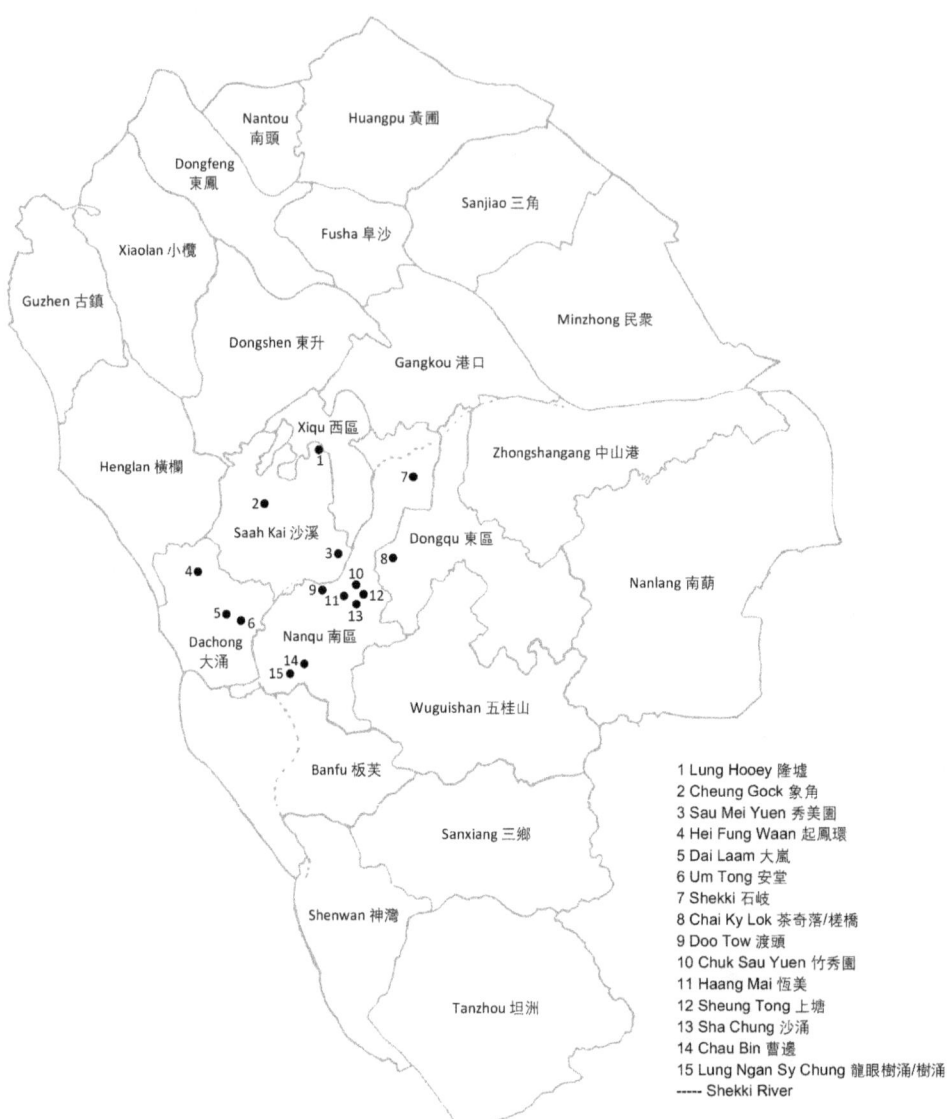

Figure 0.9 Chung Shan (中山).

Maps

Figure 0.10 Zhu Hai (珠海).

South Flows the Pearl

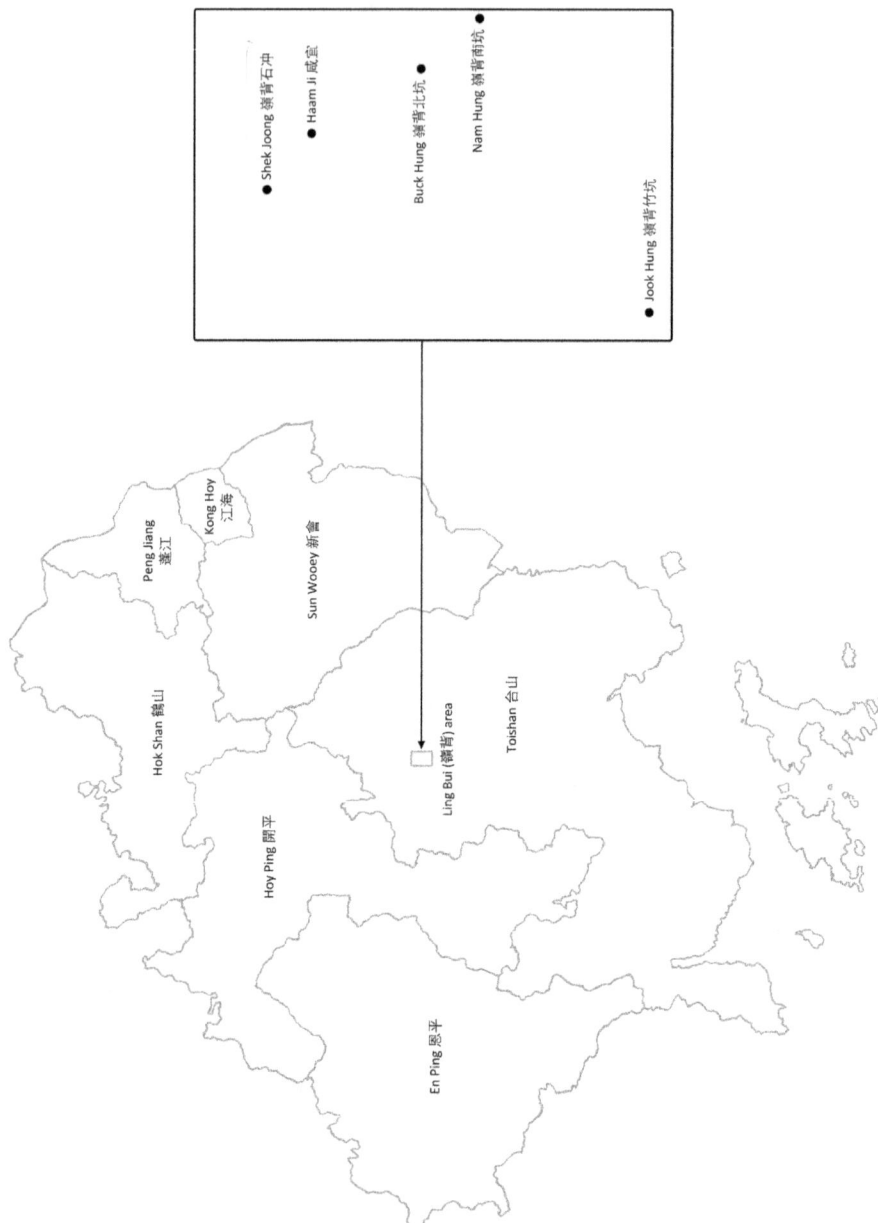

Figure 0.11 Kong Moon (江門).

A Note on the Text: Names, Places, Facts and Figures

The interviewees recalled names and places to the best of their memory and their recollection of historical events may not always be accurate, but that is both the nature of and, at times, the hazard of oral history. Discrepancies between different interviewees for the rendering of same name or place have not been amended or corrected, but have been identified by footnote if warranted. Village names in the Pearl River Delta area changed over time, and so were dependent on how the interviewee recalled the name or the dialect he or she spoke. Familiar spellings of Cantonese place names from this time period have been used throughout the book (e.g., Lung Du 隆都, Shekki 石岐, Kwangtung 廣東). Nationally known figures, such as Sun Yat-sen (孫逸仙), are rendered in conventional spellings.

Two of the interviews, with Lee Sing (李成) and Leung Pui (梁社培), were conducted in Cantonese and transcribed into English by Mavis Yen. The remainder were conducted in English. Mavis transcribed the interviews from cassette tape recordings, some of which were of moderate quality as the recording equipment used was not of the highest standard. The original tape recordings have been preserved.

The landscape of China that most of the interviewees had in their mind was that prior to the Second World War. It was a predominantly rural landscape littered with hundreds of small villages linked by proximity and clan relationships, not the country of super metropolises it is today. For example, now, the city of Zhongshan (中山) in the Pearl River Delta region has over three million people across an area of approximately 1,800 square kilometres. Prior to the Second World War, the centre of the modern Zhongshan city was a large rural town called Shekki. Surrounding Shekki were numerous districts, within which were a multitude of small villages. The general area that covered these districts and villages was known to the interviewees as Chung Shan (中山) county. Today, these villages and districts are effectively suburbs of Zhongshan. The older understanding of this landscape is reflected in the maps in the book.

Mavis wrote the preface and each chapter introduction between 1995 and 2000, relying on the source material listed in her bibliography. She did not have access to the internet or digitised archival resources that are available to authors today. All her research was conducted in libraries in either Canberra or Sydney, where she lived at the time. As editors, we have made some minor amendments to Mavis' text to make it more consistent and relevant to the narratives in each chapter.

Siaoman Yen has provided the Chinese characters and the glossary for names, locations and romanised phrases. The romanisation of Chinese language throughout the text was done by Mavis Yen. Mavis generally used the Wade-Giles system and the editors have left that unchanged.

The maps used in the book have been professionally produced based on templates researched and designed by the editors. All footnotes have been inserted by the editors, who have also added the brief postscripts at the conclusion of each family story to account for the period between the date of original interviews and the date of publication.

1
'In a Nutshell'

Thelma and Leslie Chang (張)

Sitting around the Changs' kitchen table in the home they have lived in for thirty years, overlooking a cluster of yachts anchored below in Sydney's Middle Harbour, Australian-born Thelma (1914–1991) and Leslie Chang (1909–2016) present a bird's-eye view of the attraction of Australia for poverty-driven Chinese migrants in those earlier days. Thelma's great-grandfather Louey (雷), from Toishan (台山) county in the Pearl River Delta, was part of the great influx of Chinese to the Australian goldfields during the 1850s, living in Bendigo in the state of Victoria. The discovery of gold in 1851 meant that by 1859 there were over 40,000 Chinese in Victoria; when combined with those living in New South Wales, total numbers of Chinese as high as this would not be seen in Australia again for more than a hundred years. While gold was the lure, not all the Chinese were miners and many quickly saw that there was money to be made in servicing the mining communities.

Many Chinese immigrants did return to their homeland, but the cemeteries across Australia are the last resting place of many thousands of Chinese, mainly men, who stayed and made a life here for themselves and their families, or who were separated from wives and children who remained behind in China. Thelma Chang's grandfather Louey Fong Goon followed his father to Bendigo and never went back to China. He married an Irish woman and they raised nine children between them. He had various trades as a shopkeeper, food hawker and cab driver.

Leslie Chang's parents were part of the post-gold rush era. He tells how his father, Peter Chung Fung, from Tung Koon county in the Pearl River Delta, jumped ship in Sydney in the 1880s. By then the Chinese had begun diversifying into other occupations. He became a shopkeeper in regional New South Wales and was a founding investor in the famous Australian

Chinese firm of Wing On & Co. (永安果欄). Thelma and Leslie explain the sojourner mentality of the Chinese. They were poor people who simply wanted to make enough money to send back to family members in China and perhaps to go back to China themselves one day. They worked hard but not all prospered. However, many became the progenitors of successive generations of Australians with Chinese heritage.

Thelma

Our granddaughters are fifth-generation Australians. Mum's paternal grandfather, Great-Grandfather Louey, came to Bendigo in about 1850 from See Yup (四邑) (the four counties of Sun Wooey 新會, En Ping 恩平, Hoy Ping 開平 and Toishan). One of my aunts had a very early photo of him, I remember. Mum's Irish mother was first generation. My maternal grandmother's people came from the north of Ireland. They were Orangemen and they came to Bendigo too. So Mum was second generation and our grandchildren are fifth.

But we go back one generation further on the Chinese side. My grandmother Elizabeth was a fine-looking woman. She was a lovely grandmother and a really hard worker. Her husband, Louey Fong Goon,[1] used to supply all the pork to the Chinese when they went to the cemetery to worship the dead. They still have a tram in Bendigo that goes down to the Chinese cemetery. There's a temple there too. Grandfather supplied the pork to quite a few outlying places around Bendigo too. He and Grandmother would arrange for people to do the slaughtering.

At another stage, Grandfather ran a cab service to take the gamblers home at night. There used to be a lot of market gardens in Bendigo in those days. The Chinese gardeners worked hard all week and they came into Bendigo on Sundays to play *fan tan* (番攤)[2] and things like that. Even some Australians used to go and play *fan tan*. But it was only on Sundays.

Grandfather also sold tea. He went round delivering to all the shops. He should have been a wealthy man. But he died when he was fifty-six. It was his third

---

1 Recent research by members of the Goon family reveals that Thelma's maternal Irish great-grandmother Elizabeth Johnston (1861–1925) had, in fact, two Chinese husbands. She married Jim Kim Goon (born 1841 in Toishan), a hawker from White Hills, Bendigo, at St Paul's Church of England in 1879 and had three children including Thelma's mother, Florence, who was born in 1885. He deserted her and she lived with storekeeper Louey Fong Goon (1852–1907) of Long Gully, Bendigo, from about 1887 onwards, eventually marrying him in 1896 when she was able to have her first marriage dissolved. On the original tape recordings from 1988, Thelma admitted she did not have a detailed knowledge of her family history so it is possible she was unaware of her true origins and Louey Fong Goon just came to be accepted by subsequent generations as the family patriarch.
2 *Fan tan* is an ancient Chinese gambling game in which about 200 beads are placed on a table and systematically reduced until four or fewer are remaining. Bets are placed at the start of the game on the numbers 1, 2, 3 or 4.

1 'In a Nutshell'

Figure 1.1. Thelma on her mother's lap, c. 1914. Standing, left to right: Lucy and Beattie Goon. Seated, left to right: Mrs. O'Hoy (family friend), Kenneth Yin, Thelma and Florence Yin. (Denise Quay)

stroke. He didn't have much time to make any money. I don't think he was a good businessman. He and Granny had nine children. Granny wasn't that old either when she died.

My own mother (Florence Goon 1885–1977), she never had much. My father's surname was Yin.[3] He died when my sister, Norma, the youngest, was only four. So my Irish grandmother had a lot to do with bringing us up, particularly my brother and myself. I always think very kindly of her. Mum couldn't go out to work and she never ever had a widow's pension, or even an old age pension. But it was very cheap to live in those days. You didn't need very much. We'd get all our vegetables, I suppose for free, from the gardens. Meat was cheap. But after we moved to Sydney there were more of us working. We ate a lot of poultry in those days. Mum would go to the auctions.

---

3   Louey Yin (Louey Ga Yeung 1874–1931) was a past president of the Bendigo Chinese Association, occasional president of the Chinese Easter Pageant Committee, and prominent in the Chinese Masonic Society in Bridge Street, Bendigo. He was a storekeeper and market gardener with interests in gardens at Echuca, where he also practised as a herbalist. He was reputed to have owned one of the first Ford motor cars in Bendigo.

I've lived most of my life in Sydney. My sister who died in 1987 lived in Bendigo all her life and knew far more about the Chinese in Bendigo than I did. Her husband used to prepare all the costumes and things for the Chinese processions.[4] When the Duke and Duchess of Gloucester came to Sydney, he was sent up from Bendigo to dress all the people who took part in the Chinese procession. He knew how to do it because he'd worked with some of the old Chinese handling costumes. He died of pneumonia in the Bendigo Hospital when my sister's third child was only nine months old. So Mum brought her eldest boy to stay with us in Sydney.

Chinatown used to be in Bridge Street in Bendigo. It could have been the first Chinatown in Australia. All the Chinese lived there. They had stores. A few made *lap cheong* (臘腸, Chinese sausages) and things like that. It was a real big community at one stage.

Leslie

Why did the Chinese come to Australia? There's only one basic answer to that. You get a See Yup person. He goes there. He settles down and makes a good living. He writes to all his friends in the village. They all come out and they settle down. There's safety in numbers. They all know each other. They write back and more and more come out. A seaman thinks a place is all right, he can make a living there, so he jumps ship, settles down and mixes with the natives. It's the same old answer: *wun sihk, hai ma* (覓食, 是嗎, make a living, right)?

Thelma's great-grandfather's surname was really Louey. But there was a lack of communication between the Chinese and the Australians. So a lot of Chinese in Australia ended up with unusual names which weren't their surnames at all. All the Australians knew was the surname came last. Now the Chinese and Japanese put their surnames first. I'm Leslie Chang. But my father was Jeong Foong (1864–c. 1930), so when I was born I became Leslie Jeong Foong. A double-barrelled surname too, Jeong Foong! I changed it back to Leslie Chang.[5]

My father came from the land. He was a rice farmer in Dai Fun (大汾) village in Tung Koon (東莞) county, Kwangtung (廣東) province. His family didn't own the land, they only rented it. Dad came to this country before Federation. He didn't come on his own initiative. He had a good friend, Leong Cheong (梁創), who lived across the street from him in Dai Fun. Leong Cheong came out here first. After he'd been here a year, he wrote to my father and said, 'I'm living in Sydney and it's not difficult to make a living here, much easier than in Dai Fun.

---

4   The Bendigo Easter fair began in 1871. A highlight was a procession through the town which very quickly included a large Chinese component involving costumed participants and the world's largest imperial Chinese dragon (*Sun Loong*) imported from China. It continues to this day as a major cultural event in the state of Victoria.

5   NAA (NSW): ST84/1, 1910/181–190. National Archives of Australia documents record Leslie's father's name as Peter Chung Fung.

You ought to come.' So my dad got his little knapsack and stick together. He got a job on a ship, where or how I don't know. He was a member of the crew, so it didn't cost him anything. As soon as the ship arrived in Sydney in 1884, like all the others, he jumped ship. As soon as the hordes got there, out they went. If they couldn't land in Sydney, they went on to Melbourne and left the ship there. They were all villagers. He could have been eighteen, nineteen, I suppose. If you're a little older, you won't do it.

There were a lot of other Chinese who came ashore at Sydney at the same time. They went to Surry Hills. They hung out all round Mary Street. Because they were all working in vegetables, they got to know each other. If you spoke Heung Shan (香山) (another county in the Pearl River Delta) dialect to a Tung Koon person, he more or less would know what you were talking about. The others would talk to you, they'd understand and use sign language if they couldn't.

In 1897 a group of them started the Wing On fruit business in Haymarket, Sydney. It was a partnership. It wasn't a family business. My father and Leong Cheong didn't know the Heung Shan Gocks (郭) from a bar of soap. They were Gock Lock (郭樂), Gock Chin (郭泉), Gock Son (郭順) and Gock Quay (郭葵), all brothers, but the other partners weren't from the same village or even from the same county. They spoke different village dialects. None of them had any money, otherwise they wouldn't have set up a partnership like that.

Ou Yeung Mun Hing (歐陽民慶) was the biggest shareholder. He had three shares. Gock Lock had two. Leong Cheong had one and a half. We had one share. Gock Son had one and a half shares, I think. Ma Joe Sing (馬祖星) had one and Pang Yoong Kwun (彭容坤) had one. Pang was from Tung Koon county like my father and Leong Cheong. He went back to China very early. Later on, Ou Yeung Mun Hing became a major shareholder in the Shanghai Wing On Company (上海永安公司), too. My father had a share too.

This is how they formed the fruit business. You took out a farm produce agent's licence. You didn't need much capital because you were selling everything on consignment. People were consigning their products to you without you outlaying any money. You sold the produce for them, got the money, returned so much to them and took out your commission. So it cost very little. That's how the Wing On fruit business began.

Meanwhile there was an opening in Tamworth in New South Wales. There were a lot of Chinese up there, all from Tung Koon county, and there were good opportunities there, my father told me. So he left Sydney and went up to Tamworth where he opened a fruit and vegetable and Chinese goods shop in the main street.[6]

---

6   NAA (NSW): SP42/1, C1903/4629. Wing Lee & Co., a mixed fruit and vegetable/cafe business located in the 'Place of Trade' building at 368 Peel Street, Tamworth, NSW. Leslie's father was often referred to in Tamworth by the name of Peter Wing Lee. It was not uncommon for Chinese men to be known by their business name.

My father must have made some money by that time. You take Hill End.[7] That's where the biggest nugget of gold in the world was found. It's a very old gold mining town in New South Wales. There were fifty-two hotels in Hill End. All they did was put up a bark hut, make a table from bush plank, put up bottles of whisky and that, and there was your hotel.

Tamworth was a gold-producing place too. But my father wasn't into gold mining. You don't go gold mining to make money. That's no way to make money. All the people who go gold mining work hard. Then they get a bit of gold. But people cheat them too. They open gambling places, the miners have no diversions, so they gamble and lose all their money. You've got to sell whisky, sell grog, or have girls. That's the way to make money in gold mining towns.

Well, my father married a girl (Isa Ken You) in Sydney in 1904 who came out with her father, also from Tung Koon county. I was born in Tamworth in 1909 and I knew Tamworth like the back of my hand. I had a bike and I used to ride up all the side streets and mix around with all the other kids. During the First World War I used to follow the soldiers, listen to the patriotic talks asking people to buy war bonds. I knew all the merchants in Tamworth. They would congregate at these gatherings when somebody from Sydney would come up and tell them how the war was going. I used to follow the Salvation Army down the streets. We only had gas light in the houses then. It was my job to light the gas frames at home every night and turn them out.

There were hundreds of Chinese in Tamworth in those days. They were mainly Tung Koon people and they were growing vegetables and tobacco. The Chinese on the flats were cultivating tobacco. All you'd see was tobacco, high, beautiful, waiting for harvesting. But Tamworth is in a hail belt. It's risky. Once they got hail or frost that would wipe the whole crop out. They reckoned they got one crop out of four. Then they'd make money. Farming's like that. When they got the crop in one out of four years, paid for everything, then they had a trip back to China. They didn't really prosper.

I remember when the Parkee family came to Tamworth. It would have been around 1917. They rented a shop in Peel Street, more like a hardware shop. Upstairs they had material used as a primer for explosives. Like caps. Us kids would take it and hit it with a hammer and it would go BANG! But they didn't do that well as it was during the war. Basil Parkee (黎宗枝) was born there and my mother gave him his name. His mother couldn't really speak English.

After the Second World War, when I had a garage business down in Double Bay in Sydney, one day I said to the mechanic, 'Where do you come from, Buck?' He said, 'I come from Tamworth.' So I said, 'What did your people do up there?' 'My father's a doctor.' I said, 'Your father's Dr Buckley?' 'Yeah!' So I told him his father was our family doctor. I was in the same class as Buck's brother, Edward. We used

---

7   The New South Wales State Heritage listed town of Hill End is a former gold mining village situated approximately 73 kilometres north of Bathurst, NSW.

1 'In a Nutshell'

Figure 1.2. Peter Chung Fung, his wife Isa Ken You and their children Charlie, Aubrey and Leslie, Tamworth, NSW, c. 1912. (Ken Chang)

to walk past their house every day. Dr Buckley gave me a book at Christmas. After that, whenever Edward came down to Sydney, he'd come into the garage and we'd chat about our childhood days in Tamworth.

While I was growing up in Tamworth, the Wing On fruit business in Sydney was thriving. It became a limited company. They sent Gock Chin over to Fiji to establish a banana business there. The Chinese merchants in Sydney now virtually controlled the banana trade in New South Wales.

I would rate Gock Lock as a genius. When he was working in the Wing On fruit business in Haymarket, during the lunch hour he would walk up to the big Anthony Hordern's department store nearby and watch how the business was run, just observe. My father told me about this. After a while, Gock Lock reckoned they could run a department store like that in Hong Kong. So Gock Lock returned to Hong Kong and in 1907 they opened the Hong Kong Wing On Company. They got all the people they knew, from Heung Shan, and others, to put in capital.

Three department stores that I knew of were set up in Hong Kong, the Wing On (永安), the Sincere Company (先施公司) and the Jun Kwong (真光) Company. They were all started by Chinese who returned from Australia. The Sun Company (大新公司) wasn't set up till later. Wing On was just ordinary shopfronts with the connecting walls torn down. It wasn't much of a place, but they did all right. They made money.

Then they decided they could do better and went up to Shanghai. Now that was a great leap. Shanghai was totally alien to them. They were southerners, and once you go into Shanghai, you're among central-south people. Anyway, they went up there and they looked around and decided they'd start a department store in the International Settlement. They selected a site, on the corner of Chekiang (浙江) and Nanking (南京) Roads. But it was Hardoon land. Hardoon was the richest man in Shanghai, he had land everywhere.[8] They negotiated with Hardoon and he said, 'Yes, I'll let you have the site for a very low rental for thirty years. At the end of thirty years the land and building revert to me.' 'That's not bad,' they thought. 'We'll make our money back in ten or fifteen years. Then we'll have another fifteen years of running it for nothing and we can give it back. We'll all be wealthy by then.' That's what they did and that's how the Shanghai Wing On Company was set up in 1917.

Back in Sydney, nobody wanted to stay here now. There were better pickings in Hong Kong and Shanghai. In 1920, when I was ten, our family went back to China by force of circumstances. My mother had died in Tamworth in 1918. There were six children and my father couldn't handle them. There were no other Chinese women around, so he said the best thing was to take us back to China where there were plenty of relations to look after us. Otherwise, my father said, we would *bin gwei la* (變鬼啦, turn into barbarians).

We first went to Hong Kong. In the beginning we stayed in the Wing On's hotel, the Dai Dong (大東旅社, Great Eastern Hotel). Then we moved to Kennedy Town, up on the hill, near Mrs Gock Quay. Gock Quay was one of the Gock brothers in the Wing On fruit business in Sydney. I used to go out during the day and I'd see her. We lived there for a while, then we went and lived in Canton. It's a very hot place! We lived somewhere near Dong Shan (東山, East Mountain suburb) where all the overseas Chinese hung around.

We stayed in Canton for five or six months. In those days, I reckon it was warlord against warlord. I didn't go to school. I had no schooling in Canton. This'll tell you how things were.

The streets in Canton were small and narrow. I was walking along one day when all of a sudden I heard shots in the distance. The shopkeepers heard the shooting and they started to put up the shutters. I didn't want to be caught in the streets, so I ran into one of the shops. I was in that shop for more than half an hour. I wasn't there on my own. There were other customers there too. Well, as soon as they got the all-clear, they opened the door, down came the shutters and it was business as usual! Of course, in those days Chinese warfare was more psychological. You fired a few shots like this. The so-called enemy knew you were shooting at them, so they ran. They never turned round. It was a joke.

---

8   Silas Aaron Hardoon was born to a Jewish family in Baghdad, Iraq, in 1851, later becoming a wealthy businessman in Shanghai prior to his death in 1931.

After that experience we moved to Shanghai where my father worked for the Shanghai Wing On Company. Leong Cheong was there too. He also worked for the company. We lived near the Leong Cheong family and grew up with the Leong Cheong children. We all went to school in Shanghai.

One of our uncles in Canton used to come up to Shanghai and would stay with us. He was a general, the chief-of-staff of the smaller warlord army of Chen Geng Meng (陳炯明) in Kwangtung. But he was a big shot. No matter how small your army was, chief-of-staff was still a big job.

We never went to my father's home county of Tung Koon. They have rich rice fields there. While my father was making money in Australia, he would send money back and ask the relations to buy rice fields. He always used to say, 'In times of stress, if you live in the city, go back to the village and you'll never starve.' He had that philosophy. So he bought polder fields.[9] He said to the relatives, 'I'm the owner, get somebody to work them and pay rent.' We don't know how much land there was because we weren't interested to go and live in the village and subsist on rice.

Tung Koon has very rich polder fields and it was well known for its community-owned rice fields. Ten thousand *mow* (畝, a *mow* is approximately one-sixth of an acre) of reclaimed rice fields were owned by Tung Koon county at a place called Maan Geng Sha (萬頃沙). These fields were originally reclaimed in an area lying between Tung Koon and Chung Shan (中山) counties. During the latter part of the Ching dynasty (清朝) (overthrown by the republican revolution in 1911), a Tung Koon fellow was found murdered there. At the time the two counties were disputing ownership of the reclaimed land. According to the law, if the land turned out to be Chung Shan land, and the murdered man was from Tung Koon, then the Chung Shan people would have to answer for the crime. So the Chung Shan people disclaimed ownership. They asserted that the murdered man was found on Tung Koon land. That settled the dispute and Tung Koon county took all the land, 10,000 *mow* of it. Probably the land should have been owned by both counties. Anyhow, Tung Koon county declared the land community property and devoted the proceeds from it to charity and education. From then on, if you had a bright child, community funds would pay for his education, even overseas, Australia too.

When the Tung Koon people came to Sydney, there were so many of them, they decided to join forces with the people from the neighbouring county of Jaang Sheng (增城). They put their money together and bought three shops in Dixon Street, the rent from which was to be used for charitable and educational purposes. Two medical students of Tung Koon origin were put through Sydney University out of these funds. In the early days, there were also dormitories in the upstairs of the Dixon Street buildings for Tung Koon and Jaang Sheng people passing through Sydney. Under the

---

9   Polder fields are low-lying, flood-prone, marshy or reclaimed tracts of land commonly cultivated in the Pearl River Delta region.

constitution of the society the shops can only be leased to a Tung Koon person at a very reasonable rental. Now, over a period of years those in charge of the society, they go bad. These properties can't be sold because they are registered in the name of the benevolent society of the two counties. It was a hell of a mix-up. Nobody can fathom it out. They held a general election to elect people to the committee running it. I went to a meeting and I looked at the list they put up and half of them were dead! Nobody else knew but I knew, you see. I said this is fraudulent.

After school I went to Nanjing (南京) University. It was based on the American system. First year you were called freshmen, second year sophomore, then junior and so on. I never worked in the Wing On Company in Shanghai, but when I returned to Sydney before the Second World War, I worked in the Wing On Company here.

In 1935, General Tsai Ting-Kai (蔡廷鍇) came to Australia to rally the Chinese community in support of the Sino–Japanese war. He was a southerner and all the Chinese here were all southerners. He was considered a patriot because his Cantonese 19th Route Army made a stand against the Japanese attack on Shanghai in 1932. The others were melting away before the Japanese onslaught. But he was not a member of the Kuomintang (國民黨). The Chiang Kai-shek (蔣介石) government notified the Chinese consuls in the different capitals here not to entertain the general in an official capacity, not to give him any support. Before General Tsai (蔡) arrived in Sydney, Dr Chen, the Chinese consul-general, put a notice in the local newspapers declaring that General Tsai was coming out in his individual capacity and had nothing to do with the Chinese government. Now that aroused the ire of the local Chinese.

That's how the consul-general got the gun. Previously he was a celebrity. Now he fell out of favour. The community sent telegrams to the Nanking government refusing to have anything to do with the consul-general. They demanded his recall. But they didn't say anything to the consul-general. He was greeted as usual while they were stabbing him in the back. The next thing was the consul-general got a notification that he was being recalled, but he never knew the local community was behind it.

During the 1920s, the Wing On Company in Shanghai went on to establish cotton mills, textile mills. By 1935 they had nine mills employing umpteen thousand people. They went into real estate and banking. But the jewel was that Hardoon land with the big department store building on it.

In the contract with the Hardoons, the rent was to be paid in Chinese currency, 268,000 dollars a year. This is what happened. The Second World War came and with it inflation. As a result, ten or twenty US dollars became enough to buy that amount of Chinese currency. That was all they needed. So Wing On was paying the annual rent with ten or twenty US dollars. But by the end of the war the lease had nearly run out. Although Hardoon had already died, his wife was there and she was the executrix. Mrs Hardoon decided this was no proposition. She decided to sell

1 'In a Nutshell'

Figure 1.3. Thelma and Leslie Chang pictured in a Sydney photo booth, c. 1936 (Ken Chang)

the property to the Wing On people. The Wing On people thought this was good. They informed all the shareholders they were making issues to buy the property. Everybody paid up for the new issues and the property became Wing On's. Then the communists came and took it. But the Hardoons already had their money. Nobody had foreseen a communist victory in 1949.

In the olden days, the average Chinese who came here didn't bring their women with them. They weren't allowed to, and they couldn't afford it anyhow. If a Chinese had a wife and kids in China, he sent money back to keep them. He came to make money, to send the money back there and make enough to go back and live in China for the rest of his days. He had no intention of becoming a permanent resident. It wasn't the rich Chinese who came. They stayed put. It was those who couldn't make a living in China, who had no jobs and saw an opportunity here. They came. That's it in a nutshell.

Postscript

Following the Second World War, Leslie owned and operated a successful motor vehicle repair and panel beating business in Double Bay, Sydney, and had a range of other business interests. Thelma Chang passed away in 1991, not long after this interview was recorded. Leslie, however, lived until 2016 and died just a month short of his 108th birthday. They had three children who went on to have successful careers. Leslie was the uncle of pioneering Australian heart transplant surgeon Dr Victor Chang (son of Leslie's younger brother Aubrey Chang), who was tragically murdered in a failed extortion attempt in 1991. Leslie's father died in China.

Thelma's large extended family from Bendigo are worthy of further exploration. Family members have been extensively researching both the Goon family origins on the Chinese side and the Johnston family on the Irish side. Two of Thelma's uncles, Fred and Herbert Goon, served with the Australian Army in the First World War. Family members also served in the Second World War. While succeeding generations have since moved away from Bendigo, many family members played a prominent role in Bendigo's Chinese community life during the 1920s and 1930s, including in the popular annual Easter pageant.

2
Memories of Sydney's Chinatown

Evelyn Yin Lo (黎鑽好)

Born in Sydney, the second of nine children, Evelyn Yin Lo (1922–2008) recreates the Chinatown of her childhood in the Surry Hills/Haymarket area of central Sydney, where her parents ran small cafes. She grew up during the White Australia period when Australia's full and mixed Chinese population slumped to its lowest level, from approximately 32,000 in 1901 to 12,000 in 1947. Evelyn tells of the taunting she suffered at primary school and how this continued in the afternoons when she helped in her parents' small cafe. She went to Sunday school regularly with the other Chinese children and became an activist in the Chinese Presbyterian Church. As a young adult she was the first female member of the Chinese Youth League (僑青社), attending their dances and social activities. The family also went to the cemetery each year to pay their respects to deceased clansmen in accordance with the practice of ancestor worship. This was the most important event in the life of the Chinese community.

The first Chinatown was situated in Sydney's Rocks shipping port area, where import-export businesses, shipping agents, boarding houses, furniture shops, eateries, gambling dens and variety stores flourished. However, with the growth of market gardening, a wholesale fruit and vegetable market developed in the Campbell Street vicinity near the existing cattle, hay and grain market. By the 1870s, Chinese merchants and traders moved into the Campbell and Goulburn Streets area. Later, the current Paddy's Market building was developed as a fruit and vegetable market and the Haymarket area became the focus for Chinese traders, with Dixon Street a popular location for Chinese businesses and shops. Meanwhile, the Chinese community began living in large numbers in an area stretching from Haymarket into the neighbouring suburbs of Surry Hills and Ultimo.

Despite the departure of the wholesale fruit and vegetable markets to the western suburb of Flemington during the 1970s and the advent of vibrant Chinese communities in a number of Sydney's suburban locations, today's Haymarket Chinatown still flourishes as a popular tourist and shopping venue, business centre and restaurant precinct. Evelyn looks back at life in pre-Second World War Chinatown, before this modern incarnation evolved.

Chinatown

My dad was the first to make spring rolls in Sydney. We used to sell them for sixpence without mushrooms and eightpence with. He made the best prawn balls in Australia. I always remember him banging the fish balls. I only wish I could have learned more from him. Dad was going on nineteen when he arrived in Sydney in 1898. He came with three other clan cousins, Lai War Hing (黎和興), Lai Poy and another whose name I can't recall. They were all qualified cooks. They came from the same village in Tung Koon (東莞) county, north of Hong Kong. Australia was the golden mountain and they came to build a new life for themselves.

When you're a kid, you don't know much. You just listen. Dad's friends said he had a pigtail when he first came. I don't know what he did at first, but eventually he went up to Tamworth where he had a little food shop. Lots of Chinese were growing tobacco there then.

Dad's name in Chinese was Lai Park Sun (黎柏燊, 1879–1945), his surname being Lai (黎), but in Australia he became known as George Lai Parkee, and it was assumed his surname was Parkee.[1] Mum was Annie Mary Chong (Jarng So Hing 湛素興, 1900–1973). She came out when she was only thirteen from Jaang Sheng (增城) county, next to Tung Koon. While she was working as a housemaid for a Chinese family, friends in the furniture business thought it would be nice if she and Dad married. Dad was twenty years older than Mum.

Their first child, Basil (黎宗枝), was born in Tamworth in 1920. They moved to Sydney when Basil was two years old, to 309 Castlereagh Street. The area was later occupied by the Department of Main Roads. I believe Dad had a little shop there

---

[1] Chinese nomenclature has the family or surname first with given names following. It was very common for Australian officials, when recording the names of Chinese immigrants, to record their last given name as their surname in Western style, as was the case for Lai Park. Officials also sometimes recorded names incorrectly by writing them phonetically or mishearing the name due to the speaker's accent, hence 'Park' may have become 'Parkee'. On occasion the official also appended an English first name or the person themselves later adopted an English first name.

but only for a short period. I was the second child, born in the Paddington Women's Hospital in 1922.

Cecil (黎滿枝) was born in 1923 while we were still living in Castlereagh Street. Then we moved to a two-storey terrace house at 92 Campbell Street on the other side of the railway in Surry Hills. We thought it was a very nice house. It had two bedrooms, one of them upstairs, and a proper staircase. There was a toilet at the back and a little courtyard. The house had guttering, which led the rainwater away. There was a laundry with a copper and a washtub. Some of those terrace houses, including the one we lived in, are still there. They look exactly the same today from the outside. They all had back entrances facing each other, though we had a factory behind us. At one time it caught fire and we were frightened the building would fall on the houses. Leslie (黎湛枝) was born in 92 Campbell Street in 1926. I remember the midwife coming. They used to have midwives in those days. Lindsay (黎金枝) was born in 1927 and Henry (黎鑑枝) in 1929.

Dad often took Basil and myself to a recreation club called the Lai Gee Wooey (黎子會), organised by the Lais. It used to be in the upstairs of one of the shops, next to the Nanking (南京) Restaurant in the downtown part of Campbell Street. We used to go up in a lift to it and Basil and I would play around there. Most of all I remember the lunch picnics the Lai Gee Wooey held. The club had a very good connection with the Chinese then. Dad probably didn't have a restaurant then because he had the time to take Basil and myself to the club. Also, I think times must have been better than in the Depression years later.

The Nanking Restaurant was started by Lai War Hing, who came out to Australia with my father. It was housed in a three-storey building midway between Pitt and Castlereagh Streets with private rooms upstairs for special parties. The building is pulled down now. The Nanking was well known in Sydney during the war years.

While we were living in Castlereagh Street, Dad had the earliest food shop that I can remember, in Harbour Street in Haymarket. This was the market area and the customers were Chinese. Not many Australians ate Chinese food then, like they do now. Dad was noted for offering a meal of rice and three dishes, including roast duck, steamed egg with minced pork and shallots, and barbequed pork or one other dish, all for one shilling! Dad did the cooking and Mum helped him. The same little shop is still there, facing the Entertainment Centre, but it's a Chinese butchery now.

On ordinary days Mum cooked for us. We always had rice, but not too much *haam yu* (鹹魚, salted fish). Dad always liked *haam yu*, but we younger ones didn't. On Sunday Basil would push the billycart down to Harbour Street to get Sunday night's tea. He would go right down to the bottom of Campbell Street and cross over George Street. There was always soup, chicken, pork, fish, prawns or whatever – the four main dishes that make up a Chinese meal. The menu varied with the chef. Dad was always giving us special food. That's why we go for food. We're used to eating the best.

As Mum was helping Dad, they asked our next door neighbour, Mrs Buck, to keep an eye on us children. Mrs Buck was an Australian lady married to a Chinese and they had a daughter by the name of Dorrie. They lived in No. 94. Mum was always busy in the shop, but sometimes Dad would come back up the hill in the middle of the day to see how we were. I used to make sure the boys didn't wreck the place, with Dad and Mum away all the time. As we grew older, we went down to the shop to get our own food and then went home again to play.

Our Campbell Street house was almost directly opposite the Sydney City Mission,[2] on the corner of Campbell and Mary Streets. Today, the same building houses the Australian Chinese Community Association. We used to go over and join the crowds inside. We had nowhere else to go. That's how we became influenced by church activities. There was a Scottish evangelist who went round with a concertina, playing all the old hymns. He had his headquarters in the mission, and he took his two daughters with him.

Mum and Dad were always busy at the restaurant. Basil was always with his friends. Besides, girls didn't get the same opportunities, so I had to entertain myself. I started going to Sunday school. I used to spend the whole day there. The boys went too, but I think they went for the company.

The Church of Christ Sunday school was just down the street and around the corner in Wentworth Avenue. It was run by Helen Wilson, a lovely woman. Her brother, Stan Wilson, used to help her. They later moved to a larger space opposite the Temple Church in Campbell Street. After Helen Wilson left, Mr and Mrs Quan Mane (關明) ran the Sunday school. They had five daughters and I became good friends with the eldest, Edna, who was about my age. The girls' grandmother came from China and I don't think she spoke English. Their uncle and auntie ran the Tientsin (天津) cafe, in the downtown part of Campbell Street. I lost contact with the Quan Manes when the Sunday school and they moved away. My young brother, Lindsay, and I were baptised in the Church of Christ.

I don't remember why, but I switched over to attending the Chinese Presbyterian Church in Albion Street, Surry Hills.[3] The Gock Chew and Wong See children and other Chinese schoolmates also went to this church. Mrs Gock Chew and Mrs Wong See were sisters and had been born in Australia. They were very active in the church and very kind to me. I was very lonely as a child. We had no close relatives and I always wished I had someone I could call 'Auntie'. I went to the Chinese Presbyterian Church for years. Cissie Young-Wai used to play the organ there. Her brother, Sammy, took the plate around. He was the treasurer. He did a lot of work for the church. Later his son took over. The Young-Wai family had their

---

2   A Christian charitable institution established by Englishman Benjamin Short in Sydney in 1862 to assist those living in poverty and inspired by the community work of the London City Mission.
3   The Rev. John Young Wai (c. 1847–1930) was born in Tung Koon county, China, and trained for the Presbyterian ministry in Melbourne in the 1870s. He established the Chinese Presbyterian Church in Surry Hills in 1893.

Figure 2.1. The wedding of Lai Parkee and Annie Chong. (Yin Lo family)

origin in Tung Koon county too, the same as my dad and all the Lais. Basil and Cecil didn't go much to church, but Cecil grew up with his little thoughts for other people. Leslie, on the other hand, became quite religious. Eventually, he was sent by the Chinese Presbyterian Church to Japan as a missionary. He married a Japanese girl, Kazue, and died in Japan and then his wife came to live in Australia.

Besides the Sunday school, the church also ran a Chinese language class. Dad wanted us to know Chinese and he sent Basil and myself to attend. The teacher would give us work to do in the class and then he would fall asleep. I liked it best when the church handed out peanuts for Christmas.

In 1931 I celebrated my ninth birthday in the lane at the back of our Campbell Street house. Dad and Mum fixed up trestle tables and all the neighbourhood kids came to the party, because we grew up together.

Dad's friends would come up to the Campbell Street house for the Chinese New Year. Dad always kept that up. He invited a lot of people to the house. They're all gone now. I was the only girl at the time and Dad's friends, having a bit of money, used to buy me beautiful dolls. They also gave us 'lucky money', *lishee* (利是/紅包), in red packets.

A half-Chinese lady with no children in Commonwealth Street always welcomed me to drop into her place. She used to serve beautiful homecooked meals in her front room. She and her husband lived upstairs and had a restaurant in the front room downstairs. I don't remember whether she used the kitchen, but she must have cooked with a fuel stove. She had a lovely set of lace tablecloths. Her dining room was very stylish, a bit classy for those days. It was the way she used to dish up the food that impressed me. She served it so nicely. She smoked too. The other kids used to be frightened of her, but I wasn't.

I used to go down the lane that ran past the back entrances to the houses in Commonwealth Street. It's blocked up now. We used to go down there to stickybeak the pak-ah-pu (白鴿票) lottery[4] in one of the basements. We were only kids. They had two drawings a day, one at ten in the morning. The man who sold the tickets arranged all the numbers and that. He used to go round all the shops to sell the tickets. 'You know you're not supposed to tell the police,' he would say to us.

I never saw the whole thing. You could win up to forty pounds, or something. It was two shillings a ticket, I think. That was a lot of money in those days. It could have been sixpence. People knew him and they would come down to the basement too. Now and again Dad bought a ticket. Dad wasn't a gambler. He only gambled because he thought he might make some money when there wasn't much business. Then he'd take a chance. I used to follow him and say, 'Dad, don't, you'll never win.'

A lot of people used to play mahjong (麻將) in those days, but this had nothing to do with the lottery.

Nobody ever closed their shop till late. There used to be an Australian who ran a mixed business at the corner of Commonwealth and Albion Streets. He used to boil up all the milk in the evening to make sure it didn't go bad. He didn't give it to you any cheaper though. We would take a billycan down. People going home late would also buy it. There were a few shops selling fruit and vegetables, as well as mixed businesses. But Mr Lum Jack Hing had the monopoly of all the Chinese business. His little shop was on the corner of Reservoir and Batman Streets, in the heart of the terrace dwellings. They're all knocked down now. He used to give credit. That's why the Australians went to him. He had a very dry sense of humour, though.

---

4 A pak-ah-pu lottery is similar to modern day keno gambling games. Players buy a ticket with eighty characters stamped on it, from which they select ten, which they hope will match the winning characters selected by the lottery promoter.

If you didn't pay your bill, then you didn't get any more credit. It was a very tiny shop with a counter and his wares on the side. The family lived upstairs. Mrs Hing came from China and couldn't speak English. Their daughter, Eileen, and I grew up together. We went to the same Sunday school. We still exchange Christmas cards. She had all boys and I had all girls.

A friend of mine lived in Mary Street. I was fascinated by the houses there. You entered the house by a flight of steps leading to what I used to call a dungeon, actually a basement floor. The lounge room was down there. Then there was a floor at street level and a floor above that, three in all.

The Chinese Masonic Society[5] – the Gee Gong Tong (致公堂)[6] – is still in Mary Street. Dad used to be a member. Like the Australian Masons, the Chinese Masons are supposed to be brothers, to help each other. All the Chinese went to the Gee Gong Tong dances, but they don't have them now.

I still go to a little noodle shop on the corner of Reservoir and Commonwealth Streets to buy *wun tun* (雲吞/餛飩, wonton) wrappers and fresh noodles. I used to work in this shop when it was a mixed business run by Chang Way Shew. A clan cousin of mine, Lai Kuen, runs it now. Lai Kuen is the grandson of Lai War Hing, who came to Australia with my father in 1898. Lai Kuen still makes the noodles the old way, by hand and by machine too.

Today the Chinese from Hong Kong are buying up property in Surry Hills. They like the area because it's close to Chinatown and to the city.

School days

Dad and Mum never had a chance to learn English properly. Mum spoke English and Chinese, but not very good English. Dad couldn't speak English. That's

---

5   Built in 1911 and located at 18 Mary Street, Surry Hills, the Chinese Masonic Society had no direct association with the European freemasonry movement but like the European movement it operated through a network of personal and business relationships. It developed out of the Yee Hing Company (also known as the Hung League 洪門), based initially in Blackburn Street, Surry Hills, in 1908.

6   Chinese secret societies, such as the Hung League, were believed to be an offshoot of the secret Heaven and Earth Society (天地会) and traditionally organised in China to express dissatisfaction with ruling dynasties. Thousands of Hung League members joined the gold rushes to California and Australia. They set up new Hung (洪) lodges on the goldfields to care for the Chinese diggers, finally merging into an overseas fraternal organisation called the Gee Gong Tong. While it supported Sun Yat-sen's (孫逸仙) republican revolution which overthrew the Ching dynasty (清朝) in 1911, as well as China's war of resistance against Japan during the 1930s and 1940s, the Gee Gong Tong had largely thrown off its overt political activities evolving into a welfare organisation. To overcome the reputation of Chinese secret societies for criminal behaviour and standover practices, the Gee Gong Tong in Sydney adopted the more publicly respectable name of the Chinese Masonic Society when it opened its Mary Street premises in 1911. Unlike the old district societies based on places of origin, the Gee Gong Tong was a fraternal society open to all.

Figure 2.2. Parkee Family Sydney, c. 1934. Left to right: Evelyn, Leslie, Annie with Edna on lap, Henry in front, Basil behind, Lai Parkee, Lindsay, Cecil. (Yin Lo family)

probably why I learned more Chinese. I can't remember how I learned to speak English. The first school I went to was St Francis' convent school. I was very young at the time. I used to go up Commonwealth Street, past the Children's Court and around the corner to Albion Street, where there was a big Catholic church.[7] The school was at the back of the church. My mother paid sixpence a week for me.

No one spoke to me in that school and I was shy. One day the nun in charge picked on me for talking. Actually, I hadn't been talking. She told me to put my hand out and she caned me. I knew she hit me for nothing. I never provoked anybody. I always did what I was told. I ended up going home crying and I didn't go back again. Looking back, I think the nun just couldn't control all those children.

Another incident at that school was a raffle ticket I bought. The prize was some mauve-coloured bath salts. I was very keen on the colour of mauve. I'd never won anything in my life before and I won it. I ran home to tell my mother. I waited

---

7   The St Francis de Sales Catholic Church and adjacent school hall, 82 Albion Street, Surry Hills.

and waited at the door but she wouldn't hurry and open it. Then, just as she did, I dropped the parcel and the bath salts scattered all over the place!

I only went to that convent school for about a month. After that I went to the Crown Street Primary School, where my brothers went. Even at Crown Street, when I was between eight and nine, I never spoke much. I still wasn't used to dealing with people. I was shy and the other children would pick on me. I never spoke much. I was always afraid somebody would hit me or want to bust me up. I listened instead. The other kids would say, 'Why don't you say something? What are you listening to?'

Whenever one of them said, 'You don't do this or I'll bash you up,' I'd be scared all day. I'd look for somebody to walk home with. Instead of going out the front door, I used to go out the back lane. I didn't know anyone who went my way. In any case I never found company with boys, and if I went with Chinese girls they'd pick on them as much as myself.

The Australian girls used to call us 'Ching Chong Chinaman' and all that. I had a lot of that as a child and I didn't like it. I didn't dare answer back. I was a coward. It was no use telling my parents. They had their own worries, so I just sat there listening. There was always one big bully when I went to school. 'Why don't you go back to your own country?' she would say.

My brothers had to fight. The Australian kids picked us to pieces. Average Australian children, they were, the same age group. They would knock you down, spit in your face.

After primary school, I went on to the Bourke Street Domestic Science School. That's where I learned what I know about housekeeping, doing the laundry and other things. My mum didn't know any more than I did. She was always busy in the business. So I'm not a very good house-person. I never had much time to spend on the house, being in business myself. My own children had to become the housekeepers in later years.

The House of Five Sons

In the early 1930s, Dad sold the Harbour Street business and bought another at 224 Elizabeth Street, right opposite the Hay Street railway tunnel. Because he now had five sons, Dad called it Ng Gee Gooey (五子館, House of Five Sons). So we left Campbell Street and lived on top of the Elizabeth Street shop. It was in Ng Gee Gooey that Dad became well known for his spring rolls and prawn balls. He also made dim sims (點心) like *siu maai* (燒賣, pork and shrimp dumplings), everything, for tuppence a piece. We sold roast duck and other delicacies too.

Every morning Dad spent hours to *daah min* (打麵, make handmade fresh noodles). He had a special heavy wooden trestle table in the kitchen for the noodles. He used a long hollow bamboo stick to roll out the dough. One end of the stick was inserted into a hole in the wall just above the table. Dad would roll the bamboo stick forwards and backwards by sitting on the other end.

We kept the live ducks at the back of the shop, locked up in a pen. The roast duck and other delicacies were displayed in the window. But when you're busy, you can't keep watch all the time. The window display was so tempting that people would break the lock and escape up the lane towards Campbell Street with a roast duck. Cecil used to chase after them. Another problem was the gas meter. We had to put a shilling in the slot in those days and someone was always breaking into the gas meter.

As business improved, Dad decided to extend the shop into a restaurant. He moved the family to 49 Foster Street, just around the corner and connected to the shop by a lane. He had an elegant staircase put in with a private dining room upstairs.

Our Foster Street house was a two-storey terrace house with two bedrooms and an attic room. We didn't use the front room as a lounge because we didn't live in it anyhow. The house faced the Salvation Army Men's Home, where they used to serve cheap meals for two shillings. While the men were waiting for their lunches, or had nothing else to do, they would sit on our doorstep. We could never use our front door. There'd always be someone sitting there. If you opened the door, whoever it was would fall inside. Anyhow, we used to come home from school to the shop. I think when the Foster Street house fell empty, Dad just took it as a second choice.

To me of course, any home was a home. I didn't take the place into consideration. I think it doesn't matter where you live. You know you're only confined in four walls.

Cemetery day

As kids, twice a year we had to go to Rookwood Cemetery[8] to visit the graves of Lai clansmen. We went at Ching Ming (清明, the season of clear and bright).[9] Rain or shine, we had to go. Dad was very insistent. It didn't matter what you had on. Girls were supposed to stay at home because they didn't count. But I went too, because I was closest to my father and he took me everywhere.

I didn't worry about girls not being counted. I was only too glad I belonged to someone. It didn't make any difference to me personally whether I had brothers or sisters. I didn't think about things like that. I knew Dad loved us all.

The graves we visited were all *seng Lai ge* (姓黎的, surnamed Lai). Dad respected this tradition. We would take the special train going to the cemetery on Sundays. We didn't have a car in those days. There were no buses either. We always

---

8   Rookwood Cemetery in Sydney is the largest necropolis in the southern hemisphere and the largest in the world still operating from the Victorian era. It contains many thousands of Chinese graves.
9   Ching Ming or Tomb-Sweeping Day is a traditional Chinese observance that falls on the first day of the fifth solar term of the traditional Chinese calendar or the 15th day after the Spring Equinox, usually 4, 5 or 6 April. Families visit the graves of their ancestors to pay respect, clean the grave site and make ritual offerings.

took a lot of food with us, *siu aap* (燒鴨, roast duck), *chaah siu* (叉燒, barbecued pork) instead of roast pork, cooked by my dad, and a boiled chicken. The chicken had to be complete with *gay tou* (雞頭, chicken head). You had to boil it yourself, and boiled pork too. Generally, Mum or Dad cooked the chicken. Mum usually went, but not when she had to look after the business. When we didn't have the business, she always went.

We carried all the food to the graves and met up with other *seng Lai ge* (Lai clansmen). They also brought roast ducks and other food along, packets of red candles and joss sticks. We went from grave to grave. At each grave we laid out all the food in front of the headstone, lit incense and red candles and burned paper money. Before each grave we placed three sets of chopsticks, three little bowls of cooked rice and three cups of *jau* (酒, wine). It had to be three of everything. This was because an odd number can't be divided and thus continuity is ensured for the family. The rice and wine we tipped out and left there. They used to say it was a meal to replenish the body. My father didn't drink, so we took Coca-Cola instead of wine. Sometimes we let off firecrackers and sometimes we didn't. After that, we moved the food away from the graves and had a picnic lunch of it. There was no pavilion like there is now, the Luk Fook Ting (六福亭, Hall of Six Blessings), where you can sit at tables. We sat on the ground.

The paper money we burned was intended to enable the spirits of the dead to buy new clothes in case they needed them. That's what people said. Big crowds used to go, not only Tung Koon people, but people from other places, especially from Chung Shan (中山) county. The cemetery would be packed out.

The visits were organised by the different county societies. We always sat and ate with the Tung Koon people. The various societies took along whole roasted pigs. These were chopped up and shared among their members.

My godfather

When I was a kid, I had a godfather who had a market garden out at Botany. He used to come to town every Saturday and he would call in to see Dad. That's how he became my godfather, not really of course, just word-of-mouth sort of thing. He was from Chung Shan county, *seng Chun ge* (姓Chun的, surnamed Chun). He used to go to On Yick Lee (安益利), a sort of headquarters for Chung Shan people. The out-of-town ones would go down there every Saturday. It was a typical Chinese import-export firm, selling herbal teas and medicines, not a grocery shop.

Cecil and I used to go out and visit my godfather on Saturdays. We went of our own accord, just to fill in time. We had nowhere to go in any case. We would take the tram to the terminus. Then we'd cross the railway line to where there were four gardens. We'd get there in about half an hour. We used to tidy up and sweep the floor of the ranch house. It was more like a haystack.

We didn't do any digging. That would have been too much for us. But we picked the tomatoes and washed down the shallots for the market, to make them look more attractive. The gardeners had a big pit with four cement walls. Some of them would use hoses and some didn't.

We thought it was lovely out there. There were four or five gardeners working there and they used carrying poles to carry the water to the vegetables. They were all pretty grubby. I used to be fascinated as I watched them sitting outside smoking their water pipes. At first, I thought it was opium they were smoking, but it wasn't.

One of the gardeners had a son there, Roy Wong. He and his father came out from China. Roy was only a young fellow. He liked comic books. We used to take him ours when we'd finished with them. We used to get them every week.

When the gardens had visitors, they used to make it a special occasion. We would have a fresh chicken which they killed themselves. We would have our tea at four o'clock and then we'd go back to town with my godfather and take some fresh vegetables with us. My godfather would then take us to the pictures for our Saturday night outing. He probably didn't understand the pictures, but he took us. He also took us to the Royal Show at Easter.

The customers

Dad had waitresses at Ng Gee Gooey, but they were very unreliable. They were only getting three shillings for half a day, from ten in the morning till two or three in the afternoon. The other shift was from four o'clock till midnight, but that only paid four shillings. Of course, that was a fair bit of money. In those days, if you had five pounds ten, you were rich.

I began to go down to the restaurant to help, when I was still too young to be able to do much. But kids can be very useful in a restaurant, washing vegetables, peeling shrimps and things like that. I used to look forward to talking to the people coming in, apart from the abusive types and the drunks. I met all sorts of people, including seamen from different boats, people from different places in China. That's how I got a bit of a twang and picked up bits of Shanghai dialect. I couldn't speak it, but I could understand enough to have an inkling of what they wanted to order.

Jack Richardson started coming to Ng Gee Gooey from the time he was fourteen. He had been adopted out by his aunt in Ashfield. When he went to sea, he always came to the restaurant first after he returned, for his food, and we would put him up. That's how he became our foster brother. Later, he joined the Australian Navy and became a lieutenant-commander. He was an extremely tall man who learned Chinese and taught his children Chinese traditions and how to use chopsticks.

In 1935, when I was thirteen and still going to school, General Tsai Ting-Kai (蔡廷鍇) visited Sydney. He commanded the Cantonese 19th Route Army in defence of Shanghai against the Japanese in 1932. I didn't know much about him but the Chinese community was very excited. Dad thought it was a great honour to cook for him. We had the private upstairs room fixed up specially for the occasion. There were four people altogether. Mentally, I can still see the general sitting up there. His name sticks in my memory. He gave me his autograph too, which I foolishly left in Hong Kong when I went over there in 1939.

We used to have a little sideboard in Ng Gee Gooey with a few drawers in it where we put the knives and forks. One day a fellow came in and he must have slipped something in the sideboard. The next minute we saw a couple of detectives arrive. 'Where's that Chinese fellow?' one of them asked.

We had a backyard that opened into Foster Lane. He must have rushed down the backyard and out through the side door that led to some little two-storey places. Apparently, he lived in one of them. He had come down to Ng Gee Gooey and waited while the police were after him. In the end, he jumped off a balcony and broke his leg, so they caught him. Maybe he put some white powder in the drawer and the police found it. I told them anyone could come in and put something there. They believed us. In those days it wasn't as bad as it is today. But things like that happened.

Even in the restaurant, people would come in and tell us to go back to China. Cecil was almost two years younger than me, but he always stuck up for me. When he was only about thirteen, he said to a man, 'Don't you dare hit my sister. I'll spit in your face!' Then the man said, 'You try!' And Cecil did. He was such a little thing too! I don't know who these people were. They just came in. I don't know whether they were drunk or not. They were very abusive. We used to get such a terrible lot of it. All because we were Chinese!

The matchmakers

A lot of matchmaking went on in the Chinese community. Marriages were still arranged. People in China who had friends here would write and say, 'So-and-so wants to come over.' Their friends would then go round trying to fix up a match with a bachelor here. At one time friends suggested Basil marry a girl in Perth. He considered the proposal, but then he decided he didn't want to leave the east and go so far away from the family. In the end, he never did get married.

Then they started on me. People would come round talking to my parents. I didn't like it at all. Cecil helped me a lot. He and I were very close. He would say to the matchmakers, 'My sister don't like you. What do you want to come to the house for?' My father used to say, 'Go inside, you. You mind your own business.'

Mum didn't say anything. Just did what Dad wanted. I think Dad wanted me to get married so he could see grandchildren. I used to get quite upset, having my father arrange a marriage for me. People were always coming round to *jouh mooi yan* (做媒人, matchmaker). When Mum wasn't around I used to tell them off. I'd say, 'Find your own daughters, find somebody else, not me.' In the end, they did. I didn't ask how though.

Figure 2.3. Paddy's Market, Haymarket, 1930. (City of Sydney Archives)

First job

I left the Bourke Street Domestic Science School when I was fifteen. Dad didn't need me in the restaurant, so he asked around for a job for me. In those days you had to be recommended. One of his friends told Dad a Chinese handicrafts firm was looking for a junior, so I became that junior.

They only paid me twenty-three shillings and threepence a week. It wasn't even enough for my lunch money, but I didn't care. I was glad to have something to do and somewhere to go. I worked in the office and answered the phone. It turned out that I knew the boss's brother. We went to the same church and he sang in the choir. It was only natural that the boss and I became friends.

However, the secretary there was an older woman who probably had her eyes on him. She must have become jealous or resented me. She used to send me out on errands. When the boss asked, 'Where's Evelyn?' she'd say, 'She's gone down the street,' and he'd think I'd gone out by myself. But I wouldn't walk off the place unless I was told to.

There wasn't much for me to do, so when I had spare time, I'd say to the fellow who did the books, 'Got anything to do around the office?' He'd say, 'Oh, yes.' Then I'd say, 'I'll help you with the figures.' I was doing all his figures for him.

At lunchtime when I got out, I was afraid to go in anywhere and sit on a chair to eat. I used to buy a sandwich or something, walk around the streets and look at the shops. Then one day, I became daring and decided I'd like to have a pie and sit up at one of those bars on a high stool. After I'd given my order, I felt a hand on my shoulder. 'Oh, no,' I thought. It was the bookkeeper. When my lunch came, he paid for it. I didn't like that. I didn't like having someone pay for my lunch. He was the only Australian working in the firm. In those days, Australians worked the books better than the Chinese because you've got to understand them. I don't suppose there would have been many Chinese who could keep books then.

Suddenly, after three months, I lost my job. Inspectors came in and the firm was fined for underpaying me. They must have been mad because they got into trouble. They gave me my back pay, but they sacked me. I was very disappointed.

Evelyn's story continues in Chapter 13
Part of Evelyn Yin Lo's description of Sydney's Chinatown appeared in Australia for Women: Travel and Culture, edited by Susan Hawthorne and Renate Klein (Geelong, Vic.: Spinifex Press, 1994).

3
Third-Generation Migrant

Lee Sing (李成)

There was no mistaking Lee Sing's (1894–1989) origins. Born in China, he spoke the purest Chung Shan (中山) dialect, sporadically lapsing into English to drive a point home. A frail ninety-five years of age when interviewed, he was the third generation in his family to come to Australia, as his grandfather, father and two uncles came to Queensland before him. Lee Sing arrived in Brisbane in 1909 in his early teens. He brought with him six years' education in the village school, during which he had studied the classics and imbued himself with the goal of becoming a Confucian gentleman. As a result, although his purpose was to work and make money, he displayed a fever for learning. Two years later, he joined the flourishing Chinese furniture trade in Sydney.

As alluvial gold supplies diminished, skilled carpenters among the Chinese diggers entered the furniture trade in the capital cities. But the competition they put up to European carpenters led to discriminatory legislation. In 1896, the *Factories and Shops Act* was passed in Victoria requiring all furniture to be stamped to show, among other things, whether it was made by Chinese or European labour. A similar attempt was made in New South Wales in the same year, but the stamping clause was deleted in parliament at the last minute. These Acts, and other similar legislation in Queensland and Western Australia, included further restrictive clauses dealing with the operation of furniture factories aimed at hampering the Chinese trade. In spite of this, the legislation proved to be largely ineffective and the Chinese furniture makers endured, with new arrivals joining them. With the introduction of the Commonwealth *Immigration Restriction Act* in 1901, however, there was limited opportunity to renew their workforce, and after the Second World War the industry ceased to exist.

Lee Sing made enough money to evade immigration restrictions and travel back and forth to China numerous times. On his first trip back around 1916, Lee Sing married and over the next ten years had three children in China. His first wife died at a relatively young age so he remarried and had a further three children, also in China. When he was finally able to bring his second wife and his children to Australia, he never went back to China again.

My home

In our village of Hei Fung Waan (起鳳環), in Lung Du (隆都) district, the second district of Chung Shan county, we are all Lees (李). Of course, there were one or two odd families with other surnames. About thirty in every hundred of the men in our village went to the Sandalwood Islands (檀香山)[1] to work as labourers. Lots of our villagers are still there. My *lo gee* (撈主, Chung Shan dialect for father) and his elder brother also went to the Sandalwood Islands before they came to Australia. To make money, of course. You couldn't make any money in the village.

The house I grew up in was built by my dad with the money he made in Hawai'i. I wasn't even born then. Granddad helped Dad to build it because Dad wasn't able to come home very often. Before that, the family lived in a much smaller house, but it did have a tiled roof. Lots of houses had tiled roofs by that time. Nobody was living in a mud hut anymore. With the money he made in the Sandalwood Islands, Ah Baak (阿伯, father's elder brother) built a house for his family too. We had one and they had one. All the villagers who came back from the golden mountains built houses. In those days, materials were cheap. Now everything's expensive. It costs a lot to build a house. The only reason why they're building houses in Chung Shan today is because they've found ways to make money.

One year Granddad, Ah Baak and Dad came home after a big fire destroyed the place where they were working in Hawai'i. So instead of returning there, they decided to try their luck in Queensland. They set off in 1898 and this time they took Ah Sook (阿叔, father's younger brother) with them. They weren't heading for the goldfields. That was an earlier generation. They just went to work. Granddad went into the fruit business and did a bit of carpentry. My dad became a fruit and vegetable hawker, working off a pony horse and cart.

Back home, I attended the village school for six years. Very few boys had that much schooling in those days. But I've forgotten everything I learned now, although I can still read the Chinese newspapers. I often ask my neighbours here to get a paper for me. I can't read the English papers so well, only a little. When I first came,

---

1 The Chinese called Hawai'i the Sandalwood Islands after the highly valued sandalwood, which was imported from Hawai'i into China to make incense.

I had no time to study. I had to work. But I have always been able to write my own letters. My dad wrote better letters than I ever did. He was very intelligent. I was lazy, only good at eating. Granddad didn't know too many characters, just some. But then, he belonged to an earlier generation.

People across the river from us say we Lung Du people are well-off because we went to the golden mountains. That's a bit of a joke. There are more people in the Lung Du district, so naturally more people from Lung Du left home. Besides, anyone who went and made a bit of money would later on take his sons. Others would follow his example. Across the river there were less people, so naturally less left home. But there were a lot of well-off people over there, especially those ones who came back from Australia and started up department stores in Hong Kong.

While I was still young, Granddad came home from Australia for good. We Chinese don't like to be idle, so he got all of us grandchildren to help him cultivate a vegetable garden. Times were good then, and Granddad lived to be over ninety.

Australia

When I reached my early teens, Dad came back. He paid someone a hundred pounds to make all the arrangements for me to go to Queensland too, so in 1909 I left with three others for Brisbane. I didn't mind leaving home. Being young, I found it all very exciting. I took a great deal of interest in all that was going on.

We had to walk the first part of our journey from the village to Shekki (石岐, county seat of Chung Shan). This took a few hours. There were no buses then. Today, of course, you can get from Shekki to our village in forty minutes. It's that close. But then there wasn't even a direct ferry service from Shekki to Hong Kong. We had to take a ferry boat towed by a launch to Macao first. From Macao we crossed to Hong Kong by a larger ferry. I had my pigtail cut off in Hong Kong. I also had a new suit made. I was wearing short pants then.

When we got to Hong Kong, we stayed in a *gum shan jong* (金山莊, golden mountain shop), a very small one, run by Lung Du people. People in the other districts had their own *gum shan jongs*. This was before the big department stores had been built. There wasn't even a Kwong War Chong (廣和昌). But there was a shop called Kwong War Hong (廣和祥).[2] We might have stayed there.

We left Hong Kong by the *Changsha*, a very small steamer. In fact, it wasn't much bigger than a ferry boat. The steerage passengers were mostly Chinese. Our group were the only Chinese travelling second class. I always travelled second class, never steerage.

---

2   Both the Kwong War Chong and Kwong War Hong were import-export firms trading with the goldfields in Australia and California and were called *gum shan jong* (golden mountain shops). There was a Kwong Wah Chong store at 82–84 Dixon Street, Sydney, run by fellow Chung Shan people that had a Hong Kong branch known as Kwong Wah Fong (廣和芳).

The ship gave us three meals a day, but I wasn't used to Western food. Even now, I still prefer Chinese food and in Australia I've always had Chinese food. Western food isn't filling enough. Besides, I don't eat much meat. In any case, it's not good for you. But I can eat cheese now. I couldn't bear the taste of cheese when I first arrived. Lamb was all right. Ice cream I liked very much. I like milk too. I have milk for breakfast every morning now. It's good for you.

The voyage took one and a half months. We called at Manila, passed Bird Island and then reached Thursday Island. From there we came straight down to Brisbane. The ship went on to Sydney, then to Melbourne, turned round and came back north again.

Mr Wong Jing Yuen met me in Brisbane and took care of me. I didn't go to school. My purpose was to earn money. My first job was in a boarding house run by *lo faahn* (老番, Westerners), slaughtering chickens. Westerners don't like doing that. When they kill a chicken, instead of eating it fresh, the way we Tong (唐)[3] people do, they hang it up. I worked seven days a week and got ten shillings a week 'pocket money'. My working day ended at nine every night, sometimes ten o'clock.

There were no Chinese restaurants in Brisbane when I was there. Chinese restaurants didn't start up there until the Second World War, when the *faar kei gwai* (花旗鬼, flowery flag barbarians, Americans) came. That's when they began Chinese restaurants in Brisbane.

There were no Italian *gwai* (鬼, barbarians) in Queensland in those days either. They came later to cut the cane. They actually learned market gardening from the Chinese after the Second World War. They would work for nothing so as to learn. Italians can put up with even more hardship than the Chinese. They economise on food too. But the Chinese, no matter how hard they work, they must eat well.

I stayed in that boarding house job for four months. Then I got another job in the vegetable market. I was in Brisbane for two years. All this time, Ah Sook was back in China on a visit. When he came back, he told me the best thing was for me to get into carpentry. He was a skilled carpenter himself. Tong people didn't have much choice in those days. They could only go into carpentry, market gardening or the fruit and vegetable business. It was the See Yup (四邑) people who ran laundries. There weren't many laundries in Sydney and they were operated by See Yup, not by Chung Shan people.

Working in Sydney

I came down to Sydney in 1911 and went to work in a very large carpentry shop in Castlereagh Street, called On Sing. There were between thirty and forty people working there. My job was to get up early in the morning to shop for the vegetables

---

3   The Cantonese called the people of China 'Tong people', after the Tang dynasty. Tong is Cantonese for Tang in Mandarin.

and then help the cook prepare breakfast. At night, after the shop shut, we readied the stock for transport. We never got to bed till midnight. It was like this at least five days a week, even on Sundays. We seldom had a Sunday off.

Several months later, Ah Sook sold his grocery business and set up a carpentry shop himself in the suburb of Waterloo. He made me one of the shop's assistants. There were seven assistants altogether. We took turns to go back to China. While four went off, the other three would stay and work. There weren't many *lo faahn* doing carpentry then. It was mostly Tong people. The *lo faahn* came to us to buy their furniture.

Although we were always very busy, we ate very well indeed. On Saturdays and Sundays, we had special food, a real *shiu jau* (燒酒, spirits, meaning banquet), much better than anything we ever got in the village. What did they have in the village that was good! The shop sent to Hong Kong for all sorts of groceries, mushrooms, dried seafood, especially dried scallop, all the goodies. We even imported our rice from Hong Kong. Not because you couldn't get rice here, but because it was cheaper that way. We had three good meals a day. There was always plenty, enough to fill you.

I had a good job. I operated the electric saw and was paid five pounds a week. That was seventy years ago, of course. A casual labourer then could only earn a little over a pound a week. In those days all you could do was work for somebody. I saved all my money and sent it back to Tong Shan (唐山, Tong mountain, meaning China). Because I was my uncle's nephew, I was naturally regarded as the shop owner's assistant, but this didn't mean I could take time off when I liked. When everybody was working, I had to work too. But I was able to go to an evening class at the Chinese Church in Campbell Street, for several years, to learn English. The teachers were Australian women. Quite a few Chinese married Australian women. It's only natural when people get to understand each other, they become fond of each other.

Later on, Dad came down from Brisbane and joined us. He did a bit of carpentry too. Then, when he was sixty, he went home for good. We took care of him. That's what you do. He had a few years at home, but unfortunately when he was sixty-six he had a fall which killed him. He didn't fall ill.

Returning to China

It took me seven years to save up enough money to go home the first time.[4] After that, I went back every few years, whenever I had enough money. The first time, I went back to get married. My first wife, Siu Gim Hee (蕭金喜), and I had three children. Unfortunately, she died when she was only thirty-two. I remarried a girl named Lam Tim Yuk (林添玉) in the next village, and we had another three children. The present Mrs Lee is my second wife.

I travelled back and forth on various ships, the *Taiping*, *Changte*, *Eastern* and others. I can't remember all their names now. Gibbs Bright & Co. was one of the shipping agents.

Whenever I was in Hong Kong, I would stay at Kwong War Hong. It had connections with the Kwong War Chong company here, they were all Lung Du people. By the time I first went home, there was a ferry boat running direct between Shekki and Hong Kong. I always travelled saloon class on the ferry boat. It cost me five Hong Kong dollars and extra for food. In Shekki I'd put up at the Wing Lock Tong (永樂堂, House of Everlasting Happiness), a hotel just a few steps from the ferry landing and the best in Shekki. The next morning, I'd cross the river to Lung Du. I still had to walk to the village the first time though. There were no buses running then.

It wasn't until my third trip home that I built a house. By that time, we had six children. We pulled down the old house and rebuilt it, with a four-storey watch tower (碉樓) at the back. It was a rather long-shaped house.

The village headman, who was appointed by the villagers, took care of village affairs. He organised the villagers to stand watch and they were paid out of contributions made by the better-off ones. Whenever bandits approached our village, we would lock ourselves in the watch tower, which was for our own use. It could hold thirty to forty people. Sometimes other villagers joined us. I used to like to sleep there whenever I went back to the village.

Those of us who went abroad were all the same. After building a house, we would invest in rice fields. It took me years of hard work to save enough money to build the house and buy the rice fields. I invested more than six thousand Hong Kong dollars in rice fields. But we lost all the rice fields in the land reform.

In 1929 I gave up carpentry and went back to Tong Shan for a visit. When I returned, I went into a partnership in a Chinese grocery in the market area in

---

4 Given Lee Sing arrived in Australia in 1909 after the commencement of the *Immigration Restriction Act 1901*, he would not normally have been eligible to apply for a Certificate of Exemption from the Dictation Test (CEDT) to travel back and forth to China as claimed. No CEDT for him has been found in the National Archives of Australia although several for a man named Lee Sing born c. 1882 have been identified from 1916 onwards, bearing a close facial resemblance to the subject Lee Sing. The ship names and number of journeys also match. It is possible he falsified his date of birth and put his arrival date back to the 1890s to evade immigration restrictions, but this is supposition only. Refer to Figure 3.1.

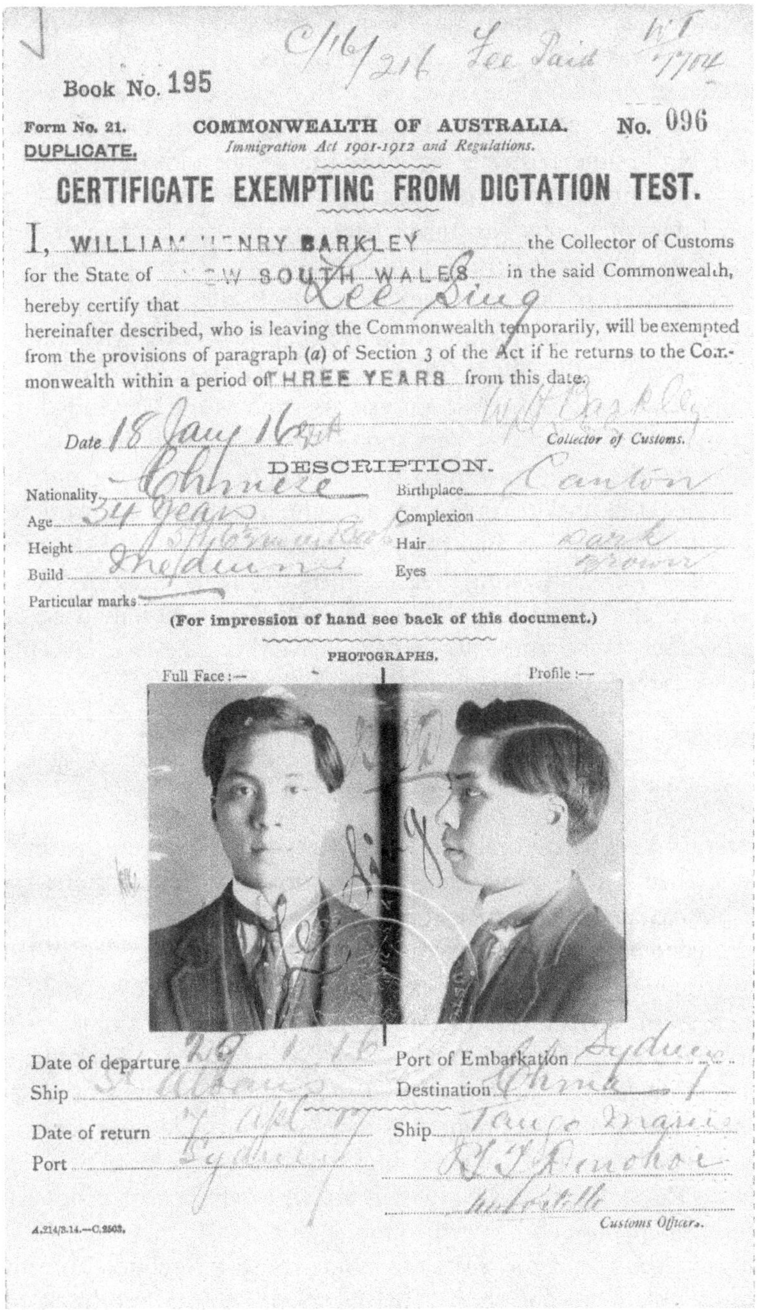

Book No. 195

Form No. 21.
DUPLICATE.

COMMONWEALTH OF AUSTRALIA.
Immigration Act 1901-1912 and Regulations.

No. 096

CERTIFICATE EXEMPTING FROM DICTATION TEST.

I, WILLIAM HENRY BARKLEY the Collector of Customs for the State of NEW SOUTH WALES in the said Commonwealth, hereby certify that Lee Sing hereinafter described, who is leaving the Commonwealth temporarily, will be exempted from the provisions of paragraph *(a)* of Section 3 of the Act if he returns to the Commonwealth within a period of THREE YEARS from this date.

Date 18 Jany 16

Collector of Customs.

DESCRIPTION.

Nationality	Chinese	Birthplace	Canton
Age	34 years	Complexion	
Height		Hair	Dark
Build	Medium	Eyes	Brown

Particular marks

(For impression of hand see back of this document.)

PHOTOGRAPHS.

Full Face:— Profile:—

Date of departure	29 1 16	Port of Embarkation	Sydney
Ship	St Albans	Destination	China
Date of return	7 Apl 17	Ship	Tango Maru
Port	Sydney		

Customs Officer.

A.214/3.14.—C.2503.

Figure 3.1. Lee Sing's Certificate of Exemption from the Dictation Test, 1916. (National Archives of Australia: ST84/1, 1916/195/91-100, photograph by Richard Horsburgh)

Haymarket. We called the shop Yat Sik; it was next door to Yee Sing (日昇) in Harbour Street. I was in this grocery for thirty years.

I had a lot of friends in the olden days. I would see them every week when I was in business. Whenever I returned to China, I would visit their villages, not only in Lung Du, but in other districts too. I used to go out a lot in those days. Now I have to use a walking stick. A lot of young people know me, but I don't know them. The reason I don't have any Australian friends is the language. You can't always remember what to say.

Altogether, I went back seven times. When the Pacific War broke out in 1941, I was here by myself. My mother, my Ah Je (阿姐, Dad's fourth wife)[5], my wife and the children were all in the village. There was no mail, no news.

Of course I worried. But it was no use. As soon as the war ended, I wrote to my family and sent them money. Very soon afterwards, I went back on a tiny ship. I can't remember the name now. As before, I went to Hong Kong and from there I took a ferry boat to Shekki. They were all right. They'd had a hard time though. Fortunately, they had some savings to live off and they were able to sell a few things. Also, the cousins were cultivating their rice fields, so at harvest time they gave my family a share of the crop. When we were first cut off, the family tried moving to Macao to live, but they found it was so expensive there they had to return to the village. That was the last trip I made to China.

My life in Australia

After my return here, I continued in the grocery shop. I was in that business for thirty years. Then I went into a fruit business for another few years. I've always worked in the city, never been to the tablelands.

There used to be a lot of Chinese here in Ultimo during the war. Whenever the *gwai jay* (鬼仔, barbarian kids) saw a Chinese they would throw stones and shout 'chow'. There wasn't anything you could do about it. The best thing was to ignore them. But it never happened to me all the time I've been living here. You know why? Because I was a local. Lots of thieves used to live at the bottom of the next street. But they had their own code of honour. They never touched local people.

My grandchildren never suffered like the Chinese here in the olden days. Except for my eldest daughter, who lives in Macao where her son is in business, the whole family is here now. I have twenty grandchildren in Sydney. The oldest is in his thirties and the youngest a few years old. Some are still in school. The others have jobs in banks, restaurants and shops. They all speak Chinese, but they can't read or write it. A few of them have even been to Hong Kong and to China and they liked it there.

---

5   Secondary wives were called *Ah Je* (big sister) by the children. Only the first wife was called Mother, including by the children of concubines.

Figure 3.2. The gravestone of Lee Sing and his two wives, Rookwood Cemetery, Sydney. (Richard Horsburgh)

After the war it became easier to bring the family out. If you had a business you could get permission for your family to come. My application was very quickly approved. So I gave up the fruit business and bought a fish and chip business in Harris Street, Ultimo, from Say Tin Fong. It was just around the corner and I bought this house at 9 Kirk Street for that reason. We've lived here for twenty years now.

It wasn't too difficult to run the fish shop. The former cook told me what to do and I hired two assistants. I always had two others working in the shop. They didn't stay very long because after my wife and two daughters came, they worked there. It all worked out very conveniently. The fish market was close by. It used to be way down at Glebe Point near the See Yup Temple where we went to *bai shen* (拜神, pray to the spirits and deities). The fish here in Sydney is very good for eating. We used to buy flathead and deep-fry it. Our customers bought fish and chips for lunch, or they bought cooked fish to take home after work.

At first the family found the life here strange, but they soon settled down. After all, I was here. Between us we ran the shop for more than ten years. That was a good few years ago, of course. It wasn't so bad, just frying fish and chips. The shop was open six days a week, half a day on Saturdays. None of them have to work now and they are still getting fed.

Mrs Lee has been here for more than thirty years now. She's never been back to China and I haven't been back for more than forty years. What was the use? We had nothing left there. All the land was gone. Even if you didn't want to leave, what else could you do? To be able to stay alive was good enough. Several years ago we were given back the house and we sold it for sixty thousand Hong Kong dollars. You couldn't sell it before then.

Australia is all right. The good thing about Australia is you can make money here. I worked very hard for my money. But every time I returned to China and saw my family and friends, I couldn't help feeling so happy. It's the language here that's the obstacle. It doesn't flow. I can't communicate so well.

People say Tong Shan is much better now. That's the way it should be. It won't do if there is no change. But I can't walk now. I can't go again, even if I wanted to.

Postscript

Lee Sing died in Balmain Hospital in 1989 within months of being interviewed and was buried at Rookwood Cemetery in Sydney on 30 October 1989. Unfortunately, at the time of publication it has not been possible to locate any of his family members.

4
A Childhood in North Queensland

Frank Lee Gee (李植良)

Believed to have been of mixed Italian and Chinese heritage, Frank Lee Gee (1910–1995) was the foster son of (George) Lee Gee (c. 1871–1944) and Elsie Kwong (c. 1894–1982).[1] Lee Gee ran a shop in Atherton's Chinatown during the maize-growing boom up to the First World War. Elsie was a daughter of the second wife of the well-known businessman and herbalist Kwong Sue Duk (鄺仕德). Chinese families without a son to perform the ancestral rites and thus ensure continuity to the family would often adopt one who would receive all the rights of a natural born son.

Although gold was discovered along the Palmer River in 1873 in north Queensland, inland from the coastal town of Cooktown, no restrictions were placed on Chinese entries to that state until their number escalated to an estimated 17,000 in 1877. This sudden rise resulted in the passing of Queensland's *Chinese Immigration Restriction Act* in the same year, limiting one Chinese arrival to every ten tons of shipping and a refundable entrance tax of ten pounds. The *Gold Fields Act Amendment Act 1878* quickly followed, excluding Chinese for three years from any new goldfield unless it was discovered by an Asian or African. However, as gold supplies diminished during the 1880s, the Chinese either returned home or took up agriculture in the new coastal settlements. They became suppliers of vegetables and fish, sugar cane and tropical fruit, particularly bananas. European settlers willingly leased them five-acre plots of virgin land in order to avoid this backbreaking labour themselves. In this way, the Chinese cleared north Queensland for today's sugar industry, before moving up to

---

[1] A lengthy description of the rituals surrounding the marriage of Elsie Kwong to Lee Gee was published in the *Morning Post* in Cairns on 3 June 1907.

the Atherton Tableland to cultivate maize. North Queensland's banana industry was also created by the Chinese, and its lucrative trade in the south became largely controlled by Chinese merchants there. In fact, it was the profits from the banana trade that led to the establishment of numerous Australian Chinese enterprises in Hong Kong and China in the first three decades of the 20th century.

Recalling his childhood days in north Queensland, Frank tells how the Chinese opened up the land for sugar, banana and maize cultivation, as well as his memories of the joss houses, the gambling and opium smoking, social and political activities, and community celebrations.

Where did I come from?

Loi lek bat ming (來歷不明, of unknown provenance; origin unclear). That's what I told some Chinese in a Sydney barber shop when they asked me where I came from. I've got no idea where I come from. All I know is I was born in Mareeba, near Cairns. The Chinese opened up, pioneered all the land up in north Queensland. They cut the trees down, sent the good ones to the timber mills and burned the rest. The ashes made the soil very rich and they grew bananas, especially around Cairns. After the bananas were cut the suckers would come up, what they call the next generation. But each plant only lasts for a few generations, so after that they shifted to new scrubland. But they didn't have to move away if they grew sugar. Then, later on, a lot of Chinese moved up to the Atherton Tableland.

I think it was about 1913 when my foster parents took me in at Atherton. They didn't have children of their own. My foster father was from Dai Laam (大嵐) village in Lung Du district in Chung Shan. He didn't tell me much about how he came to Australia but he came straight to Cairns and had nothing to do with gold mining. He lived in Cairns at first but I don't know what he did there. My foster father was in business up in the Atherton Tableland, in Chinatown. The town was only a little settlement, a one-street place, with shops and living quarters on both sides, just a dirt street, with a bit of gravel on it. When it rained it got very soggy. The maize farms around Atherton used to be cultivated by Chinese. They opened up all the land there too. One or two thousand people would come into Chinatown during the weekend, to gamble or shop. There was a joss house and a Chinese Masonic Lodge, what they called Gee Gong Tong (致公堂). Later on, they had a branch of the Chinese Nationalist Party, the Kuomintang (國民黨). In those days, more or less, everybody supported the Kuomintang when they wanted to collect money for patriotic reasons, or anything like that.

My foster father was well known. He had a house and a shop there. We lived at the back. The house had an upstairs and was done up very nicely. Not far from the

4 A Childhood in North Queensland

Figure 4.1. Kwong Sue Duk family 1907, including Elsie second from the right in the back row. (Jenni Campbell)

shop, he had a gambling place, like a casino. You could go there to play *fan tan* (番攤), *pai gau* (牌九, similar to dominoes), and even smoke a pipe of opium. A lot of the Chinese smoked opium. I've tried it. If you smoked too much, you would go off to sleep, like getting drunk with it. The authorities just turned a blind eye. As far as they were concerned, the Chinese were only smoking themselves, not doing others any harm, just like that. Sometimes the police might pinch the Chinese and fine them and let them go again, like in the gambling. They raided them now and again, then let them go and carry on. The police got a bit of money off them, that's all.

When I had a bit of sense, four or five years old, I think, if I could remember that far back, there was a young woman looking after me. She was my foster mother, Elsie Kwong. She was one of Kwong Sue Duk's daughters by his second wife.[2] He had four wives and over twenty children. He was a herbalist and came from Darwin. All his daughters and a son were living in the Atherton Chinatown, not far from our shop, and the foster mother used to send me to the grandmother.

---

2   Kwong Sue Duk (1853–1929) was a successful Chinese Australian herbalist and merchant who over a long career operated businesses in Darwin, Cooktown, Cairns, Townsville and Melbourne. He had four wives, 22 children and two adopted children. He has over 800 direct descendants in Australia and across the world. Chun Ngor Gwei (c. 1867–1924) was his second wife and Elsie Kwong had two older brothers and two younger sisters.

Every time I did something wrong, especially when I used my left hand, the foster mother would whack my left hand. Sometimes it even became swollen up. I'm still left-handed, real left-handed. Today they leave left-handeds alone. You write with your left hand. But I was beaten because I used my left hand, by my foster mother. I thought she was really my own mother. I was that young when they adopted me. I thought they were my real parents.

When it came to a festival we used to stay up all night, *ngou ye* (過夜, stick it out all night). They would put on fireworks, not just ordinary ones that go bang, a real firework display called *yin fa* (煙花). They would bring in firecrackers like that once or twice a year, for special occasions such as the new year and moon festival. Everybody would come and watch.

There was a fireplace where they roasted pork. All the firecrackers were let off in the fireplace. Then they would carry the pig up on two bars of steel and roast it in an old-fashioned way. When the pig got to a certain heat, they brought it up and used a fork to make the skin crackle. At the same time they barbecued some pork, what is called *chaah siu* (叉燒), did it all in one go. When the pig was cooked they would lift it down. That was all part of my childhood on the Atherton Tableland.

Sometimes the whole of Chinatown got on the train and went up Herberton way to have a picnic. I still remember the first time. There was a little pool there and I took off all my clothes and went in. I shouted to the girls and they ran like anything because I had no clothes on. Some of them were my cousins. In those days all the boys went in like that. The girls went in fully dressed, but the boys went in with nothing on. That's how everybody swam when I was going to school.

I used to go to a Sunday school in Chinatown, across a little street and bridge. The preacher lived there and we used to go to his place to have Sunday school. We would celebrate Christmas too.

At home I spoke Chinese. I think I started school when I was five or six years old. I learned English when I went to school. I first went to one of the schools up in Atherton in about 1916 for a year. The next was in Babinda, a sugar plantation place, where I went to the local school. I learned my times tables but I was no good at mathematics. But I learned to read and write English pretty well. I liked to read comic books, like Buffalo Bill comics. I saw movies too like Charlie Chaplin and Fatty Arbuckle. But I did have more chance to see films when I was living with the foster mother in Atherton, and only occasionally in Cairns.

Babinda

The foster mother and father had a bit of strife and the foster mother left him. She went back to her brother's shop in Babinda. She was born in Australia, she wasn't from China. She was only about eighteen or nineteen then. I think the foster father was over thirty years. She was only young. I was only six years old when she left. I was very attached to her. She used to ring me up and I always asked her when she was going to come back. Eventually, she came back and took me away with her to her brother's place. I stayed in Babinda for a long time, very seldom had contact with the foster father. I was always with her. At that time I was afraid to sleep by myself, I always slept with her. In a sort of way I was well cared for. She was cruel in a way but she looked after me. She used to make me pants, but instead of a fly I just had a little slit. I used to hate wearing those things.

A lot of Italians in Babinda went to the war on the British side. They had to conscript these Italians living in Australia to go and fight the Germans. The Italians used to work around the farms or in the hills or in town. I remember seeing them lined up and they didn't want to go. That was the early part of 1917. I was going to school there and people were talking about it.

There was a bit of a river in Babinda. One day, near the bridge, some Australian boys were playing 'prisoners-of-war'. They got me to be a German and they ill-treated me as a prisoner-of-war. They said they were going to kill me. I don't know whether they were fair dinkum or not. But they got me tied up. I was smaller than them and they were smarter than me. I was silly.

While we were in Babinda, my foster mother and her younger sister used to go around on horseback to all the Chinese cane farms selling pak-ah-pu (白鴿票) tickets. There were a lot of Chinese growing cane then. All the gambling places were around the uncle's shop there. He ran a kind of lotto called pak-ah-pu and he got a percentage of it. The two sisters got a percentage too. When you bought a ticket you had to pick a combination of ten Chinese characters from a printed list. They would be chosen, for example, from something well known like the *Three Character Classic* (三字經),[3] which everybody who went to school in China had to learn by heart.

On the second day, or even every day at night, they would open up a sealed combination of Chinese characters picked in advance. The thing was to try to pick the right combination of characters. You could pay a bit more to mark fifteen characters. If you could pick the whole ten words you could break the bank. Mostly, it was lucky if you could get up to six or seven characters right.

The uncle owned the shop, but he only had a share in the pak-ah-pu business. The foster mother might have had a couple of shares in it and all the Chinese around bought shares too. Sometimes the company made money and sometimes it might go broke. Then they had to form a company again.

---

3 Written in the 13th century, the *Three Character Classic* was the chief school primer in China and was used up to the republican revolution in 1911.

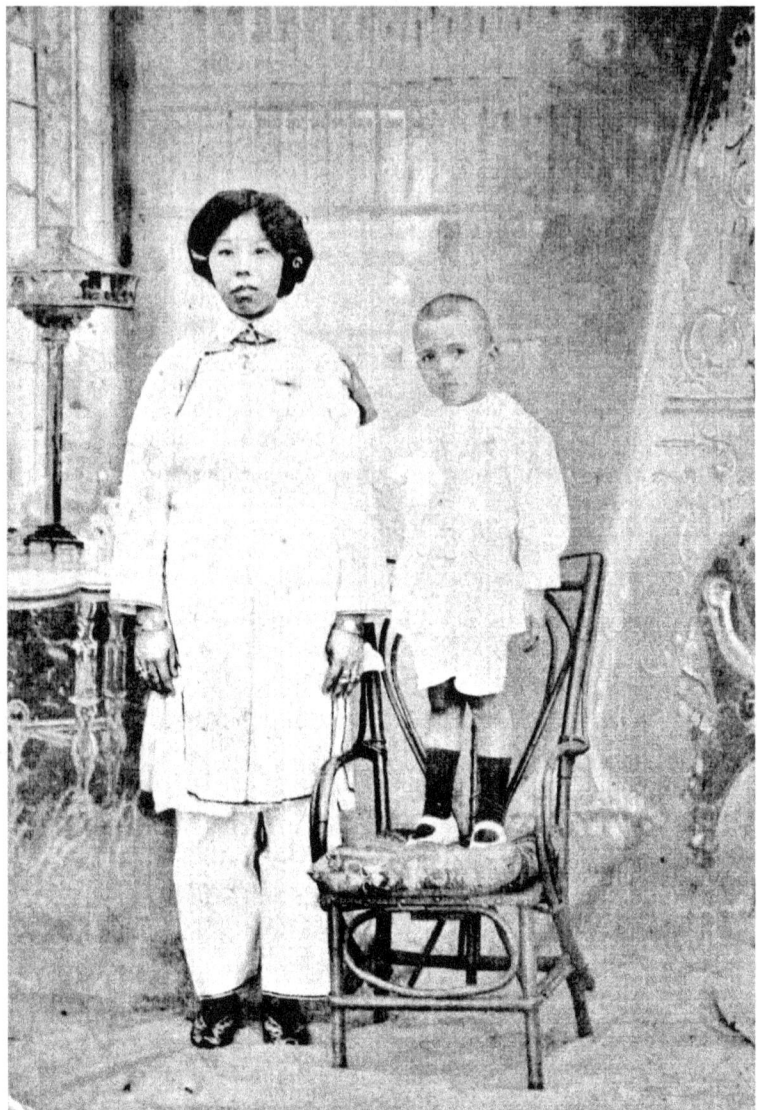

Figure 4.2. Frank Lee Gee with his foster mother Elsie Kwong in Atherton, c. 1914. (Lee Gee family)

The foster mother used to take me back to Atherton. We would stay at the youngest sister's farm there. Once when we were visiting there, her husband came out to meet the train in a horse and buggy, a sulky, they called it. Some had a front seat and a back seat, but they only had a front seat. I remember, I was just getting off when the horse started to go. The uncle was beside me. He saw the horse go, got hold of my hand and dragged me clear off the wheels. Otherwise they would have run right over me. I was only a kid.

Besides the farm, they had some chickens and a pigsty. One time they wanted to cook a chicken, but all the men were already out on the farm. There was nobody to kill the chicken and the women were too frightened to kill one. So they caught a chicken from the yard and asked me to chop its head off. I was only six! Yes, I did it. I got hold of the head and put the axe on it, but then the chicken started to run. I was terrified. It was running back towards the house, more or less chasing me, with no head on. It could still run. The nerve was still there.

I mostly spoke in Chinese to my foster mother, in the See Yup (四邑) dialect. Her family was originally from See Yup. They had moved from Toishan (台山) county to Shekki in Chung Shan (中山) county, and her father went to Darwin from Shekki. She was born in Australia and spoke good English, but she also spoke the See Yup dialect. When I was little, I could speak See Yup too. But as I grew older and got away from the See Yup crowd, then I couldn't speak it. I could still understand it a bit. I used to speak to all my cousins in See Yup.

My foster mother was always hitting my left hand. I had a toy gun, the kind you loaded by putting something in it so you could shoot at something. One day, she grabbed hold of the gun and hit me on the hand with the iron part. I think it might have cracked something. My hand swelled up and she was frightened to tell the uncle about it. She told him I fell down instead of saying she hit me. I didn't tell on her because she said she'd kill me if I told. I was afraid of her. But although I was afraid of her, in some instances, I liked her. I still treated her as my own mother. I was very attached to her.

That time on the farm she didn't take me to the doctor. One of the Chinese knew something about herbs. He went into the jungle and collected some herbs. He smashed them up and put them on my hand. But the next day it was still swollen. I think the uncle never knew what happened. The others thought I'd hurt myself.

We stayed in Babinda until the war ended. Then the uncle bought another shop not far from Babinda and he used to supply the cane farmers with groceries. Another sister bought the uncle's first shop in Babinda and my foster mother and her younger sister still worked there. But they stopped selling pak-ah-pu tickets.

When the soldiers came back after the war, they took up all the farms. The government gave the land to the returned soldiers to cultivate. The Australians eventually sold out to people like Italians and Yugoslavs who own the farms now, people who could stand up to hard work. But the English got first priority. As the Chinese had only leased the land, they had to leave. That was the end of Atherton's Chinatown.

Pawngilly

So then the uncle brought us to another place called Pawngilly. He bought a shop there. Now I had to go to another school, about a mile away, at a place called Mirriwinni, still a farming district. These were all country schools, bush schools, they called them. They had one big classroom divided into so many classes, first class, second class, and all that, a one-room school. Mostly farming families around there, not so many Chinese. Around Babinda there were a lot of Italians. A few years ago, when I was visiting Queensland, a friend of mine took me past the school. It still looked the same.

I enjoyed school in a way. I used to walk to the Mirriwinni school with a cousin, my foster mother's younger sister's son. He was a bit younger than me. He started school in Mirriwinni and I had to take him to school every day. One day when we were coming back he messed his pants up and I took him to the creek and washed him. He could have been five years old and I seven then. Before he went home he put on the wet clothes again. After we went home they all knew about it.

We could come home along the road, or we could walk along a railway track. There was a railway going through but only up to a certain point until a bridge was built. Before the bridge was built, a ferry took all the motor cars across. You went from Cairns to that point. After you crossed to the other side you got on another train that was waiting for you to go further down to Innisfail. The train went right down to Brisbane.

I stayed in Pawngilly until I had to go back to the foster father quite some time after. My foster mother had met an Italian man and got into trouble. The baby was born in the shop, we could hear it. Childbirth was very painful in those days and women suffered. Women would cry out 'Kill me, kill me. I want to die', you know. Afterwards they love the baby but curse the husband! Then she left with the baby and went to work doing housework for an Australian cane farmer as the foster uncle didn't want her there anymore. She couldn't keep me too so the foster uncle arranged for me to go back to my foster father.

By then he had left Atherton and moved to Mossman. In those days you could get to Cairns on the train or on a bus, but I had to wait in Cairns for the foster father to come over and take me back. I stayed at one of the foster father's friends. He lived at the Gee Gong Tong, the Chinese Masonic Society. I shared his bed too. I never slept by myself, always with somebody else. I was always afraid to sleep alone. Even when I went back to the foster father, I slept with him.

I didn't see my foster mother for a long, long time after I went to Mossman, not until during the Second World War when I came back to Australia from China. I did hear that my foster mother had met another Chinese man and went to Townsville and he conned her into sort of marrying him. I think the baby must have been adopted out, as I don't think this man wanted another man's child. This man took her back to China, to Shekki, but he had a wife back in a village there that the foster mother knew nothing about. He then got all her money and jewellery, took everything. Luckily she had a stepbrother in Nanking who had a government position. The Kwongs (鄺) were well educated. So he arranged for a local official to arrest the man for mistreating her and threatened him with execution if he didn't give her back all her money. He was so afraid he gave everything back and she came back to Australia in about 1927 or 1928.

Figure 4.3. Frank Lee Gee in Atherton, c. 1914. (Lee Gee family)

As a child I never experienced racial discrimination. They didn't call me names, like they did all the other Chinese kids. They used to sing a song. It went, 'Ping pong, Chinaman, very, very sad'. I can't remember it all now, but it went on to say, 'and they washed their face in a frying pan'. It rhymed too. Even in Mossman when I was a kid, they would say, 'Oh, you're different, you don't look Chinese'. It was like that all the time. But I think they regarded the Chinese better during the Second World War.

5
Chung Shan County

Frank Lee Gee (李植良)

In 1152, islands at the mouth of the Pearl River were officially designated as Heung Shan (香山) county. However, with the continuous washing down of silt by the West, North and East Rivers, by the time of the Ching dynasty (清朝, 1644–1911) the northern part of the county had been transformed into polder fields. Added to the already long-existing polder fields in the county's southern area, Heung Shan county became the richest rice-producing area in the Pearl River Delta.

Criss-crossed by waterways, streams and canals, Heung Shan county lay at the juncture of two worlds. In 1557, the Ming dynasty (明朝, 1368–1644) allowed the Portuguese to establish a settlement on a stony island at the southern tip of Heung Shan county, part of which they had already occupied in 1553. Historians believe this act was in appreciation of the Portuguese contribution in putting down pirates infesting the area. The Portuguese called the island 'A-Ma-Gau' (媽祖閣) after the Ma Kok Miu (媽閣廟) temple they found there, dedicated to the Goddess of the Sea. Eventually the Portuguese shortened the name to Macao. They were the first Europeans to set up trading relations by sea with China, arriving there early in the 16th century, after the discovery of the Cape of Good Hope by Vasco da Gama. The first English ships did not reach the seaport of Canton, the capital of Kwangtung (廣東) province in the north of the delta, until 1637.

However, the tottering Ching dynasty (1644–1911) lost the First Opium War (1840–1842) and had to cede Hong Kong to Britain. Located some sixty-five kilometres west of Hong Kong, until then Macao had served as the centre of Western trade. Faster European steam shipping during the mid-19th century made possible the massive migration of Chinese labourers to Australia, the United States, Canada and other Pacific countries. Both Macao and Hong Kong became points of departure.

Although the older Chinese always referred to the county as Heung Shan, in 1925 it was renamed Chung Shan (中山) in honour of Dr Sun Yat-sen (孫逸仙), who had inspired the republican revolution in 1911. However, the republican forces were weak, and tempestuous days of warlordism and banditry followed.

During this period, one of the most chaotic in China's history, Frank Lee Gee arrived in his foster father's village of Dai Laam (大嵐) in Chung Shan county in 1923 at the age of thirteen to learn Chinese. First he attended the village school, then later studied in the county centre of Shekki (石岐) and in Canton. This was a turbulent time, when Canton was the centre of China's nationalist revolution.

First impressions

In 1923, when I was thirteen, my foster father put me on a boat and sent me to China. I could speak a bit of Chinese then but my English was better. I wasn't any good at mathematics but I could write a letter.

The foster father's brother, my uncle, met me at Hong Kong. We caught a junk ferry, the *Ki Kong Dou* (岐港渡), to Shekki. 'Ki' was short for Shekki and 'Kong' for Hong Kong. 'Dou' means ferry. That's how they shortened names in Chinese. From Shekki, we went straight to the Lee (李) clan village of Dai Laam in the Lung Du (隆都) district of Chung Shan county. We took a small steamer boat from Shekki to Um Tong (安堂), where there was a little jetty and from there we walked to Dai Laam.

In a way, compared with Australia, it was a bit strange. The buildings were different. The food wasn't much different because all my life I was reared as a Chinese. Most of my meals were Chinese. The climate wasn't much different either. I suppose the villagers must have thought I was a strange being from another world. My clothes were different. I used to wear short pants and ordinary English shoes. It was a very simple life in the village. I don't think I could stand it if I had to go back there now.

The furniture where we lived was very simple. The whole family slept two or three to a bed. I shared a bed with an auntie. She cooked all the meals. I didn't have to do anything. When I got more used to the village, sometimes I helped fetch the drinking water from a spring not far away. The water in the well near the kitchen was considered only good enough for washing. The cousins usually fetched the water, a boy and a girl, about my age. The girl was the eldest of Uncle's children. We used a carrying pole, but it hurt my shoulder when I first tried it. I had to get used to it.

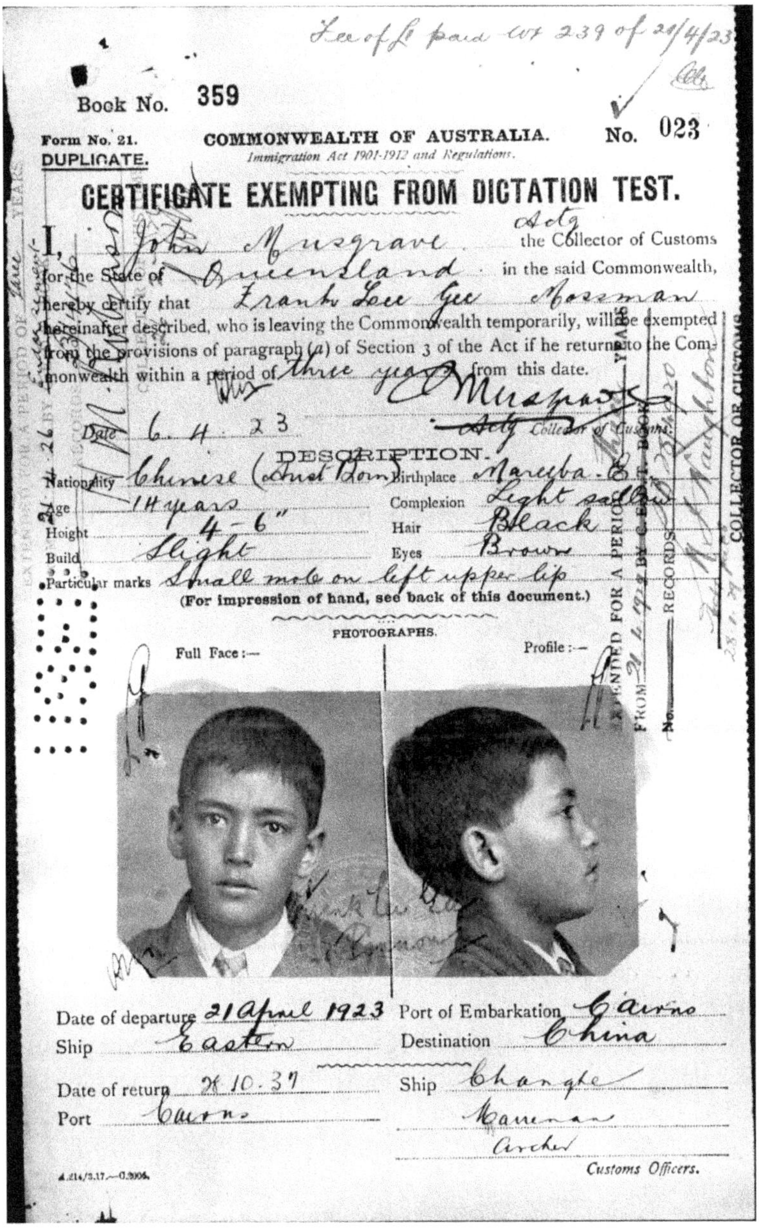

Lee of L paid Wt 239 of 21/4/23

Book No. 359

Form No. 21. COMMONWEALTH OF AUSTRALIA. No. 023

DUPLICATE. *Immigration Act 1901-1912 and Regulations.*

CERTIFICATE EXEMPTING FROM DICTATION TEST.

I, John Musgrave Actg the Collector of Customs for the State of Queensland in the said Commonwealth, hereby certify that Frank Lee Gee Mossman hereinafter described, who is leaving the Commonwealth temporarily, will be exempted from the provisions of paragraph (*a*) of Section 3 of the Act if he returns to the Commonwealth within a period of three years from this date.

Date 6.4.23 J Musgrave Actg Collector of Customs.

DESCRIPTION.

Nationality Chinese (Aust Born) Birthplace Mareeba

Age 14 years Complexion Light sallow

Height 4-6" Hair Black

Build Slight Eyes Brown

Particular marks Small mole on left upper lip

(For impression of hand, see back of this document.)

PHOTOGRAPHS.

Full Face:— Profile:—

Date of departure 21 April 1923 Port of Embarkation Cairns

Ship Eastern Destination China

Date of return 28.10.37 Ship Changte

Port Cairns Cameron

Archer

Customs Officers.

Figure 5.1. Frank Lee Gee's Certificate of Exemption from the Dictation Test, 1923. (National Archives of Australia: J2483, 359/23)

Village life

There was a bit of a hill near the village and the family had an orchard of twelve lychee (荔枝) trees there. But after one season, the grandfather sold the orchard.

Grandfather's name was Lee Yit Wah. He used to be like a foreman of some rice fields for a big landlord. He was called a *lo ba* (老闆, manager of rice fields). Before my foster father came to Australia, he used to hawk *haam yu* (鹹魚, salted fish) around Shekki and all over Chung Shan county. The foster father asked the grandfather to put up the money so he could go to Australia. How he came, I don't know. He didn't tell me much about the early days. But I learned the grandfather had to sell part of his *tin* (田, rice fields). The grandfather was only a small owner. He didn't come to Australia.

The village clan also owned rice fields which were rented out. Every year the clan distributed a share of roast pork to all the men and boys, but none to the women or girls. In some parts of Lung Du the girls didn't even take part in worshipping at the graves. But down in Tong Ka (唐家), a district close to Macao, they did. Not all the women in Lung Du had their feet bound. That depended on the parents. Even though foot-binding was already outlawed, people still bound their girls' feet in the outback places, right up to the People's Republic. But the Teng Ka (蜑家) people, the people who always lived on boats, they didn't bind the feet of their women.[1] Nor the Hakka (客家) people either.[2] Because they were all working people. They had to go down to the fields and up the mountains to collect firewood, *chai* (柴). They called firewood 'hard fuel'. 'Soft fuel' meant anything soft, like grass.

During the Chinese New Year festival I just watched the preparations of holiday food. At mealtimes we had more things on the table than usually. At least we had some pork, a duck or a chicken. When the holidays began I went out with the cousins. I used to watch people flying kites. There were two kinds, some very huge ones. Most were handmade. They also had a 'fighting kite', a smaller one with no tail. All the others were display kites. They had a tail, but not the fighting kites. The fighting kites would fight to see which had the sharpest thread on it – that one would win. Sometimes the fighting kites would get tangled up with the display kites and cut their cord, and they'd be flying away. But I didn't ever compete with the kite fliers. I just watched.

Dai Laam was a medium-sized village, with under a thousand population. Not like some villages which had about three or four thousand people. There was a market in Dai Laam, with all sorts of things on sale. You could get fresh fish every day, and at night time you could go there and have some *wun tun* (雲吞/餛飩, wonton) or noodles.

While I was in Dai Laam I went to the village school in the *chee tong* (祠堂), the ancestral hall. There was no such thing as a proper schoolhouse. There were about thirty or forty pupils. All the tablets of the clan forefathers looked down on

---

1 The Teng Ka are considered descendants of an aboriginal tribe in south China.
2 The bulk of the Hakka people arrived in Kwangtung province in the Sung dynasty (宋朝, 960–1279). They retained their own dialect and customs. They were dubbed 'hak ka', meaning guest people. They did not bind the feet of their women.

us and incense was burned every day. We had to go to school at six or seven o'clock in the morning. You didn't have any breakfast. You went straight to school. About ten o'clock you came back and had your breakfast. Then you went back to school until you came back for your evening meal. In those days in the village there were only two meals a day, at ten o'clock and four o'clock. Those were big meals. You only got three meals a day when it was harvest time. You had lunch as well then.

The rice was cooked in a big wok with a wooden frame across the top, so that while the rice was steaming, the pork and fish to go with the rice were also cooked. You might have another utensil for cooking vegetables. We burned soft fuel, grass. The cousins used to gather the grass. I didn't go. I just went to school seven days a week. There was no such thing as a weekend.

I went to the village school for less than two years. I started on simple characters first. I learned a good few characters there. In those days there was no such thing as first year, second year. I was never good at figures. That's why I never became a businessman. I was a dunce, and when I was in the Australian schools I was kept back in a way through the sums. Even later when I was going to middle school in Canton, I didn't like arithmetic. I used to like history and geography. In middle school I used to write articles, but if you ask me to now I don't think I could.

Now and again I went up to Shekki by boat or you could go to a nearby village and hire a rickshaw. There was a track leading right down to the waterfront opposite Shekki. It took less than an hour to get to town. I would go window shopping and have a look around Shekki.

Shekki

In 1925, I went up to Shekki to continue studying there. There was great turmoil then, especially in Lung Du where there were a lot of bandits. They were kidnapping people from overseas and holding them for ransom. They could see I was one of them. In fact, I was almost kidnapped once. If you were kidnapped and didn't pay the ransom you'd be killed. My foster father was still in Australia, so the uncle thought it better to send me up to Shekki. I remember Dr Sun Yat-sen died in 1925, the year I went to Shekki.

During 1926 and 1927, there was a united front between the nationalist and communist parties and there was a great upheaval in Shekki. Drives were conducted against the local village bullies and corrupt officials. There were a great deal of strikes too. A lot of new Marxist ideas were being spread. In a way, that's how I became interested in politics. One of my teachers became the secretary of the Shekki Trade Union Federation. Although we studied the normal textbooks, looking back I can see that a lot of the teachers had Marxist attitudes.

The school I went to had to give up its premises because the army wanted to take it over for a headquarters. So the school moved to the city's southern gate where there was a big market called the Nam Mun Gai See (南門街市, South Gate Market). I had no

Figure 5.2. Shekki, China, c. 1932. (Agnes Breuer papers, courtesy Liz McNamee)

home in Shekki, so at first I shared a room with another chap and we cooked together. After we had to shift out, I had my meals with the family of one of the teachers.

Life in Shekki was different to the village. It was a busy town. There was a picture show there, no sound movies of course. It was all silent movies and very primitive. Sometimes I used to go with a friend. There was only one wide street and one bookshop. While I was there they started to widen the main street. There wasn't even a hospital until somebody came from America and started one, about 1927, I think. There was a Catholic church and a foreign priest too. There weren't any other foreigners living there that I remember.

If you wanted to travel, you had to rely on the waterways. There were no highways. There were junks towed by a steamer launch going to Canton, like the ferries going to Hong Kong and Macao. Now and again bandits would seize the junks. The launches would cut the ropes towing the junks and leave the passengers to the mercy of the bandits.

Canton

After two years in Shekki, I completed the regular primary school curriculum. I then went up to Canton and became a boarder in a very well-known private school, called Foo Yung Middle School. Foo Yung used to be co-educational, but after Chiang Kai-shek (蔣介石) came to power, the policy was changed again. By the time I went there, they had restored separate boys' and girls' sections. I enjoyed studying at Foo Yung and being in Canton. While I was there, the foster father returned from Australia and I would go back to the village for the holidays.

After his return my foster father remarried and decided to start a business in the township of Heung Chow (香洲), near Macao. Because of Heung Chow's favourable location, there had been talk of turning it into a deep-water port for international trade, to compete with Hong Kong and Macao, but there wasn't sufficient support for the project. The business my father started was a *jau mai pou* (酒米鋪, wine and rice shop). He hired somebody to make the wine and also sold rice. But when I went back to Heung Chow at the end of my third term at Foo Yung, my foster father suddenly told me I wasn't going back to school anymore. I got such a shock. I nearly put up a fight, but I knew it wasn't any use.

I knew it was my father's new mother-in-law. She'd nagged him not to waste money sending me to school anymore. You see, he might have offspring from her daughter and they would have to be looked after. So why not get me to work in the shop or even send me back to Australia? Actually, I was dying to come back to Australia. I did put up a bit of a struggle. I boycotted the foster father and his wife. I wouldn't eat. I wouldn't do a thing for the place. I could have helped round the shop, but I wouldn't. I wanted to go back to Canton to continue at school. If I had finished junior middle school, I could have done a bit of teaching in primary school. I still had the right pronunciation as far as English was concerned. I was just twenty then. So from then on, I just stayed in Heung Chow, doing nothing. I became what the Chinese call a *faai yun* (廢人, useless person). My father tried to get me to work in the shop, but I didn't want to. I became more or less unemployed.

While I was doing nothing, I used to go off to visit an old schoolmate from Canton who lived in Tong Ka, not far from Heung Chow. Like me, he and his eldest brother couldn't continue going to school as their father had died. Sometimes I stayed with them for a week or so, more or less sponging on his mother. Finally, somebody took the eldest brother to Shanghai to learn the tea business. The Tong Ka people were in the tea business. The younger brother only had one eye so it wasn't so easy for him to find something to do. I made some good friends in that little town.

The foster father's shop had a bicycle. I used to take it out and ride all over the place. But in the shop, they didn't like me using the bicycle and they went and sold it. If I had had that bicycle I could have travelled down to Macao and brought stuff back. I could have earned a bit of money. They just sold it and then I didn't have it. Oh, I used to love that bicycle.

My father wasn't all that strict. But he couldn't make me work because I didn't want to. I think the wife had a lot to do with it. She used to have her brother working in the shop. Sometimes I used to take a few coppers out of the till while

Figure 5.3. Frank Lee Gee (top right) and school friends, Canton 1928. (Lee Gee family)

I was selling the wine. I might take ten cents, or twenty cents. I used to save it up and when I had twenty or thirty or forty cents, I would go down to yum cha (飲茶). I loved yum cha in those days. I still like to go to yum cha in a sort of way, but you do get sick and tired of it. I'd go and sit in the teashop for a couple of hours, chat with someone, have a few *bao* (包, buns). I'd be watching people and thinking. Or sometimes I took a book there and read. I used to like reading modern Chinese literature. I couldn't read the classics. You have to study that subject to be able to understand them. I wasn't interested in girls. In any case, you couldn't take them out. You hadn't got the money to spend on them.

My father had a partner, a cousin from the same village. Father had put up the money to buy the shop. But the other bloke went and borrowed money to start the business and then he didn't put any money in at all. I don't know how the foster father got into this. The partner could have said, 'If you trust me, I'm not going to use all the money for the shop. I can put half the money in.' But instead, as he had to return to Townsville, he said he was going to send the money to keep the shop going. But he didn't send anything. Mind you, he was a cousin from the same village. So, when the time was up, the creditors sued the foster father. He had to give up the shop. They took everything. That was when he had to go back to hawking salted fish.

Frank's story continues in Chapter 10

6
Two Worlds

Harry Gock Ming (郭桂芳)

In 1910 Harry Gock Ming's (1911–2002) Chinese father William Gock Ming (c. 1877–1940) married Harry's mother Mabel Jenkins (1879–1925), a seamstress. Gock Ming was the manager of Wing Hing (永興) & Co., a fruit and vegetable business in the Chinatown area of Western Australia's capital of Perth. At twenty-six years old, William Gock Ming had come to Perth from Queensland via Sydney in 1903 to take over his older brother's share in the store. Mabel had arrived in 1901, aged twenty-two, from Bendigo in Victoria with her widowed mother and three unmarried sisters to explore job opportunities in the growing city.

The number of Chinese living and working in the state of Western Australia remained relatively small throughout the 19th century. Following the first recorded arrival in 1829, the Chinese were principally employed as farm labourers, cooks and gardeners. Hundreds, perhaps thousands, came to perform this work under contract arrangements organised by the colonial government through Singaporean agents, one of the main recruitment centres for the so-called coolie trade. When gold was discovered, legislation was introduced to prevent Chinese from obtaining leases on any new goldfields for a period of three years. However, from the 1880s into the first decade of the new century, there was a steady increase in Chinese employed in service occupations – as shopkeepers, tailors, bootmakers, furniture makers and market gardeners. The coastal towns of Broome, Carnarvon and Geraldton had small communities of Chinese shopkeepers by the end of the century. Broome, in particular, had a high concentration of Asian residents following the establishment of the pearling industry in the 1880s, mainly Japanese and Malays but also Chinese.

There was a constant trade of foodstuffs and goods between Chinese shopkeepers in Perth and these coastal towns and inland agricultural and beef cattle properties. Harry's father was one of these suppliers. The population of Perth grew from approximately 10,000 in 1880 to over 116,000 by 1911 and the Chinese residents, while only making up about one per cent of the state population, were by far the largest non-European community. Perth's Chinatown at that time was located around James and William Streets, in what is now the inner-city suburb of Northbridge.

Harry was born in Hong Kong in 1911 during an extended two-year honeymoon visit by his parents to his father's ancestral village in Chung Shan (中山) county in the Pearl River Delta. Returning to Perth in 1912, Harry's mother instilled in him a deep sense of pride in his Chinese ancestry as well as a firm belief in Australian values, particularly the principle of a 'fair go' for everyone. His story is about the two worlds he grew up in.

The Gock clan

Chinese in Australia in the olden days were a community under siege. They had no roots here, no one they could rely on. Because of their industry, efficiency and thrift, they were feared. The Australians thought the Chinese would take over the country. But the Chinese had no such ambitions. Until the outbreak of the Second World War, when two Chinese met their first words were 'Are you well?' and 'When are you going home to China?'

All the Chinese wanted was to gather some money, no matter how hard the process, then return home to enjoy the fruits of their labour. Before the Depression in the 1930s, a Chinese could work for three to five years, save enough to go home for two years and then start all over again.

The money they earned was a great boost to the economy of many towns and villages in the Pearl River Delta. It also created a great many *tai jee jay* (太子仔), crown princes or wastrel sons and grandsons, who bludged on the labours of their fathers. But under the *Immigration Restriction Act* of 1901, no new Chinese were allowed into the country. Thus, by the 1930s Australia's Chinese population had dwindled to a very small number indeed.

My grandfather came to Australia in about 1860 from Chuk Sau Yuen (竹秀園) – Beautiful Bamboo Garden, that was the name of the village – in Heung Shan (香山) or Fragrant Mountain county, in the Pearl River Delta. The county was renamed Chung Shan in 1925 in honour of Dr Sun Yat-sen (孫逸仙), who became Provisional President of the Chinese Republic on 1 January 1912. Dr Sun's home village was in Heung Shan too, within walking distance of Chuk Sau Yuen.

6 Two Worlds

Originally, Chuk Sau Yuen was the smallest of a cluster of three villages. Later, another village grew up alongside and so they became four. They were Sha Chung (沙涌), Haang Mei (恆美), Chuk Sau Yuen and Sheung Tong (上塘), always referred to in this order because in China seniority counts. Sha Chung was the oldest village, set up in the Sung dynasty (宋朝, 960–1279) and home of the Ma (馬) clan. Haang Mei was the largest and wealthiest. Its people were surnamed Lee (李). It was set up in the Ming dynasty (明朝, 1368–1644). Chuk Sau Yuen was also set up in the Ming dynasty but later than Haang Mei. Sheung Tong was established comparatively more recently by people who wanted to enter the three villages but couldn't, so they settled down alongside them. Sheung Tong was multi-surnamed.

Chuk Sau Yuen was a distance of three miles from the county centre of Shekki (石岐). Everyone in this village was surnamed Gock (郭, also romanised as Kwok). My grandfather was a Gock. The village was formed when two brothers moved over from Chai Ky Lok (茶奇落) village, halfway between Shekki and Chuk Sau Yuen, from the Gock clan there.

The Chinese like to play on words with a similar pronunciation but different meaning. One of these two brothers became known as the 'Blue Sky' ancestor and his progeny the 'Blues'. The other was styled 'Hundred Years' ancestor and his descendants the 'Whites', because the character for white has the same pronunciation as that for hundred. Baak Sooey Goong (百歲公), hundred years ancestor, lived till over a hundred. My grandfather, we called him Ah Goong (阿公), was a White. I never knew his proper name in Chinese, but in English, on my parents' marriage certificate, it was Ken Joy.[1] He died in about 1880 when my dad was four by traditional Chinese reckoning. Ah Goong's bride was a Ma from the neighbouring village of Sha Chung, and her given name was Doong Chee, meaning persimmon. Ah Goong's family couldn't have been poor because Ah Paw (阿婆), my grandmother, had bound feet. Such women had to have servants work for them. Their first child was a girl, a strong and healthy child, whose feet were bound as soon as she became old enough. Then they had triplets, an event so outstanding it was remembered among the Gocks of the day. Only one survived, a boy, and he was named Sek (锡).

The new gold mountain

There was a lot of talk in those days about gold being picked up off the ground in California and Australia. California was dubbed the 'old golden mountain', and Australia the 'new golden mountain' because the Chinese rush took place to California first. Ah Goong took off for Bendigo in Australia in about 1860. By then

---

1   The name Ken Joy remains a mystery to Harry Gock Ming's family, as there is no reference to the clan name of Gock on the marriage certificate and no person of this name has been found in the National Archives of Australia.

Chinese were no longer allowed to mine for gold.² So he and others went into market gardening around the goldfields. Ten years later, Ah Goong returned to Chuk Sau Yuen with a bag of gold. Now he was Gock number one, the richest man in the village. He built the village's first brick house, with a tiled roof and ceramic tiled floor. Previously everyone lived in mud brick huts with thatched roofs. My grandparents had another son in 1868 named Hoy (海). He was *Saam Baak* (三伯, third elder uncle), the triplets being considered as one birth. Then Ah Goong went off to Vancouver in Canada where he spent a year working in the fish markets. Returning home, his fourth child, also a son, Ming, was born in 1877. Ah Goong only enjoyed his money for a few years. He died in about 1880, leaving the family in a comfortable position with a lychee (荔枝) orchard, a peach orchard and a grove of olives.

It was now Sek's turn to support the family. He too went off to Australia, but I don't know how or where.³ After the gold rushes declined in Victoria and New South Wales, the Chinese diggers tended to concentrate around country towns and the big cities of Sydney and Melbourne. They mostly took up market gardening, ran laundries, furniture factories, groceries, fruit and vegetable shops and import-export agencies. They followed the gold rush to Western Australia in the 1890s when gold was discovered in Coolgardie and Kalgoorlie. Although they were not allowed on the goldfields, they were able to establish similar small businesses when Sek turned up in Perth in the 1890s.

When I was growing up in Perth, most of the Chinese seemed to be from See Yup (四邑), the four counties of Sun Wooey (新會), Hoy Ping (開平), En Ping (恩平) and Toishan (台山) in the south-west of the Pearl River Delta. They had come over from Melbourne. The vast majority of Chinese in Victoria were from See Yup. In New South Wales and Queensland, Chinese from Chung Shan dominated, with large numbers from Tung Koon (東莞) county as well as other places. There were numerous county societies in the early days in Sydney. Well, Sek and four other Gocks started a fruit and vegetable shop, the Wing Hing & Co., on the corner of William and James Streets in Perth.⁴ Another partner was Pang Yee Ping. He was also from Heung Shan county, but across the river from Chuk Sau Yuen, from the village of Cheung Gock (象角) in the Lung Du (隆都) district. Our village was in the Leung Du (良都) district. They must have had some capital, so they most likely came from the east coast. Gock Wah Dung, who wasn't even a partner,

---

2   This is not true. A more likely explanation was that there was less gold to be mined by means typically used by Chinese miners.
3   No record has been found in the National Archives of Australia confirming the arrival in Australia or residing in Perth of a person named 'Sek' or 'Gock Sek'. However, an arrival record has been located for 28-year-old Seck aKok on the S.S. *Guthrie* docking at Sydney on 13 August 1888.
4   Wing Hing & Co. commenced at 71 James Street, Northbridge, in 1897 when the partners bought an existing fruit shop, On Lee & Co. It later relocated to the corner of James and William Streets in Northbridge.

6 Two Worlds

Figure 6.1. William Gock Ming, 1925, from his Certificate of Exemption from the Dictation Test, 1925. (National Archives of Australia: PP4/2, 1936/451)

whom I called Saam Gor (三哥, third elder brother), had come over to Perth from Melbourne where he had been working in the Queen Victoria Markets. Tom Chin Mook, who drove the horse and cart, came from Sheung Tong village. He'd been all over Australia. Actually, his surname was Chun. I don't know how it became Chin.

The next in our family to go to Australia was my own third elder uncle, Hoy.[5] He went in 1888. But he was a disaster. I am entirely ignorant of his movements but suspect he lived in Sydney at some point. He never contributed a penny towards the upkeep of his wife and child when he married years later.

Father's arrival in Australia

Then came my dad, Ming's (明) turn. He went to Queensland because Chinese were no longer admitted to New South Wales, unless they paid a poll tax of one hundred pounds. Ming arrived in Cairns in 1897. He was nineteen at the time by Chinese reckoning. Chinese babies were considered one year old at birth and two years old by their first Chinese New Year. Even if they were born the day before.

When Ming produced a landing permit bought from a sixty-year-old returnee,[6] the customs officer laughed.

'What's your name?' he asked.

'Gock Ming (郭明).'

'All right, I'll give you an English name, William, William Gock Ming.'

The surname Gock acquired various renderings, including 'Gork', 'Goq', settling down as 'Gock', and eventually 'Kwok'. Today in Mandarin it has been altered from Kuo to Guo.

At first Dad worked in the sugarcane fields, later on at a station doing fencing, tree clearing and any other job available, for ten shillings a week. Here he became a great admirer of the horsemanship of the Australian stockman. He told me that when an Australian sat on a horse you could not distinguish where the horse finished and the man began. He particularly admired one young rider recognised by his peers as the champion. Unfortunately, this young man was breaking in a horse one day when it unseated him and kicked him to death. That left my father with an abhorrence of horses. It also left him with a philosophy that he impressed on me once. Always strive to achieve in what you do, but do not become the best because there is always someone better who will cut you down.

After a few years in the bush and saving his meagre pay, Dad joined with four others, one a first cousin named Gock Hoy Buck, to cross the border at night-time with a guide into New South Wales to avoid the tax. Then the guide left them but as soon as they walked into the border town of Tenterfield, the local policeman

---

5   NAA: K1145, 1916/102. A CEDT for Gok Hoy in Perth is listed in the National Australian Archives. Both his date of birth and departure from Australia in 1916 match other information known to Harry Gock Ming. Ann Atkinson in *Asian Immigrants to Western Australia 1829–1901, The Bicentennial Dictionary of Western Australians* states that his address is John Street, Leederville. At the time his brother Gock Ming lived at 88 John Street, Perth, on the border of the suburb of Leederville.

6   This story was handed down through the Ming family but cannot be verified, as no records of the arrival of Gock Ming in Queensland in the 1890s have been found. The use of another person's immigration papers, however, is not unusual – see chapter 16.

arrested them. Hoy cried all night at the disgrace of being locked up. The next morning the copper ordered them to chop a supply of firewood. Ming refused. 'Me no thief, no chop,' he said. 'All right,' said the copper, 'no wood, no tucker'. So he got his wood. They were allowed to send a telegram to Sydney to Hoy Buck's brother, Hoy Gei, who was then working in a banana store. Hoy Gei telegraphed a Tenterfield solicitor to defend them.

When the solicitor questioned the reason for their arrest, the policeman said it was obvious they were illegals from Queensland because the soles of their boots were worn out. The solicitor took the policeman into the street and asked the first five white men passing if he could look at the soles of their boots. Their soles were worn out too. The Chinese were released and proceeded on their way to Sydney.

Chinese businesses in those days were mostly loose partnerships. When one partner wanted to return to China, he sold his share and found another on his return. As long as you could afford a share in a business, you did well. But if you had to hire out, you got a rough deal. Ming was offered work in Sydney by his fellow Gocks, but he wasn't impressed with the pay and the conditions. Instead, he bought two Chinese baskets and a carrying pole and began forestalling in the Sydney markets. He would buy his produce early and resell at a profit. He soon developed a skill in estimating market conditions. Among Ming's fellow Gocks clan cousins were James Gock Lock (郭樂) and Philip Gock Chin (郭泉), two brothers, of the Wing On (永安果欄) fruit merchants business. Gock Lock would scoff at Dad and say, 'You call that a business!' But Dad would only smile and say, 'I'm eating.'

The uppermost thought of every Chinese in those days was when he could afford to go home to China. During the 1900s, Sek decided he had enough money to do so. He was also under pressure from his mother to return and get married. Sek's sister had already married a man surnamed Lo (劉) in the village of Lung Ngan Sy Chung (龍眼樹涌), Lung Ngan Tree Creek, when she was sixteen, before Ming was born. *Lung ngans* (龍眼) are a brown-shelled fruit similar to lychees and valued for their medicinal properties. I called this sister Gwoo Moo (姑母), meaning father's elder sister. Her son was older than Dad and he also went off to Australia where he had a fruit and vegetable business in Charters Towers in Queensland.

One of the greatest highlights of a Chinese mother's life was when her eldest son married. But Sek didn't want to give up his interest in the Wing Hing & Co. So he sent for Ming to go to Perth. Ming was to retain a share of the profits and remit the balance to Sek in a constant flow of funds. Dad must have gone to Perth in about 1903 when Sek returned to Chuk Sau Yuen. His mother had already picked out a bride from Doo Tow (渡頭) village, a mile from Chuk Sau Yuen. Everyone in Doo Tow was surnamed Louey (雷). Anyhow, Sek went home, got married and had a son and two daughters. But the quiet village life didn't appeal to him and he made constant trips to Hong Kong to enjoy the good life there. On one of these trips, he contracted double pneumonia and died.

With Sek's death, responsibility for the family fell on Ming's shoulders. He became a full partner in Wing Hing. Although the business was maintaining itself, he thought it was inefficient. Every evening after the shop closed, Ming would argue with the other partners. But they regarded him as a young whippersnapper and took no notice. Then Gock Yea, one or two years older than Ming, began to side with him. The arguments became more heated to the point that the partnership itself became intolerable. When a shop became vacant a few doors away, the two of them took it over. They not only withdrew from Wing Hing, but captured three-quarters of its business through better buying and management practices and elimination of waste. The older partners in Wing Hing began to panic. Through Gock Yea, they put out feelers for a reconciliation. They were cousins, uncles, nephews, they should stick together, they reasoned. Agreement was reached. Ming was to be the new manager and Wing Hing prospered as never before.[7]

Marriage and family

After the reconciliation, Ming and Yea enrolled in a church-funded night school run by two Australian ladies, trying to teach Chinese the rudiments of English as well as convert them to Christianity. Ming's understanding of English was basic at best and he realised that without better language skills he could not progress very far. Even his written Chinese ability was not high as back in the village he preferred flying a kite to attending school. The younger teacher, Mabel Jenkins, came from Bendigo. She was a devout Christian, a leading member of the Congregational church, and she abhorred strong drink and the loutish behaviour of many white men of the time. She was a handsome woman, very prim and proper. She was about five foot two inches tall and Ming was only about half an inch taller.

By early 1910, Ming and Mabel decided to get married and go to China for their honeymoon. But when Mabel took Ming down to her Congregational minister to discuss the wedding he was horrified and refused to marry them. Her mother didn't approve either. However, the Congregational church in Melbourne had a more liberal attitude. So Mabel took passage on a ship to Melbourne and Ming followed on the next boat. She later said, 'I would not travel with him and would not allow him to go first, so no one could say I chased him across Australia.'

After my parents' marriage at the Congregational church in the suburb of Richmond in Melbourne, they visited Sydney. They stayed with Mr and Mrs Harry Gock Gew, who had a fruit and vegetable shop near today's Broadway in Sydney.[8] Mrs

---

7   At its peak, the Wing Hing & Co. shop complex comprised four adjoining shopfronts on a prime corner location – at 207 William Street and at 61, 63 and 65 James Street, Northbridge.

8   NAA: SP42/1, c. 1936/1860. This National Archives of Australia file records that Harry Gock Gew, also known as Jim Lee, worked at Wing On & Co. in Sydney from 1906 to 1910 and from 1910 to 1930 was the proprietor of a fruit shop at 530 Parramatta Road, Leichhardt.

6 Two Worlds

Gock Gew was also Australian. Both she and her husband, a childhood mate of Dad's in Chuk Sau Yuen, were so kind to Mum and Dad that I was named after Harry.

After the gold rushes in Queensland, instead of concentrating in the big cities as in Victoria and New South Wales, the Chinese diggers who stayed on moved into agriculture. Coming from the Pearl River Delta, they were well experienced in handling tropical crops and they built up a flourishing banana-growing industry, with huge exports to the south. As a result, by the early 1900s, the Chinese fruit merchants in Sydney and in Melbourne virtually controlled the distribution of this fruit. They had also become the leading members of the Chinese communities.

Among the wholesale banana distributors in Sydney were the Wing Sang (永生), the Tiy Sang (泰生) and the Wing On companies. They were not only marketing Queensland bananas, but in about 1904 they had formed a three-company syndicate, the Sang On Tiy & Co. (生安泰公司), to both cultivate and purchase bananas in Fiji. The syndicate was managed by Philip Gock Chin (1875–1966), a younger brother of James Gock Lock (1872–1956). Through the banana trade, the humble Wing On fruit merchants store had blossomed out into a registered limited company. The Wing Sang company was even older than Wing On, having been set up in 1890, the same year that James Gock Lock arrived in Australia.

One of the founders of the Wing Sang company was Ma Ying Biu (馬應彪, 1860–1944). He was from the village of Sha Chung, where Dad's mother came from. Ma started out working in the tin mines and became converted to Christianity. He was well known for his Christian endeavours. When one of the partners in Wing Sang was preparing to retire to China, Ma advised George Gock Bew (郭標, 1868–1932), a labourer in Wing Sang, to buy this partner's share. George asked his Gock cousins in Wing On to loan him the necessary money. But they only laughed at him. So Ma lent George the money and George later became a very successful banana merchant.

One of the fascinations for the Chinese in Sydney in those days was the large Anthony Hordern's department store on the edge of Chinatown. A department store where everything was sold at fixed prices was unheard of in China. After Ma returned home, he decided he would like to run such a store in Hong Kong. He persuaded others to join him in setting up the Sincere (先施) Company Ltd in 1900, the biggest shop in Hong Kong at the time.

Over in the Wing On fruit business, the same idea was entertained by James Gock Lock. So, in 1907, he dispatched Philip Gock Chin to Hong Kong to follow Ma Ying Biu's example. With the assistance of compatriots with Australian experience, the Wing On department store was set up and grew rapidly. Soon afterwards, James Gock Lock returned to Hong Kong to become the managing director. So by the time Mabel and Ming passed through Hong Kong in 1911 on their way to Heung Shan, both the Sincere and Wing On companies had already become influential commercial forces there.

Figure 6.2. Mabel Jenkins in Bendigo, c. 1899. (Gock Ming family)

Honeymoon in Heung Shan

Mabel must have found the transition from Australia to Chinese village life very strange. While her mother-in-law may have had reservations about her son's foreign bride, when she was told Mabel was pregnant she was ecstatic, for more grandchildren was the only aim in her life. Although an object of great curiosity to the Chinese women, she was waited on hand and foot and soon settled in. She was never heard to utter one word of complaint about her stay of two years in the village. As for Ming, back home at last, after an absence of more than ten years, he set about building three new houses, one for his mother, one for his sister-in-law and one for himself.

It was essentially one large house with two wings. The centre one, his mother's, featured the common front door, a massive double door about four inches thick. This was left open all day but barred at night. Immediately inside the front door was a large room serving as a living room for all, where visitors were received. Behind this were two private rooms for his mother's use, and behind again the common kitchen. The wings on either side were identical, each consisting of four rooms, with connecting doors to the centre house in the front and back rooms. Outside the kitchen door in the centre house was a well for washing, bathing and general cleaning purposes, but the water was not fit for human consumption. All drinking water and water for cooking had to be carried in large Chinese wooden buckets, or two large kerosene tins, two to a pole, from a mountain spring half a mile away to the east of the village.

A high brick wall enclosed the small backyard, with an outhouse in the north-east corner. The facilities were a deep pit over which one squatted, and a box of ashes to be sprinkled after each usage. These double brick houses had a high-pitched tiled roof and floors of ceramic tiles. They are still standing today.

Fuel was fast-burning dried grass gathered from the mountains. Most of the carrying of water and gathering of grass was done by the women. Ming's mother and sister-in-law had small feet, so he had to employ labour. Mabel was not required to do any work at all.

In July 1911, Ming and Mabel returned to Hong Kong, where I was born at 8 am on 8 August 1911 at the Nethersole Hospital. This was the twelfth day of the intercalary sixth month in the year of the pig. The Chinese lunar year falls short of the solar calendar by several days. An intercalary month is therefore inserted every few years to bring the lunar calendar into line with the seasons. I was registered at the Hong Kong Registry Office and issued with a birth certificate in the name of Harry Gock Ming.

My early diet consisted of Borden's condensed milk and Arnott's milk arrowroot biscuits, purchased in Hong Kong. Dad and Mum now went back to the village where my mother and I were spoiled beyond description. Mabel's status soared to great heights, having given my grandmother another male grandson. After the Chinese New Year, Ah Paw registered my birth in the ancestral temple at nearby Chai Ky Lok. She gave me the name of Gock Kway Fong (郭桂芳).

Towards the end of 1912, my parents decided it was time to return to Australia. My mother's mother had died earlier in the year. We went back to Hong Kong and the Wing On Company applied for passages for us to Sydney. No passports were required in those days, except that Dad had to have his Certificate of Exemption from the Dictation Test to land. All my mother needed was her Australian birth certificate. But no shipping company would accept me on their ships despite my Hong Kong birth certificate. A deadlock held us up in Hong Kong for a considerable time. Finally, one of the shipping agents came up with a solution. Traditionally, Chinese women retained their maiden names after marriage. He suggested my mother book a first-class passage in the name of Mabel Jenkins and child, while my father travel steerage on the same ship. So we arrived in Sydney in November 1912 without a hitch.[9] Then we sailed across the Bight to reach Perth.

Growing up in Perth

We lived for a while in Fitzgerald Street in West Perth, just three blocks from the Wing Hing shop. Next, we moved around the corner into James Street and finally to 6 Randall Street in North Perth, much farther away. It was owned by my auntie Ellen (but called Sheila by everyone), Mum's older sister. Dad had to walk to and fro. I had no playmates until my sister, Eunice (Una), was born in 1914.

Because Mum was married to a Chinaman, no woman in the streets in which we lived would speak to her and she never sought them out. She was a proud woman and turned her whole life into her children. Whenever I went shopping for Mum, or for anything else, someone would call out 'chow' or 'Ching Chong Chinaman'. It was very upsetting when I was young but later I got used to ignoring it.

In Randall Street, I had a little billycart and did all my mother's shopping at the butchers and grocers with it. But Dad was feeling the strain of so much walking, so we left Randall Street and moved to 88 John Street in West Perth, where we stayed until 1925.

The John Street house was a double-fronted brick house with an iron roof. There was a small front garden, a front verandah with the front door in the middle, opening on to a passage that led straight through to the kitchen. Behind the two front bedrooms were another bedroom and a sitting room with a fireplace. The kitchen was behind the sitting room and doubled as a dining and living room for the family. Opposite the kitchen was a small back room and behind the back room a large roofed-in porch, which contained a copper for washing. Behind the porch was the WC. There was a big backyard eighty to a hundred feet deep, all sand, and behind our back fence was a junk yard.

At that time the street lighting was gaslight. A man with a long pole used to come round at dusk each evening and light the lamp post outside our house. He would return in the early morning to extinguish the light. Although electricity was already in general use, the landlord wouldn't install it for us, so we had to rely on kerosene lamps.

Mum cooked only Australian meals. We had a fuel stove and a penny-in-the-slot gas stove. The gas stove was used for boiling milk in the morning,

---

9   NAA: PP4/2, 1936/451. This subterfuge was noted on immigration files when an application was made for Harry's Certificate of Exemption in 1924.

hot water for tea and rice for breakfast. We always had rice for breakfast, with milk and sugar, as Mum wanted to train her children to eat rice. We had no ice chest, but a Coolgardie safe.[10] She baked dinners in the fuel stove, cooked stews and fried steak. She baked all her own cakes, made us a variety of baked custards with rice, bread and butter, sago and tapioca. Usually on Sundays we had jelly and blancmange. She would make these on Saturday and stand them all night in the fireplace in the sitting room.

Mum was an excellent cook. But I took to Chinese food. From the time I was big enough I seized every opportunity to go down to the Wing Hing shop for the evening meal prepared by one of the staff. I learned my table manners there from Dad. Once I was sitting at the table, my rice bowl on the table and my left hand hanging down at my side. I was using chopsticks in my right hand. All of a sudden, Dad growled, 'Is your left hand crippled?' I lifted up my left hand and said, 'No, it's all right.' 'Then pick up your bowl and hold it when you eat,' he ordered.

Another time I was busy picking out all the titbits on the table and neglecting to eat my rice. Suddenly, Dad reversed his chopsticks and hit me across the knuckles with them. 'Eat one mouthful from the table and one mouthful of rice,' he said. To this day I automatically do so.

When we first moved into John Street, for two or three Christmas days running, the men from the shop would come in early on Christmas morning and take over Mum's kitchen. They killed chickens and ducks and cooked a real Chinese feast. They gave Mum a break and we all enjoyed the Chinese food. Mum used to boil up the Christmas puddings in November and hang them from the back porch. She used to put threepences in two of them and sixpences in the others. I think it all stopped because the old partners were returning to China, leaving Dad to take care of the business. Now Dad had to take on men not from our district, with different customs and even speaking a different dialect. As I remember there were about seven staff in all working at the shop. One, Gock Wah Dung, looked after the retail shop full time. Henry Louey, an Australian-born Chinese, was secretary and Andrew Fong, who bought into the business, was assistant manager to Dad. All the others worked packing and carting produce from the markets and to the railway goods yard.

Dad's business

The Wing Hing shop faced William Street and behind the shop was the office. Just outside the office were four lidded wooden bins containing peanuts, walnuts, brazil

---

10   The Coolgardie safe, invented in the Western Australian mining town of Coolgardie in the 1890s, was a common domestic device in Australia to keep perishable items prior to refrigeration. It was essentially a metal frame with hessian inserts on the side that were kept wet from a water reservoir on top. The process of evaporation maintained a cooler inside temperature.

Figure 6.3. Harry and Edna Ming in Perth, c. 1923. (Gock Ming family)

nuts and almonds. There was a staircase behind the office leading to the second storey, which served as a dormitory for the partners and workers.

Adjacent to the front shop were two more shopfronts facing James Street. They were used for packing produce for the wholesale business, country orders and the export trade that Dad was building up. The large back room of the centre shop was a combined kitchen and dining room. The back of the third shop contained two gas ripening rooms for the bananas imported from Java. Behind this room was a furnace and a revolving iron drum for roasting peanuts imported from China.

6 Two Worlds

Anzac Day 1919 was a very quiet day in the shop. At 7 pm Dad decided to go home. He told Gock Doh to close up, but Doh said he'd stay open till nine as he might pick up a pound or two. At about half past eight, a mob of drunken returned soldiers invaded the shop, mouthing abuse about dirty chows. They began throwing the fruit and vegetables into the middle of William Street, so Doh phoned the police. A party of police arrived and formed two files, one on each side, as the ex-soldiers emptied the shop of its stock and ground it into the road. But no action was taken.

Ever since his return to Perth, Dad had been expanding the business. He was importing tea and fireworks from China and had started exporting sandalwood to China. But some time in 1922 or 1923, the West Australian government passed an Act permitting only white Australian companies to export West Australian timber.

We became very friendly with the Hoy Poy (靄培) family. Mr Hoy Poy[11] had a cabinet-making business. He came from the same village as Mr Pang Yee Ping, one of the original founders of the Wing Hing business, from Cheung Gock village. Mrs Hoy Poy was an Australian. She and Mum, both being white women married to Chinese, suffered ostracism from their own kind. The Hoy Poys had a big house at Nedlands, a riverside suburb. Mrs Hoy Poy used to drive her horse and trap over to our place and take Mum and myself and my sister Una to Nedlands for the day. We seemed always to be there. We spent the days playing on the beach and as we grew older, wandering in the bushland. When we were not at Nedlands, the Hoy Poy children would be brought to our place and we would go down to the cabinet-making factory to play. The partners there allowed us the run of the place. Nedlands and the neighbouring suburb of Crawley are my most pleasurable memories of Perth. I went back to Crawley in 1980 and it still smelled the same.

There was another cabinet maker near Wing Hing. He was also from Heung Shan. I remember going to a farewell dinner at his place for one of the partners retiring to China. I met a Chinese boy about my age there whose father was a market gardener. I was looking forward to seeing more of him but he lived a long distance from us and had to help his father before and after school. Some months later he hanged himself in the toilet. No reason was ever given. Some said he couldn't stand the racist treatment of his schoolmates.

War and school

When I was four and a half, Mum sent me to St Brigid's convent school, about two hundred yards up from where we lived. The Irish nuns there were very kind, but most of the instruction was religious. If we weren't in the Nun's Chapel we were being marched around to the main church on the corner of Fitzgerald and

---

11 His proper name was Yuen Hoy Poy (阮靄培), but as was often the case his surname became Hoy Poy in Australia.

Aberdeen Streets. One afternoon, I went home and asked Mum for permission to turn Catholic. Mum had stopped going to the Congregational church after the controversy about her marriage, but she remained deeply religious and said she would not rear a papist in her house. She told me if I still wanted to when I was twenty-one, I could do so. The next term Mum sent me to the Newcastle Street State School, two blocks away. At first, I ran home to Mum crying that the other kids had called me 'chow'. Then I learned to fight, and after that I was all right.

The standard of teaching at the state school was high. I soon mastered the alphabet and learned to read. First it was the comics, then boys' weekly magazines such as the *Magnet*, *St Jim's* and *Sexton Blake*. Later, I graduated to westerns and adventure stories. Newcastle Street was a big school for both boys and girls, with separate playgrounds for each sex. Behind the school there was a large paddock, ideal for playing cowboys and Indians. One corner was fenced off with wire and no one was allowed in, except the big boys. They were taken there at playtime, morning and afternoon, during lunchtime and for a period after school, when they practised shooting with .22 rifles. The First World War was still on.

I made friends with a boy at the state school and he used to come down and play with me in the backyard after school until dark. His family had a junk yard next to the West Perth station, about three blocks away. One night, instead of using the overhead rail crossing, he crossed the lines directly to his home as he usually did. But there was a stationary train in the way, blocking his view. The Fremantle express charged down from the other direction. His was the first funeral I attended and how I grieved for him!

Not long after this in 1918 my sister Una, who was born in 1914, took ill with scarlet fever, which developed into diphtheria. This was a notifiable disease and she had to be admitted to the isolation hospital at West Subiaco. We visited her every night but only Mum and Dad were allowed into the isolation hospital, with special gowns and masks over their faces. I had to wait outside. She died within a week or ten days.

When the war ended in 1918, there were great celebrations in Perth. The town was all lit up and decorated and at night we could see the fireworks being let off in Kings Park from our front verandah. The soldiers started to return and 'welcome home' signs were hung out in front of the houses. But the next day they were replaced by 'quarantined' signs. Spanish flu had broken out. Sufferers were taken to a hastily constructed tent hospital at Blackbuoy to the east of Perth. Mum had a friend with a son just returned from the war and he was stricken with the flu. This lady had another son who drove a baker's cart and had breakfast with his mother every morning. Now he couldn't go to his mother's place anymore, so Mum gave him his breakfast until the quarantine ended. He used to let me sit beside him as he made some of his deliveries. It was a great thrill for me, after the slow plodding of Wing Hing's semi-draught lorry. I was very sorry when he went back to his mother's for breakfast.

6 Two Worlds

As I grew older, I got in with about six boys at the state school and we used to play down near the cattle pens at West Perth station. We did this after dark because in daylight the watchman would chase us. We knew no fear then.

Later, I mated up with a boy and we built a tin canoe with flattened-out kerosene tins. We had to do it at his place because I didn't want Mum to know about it. This boy's elder brother soldered the tin for us and sealed off a tin so that we had a tin of air for buoyancy. We wedged this tin in the bow of the canoe. Then one day, we wagged school, carried the canoe between us down to the esplanade and launched it. We paddled right across the Swan River to Mills Point and back again. It was exhilarating but tiring, and we never tried it again.

During the summer months the school took us on special trams to Crawley to teach us swimming. In the first two years all I learned was how to float. Then Mr Hoy Poy's Chinese foreman invited me to his place at Crawley for a week. He had married a Welsh girl who stayed with us before they married. I went down to the beach every morning and taught myself the overarm stroke and to breathe. There was no keeping me back after that. I went to the Crawley baths at every opportunity. Mostly I travelled by tram, but when wagging school I would walk through Kings Park and down to the baths.

Mum had three more girls, Mavis in 1916, Edna in 1917 and Sheila in 1922. She had all her babies at home, with a Dr Moss in attendance. Every year she would take me and the girls to the zoo on Easter Monday. In the summer we went on picnics at Point Walter on the Swan River, the highlight of the summer for me. Then as I grew bigger, I had to take my sisters to Sunday school in the Oddfellows Hall in William Street. I used to look forward to the Sunday school picnic held every year in the foothills of the Darling Ranges.

I was ten years old when Mum gave me a No. 2 Box Brownie camera for Christmas. From then on, I took a great interest in photography. I read up on the subject and learned to do my own developing and printing. Now Mum decided I should learn to play the piano. She shopped around and bought a second-hand piano, a 'Cord' of French make, and she found a young woman to teach me and paid me a shilling a week pocket money to practise. Another shilling a week was to chop the firewood, mostly fruit boxes from the shop. Later she changed my teacher, and arranged for my Aunty Beatrice to teach me. She had an only daughter about my age, my cousin Selma, who had a good singing voice and ambitions for a singing career.[12] To supplement the fruit boxes, on Saturday mornings I would go to a nearby sawmill and for one shilling I would fill up a billycart with blocks of wood and offcuts. A few times a year I took my little cart into the bush and gathered blackboy cones and bush timber.

Meanwhile, Dad required me to help in the shop during the school holidays, on Monday, Wednesday and Friday. I wasn't paid anything but was allowed to eat

---

12   Selma Inez Bergstrand (1910–1983) enjoyed a career as a professional opera singer on radio and on stage during the 1930s and 1940s.

anything I liked, provided I asked permission first. I didn't mind, because it meant I was guaranteed a good Chinese meal at teatime. My job was to serve the customers so that Cousin Gock Wah Dung could stack up the fruit in the window. I addressed him as Saam Gor (third elder brother).

Dad wouldn't let me go to the pictures. He considered dancing and picture shows sinful. One Saturday, however, a picnic had been organised to leave from our house. But it rained all morning. Mum gave us lunch, but the rain continued, so the picnic had to be abandoned. A bigger boy who was sixteen or seventeen suggested we go to the pictures. After much pleading, Mum agreed. From that day on, I became a picture nut. In those days a child could go to the pictures up to 6 pm for threepence. The shows were continuous. I saw all the cowboys, William S. Hart, Tom Mix, Hoot Gibson, Harry Carey and so on. There were five picture theatres in Perth in those days: the Pavilion, the Palladium, the Majestic, the Theatre Royal in George Street and the Grand, which had entrances in both Murray and Barrack Streets. Later on the Prince of Wales was built in Murray Street. It had a perfumed fountain in the foyer and was very posh. Once I started at 11 am, hurried next door as soon as the first program was over, then up the street and finally across the street. I saw four full programs in one day for one shilling.

I had been brought up to believe that all Chinese hated the Japanese for their attitude and actions in China. After I had seen a film called *The Mikado*, I told Georgie Mook, who drove the horse and cart in Wing Hing, that I had seen a very good Chinese picture. That night he went to see the film. The next time he saw me he abused me for not being able to tell the difference between Chinese and Japanese.

Dad's only recreation was playing *tin gau* (天九, Chinese dominoes) practically every night and on weekends. When others came into the shop and tipped him on racehorses, he would abuse them. He never played mahjong (麻將), but he was an expert at dominoes. In years to come when Dad took us on an extended visit to Chuk Sau Yuen, two big funerals were held while we were there. All the bigwigs in Wing On in Hong Kong came down for the funerals and their wives stayed on for a while afterwards. Dad played dominoes with them every night and won a lot of money off them.

In 1923 Mum decided to send me back to St Brigid's convent school. I was picked out to join a special class for the state scholarship and high school entrance exams. I really learned something that year. Class began at eight o'clock and finished at five o'clock. Our teacher was an Irish nun, Sister Ignatius, who was a bit of a tartar. Both Mum and Dad advised me to work hard, but not to accept a scholarship. Dad was planning to take the family to China so we children could learn Chinese.

Planning to leave

Meanwhile, Dad went off to China in 1922 to have a look around. During his absence, I found I had more freedom. Mum bought me a football, which he would

Figure 6.4. Wing Hing Fruit and Produce Merchants at the corner of James and William Streets in Northbridge, Perth, 1932. (Chung Wah Association, Perth)

not allow. I could borrow a bicycle from the shop on Sundays. Also, Mum allowed me to sell football programs on a Saturday afternoon. From the programs I earned about five shillings a week. With the two shillings from Mum and a two shilling book allowance, I was nearly a millionaire. I persuaded Mum to let me withdraw from Sunday school and attend the morning service at the Church of England instead. I then developed the habit of going to the cinema every Saturday night.

My youngest sister Sheila was born in December 1922 while Dad was still away. Mum had her confinement at home, but was very ill afterwards, and had to hire a trained nurse to attend her for about a fortnight and also hire a woman to do the housework. I suggested Sheila for the baby's name as Mum's oldest sister Ellen, who we all loved very much, was nicknamed Sheila. I was a bit surprised when she agreed to the name because she had no time for the Irish.

Dad returned from China just after Christmas in January 1923. He was bubbling over with enthusiasm about Shanghai. He had nearly bought a block of land in Bubbling Well Road (南京西路, now Nanking Road West), a prime site, when he saw a dog dragging a human bone. That turned him against it. There were no hills in Shanghai, so the graves were in the fields. I passed the high school entrance exams but didn't win a scholarship. Instead of entering high school and breaking off to go to China, Mum decided to have me stay on in the school's commercial class. I was the only boy in the class. The girls were very nice to me at school, but outside on the street they didn't know me, a Chinese boy.

Dad set about converting Wing Hing & Co. into a limited company and selling off most of his shareholding. I'd developed some skill at typing, so Dad required me to go to the shop after school and type out the articles required in the conversion.

Then we struck trouble with the Australian government. Dad applied for his Certificate of Exemption and Mum, married to a Chinese citizen, was issued with a Chinese passport by the Chinese consul general in Melbourne. The three girls could travel on their birth certificates endorsed with their photos and fingerprints on the back.

But I was a different kettle of fish. Where did I come from? How did I get into the country when I was born in Hong Kong? Could I be deported as an illegal immigrant? Dad got a solicitor and squashed all that. A customs officer came to our house asking how I was brought into the country. They were very relieved to know the port was Sydney and not Fremantle, so the Western Australian authorities were not responsible for any mistake. The problem was, if I left the country, I may never be let back in. Desperate and frustrated, Dad finally contacted the Wing Hing customs agent in Fremantle, who said, 'Why didn't you come to me before, William, and I could have saved you all this trouble. I helped get the Minister for the Interior elected last year so leave it to me.'

A few weeks later we received a letter informing us that I would be granted a Certificate of Exemption. Dad bought two copper jardinieres for ten pounds each. One for his customs agent friend in Fremantle and one for the minister.

When all preparations were completed, Dad booked passages for us on the MS *Centaur*, a motor ship of 3,000 tons of the Blue Funnel Line that was making its maiden voyage from Fremantle to Singapore.

7
The Great Adventure

Harry Gock Ming (郭桂芳)

In 1925 Harry Gock Ming's parents took the family to China so the children could learn Chinese and more about their heritage. He describes life in the International Settlement in Shanghai and the Wing On business empire that was started on the profits of the banana trade in Sydney.

Following China's defeat in the First Opium War (1840–42), Hong Kong was ceded to Britain and five treaty ports opened to Western trade. A string of other privileges included concession areas and extraterritoriality, which placed British, American and some other nationals under their own consular jurisdiction. By the end of the Second Opium War (1856–60), eleven more treaty ports were added and foreign control of China's customs was legitimised.

While Hong Kong remained a British colony, Shanghai was the largest of the treaty ports. Its foreign concessions, the International Settlement administered by the British and the French Concession, ensured a virtually independent city state run by Western merchants. In the face of political disorder and banditry, Shanghai provided stability for the development of commerce and industry. It became China's greatest trading port and industrial centre. Wealthy Chinese were attracted to Shanghai for the protection and political dissidents for the freedom it offered them.

Also drawn to Shanghai were the successful Chinese banana merchants from Australia. By the early 1900s they had established a number of modern department stores in both Hong Kong and Shanghai. Their interests had further expanded to include textile and other light industries, real estate, banking and insurance. Despite Shanghai's numerous places of interest and historic sites, as far as the Chinese public was concerned, the department stores had become the greatest attraction of all.

It was an eye-opening experience for Harry and his three younger sisters to move from sleepy Perth to the bustling, multicultural metropolis of Shanghai as it was transforming into the Asian region's commercial and financial centre. However, it was a move also framed by tragedy.

Steam boat to China

We sailed from the port of Fremantle on 1 March 1925 on the SS *Centaur*. All Dad's Chinese friends, Mum's sisters and families and the Hoy Poy (靌培) family came to see us off. The streamers stretched from the ship to shore as the boat moved away from the wharf and I felt very excited at the thought of what great adventures lay ahead.

The next day we were in Geraldton. Practically the whole Chinese population came down to meet the boat and to see Dad. Mr Sydney Fong, a cousin of Andrew Fong Bean, who had taken over Wing Hing (永興), took us to his home for the day. Mr Fong came from See Yup (四邑, four counties in the west of the Pearl River Delta). Dad could understand the See Yup dialect, although I never heard him speak it.

From Geraldton onwards, we had our first experience of difficulties with water. No tap water was to be drunk. All water had to be boiled first. It was the same in all the towns along the north-west coast of Western Australia and later in Singapore. So tea became our standard drink.

A couple of days later we docked at Carnarvon. I was warned by an old Chinese on the wharf not to skylark with some Chinese boys who had come to greet us. He said if I fell into the water there was a ninety per cent chance a shark would get me immediately. From Carnarvon we continued our way up the coast. At every port of call we went ashore to meet the Chinese businesspeople. They all came from the Pearl River Delta and spoke Cantonese.

Our cousin, Gock Wah Dung, was also making the voyage on the same ship, although he was travelling second class. At ports we went ashore together. At one of the ports, a horse-drawn tram conveyed us from the wharf into the town. Finally, at our last Australian port, Derby, the mosquitoes attacked us in droves. When we returned to the ship in the afternoon, it was high and dry. The tide was out and there was no water in sight. Then a little later, the king tide came in with a rush, and we sailed away from Australia.

Singapore

After two or three days we reached Sourabaya and a day later, Batavia. Dad hired a car in both places to drive us around sightseeing. Another couple of days later,

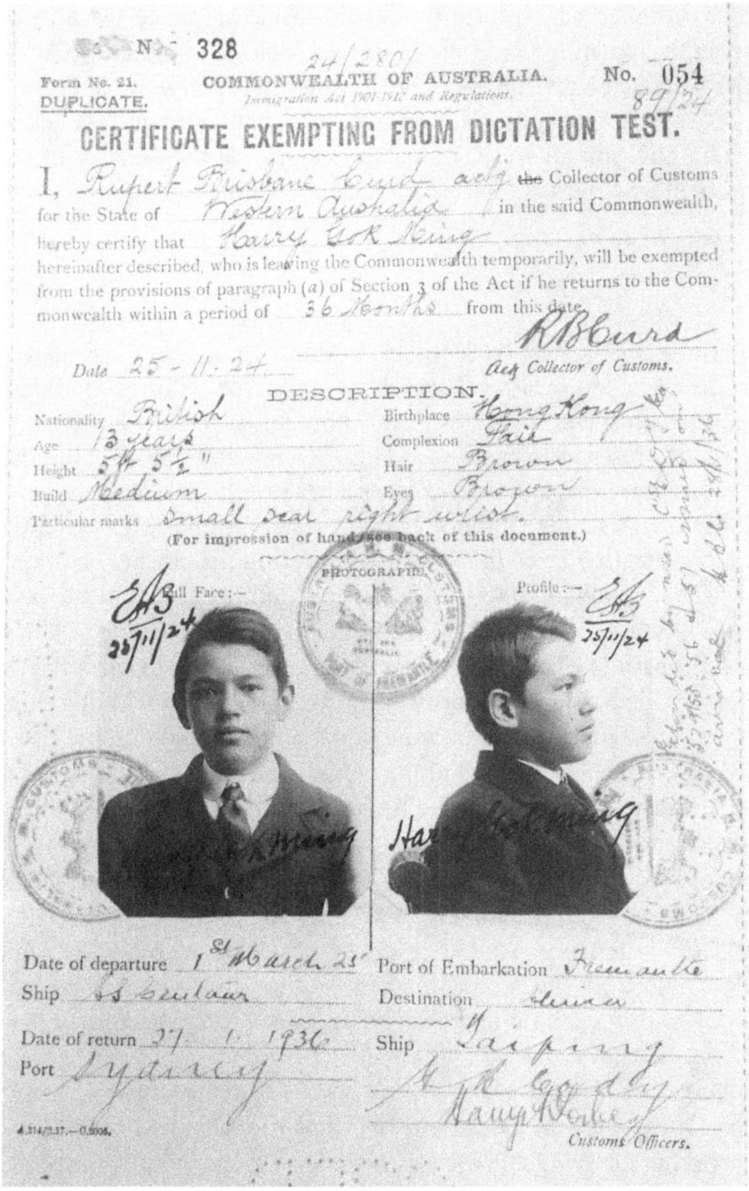

7 The Great Adventure

Figure 7.1. Harry Ming's Certificate of Exemption from the Dictation Test, 1924. (National Archives of Australia: K11/45, 1924/89)

we reached Singapore where we were greeted by a fleet of canoes, the occupants of which dived for silver coins.

In Singapore the heat was oppressive. We stayed in a Chinese hotel, waiting for a ship to Hong Kong. Dad wouldn't let me buy drinks off the stands or the luscious-looking pineapple displayed everywhere. Typhoid was the threat and all water had to be boiled which meant the main drink was again tea. I would sit on the balcony in the mornings and watch Chinese, Malay and Indian workers on their way to work. A courteous Chinese clerk at a shipping agency looked after us when we were booking our passage to Hong Kong, but when an English lady came up to the counter an Englishman on the other side snapped at the clerk for not attending to her. 'Let them wait,' he said. I was furious, but Dad told me to keep quiet.

Hong Kong

It took us three and a half days to reach Hong Kong on a German ship, the SS *Saarbrucken*. The food was excellent, but we had some difficulty understanding the German stewards. Hong Kong was warm but not as hot as Singapore.

There was no customs inspection as Hong Kong was a free port, but there was a constant lookout for arms and drugs. All except one big packing case went through without question. A senior Chinese woman, wearing a black jacket and trousers and an armband with a large brass badge indicating her official position, wanted this case opened. Dad had gone ahead, leaving Mum and me and the baby on the wharf. The Chinese lady couldn't speak English. She kept saying '*hoi*' (開, open) and kicking the case. We had four coolies standing by, ready to carry the case away, but they feared this woman's authority. Mum tried to reason with her but her only response was '*hoi*!' Finally, Mum became impatient, and nudging the case with her foot, she said '*yee shong*' (衣裳, clothing). The woman was so surprised to hear a white woman speak Chinese, that she hesitated and stepped back. Thereupon, the coolies hoisted the case on their bamboo poles and whisked it away.

Dad booked us into the Great Eastern Hotel (大東旅社), a Wing On (永安) subsidiary next door to the Wing On department store in Connaught Road, along the Hong Kong waterfront. We had a large front room with a wide verandah on the first floor, and from the verandah a view of the whole Hong Kong harbour. Of course, today, with the silting up of the Pearl River, Connaught Road is no longer the waterfront.

Throughout our stay of two months we had a constant stream of visitors, mostly Gocks (郭). One of the non-Gocks was Ma Chor Kin, also returned from Australia and then working for Wing On. He was from Sha Chung (沙涌), next to Chuk Sau Yuen (竹秀園), my grandmother's village. He visited us constantly and had a lot to say. Dad and the others referred to him as Din Ma (癲馬, Mad Ma). Later, I learned this was a common nickname given to the Mas (馬) who worked for Wing On.

Hong Kong was my introduction to the Wing On interests. Starting as a humble fruit merchants' store in Sydney in 1897, Wing On was fast becoming an empire. At the top of the hierarchy was James Gock Lock (郭樂), managing director of all the Wing On enterprises and founder of the company. He had already moved his headquarters to Shanghai. He was a man of tremendous intelligence. His younger brother, Philip Gock Chin (郭泉), was managing director of the Hong Kong Wing On Company. He was a thin, aesthetic looking, hard man of no mean ability and a great influence on his elder brother. The youngest brother, William Gock Son (郭順), who had been in charge in Sydney till recently, was now managing director of the Wing On cotton mills in Shanghai. The mills were employing fourteen thousand people and planning further expansion. He was a hail fellow well met type.

Gock Chin welcomed us at a banquet of twenty courses. At this dinner, which I thoroughly enjoyed, I met his eldest son, Gock Lum Song (郭琳爽). He was a graduate of Lingnan (嶺南) University in Canton and spoke excellent English. He explained all the different dishes to me, one of which was a soup made of frogs' tongues.

Dad had to return to the village to see his mother, but thought it unwise to take the family. The 1911 revolution which took place following my birth had ousted the Manchu Ching dynasty (清朝). But although a republic had been declared, a long period of anarchy and unrest had followed. The countryside was plagued with bandits, while outside the walled cities and towns kidnappings were a daily occurrence. Dad went off on a junk towed by a tug to Shekki (石岐), the county seat of Heung Shan (香山). From Shekki he travelled by foot along the mountain path to Chuk Sau Yuen, as the path along the riverbank was no longer safe. He was told to pick up a revolver from the Wing On Bank in Shekki to carry as protection.

While Dad was away, Mum, the girls and I explored Hong Kong by riding on the double-decker trams to the terminuses and back. Every afternoon, I would watch the Canton ferry arrive from our balcony. It docked in front of our hotel. Then hordes of coolies with bamboo poles would push their way onto the boat to carry away a portion of the cargo, mainly fresh fruit, vegetables and live fish. They had to fight a constant tide of others looking for jobs. A few Sikh policemen were there to keep some sort of order and would lay heavy canes across the backs and heads of the coolies. This upset me, but there was nothing I could do.

Dad returned after an uneventful trip of ten days. It was now warm enough for us to proceed to Shanghai and he booked passage for us, this time on a Japanese ship, the *Shinyo Maru*.

Shanghai

Our first sight of Hong Kong had been drizzling rain against a backdrop of hills and harbour and the spray of salt water. The coolies unloading the ships wore straw hats and straw raincapes. By contrast, Shanghai's landscape was flat and the river was a yellow muddy colour. We had to transfer from the ship to a lighter to proceed up the Whangpoo River (黄浦江) to the city.

Old friends of Dad's met us at the customs jetty and whisked us off to Wing On's Great Eastern Hotel in the heart of the International Settlement. The hotel was in Wing On's seven-storey building put up in 1917 and occupying a whole block.

We were given a large corner room on the first floor of the hotel, overlooking Chekiang Road (浙江路). Chekiang Road linked Nanking Road (南京路), the main street leading to the riverfront, with Kiukiang Road (九江路). In Hong Kong, the hotel's floors were tiled. Here they were of polished wood. We had hot and cold running water and steam heating, comfortable armchairs with white drill covers. Downstairs we could buy fresh bread sealed in waxed paper and English-language newspapers, complete with American comic strips. Shanghai, we were to learn, was the most modern city in Asia.

As in Hong Kong, we had many visitors and they invited us to their homes. The people we met in Hong Kong seemed closer to the village and old traditions. Here they were more sophisticated. Mrs Gock Son, wife of the managing director of the Wing On cotton mills, made us particularly welcome. She was Australian-born. Her father, Lee Goon Ick (李觀益), was a banana merchant in Sydney and came from Haang Mei (恆美) village, next to Chuk Sau Yuen. The Gock Son family had not long returned from Sydney, where Mum had stayed with them. They had two boys – Alan (the same age as myself), Raymond (a year or so younger) and three little girls. We visited them several times, and Alan and I found much of common interest.

We also visited the family of George Gock Bew (郭標). They had returned earlier from Sydney and were living in a Western-style mansion. The Wing On Gocks had prevailed on Gock Bew to join them instead of going to the Sincere Company (先施公司). He was now the vice-director of the Shanghai Wing On department store.

Shanghai was then divided into three areas of control. There was the International Settlement controlled by the British, with some Japanese influence. There was the French Concession ruled by France. Those areas outside the foreign concessions were ruled by the Chinese authorities. Wing On's department store was located in the International Settlement, the major business centre and providing a stable environment for trade, particularly with the turbulence and warlordism that had followed the 1911 revolution.

30 May 1925

I shall always remember the day of 30 May 1925. That morning, Alan Gock Son came to see me about eleven o'clock. It was hot and humid. After Mum had given us lunch, Alan took me out to show me some of the sights. We went through the hotel lobby into the Wing On store and out through the main door into Nanking Road. We found the street packed with a mass of shouting, gesticulating people. Not knowing what it was all about, we followed the crowds along Nanking Road. It turned out to be a protest demonstration by cotton mill workers against the killing of a mill worker earlier in the week in a Japanese-owned cotton mill.

7 The Great Adventure

Figure 7.2. The Ming Siblings in Perth, 1924. Harry standing. Seated from left: Mavis, Sheila and Edna. (Gock Ming family)

The workers had held a meeting that morning outside Wing On, which was in the city's busiest intersection. Twenty-five people had already been arrested. Now hundreds more had appeared and were demanding their release. The police were trying to disperse the crowd. But their numbers were swelling and they were resisting. The police were outnumbered and were retreating before the mob we were following. After we had moved some two hundred yards down the street, police reinforcements arrived and mounted a baton charge against the leaders. This caused a panic and the mob charged backwards, almost engulfing Alan and me. We dived into the open door of a shop to avoid being trampled on. The shopkeeper drove us out and began putting up shutters over his plate-glass windows.

Alan and I were now caught between the mob and the line of police carrying rifles. The mob re-formed and advanced on the police again. We squeezed ourselves against the shop windows to let the demonstrators pass us. The police retreated, so we walked along behind six files of demonstrators.

'Why don't they shoot?' Alan asked me, meaning the police. Out of my own book knowledge, I said, 'They don't dare. It would cause an international incident.'

But I had no sooner spoken, when there was a loud bang. The police fired a volley of shots into the crowd. The crowd started running backwards and Alan and I were terrified. In a fraction of a second, the road in front of us was cleared. We could see the police with rifles levelled at us and bodies and blood on the ground. As the people thinned, a side road opened up to our left. Alan and I ran into this side street. We never stopped till we reached the hotel foyer. Instead of waiting for the lift, we ran upstairs to our room and collapsed in armchairs.

Mum had heard the shooting and was worried. After I told her what had happened, between gasps for breath, she said, 'Serve you right! You're always talking about guns. Now you know what happens when you're on the wrong end of them.'

There was another demonstration on the Monday morning, this time in Chekiang Road. The noise of the shouting drew me out onto the balcony. This crowd was far more militant than Saturday's. They pelted the police with wooden blocks and stones from road repairs that were in progress. The police returned several volleys of rifle fire and the mob disappeared. I saw a rickshaw coolie lying between the shafts of his rickshaw. I could see the hole behind his knee where he'd been shot. Blood was pouring out of the wound. After some minutes, the police came into view, rifles still at the ready. There were many bodies lying in Chekiang Road, but beyond my view. The police examined the wounded coolie, who was fully conscious but in great pain. They bundled him into his rickshaw and wheeled him away. The next morning, I read in the English-language paper that a Chinese, wounded in the calf, had died in hospital from loss of blood. I think in all, thirteen demonstrators were killed.

This was the May Thirtieth Incident and there was a lot of trouble after it. The incident marked the rise of Chinese nationalism and the decline of the concessions won by the foreign powers in the two opium wars. There were nationwide protests, demonstrations and strikes. In Canton, a demonstration opposite the British concession of Shameen (沙面) led to shooting between Anglo-French forces and Chinese military cadets, in which more than fifty Chinese were killed. A general strike lasting fifteen months paralysed Hong Kong.

7 The Great Adventure

In Shanghai, the British-controlled Shanghai Municipal Council declared a state of emergency and a curfew from nine o'clock each evening until daylight. The Chinese people declared a boycott of British and Japanese goods. The anti-British boycott lasted over a year. But in the case of Japanese goods, the boycott never ended until the Japanese occupied the eastern coast of China, just before the Second World War.

The state of emergency in Shanghai lasted for several weeks. We had to stay on in the hotel until Dad could find us a house to move to. Meanwhile, Dad took on a job as a supervisor in the Wing On store, in charge of the fabric piece-goods department, the *putt to bu* (疋頭部). It was a big department and took up half the first floor of the building. The other half was the silk department. Dad was very cranky at the china and glassware departments because they charged four and five times their costs. They made tremendous profits. Dad said, 'That's not right. I've traded in Australia and made three and four per cent.'

Several of the old Wing Hing people who used to spend Christmas with us in Perth had good jobs in Wing On. Dad had left his run too late. Gock Yea was now general manager of the fire insurance department. Pang Son, the nephew of Pang Yi Ping, who had worked with Dad for years, was manager of the Wing On Life Assurance Company. Gock Baat Ming was Pang's assistant. Gock Kwan Ju had retired but his son was manager of the Wing On Savings Bank. They were all ground floor partners in Wing On, the same as Dad.

Late in June, Dad rented a new house in Foong Lock Lee (豐樂里) in the Hongkew (虹橋) district, near the Dixwell Road (溧陽路) junction with North Szechuen Road (四川北路). Apart from the local Chinese community, the Hongkew district was heavily populated with Cantonese, Japanese and Eurasians. Rented Chinese houses in Shanghai at this time all followed the same pattern. They were built in complexes of fifty or a hundred houses, surrounded by high brick walls, with the landlord providing a watchman.

The houses were two-storey, built in terraces, with brick walls and tiled roofs. The front of the house was enclosed in a high brick wall with a heavy double wooden door in the centre. Inside the door was a small courtyard, then a front room, the front of which consisted of doors set in wood and glass panels, the full width of the house. The back wall of the front room was brick, with another room behind it, then a stairwell and staircase, and at the rear a kitchen opening on to the back lane. Upstairs there was a large front bedroom, behind it a bathroom, and over the kitchen a small back room. Above the back room was a flat concrete area enclosed in brick walls, about three feet high, for drying clothes.

Just at this time the province of Kiangsu (江蘇), of which Shanghai was the seaport, was controlled by a warlord, a northerner named General Sun Chuan Fang (孫傳芳). The Manchurian warlord Marshal Chang Tso-Lin (張作霖) had invaded the province, but there was no fighting as Sun (孫) withdrew his soldiers before the superior numbers of Chang (張). After successful negotiations, Chang went back north.

However, during the Marshal's advance, his soldiers had raided a girls' boarding school and two of the girl students were raped. In order to reassure the public, Chang had two of his soldiers beheaded and their heads exposed on spikes over the iron gates of the Shanghai North Railway Station (上海北站). Alan Gock Son asked me to accompany him to look at the heads, but I declined.

Tragedy

Now the most traumatic event in my life took place. Three weeks after we moved into the new house, Mum became very ill. The doctor diagnosed smallpox and she was taken to a Western-style hospital. Unfortunately, Western medicine was not yet capable of dealing with this disease. The hospital gave her a hot bath on admittance. She contracted pneumonia and died within a few days. Her death left me like a ship without a rudder.

We had a very hard time at home after Mum's death. A lady came in every day to cook the food as no woman would stay in a house unchaperoned with an unattached male. Then two aunties came to live in as a stop-gap solution.

Dad had a long talk to me one night about our problems. I suggested we go back to Perth but he dismissed this. He told me the only solution was for him to marry again. In those days, marriages were arranged. The professional matchmakers finally came up with a suitable candidate, the daughter of a bankrupt Cantonese merchant. After a great deal of negotiations, agreement was reached and Dad married her. She was only several years older than me. I wasn't very happy about this at the time and our relationship was never much better than an armed truce, but when you consider the great difficulties she had to work under, I reckon she did a pretty good job.[1]

Schooling in Shanghai

With the approach of the school term in September, Dad enrolled me in a Cantonese school near where we lived. As I couldn't speak Chinese I had to join a very low class with children of seven and eight. I became the object of much merriment and my presence disrupted the school, so I had to withdraw. I was next sent to a private class of about fifteen children run by an old gentleman near Woosung Road (吳淞路), just north of the Soochow Creek (蘇州河), which separated the Hongkew district from the city. Still, I couldn't make much headway with the language but persevered until the end of 1925.

---

1 Ming family research reveals that Gock Ming's second wife was from a family named Chan. The children were told to call her 'Ayee' (阿姨) or Auntie. She later took the English first name of Daisy.

7 The Great Adventure

My sisters, Mavis and Edna, were sent to a school teaching English for young Chinese girls run by the American Central Methodist Mission. They were not terribly happy there either as the Chinese girls tormented them, calling them *fan kwai mui* (番鬼妹, foreign devil girls) and generally chasing and annoying them.

Then, early in 1926, Dad and several other fathers in Wing On arranged for a tutor to come from Canton city to teach twelve boys in a classroom above the Wing On Bank in North Szechuen Road in the Hongkew district, as we all lived there anyhow. There were Alan and Raymond Gock Son, Leslie and Aubrey Chang,[2] all from Australia, two sons of Gock Yea, a son of Gock Hou and others. Our teacher was an eminent scholar of a gentle disposition. He made a very good start. Our only subject was the Chinese classics. Mr Ho (何) would go through each word with us, explaining its meaning and use, then we would learn the passage by heart. We had to recite it over and over again till we knew it vocally. Then we had to write it out repeatedly. The next morning we each had to recite to Mr Ho individually, after which we had to sit down and write out the passage from memory. Even now I can still remember some of the passages, although I wouldn't be able to write them.

We lived about a mile from the school. Dad provided me with my tram fare, but I mostly walked to save the money for picture shows and to buy English magazines. There was no shortage of English reading material in Shanghai. I began to read the *Saturday Evening Post*, *Cosmopolitan* and *Redbook* magazines.

Walking to school one morning I noticed a tramcar pull up. The Shanghai trams consisted of two cars in tandem. The front car, first class, had entrances front and rear, and the rear car, third class, a sliding door in the centre. The folding ironwork doors were locked while the tram was in motion. This particular tram was crowded. When the conductor opened the first-class compartment one man alighted. Immediately a Chinese wearing a Western suit climbed up the two steps. The conductor had called out, 'Only one,' when I noticed an Englishman place a hand on the Chinese and say, 'Now then, Chink, I'm going on this tram.' The Chinese objected that he was first, but the Englishman forcibly removed the Chinese and took his place. However, the Chinese found out the identity of the Englishman and sued him in the British consular court for assault. In those days, British, Americans and other foreigners enjoying extraterritoriality were tried in their own consular courts. This time the Chinese won the case and was awarded considerable damages. This case had a tremendous impact and after that foreigners didn't lightly assault Chinese.

I saw snow for the first time in January 1926. It had been extremely cold the night before and had snowed all night. I got up at seven o'clock, took my Box Brownie and went out to Hongkew Park, which was near where we lived. There were two to three inches of snow and I exposed a whole film of snow and water scenes. When I came home for breakfast, Dad abused me for venturing out in the

---

2   See Leslie and Thelma Chang's story in Chapter 1.

cold for no good reason. This upset me. Later that day, I had to go to Wing On for some reason to see Dad. To my surprise, I overheard him telling someone I had braved the cold to take pictures of the snow!

Another morning, I went to school without having done my homework. I worried, remembering the discipline of Sister Ignatius in Perth. But Mr Ho reacted very mildly and urged me to be more diligent in future. This was his mistake. Everyone from Australia was a bit of a larrikin, but I was the biggest of the lot. From then on, our discipline deteriorated. We would turn the clock back in the morning and put it on in the afternoon. No wonder Mr Ho resigned by the end of the year and returned to Canton.

One day Alan Gock Son asked me why I addressed his father as Elder Brother instead of Sixth Younger Uncle, like everybody else. I retorted that by rights his father should call me Great Uncle. After all, I belonged to the twenty-first generation of the Gock clan and even Alan was twenty-fourth generation. 'The next time you talk to me, you call me Great Grand Uncle,' I said.

Although the Sincere (先施) department store was started in Hong Kong in 1900, the Wing On store didn't start until seven years later, in 1907. However, by 1917, Wing On had caught up with Sincere's development. That year, both companies had opened their block-sized, multi-storeyed stores in Shanghai facing each other across the corners of Nanking and Chekiang Roads. A third store, the Sun Sun Company (新新公司), of a similar size, opened towards the end of 1926. It was located next to the Sincere Company, also facing Nanking Road. All three stores were started by Chinese from Heung Shan county who had returned from Australia. Every evening the three buildings glittered with lights. With their roof-garden amusement centres offering film shows, Chinese opera and other forms of entertainment, to the Chinese population these three stores were the showplaces of Shanghai.

Meanwhile, down in Canton, trouble was brewing. Chiang Kai-shek (蔣介石) was preparing to march north to unify China. Strikes were taking place in the main cities in central and south China. Thus, in 1927, the three department stores in Shanghai were hit by a strike of shop assistants. Most of them were local Shanghai Chinese, very poorly paid and not very well treated. We Cantonese tended to regard the local Chinese as inferior beings. The strike was costly and inconvenient, but the three stores decided to remain open. In Wing On, the older sons of the staff were asked to help out.

I was assigned to the blanket department. I wasn't of much use. I couldn't speak the local dialect and only had a smattering of Cantonese, but I enjoyed the experience. The store was open seven days a week, from nine in the morning till eight in the evening. After tea every night, Leslie Chang would come down from the toy department where he was working, with two air guns. We would then have a competition shooting out the external lights of the Sincere Company opposite.

7 The Great Adventure

A week or so later, the strike was settled. There was a light wage rise but, more importantly, an end to work on Sundays.

After Mr Ho left for Canton, and acting on advice from others, Dad had me enrolled in an English school – this time the Thomas Hanbury School for Boys. It was run by the Shanghai Municipal Council for Chinese and Eurasian boys. The teachers were from England. But I found the curriculum inferior to that in my primary school in Perth. So, after the summer holidays, I applied to the headmaster of a similar school, the Public School for Boys, to be admitted there. The school accepted European and Eurasian students, no Chinese, but using my Certificate of Exemption I was admitted as a British subject. I found this school run on lines very similar to the fictional schools I had become familiar with in my schoolboy reading in Perth. The teachers were excellent. Although discipline was strict, it was carried out in a relaxed manner.

The headmaster assigned me to Five Upper, to study for the London Chamber of Commerce Junior Commercial Examination the following year. Most of the boys in my class were Eurasian, a couple were Russian, one was an Arab and another was George Chue, whose grandfather was a well-known lay preacher among the Chinese gold diggers in Victoria. I settled in very well and made lots of friends. I nearly got a flogging for striking a prefect, but was saved by the sports master, Mr Billy Tingle, a former Australian feather-weight boxing champion. I think he explained the situation in Australian schools.

The school had a cadet corps, which I immediately joined. We were drilled and trained after school by non-commissioned officers from the regular British Army, and had monthly firing practice on a 1,000 yard rifle range just behind the school. I was promoted to lance corporal and later to corporal. The sergeant, a Russian boy, myself and two others were chosen to be attached to the field artillery battery, an adult unit. We had to attend a weekly parade at night, and paraded every Sunday for field exercise with the guns. There were four 4.5 inch howitzers in the battery, and each gun and ammunition tender was drawn by a team of six horses. We were issued with riding breeches and leggings, which we wore on every possible occasion, swaggering around the school. We were initially taught to ride and do mounted drill, after which we rode the middle pair of horses on Sundays, drawing the guns. We were issued Mark VII modern rifles instead of the Mark VI Lee Enfield rifles given to the other cadets.

Early in May 1928 we sat for the Chamber of Commerce Junior Commercial Examination. After the papers were sent to London for marking and returned to Shanghai, the results were announced. There were two or three failures but all others passed. Much to the surprise of the teachers, it was announced that I was the only student who passed the history exam with honours.

Early in 1927, the rumblings from Canton grew louder, as Chiang Kai-shek prepared to march north. The foreign powers began building up their military forces in Shanghai. The British brought in the Coldstream Guards, the Durham Light Infantry, the first battalion of the Middlesex Regiment, some Punjabi

Figure 7.3. Harry Ming at Shanghai School for Boys, 1928. (Gock Ming family)

regiments and Gurkhas, artillery units and the Royal Army Service Corps. The Americans brought in marines and army units from the Philippines. The Japanese shipped in a large force of marines and the Portuguese dispatched black troops from Angola. In the French Concession there was a massive build-up of French and Annamese troops.

One afternoon, after the southern armies had taken Nanking, a Chinese gunboat belonging to one of the warlords sailed down the Whangpoo River from the Yangtze River (揚子江) and began shelling the Chinese city behind the French

Concession. The shelling didn't last long and the gunboat departed, but it created a panic. I saw British buglers seated in rickshaws racing through the streets blowing recall to the British troops who were on leave in the city.

By the summer, the southern troops reached Shanghai. There was some fighting between them and the troops of the local warlord. The foreign settlements were sealed off and a state of emergency was proclaimed. The Shanghai Volunteer Corps was called up to help police the International Settlement. British soldiers were billeted in the Shanghai Public School at the bottom of North Szechuen Road and other troops on the rifle range behind the school. We cadets weren't called up.

All day long British army trucks raced up and down North Szechuen Road. A segment of this road was bordered by Chinese-administered territory on both sides, where Chinese snipers took up positions. Several English soldiers were wounded in the trucks. One afternoon in the school, I saw the body of a Punjabi soldier who had been shot on the road. He was already dead but his body kept moving in spasms.

Not long afterwards, the trouble subsided. Then there were some changes. The Chinese railways had been controlled by the British in respect of loans made to previous governments. Now the Union Jack that used to fly over the Shanghai North Railway Station was replaced by the nationalist flag. Similarly, the maritime customs receipts had been controlled by the British with an export duty of ten per cent levied on all exports from China and a flat five per cent import duty on all imports. These were revised, but full customs autonomy wasn't returned till 1933. The signs forbidding entrance to 'dogs and Chinese' also disappeared from the parks in the International Settlement.[3]

After the situation had quietened down, Dad invited his mother, Ah Paw (阿婆), his sister, Gwoo Moo (姑母), Sek's (锡) widow and Sek's son, Hoon Mun (煥文), to visit Shanghai. We called Sek's widow Baak Moo (伯母) because she was the wife of Dad's elder brother. Ah Paw had been urging Dad to bring the family to the village so she could see us all before she died. She was eighty-four at the time. None of the women had ever been further than the county centre of Shekki, three miles from the village. They all had bound feet too. They travelled by junk to Hong Kong and then by steamship the 1,800 miles to Shanghai. Of course, they were helped by the Wing On Gocks all the way.

Dad spent a lot of time showing them around, in the course of which he struck a few problems. When he took his mother to the piece-goods department where he was the supervisor, she wanted to bargain for a lower price. But the department

---

3   The Municipal Council had posted ten regulations in 1917 at Whangpoo Park (黃浦公園). The first stated that the park was reserved for the foreign community. The fourth stated that no dogs or bicycles were admitted. Regulation 8 appears to allow admission of amahs in charge of children. No photographic or documentary evidence exists of a sign that simply stated 'No dogs or Chinese allowed,' although it is acknowledged there are many published personal recollections of such a sign.

Figure 7.4. The Wing On Department Store, Shanghai. (Public domain)

stores had been established on the principle of fixed prices. The only way the store got around the Chinese habit of bargaining was to use a ruler that was an inch short. When the sales assistant had measured out the material, he'd reckon how many inches he'd robbed the customer of and give a bit more. The Chinese women knew this and would try to pull his finger to give more. Ah Paw complained to Dad that the sales assistant was short measuring her. Dad said, 'You think Chuk Sau Yuen is the whole world. It's much larger than that.'

One evening, Dad took the women to see the cabaret in the Great Eastern Hotel. The dancing girls were wearing sleeveless *cheong saam* (長衫) split up the sides and when the music started the blokes began to pick the girls to dance with. Ah Paw got up on her little feet. She went out to the dance floor, pushing the girls. 'Shame on you, showing so much flesh,' she muttered. They were all Shanghai girls. They couldn't understand her and they began to scream. 'Ah Ming (阿明), Ah Ming, get her away!' the manager shouted.

My contribution to their entertainment was to borrow a wooden churn and make what I considered a fairly passable ice cream. But Gwoo Moo asked if her portion could be warmed up. 'It was a bit too cold,' she said.

Harry Gock Ming's story continues in Chapter 9

8
'There's No Gold'

Leung Pui (梁社培)

The moral teachings of Confucius, embracing respect for learning, authority and the status quo, have exercised the greatest influence over Chinese thinking for more than two thousand years. One of the pillars of Confucianism – filial piety – requires sons to honour their parents, younger brothers to defer to elder ones, daughter to father, wife to husband and subject to ruler. In 136 BC, Confucianism was made the state religion. Schools were ordered to venerate the memory of Confucius and Confucian temples were established in every important town. The classics became the basis of the imperial examinations that produced the state's officials. Despite the republican revolution of 1911 banning the worship of Confucius and the study of the classics in state-registered schools, Confucian values are still alive today.

Appraised for their Confucian ethics of hard work and docility, Chinese labourers were actively recruited by the Australian colonies. However, with the exception of the merchants, they could not afford to bring their wives and families with them, so they developed the habit of visiting their home villages every few years, as they were able. In 1901, the Commonwealth *Restriction Act* introduced a dictation test in any language, later modified to any European language, specifically intended to halt the further entry of Chinese to Australia. Certificates of Exemption from the Dictation Test were issued to the already domiciled to enable them to make return trips home.

Leung Pui's (1914–1996) father was a commuter labourer who packed tomatoes in Sydney's Haymarket. He visited his family in Chung Shan county in the Pearl River Delta whenever he could afford to, usually once every several years. Leung Pui, who was born in China, tells how poverty drove his father and other commuters to spend a lifetime labouring in Australia. However, they did not want their children to suffer the same fate – their aim was to educate their children for a better future. Fearing kidnapping as the son of a commuter, Leung Pui lived in Shekki with his future father-in-law and attended school there and then in Hong Kong.

Lung Du commuters

Everyone in Lung Hooey (隆墟) said my dad had gone to the golden mountain. That's how I knew. But I didn't know what it meant. I only knew what Ah Paw (阿婆), my grandmother, told me. She said Ah Yeh (阿爺), my grandfather, was Leung Gai. Lung Hooey was the name of our village in Lung Du (隆都) district, Heung Shan (香山) county. People used to say the county was named after an island where you could smell the fragrance of flowers for miles around. Now, of course, it's known as Chung Shan (中山) county.

Ah Yeh died when my dad was very small. Dad's younger brother, my Ah Sook (阿叔) or younger uncle, died very young. In those days, no one lived very long. The family was poor and had a hard time making a living. Ah Paw didn't say what my granddad did. She said my dad had to start working when his father died. She sent him around the villages to collect eggs. Every family kept a few hens, and Ah Paw resold the eggs to the grocery stores and cake shops. When Dad grew older, he got a job in a cake shop in nearby Saah Kai (沙溪) village. That's where he learned to read.

I was born in Lung Hooey in 1914. I had an elder sister and a younger one. I think Dad must have gone to Australia before federation. Some clan uncles loaned him the money. Before he left, he had his queue (pigtail) cut off. It's still there in Lung Hooey. In our village, the men had their queues cut off very early, even before the 1911 republican revolution.

When I was growing up, lots of Lung Du men worked overseas and remitted money to their families for their support. Usually, the first time they returned home they got married. The second time, they built a house. By the third time, they started investing in rice fields to provide for their old age.

I don't know how long Dad stayed in Australia the first time. When he came home the second time and built a brick house, I wasn't even born. We had inherited a smaller brick house before that. Even then lots of people were still living in mud huts. We called them yellow earth houses. They were in the same style, with tiled roofs, but were smaller. The house my dad built, which I grew up in, had an upper storey with windows upstairs. It was one of a row of four houses, all built by people returned from Australia. Each was in the same style, with a little piece of ground in front and surrounded by a high wall. The front room had a sliding wooden grilled door, with a wooden half-gate on the exterior.

8 'There's No Gold'

One day, when I was still very young, a letter came from my father. He said he was returning home and wanted two persons to meet him in Shekki (石岐) to help carry his luggage. In those days it took a couple of hours to walk from Shekki to Lung Hooey. Soon after, Dad arrived in Shekki on the Shekki–Hong Kong ferry. It was a huge junk towed by a launch. He brought two large crates with him, which seemed to me to be each as large as a bed. It took four persons to carry them home on carrying poles.

That evening, all the neighbours and everybody else around gathered in our house. *Gum shan haak* (金山客, travellers from the golden mountain) always brought one or two crates of things we didn't have in the village. There would be golden mountain biscuits, golden mountain or Sydney soap. We didn't have soap in those days. We used berries from the tea trees. Dad used to bring other things like clothing, woollen material, woollen singlets. We were all very excited. We wanted to see what was in the boxes. There was bound to be something tasty and most probably we'd be given presents.

At last, the boxes were prised open. The first thing Dad took out was a leather apron. We'd never seen anything like it before. Dad said they wore leather aprons to work in. In Tong Shan (唐山)[1] we'd never dream of making an apron out of leather. Thicker cloth, for work purposes, yes, but never of leather. This leather apron had a hole in the chest. Dad said the money he earned came from wearing the hole in that apron. That's how I learned he was packing tomatoes for the vegetable market in Sydney, in Haymarket. He had to get up before dawn every morning and start carrying cases and cases of tomatoes, repack them and then carry them into the storeroom. He was doing that every day. That's why he and the other partners wore leather aprons.

He told us the market gardeners had to get up in the dark and carry hundreds of loads of water on their shoulder poles every day. They went to bed without washing their feet. But no one in Lung Hooey would dream of going to bed without first washing their feet! How could it be true!

'There's no gold!' he said. 'It's all muscle power.' But we never really believed him.

Lung Du dialect

The Lung Du district is surrounded on all sides by water. It was originally settled by sea-faring people from the Amoy area in southern Fukien (福建) province. We speak a dialect related to the Amoy dialect. This dialect is also spoken in Taiwan (台灣), in places along the Kwangtung (廣東) coast as far south as Hainan Island (海南島). For example, the Spanish were the first to come to Amoy for tea. Tea in the Amoy dialect is pronounced '*te*'. That's how the name became tea in English. We also say '*te*' in the Lung Du dialect. Tea in Cantonese and Mandarin is *cha* (茶) but

---

[1] The Cantonese called China Tong Shan, i.e. Tong Mountain, after the Tang dynasty (唐朝).

the Fukienese were the first to export tea through Amoy and the name remained tea even after tea was later exported by the overland routes to India and Europe. Today of course, the Lung Du dialect is a mixture of standard Cantonese, standard Shekki dialect and our original Lung Du dialect. We call it Shaang-Ki-Lung (省歧隆), 'Shaang' for province, meaning Canton, 'Ki' for Shekki and 'Lung' for Lung Du. It probably took our ancestors a long time to reach Lung Du. That's why the Lung Du people are inclined to be more adventurous. Wherever they see an opportunity, they will go to try their luck. You will find people from Lung Du in whatever places there are Chinese.

But the Lung Du dialect is not understandable to Cantonese speakers unless they learn it. We are bilingual because we have to speak the Shekki dialect too. Otherwise, we have the same customs. Actually, a lot of Los (盧) and Lums (林) moved across the river away from Lung Du, so the villages where they live became bilingual too. You didn't have to buy land hundreds of years ago. You just reclaimed it. Chung Shan is the richest part of the Pearl River Delta.

We Chinese used to have at least two or three names – a 'milk name' when born, a school name on starting school, a formal or style name upon marriage. Later perhaps even a name for social or business purposes. My milk name was Pui (培), which I have always used. This is a single character name. Many families use two characters for a given name, with an identifying character for the first. For example, if the identifying character 'Tin' is used for the first generation, then all the same generation would include Tin before the second character. You'd be 'Tin whatever', or 'Tin so-and-so'. The next generation might use 'Dooey' for the identifying character. If you belonged to the same clan, you'd be able to tell which generation a person belonged to. For example, my dad's name was Leung Gum Seui (梁金水), meaning Golden Water. He later shortened it to Leung Seui (梁水) because everyone called him that anyhow.

Village education

All the Chinese working overseas sent money home for their children to go to school. No matter how hard they themselves had to work, they wanted their children to be educated. They wanted their children to have better opportunities than they had. It's still the same today.

I started school when I was about eight, back in the 1920s. That was more than sixty years ago. We had a little ceremony at home beforehand. I had to bow before a portrait of Confucius and was given the school name of Chuk Saang (bring benefit to others). When I married, I was given the name of Heng Yue (meaning something to rejoice over).

The school I went to had two teachers. One, the principal, was a graduate of the Chung Shan Middle School, the highest educational institution in the county. The other was the founder of our school. He'd been in America. Both of them supported Sun Yat-sen's (孫逸仙) republican ideas, particularly on education. The village couldn't afford to build a new school. But there was an old-style village school housed in the Leung (梁) clan family temple. In any case, the temple was only used a few times a year so our teachers transformed the old village school. It became very advanced for its times.

It used to be the custom in the old-type village schools for students to bring their own desks and stools. The schools didn't provide them. At the end of the year, they carried them home again. Our school was the first to change this practice. Our founder arranged for overseas contributions to pay for new desks and chairs. They weren't as nice as school desks are today, but they had drawers and they didn't have to be locked. Nobody stole anything.

Instead of separating the sexes, as in the old schools, boys and girls attended the same school and shared the same desks. In our school, it was always a boy and a girl at one desk. There was no age limit. Two of our schoolmates were married women in their twenties. Married women simply didn't go to school before.

Every morning, we did exercises. This was also unheard of before. We wore a uniform. I wore a white cloth hat, a white top and long white trousers. The girls wore skirts. This was all very revolutionary. We had sports and played volleyball – something new too! We studied the new modern textbooks, instead of the old classical books. On the walls we had pictures of world-famous figures and maps of other countries. Our drawings and essays were displayed along the walkway outside the temple hall, which was the classroom. At that time, the national flag was five horizontal stripes of red, yellow, blue, white and black.[2] These colours were used on a chart at the school entrance, assessing the performance of each student. After the May Thirtieth Incident in Shanghai in 1925, when unarmed demonstrators were shot by police in the International Settlement, our little school joined the nationwide protest by staging a demonstration in Lung Hooey.

The cost of running the school was covered by contributions from the Leung clan and the school fees. You couldn't charge too much. Some families couldn't afford to pay fees. Some of the money came from overseas. There were two other schools in our village, one of which was later upgraded to become the Lung Du District Middle School. This meant that after completing our little primary school, you could attend middle school right in Lung Hooey. But Confucianism still remained the ideology of the state. We still continued the traditional practice of marking Confucius' birth every year, by kneeling and paying our respects to his memory.

While I was attending the village school, we constantly worried about bandits. Kidnappings were particularly bad in Lung Du and families receiving overseas

---

2 This was the flag of the Beiyang government (北洋政府) based in Peking and used from 1912 to 1928. When the Kuomintang (國民黨) army led by Chiang Kai-shek (蔣介石) defeated the Beiyang warlords (北洋軍閥) in 1928, the capital of the Kuomintang government shifted to Nanking and a new flag was promulgated. It is interesting to note the use of the Beiyang (北洋) flag in the Nationalist stronghold of Kwangtung province during the 1920s.

Figure 8.1. Leung Pui far left with fellow students in Shekki, 1931. (Leung Pui)

remittances were the main targets. The villagers had very little money and anybody with overseas connections was regarded as wealthy. If a family didn't have a thousand dollars, it might be good for eight hundred. For this reason, families who could afford to, were moving to the security of Shekki, the county centre. There used to be huge mansions in Shekki put up in the past by the ruling officials. But when later generations squandered their family wealth, they had to sell their homes. Real estate dealers were buying up these broken-down homes and rebuilding smaller dwellings. It was mostly the Lung Du people who could afford to buy or rent them. The villagers began to say I'd be kidnapped if I stayed on in the village. But we couldn't afford to move to Shekki and, after all, Dad had built the house we were living in.

　　Dad had a good friend, surnamed Lum, who came to the rescue. He was a fellow villager and he was working in the Newcastle area in New South Wales as a hawker. He'd been kidnapped on the very eve of his marriage. It cost a few thousand dollars to get him released. He'd already moved his family to Shekki. He invited me to stay with his family and continue my education in Shekki after I finished the village primary school. That's how he eventually became my father-in-law, my Ngoi Fuh (外父, external father).

　　During my last year in the village school, lots of the students were preparing to sit for the entrance exams to the Chung Shan Middle School. Dad didn't have any ideas about such further study for me. He wanted me to learn to read and write and get an office job. So after I finished the last year of primary school, I went up to Shekki, where I studied the Chinese classics under an old-fashioned private teacher. I also began studying English at a school run by a Mrs Jessie Lee, called Jessie's School. Her school was very popular. She came from Australia. She was a very pleasant lady, short and a little plump. Years later in Sydney, I met a young man in the markets who looked exactly like her. When I told him, he laughed and said, 'That was my mother!'

Shekki

Shekki is more than five hundred years old. There used to be a wall around it, with east, south, north and west gates. The main street, Sun Wen West Street (孫文西路), was named after Dr Sun Yat-sen, who was a native son of Heung Shan county. It leads into Sun Wen Central (孫文中路) and finally Sun Wen East Street (孫文東路). This street used to be called Sahp Baat Gaan (十八間, Eighteen Shops). It was full of shops, running eastwards from the riverfront.

You can still see traces of the old city wall near the east gate, where there's now a large People's Hospital (人民醫院). The old Confucian temple, the Hok Goong (學宮), used to be here. It was destroyed during the Cultural Revolution (文化大革命). There used to be a lot of ancestral temples near the north gate. Shekki also had another name, Tit Sehng (鐵城, Iron City). There was once a private hospital in Shekki, called the Tit Sehng Hospital. People from other counties were attracted to move to Shekki because it was easier to make a living there. It was closer to Macao, and Chung Shan was always considered a good appointment for a county magistrate. He could make a good income there. Tang Shao-Yi (唐紹儀) asked for the job of magistrate of Chung Shan and held it for five years before the Second World War. Just imagine, he was a prime minister under the Yuan Shih-Kai (袁世凱) government after the republican revolution in 1911! His home was in Tong Ka (唐家), in Chung Shan. He was one of the first Chinese students sent to the United States by the Ching dynasty (清朝) government in the 19th century.[3]

Father-in-law

As a hawker, my father-in-law, whom I called Ngoi Fuh, went from door to door, not selling fruit, but clothing and things like that. He always carried two suitcases. He was about the same age as Dad, not much younger. Most of the hawkers in the Newcastle area were from Lung Du. Ngoi Fuh worked in the Cessnock coal-mining

---

3   Tang Shao-Yi (1862–1938) was born in Chung Shan county and educated in America. He was the first premier of the Republic of China in 1912. In 1938 he was assassinated by the Bureau of Investigation and Statistics, the nationalist government's security agency.

area as well. He operated on a kind of credit or time-payment system. For example, if a customer bought a singlet for one pound and couldn't pay straight away, he paid two shillings, and the following week he paid another two shillings. The buyer got the goods immediately. This meant he would buy more at one time. For a pound, he might buy some socks as well, and every week Ngoi Fuh would collect payment. Usually someone would buy something new and another would pay for what he'd already taken.

Ngoi Fuh and his customers were just like friends. He never collected all the money owed him. Even when a customer paid up what he owed, say for a shirt, he would take a singlet or two pairs of trousers. Ngoi Fuh was forever extending credit. Chinese businesses usually operated that way. Even today, the Chinese country stores extend credit first and collect payment later.

Ngoi Fuh would work like that for a few years and lots of people would be owing him money. When it was time for him to return to China, he would lease his business to someone else. Say he was owed three thousand pounds. Someone would give him three thousand pounds and take over the business. After Ngoi Fuh returned, he would take back the business and the other man would go home.

Socially, hawking was graded higher than packing tomatoes or market gardening. You went into people's homes, so you had to wear a suit and a tie. Dad and Ngoi Fuh were totally different. Dad worked in the markets, so he dressed any old how. But even though he never went to school, he could always read the letters he received. When it came to writing though, he had to ask someone to help him. Strangely enough, he never asked me to either read or write for him. Ngoi Fuh, on the other hand, could read and write. He even learned some English. He always wore a well-pressed suit. When he returned to China, he still dressed the same way, with highly polished leather shoes, even in the village. When Dad came home, he wore Chinese clothes and cloth shoes. Everybody in the village wore home-made cotton suits, with a padded jacket for warmth in the winter.

Work

However, both Dad and Ngoi Fuh shared one idea in common. Neither wanted any of their children to go overseas. Dad always urged me to study hard and not to think of going abroad. It took me a long time to understand why. Dad never had the chance to go to school. He didn't want his children to be like him, illiterate and slaving for a living. In Ngoi Fuh's case, he said he would never allow any daughter of his to marry a traveller from the golden mountain. To do so, he said, was as good as to condemn her to the life of a widow. I never thought I would one day go to the golden mountain. Eventually, my elder sister married a man who went off to Peru. He returned though and died in Macao during the war. She is now living in Kweilin (桂林), where her daughter is a lecturer at Kwangsi (廣西) University. My younger

8 'There's No Gold'

Figure 8.2. Leung Pui in Hong Kong. (Leung Pui)

sister attended normal middle school and became a teacher. She married a fellow student and they are now living in Hong Kong.

By the time I was born, the Chung Shan Chinese returning from Australia had begun to invest their money in business companies and manufacturing enterprises. Four very successful department stores had been set up in Hong Kong and Shanghai, modelled after the big Anthony Hordern's department store in Sydney. All four stores were established by people from Chung Shan county.

Whenever Dad visited us every few years, his friends and relatives would urge him to invest in the new companies. That is why my dad never bought any rice

Figure 8.3. The Japanese Army marching into Hong Kong, December 1941. (Public domain)

fields. He bought some shares in a smaller department store, called Jun Kwong (真光), which was set up by Lung Du people in Hong Kong. Dad ended up with lots of share certificates. He also invested in the Wing On (永安) cotton mills in Shanghai, the largest of their kind in China at the time. All this growth in trade and manufacturing created jobs in offices. Working with a pen was now looked upon as a more elegant occupation. So, after studying in Shekki for two years, I went down to Hong Kong and entered St Paul's College, an English school for Chinese boys. I stayed with my *Kou Fuh* (舅父), the younger brother of my mother.

Dad returned home for good by the late 1930s, when the Japanese were extending their invasion of China. But he had to sell his cotton mill shares in order to live, while the other shares turned out a dead loss. I had to discontinue my studies and went back to the village and Shekki. As there wasn't anything I could do there, I returned to Hong Kong. By then my *Kou Fuh* had set up a boarding house in West Point (西角), near the Saam Kwok Jetty (三角碼頭) and Salted Fish Lane (鹹魚欄), west of the central district. I helped him take care of the books and do other odd jobs. Then in 1938 the Japanese took Canton and went on to occupy Chung Shan. So I moved the family to Hong Kong. I worked there up to the surrender of Hong Kong to the Japanese on Christmas Day 1941.

Leung Pui's story continues in Chapter 14

9
The Ancestral Home

Harry Gock Ming (郭桂芳)

Harry Gock Ming describes the two years (1928–30) he spent in his father's home village of Chuk Sau Yuen in the Leung Du (良都) district and the regional centre of Shekki (石岐), where he studied Chinese and made friends with others also visiting from Australia. Many of the Chinese immigrants who settled in Sydney in the late 1800s came from the districts surrounding Shekki, the biggest town in Chung Shan (中山) county in the Pearl River Delta. Now the centre of the modern city of Zhongshan (中山), Shekki was then a busy river town and an important link between many Chinese living in Australia and their families in the neighbouring villages. Banks and clan stores in Shekki were the clearing houses for letters and money sent back from overseas, and Wing On & Co. (永安果欄) had a regional store there. The two nearby districts of Lung Du (隆都) and Leung Du on either side of the Shekki River contained over one hundred villages that had sent thousands of their young men to make a living abroad. In return, money was remitted to support families, homes and village infrastructure.

Despite the reforms introduced by the 1911 republican revolution, Harry tells how life went on much like before. Up to half of a village's rice fields were owned by the clans. The clan took care of the ancestral temple, education, road and bridge building, and also ran businesses. Law and order, including defence against bandits and the militia, was maintained by village elders from the better-off families. It was a paternalistic relationship that stressed loyalty to the family and clan.

Journey to Chuk Sau Yuen (竹秀園)

Gwoo Moo (姑母), Baak Moo (伯母) and Hoon Mun (煥文) returned home in the autumn of 1927 while Ah Paw (阿婆) stayed on in Shanghai. The following June, Dad gave up his job and took the whole family to the village. We sailed from Shanghai to Hong Kong on the Canadian Pacific liner *Empress of Russia*. The first night out a gale was blowing and we ran into the tail end of a typhoon. I went up on deck after dinner and in no time I was seasick. I dragged myself back from the rail and found a seat in the lee of the superstructure. When I looked up I saw Ah Paw, in her tiny feet, standing by the rail and really enjoying looking at the sea. I felt I should pull her back. But the ship was rolling and pitching, and I couldn't stand up. Then one of the deckhands, an elderly Chinese, took her arm and said, 'Grandmother, come back here.' At first she objected but finally she allowed him to help her inside.

The trip to Hong Kong usually took thirty-five hours but we were late arriving. For the next few days, I instinctively halted my foot six inches from the ground, waiting for the ground to come up and meet it. While we were on shore we bought presents to take to our people in the village. But by the time I had recovered my shore legs, we had to leave by the junk ferry to Shekki.

We sailed at four o'clock in the morning. Once on board, all passengers were confined to the interior of the junk. Our accommodation was in small cabins with bunks. This was first or saloon class. The central area of the junk had only deck-chair passengers. No one was allowed on deck. On the decks, fore and aft, were muzzle-loading cannon for protection against pirates, and the seamen were very surly.

I entertained myself looking out of the porthole. Halfway across the mouth of the Pearl River, we halted and a launch came alongside. I heard someone humming 'Singin' in the Rain'. Then I saw a European on the launch. I asked Dad if we were still in Hong Kong. He said, 'No, this is China, Ling Ding Shan (伶仃山).' 'Then why was a green-eyed red beard in charge?' I asked. Dad said he didn't know.

Ling Ding Shan was Ling Ding Mountain or Lin Tin Island (內伶仃島). The islands in the delta were mostly rocky hills and were called mountains in Chinese, rather than islands. We had stopped in the Lin Tin anchorage. In the olden days, all foreign vessels were required to wait here for permission to proceed to Canton. Later on, during the opium running days, the opium was smuggled from overseas vessels here. By 1928, Lin Tin Island was an important Chinese maritime customs station, controlling the entrance to the Pearl River. China's customs service was then administered by a British inspector-general and the senior staff were Europeans. The revenues collected went to pay China's indemnities to foreign governments, secure loans and support the Chinese government, first the Ching (清) government, then various warlords and finally Chiang Kai-shek's (蔣介石) government at Nanking.

9 The Ancestral Home

As we crossed the sea from Hong Kong to the mouth of the Pearl River, the junk was propelled by a tug tied alongside it. But once we reached the delta the tug went forward and took the junk in tow because of the narrowness of the river. This was necessary to fit in with the tides.

We came up the estuary of the river, then turned left and came around the Shekki River. Everywhere I saw green mountains with silvery water flowing down their sides. Heung Shan (香山) looked truly beautiful. The name had now changed to Chung Shan county, in honour of Dr Sun Yat-sen (孫逸仙). In his early revolutionary days before the 1911 revolution he had to seek shelter in Japan, where he had adopted a Japanese name, Nakayama (中山), the two characters that read Chung Shan in Chinese.

After a twelve-hour trip, our junk tied up on the east bank of the Shekki River, almost opposite Dai Ma Loo (大馬路, Big Horse Street) – in other words, Shekki's main street. We made a brief visit to the Wing On Bank in the main street, had a good dinner in a restaurant and spent the night in a hotel on the waterfront. The very next day, Dad had all our luggage and paraphernalia transferred to a paddle-wheel junk to take us to Chuk Sau Yuen.

The junk to the village looked exactly like the Hong Kong ferry junk but was much smaller. It was just big enough to ferry passengers and produce between Shekki and our cluster of four villages – Sha Chung (沙涌), Haang Mei (恆美), Chuk Sau Yuen and Sheung Tong (上塘). But instead of being towed, it was propelled by men working a treadmill that turned the paddle. All of them were Gocks. It was a Gock enterprise that belonged to Chuk Sau Yuen. We were allowed to move around the junk freely and I found this last journey fascinating.

A strong and dazzling sun shone on the yellow waters of the Shekki River. All water in Chinese rivers then seemed to me to be yellow. On the left or eastern bank of the river as we slowly moved southwards, green rice fields stretched as far as one could see. The tall green mountains in the background came closer as we moved south. On the right bank of the river was the Lung Du district with scattered villages. The mountains on that side were closer. Dad explained to me that Lung Du was where the bandits lived. The bandit situation had improved but it still wasn't safe to take the riverside path between Shekki and Chuk Sau Yuen.

After two hours we turned into a creek on the left. Very soon we passed a landing stage where a launch was tied up. The launch provided a service to Shekki and was operated by the Lee (李) clan of Haang Mei village. The launch only took half an hour or less to reach Shekki. Both the launch and junk services were safe. The launch was too fast for the bandits and the junk employed a lot of men. A hundred yards past the launch we tied up at a stone landing stage. Beside it was a wooden bridge giving access to the rice fields beyond. This was Chuk Sau Yuen village. Men and women were waiting with bamboo poles and baskets. We weren't required to carry anything. It was our first sight of the ancestral home and I was very excited.

Figure 9.1. The Gock Ming Family Home in Chuk Sau Yuen, photographed in 2000. (Yen family)

We followed the luggage bearers along a gently rising path towards the village proper. On our right was a large lychee (荔枝) orchard, its trees laden with fruit. On the left there were more rice fields. Soon we came to a junction, towered over by a magnificent banyan tree, hundreds of years old. It turned out to be a favourite meeting place for the old men of the village. I was to hear an old 'forty-niner' from the Californian goldfields sing his version of 'Clementine' here. A path led off from here to the left in an east-northeast direction towards the boundary of the village, then along the fringes of the mountains to Shekki. Just inside the village boundary was a circular fort.

We continued our way straight ahead, the ground rising slightly again into the village proper. We passed rows of grey brick houses that opened on to lanes branching off from the main path. Now the path was paved with granite slabs. All the houses faced south, the front of one looking on the high back wall of another. There were about ten rows of houses on the left and then the land began to rise again. On the right, however, another paved lane led to two shops, the village school housed in the ancestral temple and then on until the buildings of Chuk Sau Yuen merged with those of Haang Mei and Sha Chung villages. I was never able to tell what were the boundaries of these three villages although they certainly existed.

The three houses that Dad had built before I was born were about a hundred yards up from the banyan tree. They were on the corner of the main lane and another lane on the right leading to Haang Mei. Sek's widow was waiting to greet us, together with her son, Hoon Mun, and his wife. Also, Saam Baak Moo (三伯母), Hoy's (海) wife, and their eleven-year-old daughter.

There was one more row of houses in front of ours. The path fronting these was the southern boundary of Chuk Sau Yuen. Dad later took us to visit in two of the houses in this row which faced Sheung Tong village across a hundred yards or so of vacant land. These two houses were occupied by the families of Hoy Gei and Hoy Buck, Dad's closest relatives. Our arrival in the village was a very happy time for Dad. Both Hoy Gei and Hoy Buck were back from Australia. The three of them had grown up together.

The western wing of the house was allotted to us, the eastern wing being occupied by Baak Moo and her son and daughter-in-law. The middle wing was occupied by Ah Paw, Saam Baak Moo and daughter. There was plenty of room and we settled in comfortably. But I found it difficult to get used to the primitive latrine.

There was no electric light in the village then. However, we were familiar with kerosene lamps because they were our only source of light in John Street, Perth. Nor was there any street lighting. Anyone venturing out after dark had to carry an electric torch. Electric torches were also kept at bed heads in case of emergency.

The first thing we had to adjust to was the village eating habits. There was no breakfast. Tea was always available in a tea pot enclosed in a padded basket. The first meal of the day was about 10.30 am and the only other meal at 4.30 pm. We ate around a large table in the reception or front room in the middle house.

Saam Baak Moo did the cooking and, for that matter, the lion's share of the housework as she didn't have bound feet. She was a most unfortunate woman. When I was very young, Ah Paw had insisted that Dad send his older brother, Hoy, back to China to get married. Dad had provided the money to find Hoy a wife, paid for the wedding expenses, and through his mother enough money to live on for two years. Then Dad sent Hoy his fare back to Sydney. But after Hoy left his wife with a baby girl, she never saw or heard from him again. Eventually he died in Sydney[1] and Saam Baak Moo was provided for by Dad for the rest of her life. She had to carry the drinking water from the mountain spring, gather and carry all the grass fuel as well as do all the housework. To supplement the meagre money doled out to her by Ah Paw, she was allowed to keep a sow and sell its progeny while the fruit from the peach orchard was entirely hers.

The second day of our arrival, Dad came in just after midday with a man carrying a basket full of lychees, freshly picked from the orchard on the banks of the creek. The basket contained a 'load' (擔), one hundred catties, the normal load a man was expected to carry. The basket was set down in the centre of the front room. The whole family, grandmother, aunts and everyone else sat around and ate them. The skins and seeds were discarded on the floor. When all the lychees had

---

1   Gock Hoy died alone and destitute in Sydney on 14 March 1927. He had been admitted to the Lidcombe Asylum for destitute men one month previously. He is buried in an unmarked grave in Rookwood Cemetery.

been consumed, the basket was returned to the orchard. Saam Baak Moo and Hun Mun's wife swept up the mess and then washed down the tiled floor. It was a feast of a superb fruit.

Lychees in our village came in five varieties, the best being called *nor mai chee* (糯米枝). This very large fruit with a tiny seed has a delicious flavour. It wasn't grown locally. The ones we consumed were number-two grade, called *gwei mei* (桂味), smaller and with a slightly larger seed. There was a third crop, smaller and with a small stone, called *haak yip chee* (黑葉枝), that ripened much later.

Village history

A popular story was told in the village about the earliest ripening variety of lychee called *saam yuet hoong* (三月紅, third-moon red). It is seventy per cent seed and often sour. When the Mongols invaded China and subsequently founded the Yuan dynasty (元朝, 1271–1368), the last heir to the Sung (宋) throne was driven from its court-in-exile in Hangchow (杭州) to the Pearl River Delta. He and his court spent one night in Sha Chung village. Sha Chung is the oldest of our cluster of four villages. The young emperor complained that, although the lychee trees were laden with fruit, none were ripe. So that night the Ma headman went to the ancestral temple, the Ma Ga Chee (馬家祠, Ma family temple), and prayed all night.

The following morning, the fruit in one orchard had turned red. This was considered a miracle. It was only the third moon, in April, and the fruit wasn't due to ripen till the fifth moon, about the end of May. The boy emperor was so moved that he commanded the Ma clan to rename their ancestral temple Ma Ga Dai Chee (馬家大祠, Ma Family Great Temple). The emperor and his court left Sha Chung, but shortly afterwards they were overtaken by the Mongols near the mouth of the West River (西江). Rather than surrender, the young boy emperor was carried on the back of his prime minister into the sea, where they both perished.

The original founder of the Gock (郭) clan, probably a minor official, was Jee Jeng (致政). He moved from Nam Yung (南雄) (pronounced Nam Hong in Cantonese) to the south of Shekki sometime between 1265 and 1275. He came during the heaviest migration period into Kwangtung (廣東) from the north. This was after the Mongols had driven the Sung dynasty (宋朝) court to Hangchow, during the period of the Southern Sung dynasty (南宋, 1127–1279). The migrants poured over the Nanling ranges (南嶺山脈), through the Meiling Pass (梅嶺關), to reach Nam Yung on the border of Kwangtung and Kiang Si (江西) provinces. Nam Yung was the staging point from where they moved further south.

After the Mongols overthrew the Sung dynasty, they set up the Yuan dynasty (元朝, 1271–1368). It was during this dynasty that two fourth-generation Gocks moved away from the south of Shekki. One of them, Louey Joong (侶翁), moved to nearby Chai Ky Lok (茶奇落). Later, a tenth-generation descendant, Joong Jau (宗周), moved from Chai Ky Lok to Chuk Sau Yuen in the Ming dynasty (明朝, 1388–1644).

As the oldest of the four villages, Sha Chung was well established. The Sha Chung Mas were originally a branch of the Ma clan in Sun Wooey (新會) county. One of their forefathers was magistrate of Sun Wooey at the time the Sung dynasty moved its court to Hangchow in 1127. When the Southern Sung dynasty was finally overthrown and the Mongols started to carry out reprisals, the clan had to disperse.

The Lees of Haang Mei moved to our area, also from Sun Wooey county, during a period of distress in the Ming dynasty. They named their new village after their old one. Historically, Haang Mei was the largest and wealthiest of the four villages. But by the 1920s, with the backing of the Wing On enterprises in Hong Kong and Shanghai, Chuk Sau Yuen had become one of the most affluent villages in Kwangtung province.

Village life

In 1929, life in China was still regulated by the lunar calendar, especially in the villages. Three festivals were strictly observed each year. The first was Chinese New Year's Day; the second was the fifth day of the fifth moon, the boat-race festival (端午節) in mid-summer; and the third, the fifteenth of the eighth moon, the mid-autumn festival (中秋節).[2] The day before each festival, debts became due and anyone who did not settle up lost all credit.

On the fourth day of the fifth moon, a few days after our arrival, I was sent to the ancestral temple with a small basket to collect our share of roast pork. The day before each of these festivals, the temple distributed free roast pork, according to the number of males in each family, to all the Gocks in the village.

The following day was the dragon boat festival. There were dragon boat races in Shekki as well as other celebrations. Dad took us all up to Shekki by the launch service to see the fun. I was commandeered by my cousin, Hoon Mun, who with others had hired a small boat and we went out to watch the boat races. I still remember the long sleek craft manned by up to twenty men, each with a paddle, a dragon's head in front and a dragon's tail at the rear. There was great excitement, shouting, drum beating and the letting off of firecrackers.

Next, Hoon Mun took me on a tour of our family property. We left the village by a path that crossed the land between Chuk Sau Yuen and Sheung Tong, in a diagonal easterly direction. We came to the foot of a mountain that rose straight up to a height of several hundred feet. The rise was fairly steep for a short distance, then levelled out onto a peach orchard of up to a hundred peach trees. The trees

---

2 Chinese New Year usually falls in late January or early February, the dragon boat festival usually in June, and the moon festival usually in October.

were heavy with a flat type of peach. They looked delicious, but Dad had forbidden us to touch them. They were part of Third Aunt's income. To the left of the peach orchard, the ground rose to a small knoll with a single olive tree. Hoon Mun said this olive tree belonged to me.

We returned through the peach orchard and on the rising ground behind it was our lychee orchard. There were about a dozen or so trees there, but they had been sadly neglected. They were of a type called *wai chee* (淮枝), the equivalent of number three in quality. They were damaged by a pest called *gompooyie* (金背), very similar to a locust, which emitted a liquid that burned the skin. All these orchards had been left by our grandfather and were now controlled by Dad, he being the head of the immediate family.

The path to our peach and lychee orchards was a deviation from the main path, which led straight up the mountain. Some three or four hundred yards up this mountain was the spring which supplied the drinking water for our village and Sheung Tong. I walked up to the spring every day after that, just to enjoy the beauty of it.

The spring was a waterfall, the water cascading down from high above and draining through rocks at the base into the ground again. The women of the village came every day with two kerosene tins, one on each end of a bamboo pole. One day I tried doing this too, only half filling the tins, but by the time I had descended to level ground the water had splashed out from both tins and my right shoulder had lost most of its skin. But my eleven-year-old cousin, Saam Baak Moo or Third Aunt's daughter, carried two full tins back to the house without spilling a drop!

The mountain on the eastern side of the village was the dominant feature of the landscape. It was a beautiful sight, rising straight up and towering above us, all green, spotted with black rocks and a silver ribbon of spring water tumbling down. I couldn't persuade anyone to accompany me to the top. Everyone thought I was mad – all that energy with no reward! Wherever I went in south China, the mountains were beautiful, each with its own waterfall, but with one fault – the many graves cut into the mountains, in the shape of a horseshoe. These graves were constructed with great care and in accordance with *fung shui* (風水, geomantic principles) to secure good influences. But I thought they spoilt the landscape.

Dress in the village was standard ankle length pants and a matching top jacket. The top for a male buttoned down the middle and for females the top buttoned from the centre at the throat diagonally down under the right armpit and then down the right side. The material widely used was a glossy black lacquered silk, black on the outside and brown on the reverse. It was very strong material, hard-wearing and reputed to be cool. Women with bound feet wore silken slippers, some men wore silk or cotton slippers and some Western-style shoes, but by and large most people went barefoot. After the evening meal, you washed your feet in warm water and then wore wooden clogs. Headgear was almost universally a wide round cane or cane-grass hat about three feet in diameter. The edges were woven into a piece of stiff cane and turned down about three-quarters to one inch. The

9 The Ancestral Home

Figure 9.2. Left to right: Edna, Sheila and Mavis Ming standing in the Chuk Sau Yuen Village Fields, c. 1929. (Gock Ming family)

hat was almost horizontal from the edges until about six inches from the centre when it rose to a peak, like the top of a pagoda. The whole hat was glazed, with a head piece on the inside. It provided maximum protection from the sun and was an excellent umbrella when it rained. Most people painted their names on the outside in large characters. There was another type of hat, of the same material, narrower, of a conical shape, and sloping straight down from the centre to the edge. I favoured the second hat because it was lighter, did not take up so much room when removed, and because it differed from the norm.

There were no wheels in the village. Everything was carried by shoulder pole. You either walked or travelled by boat or sedan chair. Each chair was suspended on two poles and carried by four men. Mostly the chairs were used by women with bound feet, by brides on their weddings or by rich men.

Fuel for cooking was still dried grass gathered in the hills and surrounding mountains. Each morning you could see the women going out with their poles and ropes to gather the grass, and each evening they would return laden with two massive bundles. They would travel many miles a day.

Meat, vegetables and fish were obtainable in a market on the border of Sha Chung and Haang Mei villages. The village's two shops were housed in one building. They belonged to Gock Pui Heen (郭沛勛), the father of Gock Lock (郭樂), Gock Chin (郭泉) and their other brothers. One of the shops sold Chinese groceries and doubled as the post office and village bank. It also sold various herbs. The other shop sold Chinese whisky, double distilled and triple distilled on the premises. It was famed throughout the area as the best quality whisky in the delta. People came from far and near to buy it.

One day, Dad and I were sitting outside the house when a bloke came up the lane from the creek where you caught the boat to Shekki. He was wearing a Western suit, with a waistcoat and everything. He was stickybeaking here and there, and all of a sudden Dad shouted, 'Hey there! Stealing chickens, are you?' The man started and looked around. He came over and said, 'Ah Mung, Ah Mung!' (village dialect for Ah Ming 阿明). He sat down and they had a good yarn. 'This is my son, Ma Sin Saang (馬先生, Mr Ma),' Dad said. He was Mr Ma Ying Biu (馬應彪), the managing director of the Sincere Company (先施公司), on his way to Sha Chung.

Law and order

One of Hoon Mun's sisters had married into the Louey (雷) clan in the nearby village of Doo Tow (渡頭), where her mother had come from. She came to meet us and invited me to visit her whenever I could. I did so on several occasions. Doo Tow was a large village on the main riverbank about a mile or so west-southwest of Chuk Sau Yuen. The main river, after passing the mouth of the creek to our four villages, wound around towards the west. There was a very large jetty at Doo Tow. The boats to Macao stopped here, and there was much traffic to Shekki and across the river from here to the Lung Du district.

After my first visit, my cousin insisted that her brother-in-law escort me home, at least to the point where the path left the river and proceeded inland. She explained there was still danger of being kidnapped by bandits from across the river. Her brother-in-law was in his early twenties, dressed in the traditional black silk pants and unbuttoned top, and a white singlet which overlapped the top of his pants. He was about my size but more muscular. I couldn't see what protection he was giving me, but I said nothing. A week or so later, he again escorted me. Halfway along the path, where no one else was about, he said, 'I'll show you something.' He put his hand underneath his singlet and produced a huge Mauser pistol. It was practically invisible when he was wearing it. Instead of tucking it into his belt, barrel down, he had it tucked, barrel up, in his belt.

There was no police force in the village. The village elders had to provide their own law and order. The one great problem after the fall of the Manchu Ching dynasty (清朝) in 1911 was banditry. I was born in the last year of the Ching dynasty. It was still reasonably peaceful then. Everything was in place. Mum never spoke of bandits while she was in the village. But when I was growing up in Perth, we got news from China all the time about the bandits. The Lung Du district across the river from us was a large area of seventy-eight villages. The people there spoke an entirely different dialect closely related to the Amoy dialect. When the Portuguese settled in Macao, the local fishing people spoke the same dialect. Although there were large areas of rice fields in Lung Du, the land was owned by a handful of rich families. Consequently, there was little opportunity of employment for the constantly growing population. The chances of emigration were nil,[3] and as most of the population had little education, employment in the big cities was minimal. The young men grew up idle and bored, their only recreation being the practice of martial arts. It wasn't long before they turned to banditry, and in the years following my birth they terrorised the countryside.

Our four villages were the constant target of these bandits. They regularly raided, mostly at night, looting, burning and killing, and carrying off those they could hold for ransom. There were only eighteen villages in our district and each of them erected a blockhouse or fort, like the turret of a Norman castle, to ward off attacks by the bandits. But they were mostly ineffective. At Chau Bin (曹邊) village, a mile or so to the south of Chuk Sau Yuen, the Leung (梁) clan there built an underground tunnel, leading a distance of fifty yards from the blockhouse into the open, to provide an escape route. So the Gocks decided to build a round fort instead. Dad paid his share from Perth. They built a great white round structure on the north-eastern side of the village. It looked like the lighthouses off the Australian coast. This round fort had slits cut into the walls all the way up. A machine gun was brought in piece by piece and installed at the top. The round fort dominated the landscape so that the whole area to the west and north could be kept under observation and fire. Once the fort was completed, our villages were no longer raided. The villagers paid selected clan members to man the watch tower (碉樓), apart from the people paid to keep watch when the lychees and peaches ripened.

---

3   This was not true, as Lung Du district was a prime place of origin for emigration.

But the path along the river to Shekki was still unsafe. Two or three armed people could very quickly cross the river and seize a lonely traveller. There was a saying that it was more profitable to kidnap a woman than to raise a pig.

Another problem was the standover man. In 1928 the standover man was Ma Shong of Sha Chung village. I met him one night when I went with my cousin, Hoon Mun, to the post office-cum-liquor shop where he was playing mahjong (麻將). Ma Shong was a chunky young man, dressed in a white silk coat and jacket, with silk socks and silken slippers. Underneath his coat he carried two revolvers in leather holsters. He seemed a jolly, outgoing young man, smiling, laughing and with much to say. His predecessor, a Lee from Haang Mei village, had lasted several years, until he outlived the patience of the villagers. They finally put a price on his head. Early one morning, three Lees grabbed him while he was still asleep. They tied him up hand and feet, slung him on a pole, carried him miles up into the mountains, shot him and buried him. They claimed their reward but had to leave the villages immediately.

Well, Ma Shong lasted several years too. They put up with him at first. He kept the peace. You only had to deal with one. Then they went up to Shekki and complained. So the county magistrate sent a party of soldiers to arrest him. But the kids regarded Ma Shong as a hero and alerted him. In his hurry to escape, he vaulted over a low stone wall, slipped and fell unconscious. He lay there unnoticed. Meanwhile, the soldiers' search was unsuccessful, so they left. When he regained consciousness, Ma Shong first ascertained that the soldiers had gone. Then he paraded through the villages, threatening anyone who dared harm him. He got even worse after that. Finally, it was circulated by word of mouth that a reward of five thousand Hong Kong dollars would be paid for Ma Shong's removal. So one day a villager ambushed Ma, shot him dead and immediately fled to Hong Kong via Macao. In Hong Kong he was given a steamship ticket to Saigon, told to collect his reward there and to stay away from China.

A village wedding

Not long after our arrival in the village, a clan cousin just a few doors from us was arranging the marriage of his son, who had returned from Queensland for this very purpose. This was called 'taking a daughter-in-law'. A huge awning of matting was erected outside the house to accommodate the large number of guests to be invited to the wedding. A framework of thick bamboo was built to the height of about ten or twelve feet at each side of the lane for forty or fifty feet. The poles were joined by tying the joints with cane grass. Then the sloping roof was thatched. This type of temporary structure was cheap and cool, with a good circulation of air, and provided protection from the sun and rain. Invitations were delivered to relatives and friends of the bridegroom's family. However, a strange custom existed there

9 The Ancestral Home

Figure 9.3. William Gock Ming, Shanghai, 1930s. (Gock Ming family)

that unless personal reminders were extended on the morning of the wedding, the invited persons would not come.

A clan cousin, Gock Chew Gum, who later became a great mate of mine in Sydney, was asked to go to Lung Ngan Sy Chung (龍眼樹涌) village to issue personal invitations. That was where Dad's sister, Gwoo Moo, lived. Chew Gum asked me to go with him. Chew Gum was a White, fairly closely related to us.

Lung Ngan Sy Chung was three miles to the south, on the bank of the main river, where the terrain was mostly flat. It was a very hot day, but the walk there was pleasant. We passed a number of villages on the way which Chew Gum pointed out to me. He also told me the surnames of the inhabitants. After delivering the reminders we called in at Gwoo Moo's house, where we had a cup of tea.

This was the first wedding I went to in the village. The bride arrived late in the afternoon in a red, totally covered sedan chair. When she alighted, she had to be led to the place of the ceremony. She was dressed in a heavy red silk robe, brocaded with gold, and a red hat with a flap covering her face, so that she could not see and no one could see her face until the ceremony began. The ceremony was very brief. As it began to get dark, large pressure kerosene lamps were lit and the feast was served outside the house beneath the temporary shelter.

During the feast, the bride and groom had to go to each table to drink a toast. Then for the next three days and nights the bride was constantly called upon, mainly by young friends of the groom, to come and serve tea and put up with banter. The wedding ceremony was probably the first time that either the bride or groom had ever seen each other, as marriages were arranged by the parents. The custom was for the bride to come practically unattended to the home of the groom among perfect strangers. She remained three nights with her new husband and on the third morning after the wedding she returned to her mother. At the end of a month from the date of the wedding, she came back to her husband and took up residence. But I learned that in Shun Tak (順德) county, just north of Shekki, the mulberry trees and silkworms provided ample employment for the female population, so the girls were more independently minded. The bridegrooms frequently had difficulty in persuading their brides to return at the end of the ritual month.

Gunslinger

That summer, Gock Yea came down from Shanghai with his eldest son, Gock Chew Hor, and Yea's brother and son from Hong Kong, on short visits to their family home. Chew Hor used to be at the school in the Wing On Bank with me. He wanted to visit his grandmother in Sau Mei Yuen (秀美園) village, across the main river from us in Lung Du. They were all Fongs in that village. His father said not to go. So Chew Hor, his cousin and I decided to go secretly. A cousin who'd been in Canada loaned me a .38 calibre revolver with six bullets. We walked to Doo Tow and caught a ferry across the river for a few coppers each. We saw a lot of young blokes lounging round the jetty on the other side. They had guns or rifles. They were eyeing us and muttering something about a *faan gwai gern* (番鬼仔, Lung Du dialect for foreign devil kid). We went a little way uphill from the landing stage. Then someone at the village gateway took us to Chew Hor's grandmother's place. We had tea and sweetmeats while all the kids hung round the door. Then it was time to leave and the kids were running around shouting 'the foreign devil kid has a revolver'.

Chew Hor's grandmother sent people with us to see that we got on the ferry all right. But when we arrived at Doo Tow, there were our three fathers, raging with fury. 'How dare you!' Dad shouted. 'It's all right, Dad,' I said. 'We're back. We're safe. Besides, I have a gun.' That was even worse. All three fathers lashed out at us again. We were very unpopular after that.

Travels with my father

Dad took me with him on several trips to Shekki in the early weeks after our arrival and on one occasion we ferried across the river to visit Cheung Gock (象角) village at the northern end of Lung Du district. Lung Du was bandit territory, but Dad said there wasn't much risk going to Cheung Gock as it was a very large and affluent village, housing three clans, the Pangs (彭), the Yuens (阮) and the Lums (林). The Yuens were fairly numerous in Perth in the cabinet-making business, Mr Hoy Poy (靍培) being one of them. We were going to call on Pang Yee Ping, one of the original partners in Wing Hing (永興) in Perth. He was in his seventies, strong and healthy, and he welcomed Dad warmly. He had retired many years before, sending his nephew, Pang Son, to Perth to service his share in Wing Hing. Mr Pang Yee Ping had acquired a great deal of land, mainly rice fields, and was living the life of a country gentleman.

I couldn't help noticing that the people in Lung Du were staring at us. Their dialect was entirely different to ours. For example, in Chuk Sau Yuen we said *yukh faan* (吃飯) for eating rice or having a meal; they said *hia puen* (吃飯).

Wherever Dad and I went with Hoy Gei and Hoy Buck, I found Hoy Gei was very popular. People would smile and say, 'You're back, Uncle Hoy Gei!' When the shopkeepers asked what he would like, he always said, '*mou chihn* (沒錢, no money),' and they would say, '*m'sai bei chihn* (不用給錢, no need to pay)'.

When Dad's father's brother married, his bride failed to produce any children. Hoy Gei was adopted. But immediately afterwards, she became pregnant with Buck. There wasn't much difference in their ages. Dad was born in between, so they became Hoy Gei Baak (伯, elder uncle) and Hoy Buck Sook (叔, younger uncle), as far as I was concerned.

Hoy Gei used to have a fruit shop in the Sydney suburb of Manly before there was a Sydney Harbour Bridge. He made his money there. I don't know what happened to Hoy Buck. But Hoy Gei bought rice fields and he copped it in the land reform in the 1950s. If anyone gave him a bowl of rice then, some lout would knock it out of his hand. He died not long afterwards.

One day as Dad and I were walking to Shekki along the mountain path, I asked him about some ruins in the distance. 'Oh, that's all that's left of Mao Yee Chut's place,' Dad said. Mao Yee Chut wasn't a local man, but he was very rich. One day when he was sailing down the Shekki River he became very impressed with the vista. He decided he'd like to build a house there. But it turned out the *fung shui*, the geomantic influences, were no good. He lost all his family and all his wealth. Everything just melted away. 'Nobody wanted to live there after that,' Dad said.

Some months later, Dad decided to move the family to Shekki and was arranging to lease a house just off Sai See Gaai (西市街, Western Market Street). The custom then was that the tenant would pay the owner a fixed sum of money, equated to the value of the house, which the owner was then free to invest as he liked. At the end of the lease, he returned the original sum to the tenant.

In July, Dad decided to visit Canton city, the capital of Kwangtung province, and took me with him. We went by junk, towed by a steam tug, identical to the craft that went to Hong Kong. The trip lasted ten or twelve hours, an overnight trip, the times of departure always depending on the tide. At low tide some sections of the small delta rivers were impassable. We were met at Canton by Gock cousins and taken to the Great Eastern Hotel (大東旅社), another Wing On-owned enterprise.

I found Canton in 1928 a large sprawling city on the banks of the Pearl River. The old traditional streets were very narrow, almost lanes, much the same as Shekki. The old city walls had been dismantled and wide roads built in their place, while other streets criss-crossing the city had been widened. Landowners on both sides of the widened streets had portions of their property resumed without compensation and were then levied to pay for the construction of the road. The penalty for refusing to comply was death, I was told.

After the overthrow of the Manchu Ching dynasty in 1911, different factions had battled to gain control of Canton. Dr Sun Yat-sen had his base here and had to fight to maintain control. It was from here that Chiang Kai-shek set out in July 1927 on his northern expedition to gain control of all China. Paradoxically, after he set up his nationalist government in Nanking in 1927, he became offside with the southern generals. In 1931, both Kwangtung and Kwangsi (廣西) provinces declared themselves autonomous and refused to accept Chiang Kai-shek's jurisdiction. The manager of the Great Eastern Hotel showed Dad and I some enlarged photographs of corpses lying in the streets after one of the battles in Canton and they were horrifying.

While walking up and down the wide street alongside the Pearl River, trying to avoid the oppressive heat in the junk the night we left Canton, I decided to explore Shameen (沙面). It was only a sandbank about 100 to 150 yards long. It consisted of one short street with offices and warehouses on each side, and wharves on the far side for ships. The British traders of the last century had been confined here during their visits to Canton. After the Opium War of 1840, Shameen became a British concession. It was then policed by the British and ruled by British law.

9 The Ancestral Home

Shekki

After my trip with Dad to Canton, it was decided that I should move up to Shekki and live in the house of Mr Pang Gin Ping, the elder brother of Pang Yi Ping. Mr Pang Gin Ping was a scholar and had agreed to tutor me in the Chinese language. In his younger days he had sat for the imperial civil service exams. He was in his seventies, a very gentle old man, who prided himself on his garden and his bees. He lived in a large old house in an exclusive street just outside the south gate of Shekki, in an area called War Gook Miu (禾穀廟, Rice Shrine). The shrine was a low stone altar dedicated to the God of Earth, but the area was known as War Gook Miu.

Mr Pang taught me selections from the teachings of Confucius, writings on the Eastern Chou (東周) States, and Tang dynasty (唐朝) poems. He also took me through the well-known *Three Character Classic* (三字經), which teaches that all men are born good but need education. I would study all morning with Mr Pang and then in the afternoon I'd go downtown to do a bit of exploring.

Shekki's landmark was a pagoda sitting on top of a rocky hill and visible for miles around. The hill, called Ki Shan (岐山, Stone Crag), gave Shekki its name. It was several hundred yards north of the main street. Chinese like balance in the landscape, so about a thousand yards to the south, along the waterfront, there was a cairn of rocks on which another lower pagoda was built. This was called Hah Ki (下岐, Lower Crag). It was not a natural formation like Ki Shan, but manmade. So Shekki was set between two crags of rock, one high, the other low, in perfect symmetry.

A block and a half or so north from the main street along the waterfront was a vacant block of land – the old execution ground. This was where criminals had their heads chopped off. In my time, they were shooting them instead. I saw bandits paraded in chains down the main street.

The old walled city was about a thousand yards east of the waterfront. The wall had been pulled down and in its place a circular road built. The main street began at the waterfront and continued along the line of the old wall to the former east gate of the ancient city. From here, you went down to the eastern villages and on to Portuguese Macao, at the southern tip of Chung Shan county.

Half a block down the main street from the waterfront, on the left, there was an intersection into a wide street called Fruit Market Street. I was forever here. All the shops sold fruit, with the exception of a rice mill owned by the Gocks. Its premises extended from Fruit Market Street through to the waterfront, with entrances on both streets. Still on the main street, a few doors further east, was the Wing On Bank. The bank was staffed by Blues and the rice mill by Whites, so Dad was always in the rice mill. The Chinese are very clannish and Dad was particularly so. If you didn't come from Chuk Sau Yuen or Sha Chung, you were an outsider. Years later, when I got interested in a girl and took her home to meet the family, Dad said, 'Where'd you find a girl like that? Don't marry an outsider.' I said, 'But you did.' 'That was different,' he replied.

Figure 9.4. Daisy and Gock Ming in Shanghai with their son Bill, on left, and others, c. 1930. (Gock Ming family)

When I went out in the afternoon, I'd first go to the Wing On Bank to see if there was any mail. Diagonally opposite the bank there was a laneway that led down to Haam Yu Laan (鹹魚欄, Salted Fish Lane), a rather smelly place. Sometimes in the daytime there was a bloke there at the crossroads, selling roasted dog meat. He had a lookout, because this was illegal. There were two separate administrations during the eighteen months I was in Shekki. When we first arrived, there were gambling shops on every corner, with *fan tan* (番攤) inside and pak-ah-pu (白鴿票) tickets on sale outside. Then they were ruled illegal.

Proceeding along the main street until just before the old city, you would reach an ancient laneway on the right called Yit Loi Gaai (悅來街, Yit Loi Street). It led to the post office, after which it continued down to the South Gate River. The brothels were at the bottom of this lane. They weren't outlawed by the new administration, but the girls were stopped from going round the hotels to sell their trade.

The businesses in the main street included two large restaurants, many small shops selling cloth, meat and jewellery, a small department store owned by the Lee clan of Haang Mei village, a picture theatre, and a church run by the Central Methodist Mission. The next intersection on the left-hand side of the main street was at the site of the old wall. Here a wide street called Sai See Gaai (West Market Street) arced around the line of the old wall to the north and east. There was a very noisy school at this intersection where scores of children were learning to use the abacus. You could hear abacuses clicking and the children shouting their tables. I attended this school for a few days, but I never got beyond the first multiplication tables. I left because I thought it was the same old thing every day, just memorising.

Proceeding along the southern line of the old city wall, the main street was intersected on the right by a medium-sized street, South Gate Street. This street led south down to the South Gate River, crossed a bridge, veered slightly west and headed south again through the southern section of Shekki and out onto the mountain path leading to Chuk Sau Yuen.

War Gook Miu was to the left of South Gate Street, just after crossing the bridge. Here there was a wide street which included the South Gate River flowing down its middle. The houses on both sides were all large old-style residences, with trees lining the riverbanks. Mr Pang's house was on the southern side.

One day when I was trying to buy a canvas watch strap in the Lee clan department store, two young lads introduced themselves to me. They were Ron and Ernie Moon from Victoria, Australia, where they were helping their father grow tomatoes. They'd come back to visit their mother and sisters. Their mother was half European. Their family was from Dou Mun (斗門) district, but they'd moved to outside the south gate in Shekki. Dou Mun is a separate county today. Ernie had been kidnapped by bandits and held in a pit covered by mats in Lung Du for six weeks. After that his brain wasn't quite the same.

We started hanging round the streets together. They brought along Charlie Fong, whose father had a business in Muswellbrook, New South Wales. We would talk and eat a bit of fruit. We played mahjong and we gawked at the singsong girls coming down the stairs of the big restaurant. We didn't have much money. Dad was only giving me sixty cents a month. Sometimes we even went to church in Sai See Gaai on Sundays.

By this time, I'd heard a lot about Macao. In 1557, the Ming dynasty government had permitted the Portuguese to settle there because they had rid the area of pirates. Except for local government and taxation, Macao was under the jurisdiction of the Shekki authorities until 1887 when it was ceded to Portugal by the Ching dynasty government. Mr Pang told me dispatch runners could make the trip from Shekki to Macao in one night. So I asked Dad to give me some money to go there.

'No proper business there, *piu, to, yin, t'sui* (嫖賭煙醉),' Dad said. Prostitution, gambling, opium smoking and drinking – the four sins for men. He refused. So one day, the Moon brothers and I decided we'd cycle to Macao. We went and hired bikes and set out on a very hot day. Instead of bells, the bikes had horns that went 'boot, boot'. We thought it was great fun when the big-footed peasant women would scatter across the road with their loads of grass. But after a mile or so of cycling we were hot and tired. We came to a place that had a big sign reading yum cha (飲茶). We stopped and went in. We had barbequed pork buns and prawn dumplings. It was lovely. Didn't cost much either. After that, we decided to return to Shekki. We never got to Macao.

Towards the end of the year, Ah Paw's health began to fail. Dad and I were visiting Hong Kong when we suddenly received a telegram to return home immediately. Not long afterwards, Ah Paw died at the ripe old age of eighty-six. We buried her on a hillside overlooking the mountain path to Shekki, near the other ancestral graves. The following year, Dad moved the family back to Shanghai.

Harry's story concludes in Chapter 11

10
'Unite to Fight the Japanese'

Frank Lee Gee (李植良)

Frank Lee Gee's arrival in his foster father's village in the Pearl River Delta in 1923 occurred during one of China's most unsettled periods in history. Two years later, following Dr Sun Yat-sen's (孫逸仙) death in Peking in 1925, the nationalist or Kuomintang (國民黨) army set out from Canton under the command of Chiang Kai-shek (蔣介石) to overcome the warlords and unify China. Also taking part in this northern expedition were the Chinese Communist Party and the warlord forces of Kwangsi (廣西) province. A new national government was established at Wuhan (武漢) along the Yangtze River (揚子江). But after reaching Shanghai, Chiang (蔣) split with the communists, set up another central government in 1928 in Nanking, and initiated a campaign to wipe out the Chinese Communist Party. The Wuhan government disintegrated and a second northern expedition led by Chiang occupied Peking in 1928. China thus became nominally united.

In 1931, during this period of unstable alliances with the warlords, Japan occupied China's three north-eastern provinces and established a puppet government in Manchuria. Chiang ordered the north-eastern troops not to resist but to withdraw. However, Japan continued its encroachments and demanded the withdrawal of Chinese troops from the Shanghai area. The Cantonese 19th Route Army was garrisoned there and fighting broke out, during which heavy losses were inflicted on the Japanese until reinforcements arrived. After the incident was settled, the 19th Route Army was transferred to Fukien (福建) province and ordered to fight the Chinese Red Army, but they rebelled and in 1933 set up an anti-Chiang government. Finally, they were defeated.

The southern warlords and other public figures opposed Chiang's policy of appeasement and pressured him to resist the

Japanese. Both Kwangtung (廣東) and Kwangsi provinces declared their autonomy. But the armed forces of Kwangtung became fragmented through defections, while Kwangsi was blockaded and isolated. Finally, in 1936 Chiang Kai-shek was forcibly detained in the north-west city of Sian (西安) by two of his own generals. He was released after he agreed to a united front with the Chinese Communist Party to resist the Japanese. The Japanese retaliated in 1937 with a declaration of all-out war.

Frank Lee Gee's greatest insight into China was gained during the mid-1930s when he volunteered to do a year's militia training. However, Frank's war was with other Chinese and he never fought the Japanese.

Last of the warlords

One of the most valuable experiences I had in China was when I volunteered to do a year's training in Chen Chai-tong's (陳濟棠) army.[1] He was the last warlord in Kwangtung province. I don't remember the exact time now, it was between 1935 and 1936, when the Red Army was on its Long March (長征) to Yenan (延安) up in north-west China. General Chen Chai-tong was in power in Kwangtung then. Actually, he did pretty good for the province. During his time, Kwangtung was very prosperous and things were cheap. For every English pound you'd get more than ten Chinese silver dollars. You could buy a ninety-kilo sack of rice for three silver dollars and that would last for months. You could buy ten *mow* (畝, six *mow* to an acre) of land for a few hundred Chinese dollars.

Chiang Kai-shek had already started conscription up north. Now in Kwangtung, every village was asked to provide one conscript to do a year's training under the slogan 'Unite to fight the Japanese'. Besides the conscripts, anybody else who wanted to could also join up. I think this was intended to offset unrest. I wasn't conscripted. I went because I had nothing to do.

The mayor of the township asked if I would like to volunteer to take part in the army training scheme. I said I wouldn't mind. I think the foster father was dying for me to go, more or less to get rid of me. So I said I'd go and the foster father agreed to it too. But when I wanted to change my mind, he said, 'Oh no, you already volunteered. If you don't go, well, you'll have to find something else to do.'

---

1 Chen Chai-tong (1890–1954) was commander-in-chief of the 1st Army Group in Kwangtung province from 1931 to 1936. Sympathetic to a united front offensive to combat the Japanese army, Chen was forced to resign for challenging Chiang Kai-shek's authority shortly before the Sian incident of December 1936 and fled to Hong Kong. Accepted back by the nationalist government during the Second World War, Chen became governor of Hainan Island, before moving to Taiwan in 1950 when Hainan came under communist control.

Instead of paying my fare for me to come back to Australia, he would rather have me join the army. Actually, he didn't want me to return to Australia then, but I wasn't wanted either. He had to keep me, but because of his wife I was a burden to them. So I said, 'All right, I'll go,' and I got ready to leave.

Mobilising

The township gave me a bit of a turnout, a *cha wooey* (茶會, tea party) with cake and things like that. After that, the shops in Heung Chow (香洲) let off firecrackers to give me a good send-off. There were a lot of villages around that area. Heung Chow was actually a little village too, but instead of calling it a village they made it a township. They were trying to turn it into a commercial centre. Some of the other villages had a bigger population, but Heung Chow had a few shops.

From Heung Chow I went to the district centre. We had another *cha wooey* with cakes and so on there. Then we all got on a bus and went up to Shekki (石岐). We were now a hundred and fifty from all over the place. More or less, all had volunteered. In the villages, they paid some to go. They would ask if someone would go if he was paid a certain amount as a bonus. I thought of it as something to do, might be a bit of experience too. I wasn't paid anything.

When we got to Shekki, the name of the county magistrate was Yang. He gave us a banquet. There were six or seven courses. It was pretty good. We had pork, fowl, duck and all that, just like any *jau lau* (酒樓, high-class restaurant). I think there were ten tables, with ten to a table. I'm not sure whether there were a hundred or two hundred people there. After the banquet we had to go down to a junk on the Shekki River, the boat to take us to Canton.

Instead of travelling *chaan lou* (餐樓, saloon class), we were put on top of the junk. We were in the army now, so we travelled up top. They didn't issue us with blankets either. All the shops let off firecrackers to send us off. We stayed on the junk overnight and the next morning we got into Canton.

In Canton they marched us to a big parade ground, which was turned into temporary accommodation for us. In the olden days it was used for training troops. In those days, besides the sitting down and writing examinations for officials, the army also had examinations. By mastering the martial arts, you could even become the head of an army. This parade ground was where they used to do their training in the martial arts. But when it came to the Kuomintang days, under the Nationalist Party, or even before, this place was used as an execution ground. In 1927, in the Canton uprising, they killed hundreds and hundreds here with machine guns.

We were housed in mat sheds raised off the ground. On the boat all we had to sleep on was a mat. So when the other blokes came on, we got together and shared the mats. We used one mat to sleep on and the other to cover ourselves. When you get two bodies together, you feel warm. It was pretty cold at that time too. It was before the Chinese New Year, round about the eleventh Chinese month, or even the twelfth month, but very cold. We still had no uniforms, but they issued us each a blanket in Canton. I paired up with a chap from another village. We became very pally. We always put our mats together, doubled our blankets and slept together. Lots of us doubled up. If you didn't, you were going to be very cool.

They didn't starve us. They gave us plenty of rice, vegetables and meat. Not much fish. When you go in the army, each person might have two pieces of meat, pork and a lot of vegetables. The only time you would get more meat, like duck, chicken and all that, was a big occasion, like Chinese New Year or the double tenth, national day, October tenth that was. Anyhow, we had enough to eat.

Chen Chai-tong put twenty cents in a day for our food, and the division headquarters paid twenty cents. That was forty cents bung in for us to eat. Out of the pay we got, we had to feed ourselves too. It wasn't clear what wages you got. Some money for the food had to come out from our army pay. I think they paid us about twelve or thirteen silver dollars a month.

Every year they might issue you with a couple of pairs of socks, a pair of sandshoes. If you wanted to keep warm, you'd need to save to buy extra thick socks, or sometimes, sandshoes. When we got up to Kiang Si (江西) province, it was very cold. It didn't snow, but it was in central China, and during the wintertime. We were going to the area recently evacuated by the Red Army.

We stayed in Canton for three or four days. After that we got on a train and went right up to Shiukwan (韶關), also called Kukong (曲江). This time they marched us into a barracks, more like an army barracks. But we couldn't come out and go wandering anywhere. We had no more freedom. Once you were in there, you had no more freedom. They thought we might run away. We saw someone guarding the barracks. They had us there.

The next day, they dumped us onto ten or twenty trucks. We travelled up to lunchtime. We stopped for lunch at Nam Hong (南雄), pronounced Nan Xiong in Mandarin. Nam Hong is a big place on the border of Kwangtung and Kiang Si provinces. I think the Red Army tried to capture it a few times, but they couldn't. It's on the traditional road from Kwangtung to the north.

After lunch, we continued on the trucks to another place in Kiang Si province, Sin Feng (信豐). The Red Army had already gone. But they might have left pockets of guerrillas in the area. Sometimes these guerrillas might raid a village for food, but the bulk of the Red Army was already on their Long March. They had left Kiang Si province and were already in Kwei Chow (貴州) or Szechuen (四川) province. Instead of having preliminary training, we were being sent straight into Chen Chai-tong's 3rd Division, to be with the real regulars. If there was to be any fighting, we would have to do it.

There was no fighting with the Japanese at the time, although we very nearly fought Chiang Kai-shek. You see, the southern militarists were putting pressure on Chiang Kai-shek to fight the Japanese. We were recruited to do one year's training under the slogan of uniting to fight the Japanese. We were to return to our villages after that and become a reserve force. That's why they sent us into the regular army to be with the soldiers who were doing the fighting. They kept their promise too, though I didn't stay for a whole year in the end.

We continued on in the trucks till we got to Sin Feng; now it's spelt Xin Feng. We stayed there for one night and early next morning we started slogging our way on foot along mountain tracks. There was no road. We weren't with the regular army yet. The division sent personnel to take us down to An Yuan (安遠). It took us two days to reach a big camp at An Yuan. The first day we marched the whole day, till we reached the top of a mountain. Up top there it was more like a tableland. There was a village and a marketplace. We stayed there for the night. It was really cold too. Another chap and I slept together on one mat. We bunged our blankets together. You wouldn't be able to sleep with only one blanket because you'd be shivering all night.

The next morning after breakfast we started to sing on top of the mountain. Then we had to go down the mountain. Sometime in the afternoon, we reached An Yuan. After we got there, they put us in different companies, about forty or fifty of us in one company. But we still belonged to the 3rd Division. We were told we weren't allowed to be promoted. We were only there for training purposes. You might have felt homesick. Sometimes you might think 'why did I join?' but you soon got used to it. There wasn't anything you could do about it anyhow. You had to go on.

Training

The old soldiers who trained us told us it would take a while to get used to army life. Actually, it was dangerous to try to run away. If the local people thought you were a deserter from the army, they might even kill you, because you had some money and they wanted to take it off you.

The old soldiers were very good to us. I got on well with a couple of squad leaders. One of the lieutenants was also very friendly. He used to ask me how to say things in English. But another one was a bastard. He came from the ranks. There were two who were more like gentlemen. They had graduated from a military academy. That's how they became lieutenants. But some came up from being sergeants and squad leaders. Actually, the sergeant was the real boss, even though he was only a squad leader.

We stayed in An Yuan for a good few months. Sometimes we went out visiting various villages. The division copied a lot of things off the Red Army in those days. Like, for instance, when they borrowed things off the people. Sometimes you might borrow a door to sleep on. The next day you had to return it or pay for it. That's what the Red Army did. We weren't allowed to take anything, not even a meal, off the people. When we billeted at a place, we had to return everything we borrowed and clean out the place before we left.

I didn't know this at the time. I read about it afterwards. Before I volunteered for the army training, I used to read about the Red Army movements in the newspapers. Chiang Kai-shek launched five encirclement campaigns against them. They broke every campaign except the fifth one. That was a failure. Naturally, the papers used to exaggerate. They would report that Chiang Kai-shek's forces had killed so many. By the time you reckoned it all up the whole Red Army had been annihilated and Mao Tse-tung (毛澤東) had been captured and executed so many times. I never believed it at all. But sometimes the papers reported defeats by Chiang Kai-shek's forces too. They would report that the Red Army had broken through an encirclement and that so many of Chiang's army had been killed.

Every morning after breakfast we would drill. Sometimes we even drilled before breakfast. It depended on the lieutenant, the company commander. He might want to see how we were getting on. After drilling, we would return to camp and do different duties. Those on sentry did sentry duty.

Army life

When it came to the weekend, they would issue us with sixty cents pocket money, silver money. That was out of our pay. When you joined the army, they held your wages back for three months. They didn't pay you all the money straight away. After the three months were up, then we got the full money. They always kept three months' money.

This wasn't only in the army. The public servants too, or teachers in government-run schools, they didn't get paid every month. When they started work, so much money would be held back. When anything went wrong, they always owed you so much money. By the time we cleared off later from the army, they still owed us three months' wages. How could we get it back again?!

Anyhow, things were cheap then, even in Kiang Si province. For instance, if we all bung in, say, three of us put in forty cents or just twenty cents, we could go to yum cha (飲茶). At one time in Macao, for fifty cents Chinese money, you could have a pot of tea. The Chinese make the tea in a cup with a lid but no handle, and you drink it out of the cup. As well, you could have two to three dishes of dim sims (點心). Even in a big place like Macao, things were cheap in those days. If you had two dollars, ten people could have a good feed.

The army didn't treat us very badly, but everybody had to look after himself. They allowed so much rice for each person. We each had a big aluminium mug and a pair of chopsticks for eating. If you lost that mug you had to scatter around and buy another one. You had to look after it. Not like the army here, where they serve you everything on a table, or in the Yankee army or European armies. We had no table. We had to squat down around a big dish. The food was divided into three sections. One was with pork, and there would be two different kinds of vegetables. There would be ten in a squad squatting around in a circle. When we started eating,

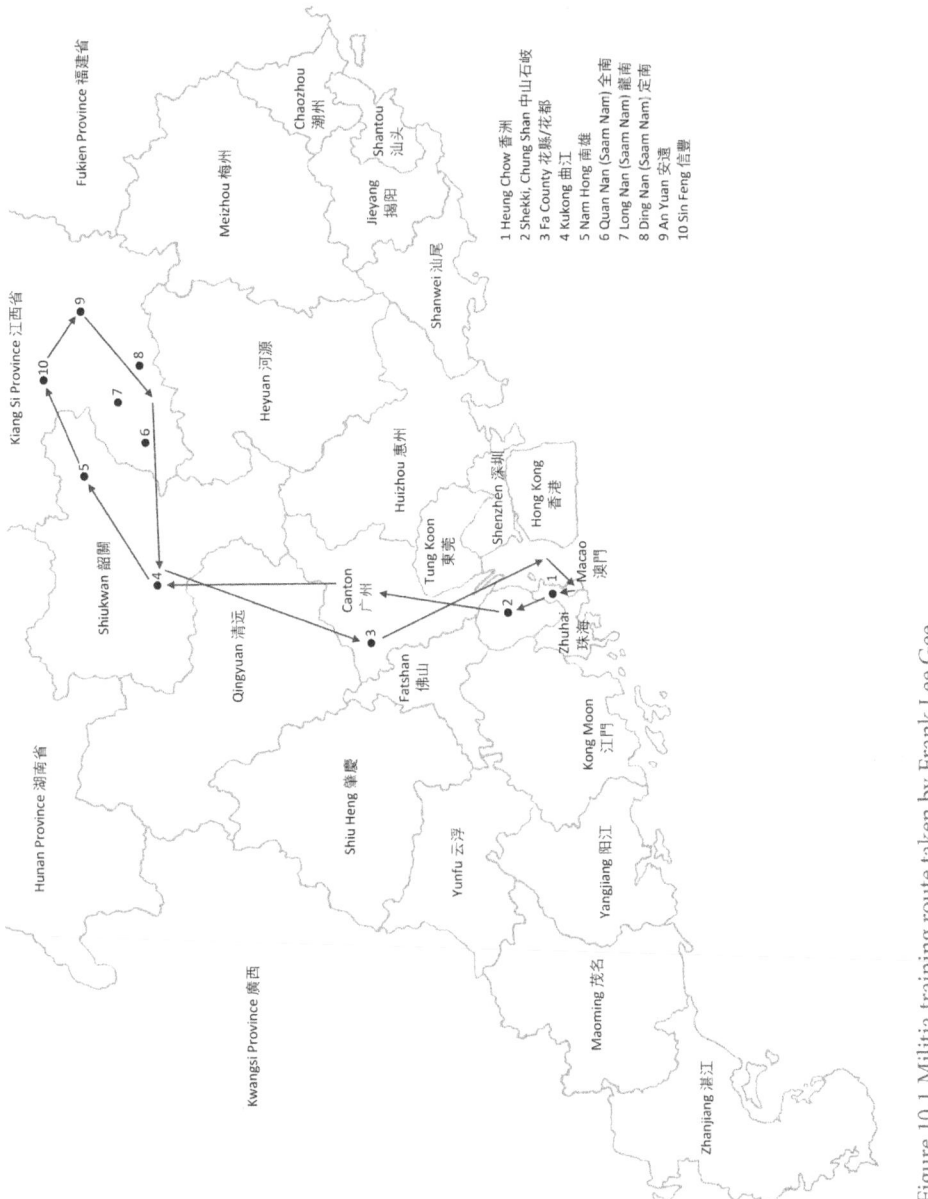

Figure 10.1 Militia training route taken by Frank Lee Gee.

we might just pick a piece of vegetable with our chopsticks to go with the rice, or something salted. But you waited until the squad leader said '*hei faan* (開飯, start eating)' before you really started eating, like that. Then we got on with the pork. We each had a piece of meat. You didn't try to eat somebody else's share. If you did, there'd be a big howl. You had to behave yourself. If it was two pieces each, you had your two pieces of pork. The squad leader took the lead. Sometimes, even other ordinary soldiers might say 'Come on,' and then we would all pick up a piece of meat each. You couldn't do what you liked.

One time when we were all lined up, one of the lieutenants that came from the ranks was talking to us and suddenly one of the soldiers answered him back. The lieutenant got hold of his stick and whacked the soldier. Then they arrested him. They were going to send him to the county jail. But all the squad leaders came and pleaded for leniency. They said, 'Don't do that,' 'Give him another chance,' 'Keep him in the company instead.'

I've seen a county jail. It was like a hell. When the Kuomintang, the Nationalist Party, broke its alliance with the communists in 1927, it started a purge of its ranks, to clean out the communists from the Kuomintang party. They called it *ching dang* (清黨, purging the party). A communist friend of mine asked me to go with him to see a chap who'd been arrested. This chap, Wong, came from a well-to-do family in a big village just across the Shekki River. He was a student at the National Peasant Movement Institute in Canton (廣州農民運動講習所), where Mao Tse-tung used to lecture.

Well, the prisoners with no money in that jail, they all had chains around their ankles. Instead of a concrete floor, they had a dirt floor, with a bit of board raised above it. I think they even had to do their business around there, it was so smelly. But for people with money, it was just the opposite. Wong had a mosquito net and his family were allowed to bring him food. They didn't execute him. They sent him up to Canton. Then during the Canton uprising in 1927, when the people of Canton broke into the jail, he escaped. Eventually he got clear and went to Shanghai for further education. The last I heard he was teaching in one of the universities in Canton. I was on a junk travelling from Canton to Shekki when the uprising took place. But I knew people who took part.

If that soldier had gone to the county jail, he would have been sunk. That's why the squad leaders spoke up for him. Anyhow, instead of sending him to the county jail, they put him in a little room near the company headquarters. The army used to commandeer ancestral temples. They jailed him in a little room and sometimes handed him a bit of food. He was treated all right, but he didn't have the freedom to go anywhere. They kept him there for a week or two and then let him go again. That's why, when they said something to you, you were not to speak back. He answered back, so he was whacked and jailed.

When you had a day off, you still had to ask for permission to go into the county town. If you were refused, you could sneak out by saying you were going to work. I sneaked out once with some others. We were caught and our punishment was to clean the toilets. We were lucky we didn't get a whacking.

At the beginning of each week, they held a memorial service. It was the same in the schools. We had to recite Dr Sun Yat-sen's will[2] and the army commander would give us a bit of a talk. Every night too, when the flag was lowered, we all lined up and recited Dr Sun Yat-sen's will. We sang a little too.

On operations

While we were in An Yuan, we used to visit different places to make friends with the local people. We called them the *lo baak seng* (老百姓, old hundred surnames). The purpose was to build up a good image for the army. This practice was also copied from the Red Army. We didn't do any fighting. There were no Japanese. The Japanese were up in the north. We were in central China. The Japanese had already taken Manchuria in 1931 and in 1932 they attacked Shanghai. But in Shanghai they were defeated by General Tsai Ting-kai's (蔡廷鍇) Cantonese troops, the 19th Route Army. Instead of making Tsai Ting-kai a hero, Chiang Kai-shek moved the 19th Route Army to Fukien province, out of the way. Chiang didn't want these troops around the central China area. They revolted in Fukien. They tried to get Chen Chai-tong to join them, but he wouldn't. I think he was trying to do better on his own.

After spending a few months in An Yuan, our division was ordered to surround pockets of communist guerrillas who were giving trouble further to the south of us. Of course, the guerrillas couldn't come out when a big army arrived on the scene. The place we went to was called Saam Nam (三南).[3] It was in Kiang Si province but very close to Kwangtung. It was a hilly area. The towns were more like villages, but they called them county centres and they were surrounded by villages.

We stayed in the Saam Nam area for about three months. That was when I got sick. I had drunk some hot Chinese wine and eaten some peanuts there. I came down with a chill and a high fever. The company had to go further on to where the communist guerrillas were, so they left all the sick behind in the county centre. Sick soldiers were left behind by other companies too.

The army doctors gave us needles. I had a high fever and I nearly died. After a couple of needles I improved. They had two first-aid men there and I got real chummy with them. They even wanted me to join the first-aid corps, but of course it wasn't allowed. We were volunteers and after one year's training had to go back to our own villages. They weren't training us to be soldiers, just reserve militia.

There were soldiers from our company and from other companies left behind with us. We had to reorganise ourselves. We had no cook, no nothing. We had to do our own cooking. I was made the buyer. I used to go to the marketplace every day and bargain for rice and things like that. In China, they have what they call *da foo*

---

2   Most likely Frank Lee Gee is referring to Sun Yat-sen's 'Three Principles of the People', broadly summarised as nationalism ('self-determination'), democracy ('rights of the people') and socialism ('people's livelihood').
3   Saam Nam is a collective reference to three adjacent counties that have the character 'Nam' as part of their names (龍南縣、定南縣、全南縣).

tou (大褲頭). Chinese-style trousers have a wide band at the top which you secure with a belt or girdle and fold over to fit comfortably. If you were handling money, by bringing down the price you could squeeze a bit for yourself. This was called *da foo tou*, folding your trouser band. They all did it. I did it too.

Because we had to do our own cooking, we learned how to cater for as many as fifty people. Even people from the front began to come back. They weren't officers. They did the paperwork but they classed themselves as officers. They didn't do any fighting. We had to cook for them too. Finally, one of our own chaps who was sick joined us and later he took me back to our own company.

It took us two days getting there from village to village. Two other companies were in the same district. The first night, this chap and I slept in the same bed in a lodging place. We had to carry a full pack, guns and everything. The next day we had to slog it out again. In the area surrounded by our division there was a creek with bamboo spikes all over it. If you were to try to get through the creek, the spikes would go right through you. The army put them there so the local people couldn't get out of the area.

After our return to the company, this other chap and I were put through a course of special training. We had to *pa shan* (爬山, climb the hills) every morning. It turned out to be very good training and restored us to health. That's how the Red Army trained their soldiers. Sometimes they even outmarched the Kuomintang army.

Suddenly we received orders to return to Kwangtung province. Two of Chen Chai-tong's three divisions had revolted against him and they raised the slogan 'Strike down Chen Chai-tong!' Chen's (陳) slogan was 'Unite to fight the Japanese'. He was a warlord but I think he was more or less a patriot, while Chiang Kai-shek was trying to appease Japan. Instead of going back to Sin Feng the way we came, we were now guided onto another track and went straight to Nam Hong on the border of Kiang Si and Kwangtung provinces, to rejoin our division there. Whenever the army was getting from place to place it had to employ local guides from the villages who knew all the tracks. It wasn't like a modern army, with maps and aerial photographs and all that. Even the Red Army had to have guides, otherwise they'd get lost.

It took us two nights to reach Nam Hong. Each company had so many men marching during the day and sleeping at night. It was my luck to march during the night and sleep during the day. When you come to think of it, it was damn ridiculous. But you'd be surprised when you got there. We would leave a big army compound at night and strike a new place early in the morning. You wouldn't imagine you could sleep while you were marching. That's the experience I had. You were that tired, you were asleep while you were marching.

Early on the second morning we struck Nam Hong. We looked all over for a place where we could camp. Then, all of a sudden, we were told to go to sleep. But how can you sleep when you come to a new place? You only want to go and have a look around. That's what we did. Three of us went to yum cha. We all put in the money. The three of us were very chummy. We had money because by that time they were paying us so much a month. We didn't spend it all. We didn't drink or smoke. The other two made me their banker. They couldn't read or write and I kept all the money for them. We were thinking that when the opportunity came to run away, we would have the money to do so. We used to go to yum cha whenever we could. It was very cheap. Compared with today in Sydney, it's like the inflation's gone wild. After yum cha we went back to camp. We tried to sleep, but how could you?! Then we started to march again, to another place where we stayed for the night.

The next morning, the company commander and the squad leader appointed myself and another chap to go back and help with the luggage. We had porters carrying the luggage, but the company supposed to be guarding it had deliberately fallen back and were holding us up. It used to happen like that all the time. The two of us went back and we found not everybody was hanging back. Some of the company were still guarding the luggage. The reason they weren't moving ahead was because they would reach a point and then find a place where they could have a smoke of opium. One of them, I think he could have been a squad leader, a pretty mature sort of bloke, invited us to join in. We didn't of course. After they'd had their smoke, then we'd start up again. Then we'd stop again.

That night we slept in a cemetery by the side of a river. We had a whole good night's sleep there. It was the best sleep we'd had. We two weren't afraid of ghosts or anything. But all the others were. In ordinary times you'd say, 'Fancy sleeping in a cemetery with the ghosts coming out all the time!' Well, I say, if you're afraid of ghosts, then the ghosts are there, that's all.

We got up early the next morning and started back to our company. The commander, a lieutenant, was waiting for us on the road outside Kukong. It was midday when he found us and took us back to the company. He gave us a bit of a talking to for being so slow. I said we couldn't catch up, that was all. We were that tired we fell asleep. Actually, we purposely lagged behind in order to have a good night's sleep.

While we were with those old soldiers, we foolishly followed their example of throwing things away. They threw away one packet of ammunition after another, so they wouldn't have so much to carry. They even cut their blankets in two, so they would only carry half a blanket. I threw my mosquito net away and that's how I got malaria later on.

We stayed in Kukong for a good week, billeted in an ancestral temple. While we were there, one of Yu Han-mou's (余漢謀) companies revolted against Chiang Kai-shek. Chen Chai-tong was still in power. Yu Han-mou was only a commander of one of Chen Chai-tong's three divisions. Anyhow, we were sent to the *jin hou* (戰壕, trenches) to surround this rebel company. We had to keep watch from the trenches and shout if we saw anybody climbing the hills. If they didn't stop, then we opened fire. When it was your turn to sleep, you lay down in the trenches. When the time came for your watch, the other fellow would wake you up and take your place. The army cooks carried all the provisions down to the *jin hou* to feed us. Our watch only lasted one night. The next morning it was all over. The rebel company surrendered and gave up their arms. These soldiers were then divided into different companies in our division.

Next, we got wind that this rebel company, instead of surrendering all its arms, had tossed their Lucas guns into the river. They called them *bok hop* guns (駁殼槍). My mate and I decided to go swimming and see for ourselves. We went down to the North River and started diving. I found the first gun. My mate, he was a Hakka (客家), he dived in and found a second one. We took the guns back to the company and handed them in. We got a reward, thirty silver dollars hard cash each. We were in luck. Others had gone looking too, but they didn't find any guns. You could get a hundred dollars easy for one of those guns if you sold them. Some local people might have wanted them. But you had to be very careful. You might get executed too. Between us we got sixty dollars and we spent some of it. We gave the lieutenant some money and he bought us a mouth organ. We also shouted some of the chaps to yum cha. All I had to put up for that was two or three dollars. Each of us still had about fifteen dollars left and my mate had me keep the rest for him.

Now Chen Chai-tong stepped down and handed over his power to Yu Han-mou. So our division was under Yu Han-mou. I think Yu (余) came from Shiu Heng (肇慶), where a lot of market gardeners in Sydney came from.

While the situation was not settled, the army more or less relaxed its restrictions and we were allowed to move around freely. One day when a few of us went out to yum cha, we heard in the *cha lou* (茶樓, tea house) that Chiang Kai-shek was arriving in Kukong that very day. We decided to go and have a look. We went out to the airfield where we saw the plane, an old Douglas, coming over. We saw Chiang Kai-shek get off the plane. They put on a bit of a parade for him. After that, he went down to Canton to talk to Yu Han-mou.

Not long afterwards, however, Chiang Kai-shek went to Sian in north-west China and he was kidnapped there by Yang Fu-sheng (楊虎城) and Chang Hsueh-liang (張學良).[4] They wanted him to fight the Japanese. That was in December 1936. Now the real turning point came in China. The Nanking government, the Communist Party and the warlords formed a united front against Japanese aggression and Chiang Kai-shek was released. Until then, the warlords in Kwangsi had been rebelling against Chiang Kai-shek. We got word that our division was going to be sent to fight the Kwangsi warlords. We didn't want to take part, so my mate and I decided the time had come for us to get away. The other mate found out, so then there were three of us.

---

4   The Sian Incident (西安事變) of 1936 occurred when two of Chiang Kai-shek's generals, Chang Hsueh-Liang and Yang Fu-sheng, detained him in order to persuade him to focus the Nationalist Army on fighting the Japanese rather than Chiang's aim of defeating the communists. Instrumental in gaining his release was Australian W.H. Donald, unofficial advisor to Chiang, whom the author Mavis Yen met and befriended in Hong Kong in 1939.

10 'Unite to Fight the Japanese'

After spending a good week in Kukong, we were put on a train. It was different to when we went into the army. Then we rode in a proper carriage for passengers. Now we were put in cattle cars. They were horse cars with temporary seating. You could smell that horses had been there. Some companies did sit in carriages and we envied them. But our company was on a freight car with a folded canvas cover in case it rained. We also had to put up with this awful smell.

We were put off the train in Fa county (花縣), near Canton. We stayed in an ancestral temple there for a week and that's where we cleared away. We didn't tell anyone of our plans, but on the train three other chaps got the idea we were going to make a break for it. They followed us around everywhere. They knew that was the thing to do. When we walked across the railway bridge to another little town to get away, they followed us. So now there were six of us. One of them didn't even have civilian clothes. He had to buy some in this town. I'd always kept mine.

By following the railway line across the bridge we went straight down to the West River (西江), where there was an arms factory, making rifles and so on. But there were some army blokes guarding the railway line there and they chased us back. After I explained we were returning to Canton, one of them told us there was a highway down the other way.

We had to climb from hill to hill to reach the highway. We threw away our uniforms up in the hills near a cemetery. As soon as we started off again, we saw a peasant pick them up. When we reached the highway, we took a bus straight to Canton. I don't remember whether we had something to eat first or not. I had to pay for all of them on the bus. One of them was from a rich family too. But he repaid me later. The others didn't.

When we got to Canton, we couldn't get rid of the other three. They followed us around like bad flies. We couldn't stay in Canton. The army could easily pick us up. We could have gone to Shekki, but that was dangerous too. Besides, we all lived near Macao. So we went to the Macao ferry. In those days you got on board first and then paid for a sailing. We didn't travel saloon class. We went steerage, *dai chong* (底艙, big hold). I was afraid they would spot who we were, so when they came round collecting the money, I quickly paid for all six of us.

When we got to Macao we were free. It wasn't like today, with the customs coming in and the Macao Immigration. In those days you could go freely to Hong Kong and Macao. Everybody in Hong Kong could go to Canton whenever they liked, just like the Macao people could go to Shekki whenever they liked. There were no restrictions, just a place to pay customs duties, that's all.

We didn't stay in Macao long. The next morning I was back in Heung Chow. When I sang out 'I'm back' to the foster father, he got a shock. He was so surprised. The local authorities knew about my return but they didn't do anything about it. As long as you got away, it was all forgotten about. You could murder somebody in Kwangtung and if you could get to Shanghai, it was forgotten about. Nobody cared.

When I went into the army, each family was given a lantern with an inscription on it. It said, 'The son of this family has volunteered for training. His family is to be protected.' But instead, the corrupt police arrested my foster father. He and the police used to work together in opium. The foster father just had a smoke now and then. He was nearly dry but would have an occasional smoke in the local coffin maker's place. A *gwoon choy lo* (棺材佬, coffin maker) was a social outcast, so to safeguard himself my foster father would sneak around there to have a smoke. He was almost broke but he still had to pay a bribe to the police to get himself off. They were going to take him up to Shekki and put him on to road construction. By then, he was so broke, he was back hawking salted fish again.

Not long after I returned, the mayor of Heung Chow gave me a job in the local militia. That's the funny part about it. Instead of being punished, I was given a job.

After the big turning point when Chiang Kai-shek was kidnapped in Sian, preparations were made to fight the Japanese. Now they had a second go in Kwangtung to recruit more volunteers into the army. They called them volunteers, but I think it was more like conscription. It was still one person from a village asked to go. The township asked me about going again. They said I might as well because I didn't finish the first time. They tried to con me, but I wouldn't have it. I was preparing to return to Australia.

Frank's story concludes in Chapter 12

11
The Fortune Teller

Harry Gock Ming (郭桂芳)

Returning to Shanghai from Shekki (石岐) in 1930 at the age of nineteen, Harry Gock Ming had completed his somewhat disjointed education after two years at the Shanghai School for Boys and a short spell in the village school, followed by his year of classical Chinese education at Shekki. He obtained his first job in the Australian Chinese Wing On (永安) Company where his father worked. Harry provides a vivid description of clerical life behind the scenes in this legendary company in Shanghai, where he lived a life of comparative privilege.

When he arrived back in Sydney in 1936 he encountered life at the other end of the social spectrum. Harry found the Chinese community confined within invisible walls. Mainstream jobs were not open to Chinese and they were restricted to working for each other. He came back with the reputation as something of a troublemaker and the Gock clan in Sydney decided he would benefit from time spent in a Chinese store in western New South Wales. Life in a small country town was not to his taste. He came close to having his boyhood faith in the Australian principle of a 'fair go' for every man shattered. It took four years of life in the Australian Army to restore his equilibrium.

Working at Wing On

Back in Shanghai, Dad took up a job as supervisor in the hardware department on the ground floor of Wing On's department store. There were now four department stores near each other along Nanking Road (南京路). The fourth, known as the Sun Company (大新公司), had originally been established in Hong Kong by Chinese from Chung Shan (中山) county, also returned from Australia. This company had gone on to set up branches in Canton. But now the profits to be made in Shanghai were too lucrative to ignore.

The four stores were universal providers, in the true sense of the term. They supplied China's freshest teas, the most valuable ginseng from the forests of Manchuria, English biscuits, Australian groceries, silk, satin, wool, the finest cotton materials from England, cameras from Germany, imported footwear and kitchenware.

My old classmate, Georgie Chue, said he could get me a job as a bookkeeper in his firm of cinema owners for a hundred dollars a month. 'Just bring a reference, and the job is yours,' he said.

I went down to Wing On to ask Gock Lock (郭樂) to give me a reference. While I was waiting in the outer office to see him, his younger brother, William Gock Son (郭順), came through the steel door connecting the company's offices with the Great Eastern Hotel (大東旅社). When I explained why I was there, he said, 'I'll give you a job. You don't need any reference. Start tomorrow.'

I protested that he wouldn't pay enough money, but he brushed my excuses aside. He assured me I'd be much better off working for the Wing On cotton mills. That's how I got my first job experience in the Wing On empire. My pay, including basic pay and bonuses, translated into about ninety-six dollars a month. This wasn't bad, but I had to work seven days a week. We also got free all our meals in the staff dining room. It was wholesome food, plenty of rice, four or five dishes on the table. When you got on a bit, those sharing a table could each put in a couple of extra dollars and add barbequed pork, roast duck and chicken.

Wing On was like an extension of the village. The Gocks (郭), the Mas (馬) and the Lees (李) were all there. They all spoke the Chung Shan dialect. It was the kind of atmosphere Dad must have longed for while he was in Perth. I still speak the Chung Shan dialect. I never did master standard Cantonese or the Shanghai dialect.

There was no doubt that Wing On saved the people of our village. In my time, their enterprises included three cotton mills employing fourteen thousand people. The brains behind it all was James Gock Lock. As a boy, he'd worked in the rice fields in Chuk Sau Yuen (竹秀園). Furthermore, he was a man with a heart. His brother, Philip Gock Chin (郭泉), was an able administrator and they worked very closely together. His eldest son, Gock Lum Song (郭琳爽), whom I first met in Hong Kong in 1925, was now general manager of the Shanghai department store. But the core to the success of the Wing On enterprises, I think, should be traced to the industry, the close-knit unity and loyalty extended by the fellow pioneers from the early days in Australia.

I worked in the head office of the cotton mills for six months. I felt they really didn't have enough work for me, that they only wanted to keep me there. So I resigned and went to work as a salesman for a foreign company. Then I had a row with them and quit. I was out of work for months. Dad must have talked to Gock Lock. The next thing I knew, I was offered a job in the Wing On Bank.

11 The Fortune Teller

I was just a bank clerk. I kept the ledgers in Chinese. The bank was on the ground floor of the department store and it had a money-changing place between the two lifts. The managerial offices, including that of the cotton mills, and the dining room were on the top floors.

After the republic was set up in 1912, the Mexican silver dollar became the basis for the Chinese dollar. It was a real silver dollar, equivalent to a Mexican dollar. When you were given silver dollars, you rang them.[1] The twenty-cent pieces were all of silver and the copper coins made of copper. The Japanese bought up the copper coins in Shanghai, re-minted them in Japan and sent them back diluted with alloy. So the value of the copper coin fluctuated day by day. Some days it'd be thirty-five to the twenty-cent piece, and sometimes it'd be forty-four.

Every six months we had to work back at night to clear the accounts, sometimes till 11 or 12 pm, using the abacus. It was Wong Mun Kut who taught me how to use the abacus. He used to be a tide-waiter in the customs. He wasn't a Gock, and he was an opium smoker. But he was brilliant with the abacus and Wing On needed someone like him. He used to pay a few coppers for a bowl of herbal tea to cool down what the Chinese call overheated blood, caused by too much rich food. When I later worked in the managerial department and had to mail parcels at the general post office, I would take an abacus along with me. My calculations always tallied with the post office charges. At first the staff in the parcels department gaped at me. We became quite friendly. But when Wong Mun Kut's health began to fail, the bank got rid of him.

One day a money changer came into the bank with a fifty-pound sterling Bank of England note which he wanted to deposit in the bank. We thought it might be a forgery, so I was sent down to the British Hong Kong & Shanghai Banking Corporation to make enquiries. They told me it was a genuine English five-pound note that had been altered to fifty pounds. The Russians were flooding the world with these notes and now this one had turned up in Shanghai. 'We'll credit you with five pounds,' the manager said.

At the time, the boycotts on Japanese goods were comparatively mild. They only intensified after the Japanese occupied Manchuria. Wing On had two top buyers. They spoke Japanese. They were very arrogant and I didn't like them. I don't remember what they did but they upset me. In fact, nobody liked them. When the cheques came in, I had to countersign them. One day a cheque came in for one of these blokes to pay $3.25 for his milk bill. I opened the ledger and he was overdrawn by close to one thousand dollars. He only had about a dollar fifty left in his account. I showed the cheque to a little bloke sitting opposite me. He said, 'Honour it, this guy's a big shot.' So I wrote on it: 'Return to drawer.'

A week later, about three o'clock in the afternoon, this buyer and Gock Lock came in to see my boss, Great Uncle Gock Yunn. I called him Yunn Goong (公).

---

1 Pure silver coins make a ringing sound when striking a hard surface, whereas counterfeit or diluted coins don't make such a resonant sound.

Gock Yunn's father was Gock Kwan Ju, who used to work in Wing Hing (永興) and spend Christmas at our house in Perth. They called the assistant manager and had a conference. Then someone shouted, 'Kway Fong, *loi* (桂芳來, come here, Kway Fong),' for me to join them. Gock Lock started by asking why I hadn't honoured that cheque.

So I replied, 'He had no money. No money, I don't pay.'

'Do you know you caused him a lot of embarrassment?'

'That's his business. I'm employed to protect the bank's money.'

Well, you couldn't argue against that. Gock Lock just looked at me. The logic was on my side.

'Why didn't you ask the manager first?'

'I couldn't leave my place. Great Uncle Yunn is always jumping on me for even going to the toilet.'

'Well, you could have asked the assistant manager.'

'He wasn't there either.'

They probably were, but I put them both in. Dad was there too, standing at the back. Gock Lock knew what it was about. But he didn't know what to do. He just snorted and stalked away with the buyer trailing him. Then Great Uncle Yunn said, 'Get back to work, you bastard.' I went back to my desk. I looked up and saw Dad coming towards me outside the railings. I got up. 'Kway Fong (桂芳), what did you do that for?' Dad asked. 'That's the right thing to do, Dad,' I started. Suddenly Dad put his hand over his mouth to hide his laughter. He ran straight out of the building towards the Great Eastern Hotel. He didn't like the two buyers either. They were that unpopular.

I sat down again. Four of us clerks were sitting together. 'You want to watch out,' one of them said. 'I don't know what's going to happen to you.' 'I've got nothing to worry about, I'm clean,' I said.

At six o'clock I went up to the dining room and had my tea. I came downstairs at half past six. While I was sitting there, a messenger came down. He was a Gock too, but he hadn't had much education. He spoke to Yunn Goong first and then he came to me, 'Kway Fong, Lum Song (琳爽) wants you. Go up immediately,' he said. As I passed Yunn Goong, I heard him mutter, 'You bastard, you deserve a good kick.'

I went up to the sixth floor to the managerial offices, walked in and said respectfully, 'Elder Brother Lum Song.' 'Oh, there you are, Kway Fong,' he said. 'Look here, your English is pretty good. What do you say to coming up here and taking care of all the English correspondence for me? All the mail, all the bills, everything in English?' He went on to ask how much I was being paid. 'So your basic pay is forty-five dollars. I'll raise it to sixty. It's a bit late now, half past seven. Go back downstairs, but report here tomorrow.' He even thanked me. Everyone downstairs thought I was getting my ass kicked. Instead, I was promoted with a fifteen-buck raise!

11 The Fortune Teller

Figure 11.1. Wing On & Co., Ultimo Road, Haymarket, 1938. (State Library of NSW)

Fortune teller

One day, Elsie Gock Bew, her dad was George Gock Bew (郭標), took a group of us to see a fortune teller, just for a lark. It was in Frenchtown. He was a fairly elderly person, a Shanghai man, and he was blind. He had a big round table and everybody who came sat round it. There was no waiting. When it came to my turn, he asked when I was born. 'The twelfth day of the sixth moon.' 'That was a very bad time,' he said. 'You were a very hard birth and your life is not going to be easy.'

My mother did have a hard time. She was in labour from twelve o'clock at night until eight o'clock in the morning. I was a breech birth and the doctor said she'd be crippled. Dad got some ginger stewed with pig's trotters and smuggled it in to her. The second day she got up and walked. The doctor was amazed.

'You were born in the year of the pig,' the fortune teller said. He made sure I understood that. 'You'll do no good in China,' he went on. 'You won't do any good in the army or in government either. Your future is in the business world.' That was all the Chinese talked about, the army, the government and the business world. 'Go abroad, go south,' he said. He didn't know anything about me, except that I was Cantonese. He said he couldn't see any more after that.

Return to Australia

To cut a long story short, I arrived back in Sydney in 1936, shortly before my Certificate of Exemption from the Dictation Test was due to expire. I stayed in Wing On's down in Haymarket where I renewed my friendship with Gock Chew Gum. He was working there, lugging bananas. It wasn't until after the Second World War when the restrictions on Chinese were relaxed that his family was permitted to join him.

Chew Gum took me out to yum cha (飲茶) in a place in Dixon Street. The tables were bare, but the serving of duck was as big as a plate, for sixpence! The prawn dumplings were enormous. The place was run by a Tung Koon (東莞) bloke. The Australians called him Old Jumbo. The customers were all market gardeners. They wouldn't come unless you gave them value for their money. It reminded me of Shekki. There were several places down the main street on the way to the eastern villages where you could go for *wun tun* (雲吞/餛飩, wonton) and noodles. They used to put samples in the window to attract the customers. The *wun tun* were bursting with prawns.

There weren't many Chinese around in those days and everybody knew everybody – who'd pinched someone else's wife and brought her out to Australia as his spouse. We all knew. There was one chap I used to buy spring rolls off. He had a second-hand car and he used to boast about where he'd been over the weekend. I soon twigged to what he was up to. He was delivering opium.

We didn't get much money in those days and to us things were expensive. The Sydney market gardeners had contracted with the racing stables for all the horse manure. They'd go in on a Saturday morning and clean out all the manure and take it back to the gardens. They didn't speak English and they couldn't read or write it. But the stable boys managed to tell them which horses were good bets. The gardeners would then go out to wherever the racecourse was and back these horses. Every time they won, they'd have a banquet down at the Shanghai (上海) or the Tientsin (天津) restaurant in Campbell Street.

I got into a conversation one day with a Lung Du (隆都) chap. I was telling him how when I was in Shekki the Canton ferry boat was blown up by bandits. For days afterwards, bodies were being fished out of the Shekki River and stored in the little pagoda in Hah Ki (下岐). He let out that he'd taken part, but I didn't think he could have played a very important part – he was a Fong but he wasn't from Sau Mei Yuen (秀美園), from another village.

Working in the outback

My first job in Australia was with a very old-established business, W.G. Pan Kee & Co. in Moree. It was a general store, dealing mostly in groceries. Wing On sent me

11 The Fortune Teller

Figure 11.2. Harry with Gock Chew Gum in Sydney, 1938. (Gock Ming family)

up there. They were all Gocks in Pan Kee. Two brothers ran the shop, Gock Geng Chew, the elder brother and boss, and Gock Geng Lum. Their father, Gock Buck, who ran the store before them, had gone back to China and died there.

Two other brothers were working there. They were part Aboriginal, but they were Gocks too. One of them was driving an old Chev truck for the shop and he taught me how to drive. There must have been a community of Gocks up there in the old days. I knew from Dad that he and Hoy Buck had tried to make ice cream to sell there, but they couldn't make it set.

Even the cook at Pan Kee was a Gock, Gock Way Kee. He wasn't a bad cook. But the steak he gave us for lunch every day would break your teeth. He was only allowed two bob a day for the meat, so he had to get the cheapest cut. Wing On in Sydney was just as stingy. The manager insisted we eat Australian rice, which was horrible. The staff wanted Chinese rice and they threatened to go on strike. Finally, he agreed to import Thai rice. At least it was better than Australian rice. It was only after the war that Australia improved its strains of rice.

When Gock Buck was still in Pan Kee, for some reason or other butter became scarce. The factory would send it down to the agent to ration out to the different stores. There were three big stores then: an Australian store where all the cockies[2] went; Pan Kee; and our competitor, Hong Yuen. The younger son of our landlord in Shekki was working in Hong Yuen. I got to know all the Chinese working there. All the Chinese in the two shops in Moree were from Chung Shan.

With the shortage of butter, the manager of the big Australian store went to the agent and said, 'There's a scarcity of butter, so why don't you give it all to us?' The agent was horrified. It was the wrong thing. He told me this himself. He said, 'Look, if you're going to be like that, I'll give all the butter to Buck, to Pan Kee.' 'Oh, you can't do that. They're only chows,' the manager said. 'But Buck's the whitest businessman in Moree,' the agent replied.

Another story I heard about Gock Buck was when the Premier, Jack Lang, closed the New South Wales Government Savings Bank in 1931. All the small businessmen, drovers and carters who dealt there had their money frozen. They thought they'd lost it. One of the drovers with a wife and five kids, who'd always had an account with Buck, was into him for quite a lot of money. He went to Buck and said he felt like shooting himself. Buck said, 'What you worry about? You go on your business. You want food for your wife and kids. You come here. I trust you. The bank will open. It's your money, not their money.' Well, Buck had a customer for life after that. All his kids too. That's the sort of people country people are.

Pan Kee traded after hours. We didn't open the front door, we opened the back door. We traded all over the weekend when everybody parked their traps and sulkies in the big backyard. The coppers dealt with Pan Kee too. Geng Chew used to shake his head over the sergeant's big bill. Pan Kee gave credit.

When I went to get a driving licence, I had to go to the police station. The sergeant was the head policeman in Moree. He said, 'I'm busy, Harry. I've got to go to the post office. Oh, you got the truck out there?' 'Yes.' 'Then drive me up to the

---

2   The Australian National University's School of Literature, Language and Linguistics defines cocky as 'A small-scale farmer. Cocky arose in the 1870s and is an abbreviation of cockatoo farmer. This was then a disparaging term for small-scale farmers, probably because of their habit of using a small area of land for a short time and then moving on, in the perceived manner of a cockatoo feeding'. Later applied colloquially to all farmers (https://slll.cass.edu.anu.au/centres/andc/meanings-origins/c).

11 The Fortune Teller

post office.' It was only a block up the street. He got out and said, 'I'll go in and get the mail. You turn the truck around and drive me back again. If you can do that …' That's how I got my licence.

I was in Moree for several months. But Pan Kee got rid of me because I was getting too big for my boots. One Sunday, we drove down to Narrabri to watch a football match. On the way, we had an accident and overturned the truck. The only person who got hurt was me. We turned the truck back on the four wheels. It went, but we'd twisted the chassis, done a lot of damage. Pan Kee had to pay for it to be fixed. I had no money.

The next thing that happened was the coppers came round and said they needed an interpreter. They had a Chinaman in the lockup for attempted murder. 'Oh, take Harry,' said Geng Chew. The case involved some Chinese living in a boarding house on the outskirts of Moree, all of them from See Yup (四邑). On the Sunday morning, a young bloke had run to the police station with blood coming out of his head. He said an older bloke had tried to murder him with a gun. So I asked about the gun. The old bloke was a very gentle man. He explained he'd never tried to murder the young man. He'd come back and found the young chap stealing his opium, so they'd had a fight. The old fellow hit the young chap on the head with his opium pipe. Now in Chinese, an ordinary smoking pipe is called a *yin toong* (煙斗) but an opium pipe is called a *yin cheong* (煙槍). *Cheong* (槍) is the same word for gun. I explained all this but the police wouldn't listen to me. They remanded the old bloke to the jail in Tamworth until the next court of sessions and pinched the lot of them for smoking opium. They all got fined.

It was then that I got a telegram from Wing On in Sydney to return there. There was a good opportunity waiting for me, the telegram said. When I got to Sydney, the manager asked me to go to Bourke. A Chinese widow up there needed someone to drive her horse and cart and sell vegetables, for thirty bob a week and keep. This was so Pan Kee didn't have to sack me. Pan Kee were paying me two pounds ten a week and keep. Moree is three hundred and thirty miles from Sydney and Bourke four hundred. I wasn't going to take that train trip up there for thirty bob a week. So I said I was afraid of horses.

I was down in Sydney for several weeks, staying in Wing On's and eating there. Then Alan Quoy got me a job in his father's market garden in Aberdeen, for thirty bob a week and keep, driving a truck around and selling vegetables. I knew Alan in Shanghai. We'd worked together for a short while, clearing customs for the fourth big department store, the Sun Company. His father's name was Yip Ting Kwei. That's how it became Quoy. He was from Tung Koon county.

One afternoon in Aberdeen, a copper came into the milk bar where I was having a milkshake and asked to speak to me outside. I followed him out, wondering what I'd done. He told me I was required to appear in court at the quarter sessions in Moree on such and such a date. I was given a rail warrant and a living allowance and I stayed at Pan Kee's for nothing. The court found the old

Figure 11.3. Harry riding his Kodak motorcycle. (Gock Ming family)

man guilty of assault with intent to do grievous bodily harm, but not guilty of attempted murder. Seeing as he had already been incarcerated in Tamworth for so many months, he was sentenced to the rising of the court. He'd already served his time in Tamworth!

I also spent some time with George Chin Mook. He then had a share in a market garden in Newcastle. One day a young copper came round to check up on the Chinese gardeners. Apparently, they were looking for seamen who'd jumped ship. The copper asked George where he was from. George told him. He'd been all over Australia, the Northern Territory, Western Australia, Queensland, Victoria. He'd seen more of Australia than the copper.

11 The Fortune Teller

The Depression was still on then and jobs weren't easy to come by. Furthermore, if you had a Chinese name, you couldn't even get an interview. Eventually, I adopted my mother's name (Jenkins). Then I got an interview and a proper job in photography, at Kodak.

Army service

When I returned to Australia, the trouble was I'd become a *tai jee jay* (太子仔, crown prince). Until then everything had fallen into my lap. It took four years in the Australian Army to finally sort me out. I learned a lot in the army, made a lot of friends too. I nearly got court-martialled at the end of the war though, when I refused an order to make a bucket of tea for the Japanese prisoners-of-war. I wasn't going to make any tea for them. Not after what I'd seen them do in China.

Whatever atrocities, whatever things are done by soldiers, I'm prepared to believe. Of course, I don't necessarily believe everything I'm told. I think as human beings we're no better than wild animals, the same as foxes or wolves or anything else in the wild. No people are honest. We've got a veneer of what we call civilisation, but you don't have to scratch very deep and that veneer disappears.

Dad was the best man I've ever met. He never gave up on his responsibilities till the day he died. He supported his mother, our family, the family of his eldest brother and Saam Baak's (三伯) widow. He once said to me, 'When my eyes are closed, I don't care what happens, but while I'm alive, I've got to look after these people.'

I think of my mother and the other Australian women like her and how they were treated. What virtues are there?

Postscript

As Harry had struggled to find permanent work outside the Chinese community in Sydney in the late 1930s, he decided to anglicise his name. He used his mother's maiden name of Jenkins, and so became Harry Jenkins. Almost immediately he obtained a job with Kodak as a motorcycle delivery man. Enlisting in the Australian Army in the Second World War, he served in the catering corps in the Northern Territory for four years. Many Chinese enlisters worked in the service divisions, as the prevailing view was that troops of Asian descent would not be suited to frontline duties in Asia as they may be mistaken for Japanese. In 1943, Harry married Mary (Nancy) Hudson and they had two children, a daughter and a son. Harry and Nancy operated a fish and chip shop at 260 Abercrombie Street, Redfern, after the war and during the 1950s. Nancy passed away in 1989 and Harry in 2002.

Two of Harry's sisters, Edna and Sheila, returned to Sydney from Shanghai during the 1930s, married and raised families. Edna Ming was the first woman of Asian descent to graduate in medicine from Sydney University in 1941 and

Figure 11.4. Harry Jenkins in military uniform. (Gock Ming family)

she practised as a GP from her home in Manly Vale in Sydney. Her husband, Louis Victor Kepert, was a prominent journalist with the *Sydney Morning Herald* newspaper and together they had three children. She lived to the age of 102, passing away in 2019. Sheila worked as a bookkeeper, raising her two children as a single mother after divorcing her husband. Sheila died in 2014. You can read about Harry's other sister, Mavis, in the introduction.

Harry's father, William Gock Ming, died in Shanghai in 1940. He and his second wife Daisy had three children: two sons, William and Duncan, and a daughter, Angela. Daisy left China in 1948 to live in the United States. Her daughter Angela also left in 1948 to live in Hong Kong, where she owned a successful women's clothing store. She later emigrated to Sydney, Australia, where she and her husband operated an independent supermarket. She currently lives on the

New South Wales Central Coast. The two sons remained in Shanghai and suffered considerable ill-treatment during the Cultural Revolution (文化大革命) after being labelled counter-revolutionaries. Later they moved to America. The eldest, William, died in December 2020 and Duncan resides in San Francisco.

12
Return to Australia

Frank Lee Gee (李植良)

Frank Lee Gee's opportunity to return to Australia finally came in 1937 when his foster father's financial situation improved. Although Frank had been born in Australia, he had been granted a Certificate of Exemption back in 1923; however, he had to wait for a fresh authorisation permitting him to land because he had been out of the country for fourteen years. Australian authorities would consider written requests to extend Certificates of Exemption for additional three-year periods while people were overseas, although at some point they demanded that individuals return or forgo that right. During Frank's absence, the categories of Chinese allowed into Australia under sponsorships had been extended to include assistants and substitutes, not only of merchants but of local traders. Chefs, cafe workers and market gardeners were also added, but wives were still excluded.

Arriving back in Cairns, Frank found he was disadvantaged by his inadequate knowledge of English. Australia was then engulfed in the Great Depression and he had to work long hours in Chinese shops for low wages. During the war, he worked in the sugar and timber industries. At the end of the war, he joined the growing Chinese restaurant industry in Brisbane. This led him to Sydney, where the postwar opening of mainstream jobs to Chinese enabled him to become a waterside worker, known colloquially as a 'wharfie'. After the war, Chinese wives were finally admitted to Australia and late in life Frank married a Hong Kong woman, Sue Yung Lee (李瑞榮).

The voyage home

By 1937 my foster father was running out of money. Fortunately, a cousin in Mexico suddenly made a bit of money and repaid a loan to the foster father, interest and all. Now he wanted to return to Australia too. The Japanese had already started bombing Canton. Every day we could see planes going over and they flew pretty low too. If anybody had an anti-aircraft gun he could have shot the lot of them down. But in those days they didn't have enough guns. The commanders of the troops guarding the area gave orders not to do that. Once you started shooting, they would machine gun you and a lot of people would get killed. While I was there, nobody got killed.

Father left in 1937. We were going to come together but we found my papers had expired because I'd been away over ten years. Three or four months later, the papers were fixed up and I had a letter asking me to go down to Hong Kong, to one of the *gum shan jong* (金山莊, golden mountain trading companies) there. I went down with the brother of the father's wife. We stayed at the *gum shan jong*, sleeping in bunk beds and having two meals a day there. The *gum shan jong* fixed up everything. The foster father had borrowed money off them. He told them what I was to bring, herbs and Chinese goods. I also brought a few books and some clothing. Hong Kong was a bit of a thrill for me. It was so different to China and especially Canton. I had always liked Canton but, compared to the village, Hong Kong was sparkling. If you could earn a few dollars a day there, you could live pretty good. There was all sorts of work there too.

The foster father's wife stayed behind. You couldn't bring your wife in those days, not like today. Not even Australian-born Chinese could marry a girl in Hong Kong or China and bring her over. You had to be in business to bring a wife out, and even then only for six months. A worker or a gardener couldn't. The foster father's old business was sold long ago. Eventually his wife settled in Hong Kong.

I came back on the *Changte*. You had to take a launch or sampan to reach the boat, which was anchored in the Hong Kong harbour. Before we sailed, the Hong Kong doctors lined up all the Chinese passengers and Chinese crew to examine our eyes for *saar ngan* (沙眼, trachoma). This was only done to the Chinese. They were very cruel. The doctor who examined me, who was also Chinese, reckoned I had a bit of trachoma. He wanted me to stay behind and have it fixed up before leaving. I think he must have wanted a handout or something like that. But the ship's doctor, an Australian, said 'Oh, that's all right, let him get treatment on board the ship.' So a Chinese steward came down every day to put drops in my eyes. It was all Chinese stewards in those days. I was the only one suspected of having trachoma.

There was no such thing as bunks in steerage. You just put a mat down. I slept on the same common bed with everybody down in the hold. But they did open up the hatch so we could get plenty of air. When we got to Manila two days later, they used the lower deck to load up. When the loading was finished, they closed up the

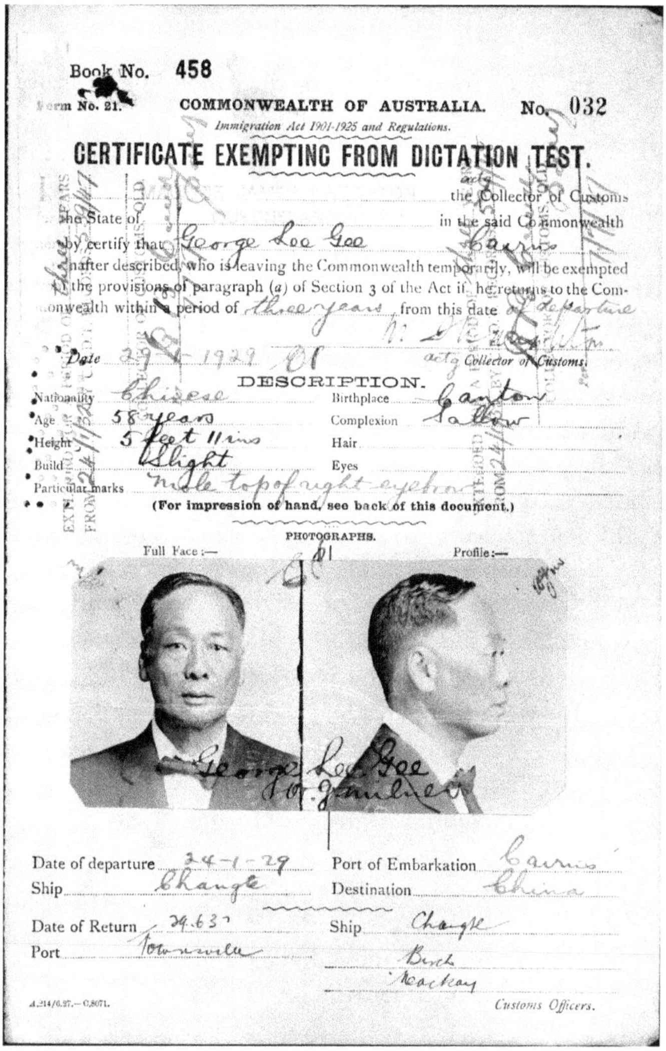

Book No. 458

Form No. 21. COMMONWEALTH OF AUSTRALIA. No. 032

Immigration Act 1901-1925 and Regulations.

CERTIFICATE EXEMPTING FROM DICTATION TEST.

the Collector of Customs for the State of ... in the said Commonwealth hereby certify that George Lee Gee ... hereinafter described, who is leaving the Commonwealth temporarily, will be exempted from the provisions of paragraph (*a*) of Section 3 of the Act if he returns to the Commonwealth within a period of three years from this date of departure

Date 29-1-1929 ... acting Collector of Customs.

DESCRIPTION.

Nationality Chinese — Birthplace Canton

Age 58 years — Complexion Sallow

Height 5 feet 11 ins — Hair

Build Slight — Eyes

Particular marks mole top of right eyebrow

(For impression of hand, see back of this document.)

PHOTOGRAPHS.

Full Face:— Profile:—

George Lee Gee

Date of departure 24-1-29 — Port of Embarkation Cairns

Ship Changte — Destination China

Date of Return 24.6.31 — Ship Changte

Port Townsville

Birch

Mackay

Customs Officers.

Figure 12.1. George Lee Gee's Certificate of Exemption from the Dictation Test, 1929. (National Archives of Australia: J2483, 458/32)

deck again and put tarpaulins over the hatches. They also put up tables and chairs where we had our meals.

We weren't allowed to go ashore at Manila. I didn't see Manila until 1959, when I was returning after a short visit to China on the *Changsha*. One of the passengers knew an old man from his father's village, so we went to see him. A nephew of the old man took us around and we had a good time. They asked my passenger friend, 'Did you bring any ham or bacon?' because Australia was famous for that.

Cairns

The foster father and his partner came down to meet me in Cairns. They were planning to set up a herbalist business. The partner knew a lot about herbs. I brought about half a dozen baskets of Chinese herbs and different Chinese groceries from the *gum shan jong* in Hong Kong and they fixed up everything with the customs. I was penniless. I had nothing.

Well, the first thing when I landed, they gave me five pounds. That used to be the Chinese custom in those days. If anybody went back to China penniless, before he left all his friends would start him off again. This one would lend you twenty pounds, that one thirty pounds. In those days you didn't go by the hundreds, only by the tens and twenties. If you had fifty pounds in your pocket, then you'd be rich. That's what they used to do.

There was a shop dealing with the other Chinese shops and it had a dormitory where you could stay. You had to pay so much for your keep, but you didn't have to pay anything until you started off. They would give you credit. They would always lend you money to start up your garden again, if you were a market gardener. It was a fellow countryman relationship. For instance, if you came from Chung Shan (中山), then a Chung Shan shop would look after you; if you came from See Yup (四邑), a See Yup shop would look after you. Just like here in Sydney, the Kou Yiu (高要, a county on the western rim of the Pearl River Delta) people have a shop in Dixon Street like that. People say the Bank of China allowed their shop to put up a four-storey building in Canton to handle all the remittances they are sending back to the villages now. It's like the *gum shan jong* in the olden days. You could send money back through them to another *gum shan jong* in Shekki (石岐). They did the banking for you. They would tell you what the current rate of exchange was for the English pound and they always gave you a better rate than the banks. At one time you could get up to two hundred Chinese dollars for ten English pounds.

I went down to see the uncle on my foster mother Elsie Kwong's side. The auntie, my foster mother's sister, had already died in about 1925. She died very young from an abortion – had too many kids. But all the cousins were there. I helped around their shop and Uncle would give me two or three pounds. No such thing as talking about wages then. I had just come back. Every now and then whoever you worked for would give you a bit of money.

Now the foster father and his partner set up their shop. All those herbs and groceries I had brought were part of the capital. The partner had one of these old Dodges he was going to put in as capital. It was only an old bomb. He wanted me to go around in the old Dodge and sell vegetables and be part of the shop. But I wouldn't be in it. I didn't know how to drive and I wasn't going to go around selling vegetables.

I was learning English by myself then and the partner used to make sarcastic remarks about it. He would say, 'When you're thirsty, you begin to dig a well,' and 'When a young girl wants to marry, she starts piercing her ears'. He meant I wasn't a child any longer; instead of trying to learn English I should get straight down to working. All the English I know now, I had to pick up by myself. I never had a chance to have an English education. I had to use a dictionary and teach myself how to read. Even the Chinese I know, I learned through reading. When I came back to Cairns, I could only speak simple English. I would meet people who used to know me as a child and they would say, 'Oh, you're grown up now!'

Before my arrival, the partner had been working in Atherton. Now he and I took the train up there, where he packed up what he wanted and sold what he didn't want. The old joss house was still there. I didn't even recognise the joss housekeeper. We called him the *miu jok goong* (廟祝工, temple worker). I used to know him as a kid but he didn't recognise me either. He said, 'You're a man now!'

We drove back to Cairns in the old Dodge. The partner drove, I wouldn't learn. The Dodge is a funny car, it's worse than an ordinary car. It has to be reversed to go forward.

Mossman

When we got back to Cairns, I was offered a job as a grocery boy in Mossman for three pounds a week and I agreed to take it. Actually, the shop used to be my father's shop before I went to China. The foster father had two other partners then, but because he did all the work, he had all the say. He got the money to go back to China by selling his share in this shop. In China they called him a *choy gee lo* (財主佬, rich fellow), but he wasn't all that *choy gee* (財主, wealthy).

At one time you had to go to Port Douglas from Mossman to get a boat to go to Cairns. Now there was a road going through from Cairns to Mossman. A passenger car would take you there. I'd already saved up a few pounds, so I took the passenger car over to Mossman. The Mossman shop sold groceries, clothing and all sorts of things, mostly for the Australian cane farmers. There were very few Chinese goods. When my father occupied the premises, it was just an ordinary shop. But these people had a motor car and a truck and delivered to all the farms. The farms might order a bag of corn, a couple of bags of sugar, flour and so on. I helped with the delivering.

I had to pay my own fare over to Mossman. Before I went, the boss said he'd pay me three pounds a week. But the day after I got there, he said, 'You're pretty green,' and he cut my pay in half.

I had to do all the delivering. I had to get up early in the morning, water and feed the horse, all by myself, before breakfast, and then start work in the shop. When the boss had a tin full of water, instead of carrying the tin himself, he would sing out to me to carry the water for him. He treated me more like a slave. All right, so I did it. There were two daughters. One had been in China for a few years. She was younger than me. She used to take off her stockings to look at the sores she had on her legs from mosquito bites in China.

At night, after the shop had closed and all the others had gone and I should have knocked off, the shop gave me evening jobs. 'Bottle the kerosene,' 'Weigh this out, weigh that out,' I was told. That's how the Chinese exploited their Chinese staff.

Another girl, Ella, used to drop into the shop and chat with me. I think she must have been about sixteen. On Sundays I used to go to her family's place, have a good roast dinner and talk with the girls there. I also became friendly with a cane cutter, Peter Atkinson. He was the first Australian I knew who was a member of the Communist Party. I would visit him in the evenings at the weekend. I only had a very limited knowledge of English, but we got by. Whenever I had a chance, I would go to a picture show. I picked up my English from the picture shows and from associating with Australians. I preferred their company.

Well, one night when I was chatting with Ella, the daughter went crook. She said, 'Why don't you do your work? Go on, get something to do.' She just didn't like me talking to Ella. Then my temper came up. I've got a rotten temper. I said to the daughter, 'When your father comes back, I'm going to leave.'

It just happened that her father had gone over to Cairns. I made up my mind I was going to leave, and the next day I got hold of Peter Atkinson and told him all about it. 'All right,' he said, 'I'll fix it up for you'. He rang over to a waterside worker in Cairns specially for me. 'When you go back to Cairns,' he said, 'go and see this person'. The boss and his wife thought I wouldn't get by because I had a limited knowledge of English. They said to me, '*Gong de m'wooey gong, paa nei meia* (講都不會講, 怕你什麼, Can't even speak English, why would we fear you)'.

I went back to Cairns and I went down to see the waterside worker Alan Tucker, another communist. Alan took me down to the labour bureau and they sent someone in a car to Mossman to investigate, to find out why I wasn't paid proper, only thirty shillings a week and things like that. As a grocery boy I should have been getting four or five pounds a week. The shop people intended to say I hadn't worked there. But the man from the labour bureau told them I had witnesses. The labour bureau got me ten pounds off them and they were very sore about it. I had worked in the shop for a good few weeks when they started to get tough with me and my temper came up.

The husband and wife said they were going to blackball me in Cairns. That's what they told me. They did come over to Cairns and tell the Chinese shops how bad I was. They said I had *gou keui deih* (告他們, reported on them). They wanted to stop me from getting another job. Actually, this couple had a bad name in Cairns. I still got another grocery shop job and had my meals there. It was only for two or three pounds a week. That was very little, but in the Depression Chinese working for Chinese shops in Cairns were only getting three pounds a week. They had to stay back and do a bit of stacking after the shops closed, for no extra pay.

Australians who were in the union got about five pounds for the same job. At that time I didn't know anything much about unions. When I first got back to Australia I found there was a Labor Party here, a workers' party. But later on when I knew a bit more I realised it really wasn't a workers' party but a capitalist party in the service of capitalism. They give the workers a bit but don't change the system.

I delivered all the groceries on a bicycle. I had a big box at the back and a basket in the front. I had to balance between two and three hundred pounds on the bicycle.

12 Return to Australia

It wasn't so bad if the wind was going with you. But if the wind was against you, you had to pedal as hard as anything.

When I was in Cairns I lived at the father's shop but I didn't work for him because whatever little money I earned, he always wanted to take some off me. The making of me was I wouldn't be exploited. I was saving money even when I was only earning thirty shillings a week. I didn't drink, I didn't smoke or gamble. There was no such thing as yum cha (飲茶) in Cairns. What I need I would buy but I didn't waste money.

Kuranda

Not long afterwards a Chinese chap recommended me to work as a gardener and kitchen boy in an Australian hotel in Kuranda, a scenic spot not far from Cairns, for three pounds a week. I didn't know anything about gardening, but I knew how to ripen bananas. The hotel had some banana plants but the Chinese working there before hadn't taught them how to ripen the bananas. They knew the Chinese put incense in a big drum with the bananas and covered it up. But when I went to have a look, I found the incense wasn't lit. They knew to put in the incense, but they didn't know they had to burn it.

Burning the incense wasn't a secret. In the old days, when you wanted to ripen bananas you had to pack the incense with the bananas in a circular drum and cover the drum up well, so that the fumes from the burning incense would circulate. The bananas were ripened by the fumes. But the Australians in the hotel thought the bananas ripened on the plant. They didn't know that after you'd picked the bananas when they were nearly ripe, you had to use incense. Nowadays, when the bananas are nearly ripe, they use gas.

Sometimes you might put half a dozen sticks of incense in the drum, but you didn't pack it the way they did. You had to stack the bananas so the fumes would circulate and ripen the bananas. The fumes turned the bananas a brownish colour. It was all very simple. I knew because I had heard people talking about how they did it and that's what I did up there. They wanted me to do the garden too, but I couldn't. They wanted me to grow vegetables and light the kitchen fire.

They knew I had a bit of Chinese in me. Well, we had our meals in the kitchen at a big, long table. All the waitresses sat there and I thought I should have been sitting together with them, but they put me in a corner and I thought it was discrimination. Much later on, I heard that even down here in Sydney, the kitchen hand doesn't eat with the cooks. Cooks could eat with the waitresses and the waitresses with them, but not kitchen hands. But at the time I thought the reason was racial, so I left that job after a few weeks. I went back to Cairns to the grocery shop, and I worked there for a good long while.

Figure 12.2. Frank Lee Gee and a cousin in Cairns, 1938. (Lee Gee family)

Cane cutting

During the war I went cane cutting. All the sugar cane farms then were Australian. There were no more Chinese farms. That was in the early days. I only lasted for one season. A season is five months. I could have stayed on because I was a part-time cook because each gang had a cook, but I couldn't stand it anymore.

When you're cutting, they always have a pacer, a fast one in front. You have to follow the fast one and then they've got somebody at the back there, another fast one to push the one in front. You work in a gang and they pay you by contract. The faster you cut, the more you cut, the more money you make out of it. In those days a cane cutter could earn about ten or twenty pounds a day. It was good money. After you cut the cane, you have to load it. You might get bitten by a snake. Before they cut, they burn the cane to get rid of all the trash. They make a break, start from the break and see how the men go. They did the burning in the evening, only a certain portion which had to be cut the next day. They couldn't leave it. If the cane went, you wouldn't get the price for it.

I was just an average cutter. They kept me there because I knew how to cook. I cut the cane first, loaded up, and then they would send me back to get the meal ready and the other cutters finished my job. That's the only way I kept going. I cooked all sorts of things for them, a bit of Chinese food, a bit of stew and sometimes I made a roast. I still got the same share of money. Somebody had to cook and we shared the money equally. But after one season, I couldn't stand it anymore. Instead, I went to work in a saw mill, in the timber yards, and on the floor.

It was during the war after I'd left Cairns that I saw my foster mother Elsie Kwong for the first time since I had left Australia. About the time she had come back to Australia from China in 1928, one of her uncle's wife had died in Cairns, so he said, why don't you come and look after my kids? Later, she moved to Bowen, where a sister and her husband had a big shop that supplied all the cane growers. Eventually she lived in Townsville on her own on the pension.

Wirth's Circus

Towards the end of the war, I moved down to Brisbane and worked in a Chinese cafe as a grill cook. They served both Australian and Chinese food. The Australian food was mostly steak and eggs. I picked up Western-style cooking in the restaurant. I did cafe work for years until some of us got together and ran our own business cafe serving the same, Chinese and Australian food.

While we had our own cafe, the boss of the Wirth's Circus[1] used to come in to eat. When we sold the business, he asked me if I would like to work as family cook for the circus, not for the men, but for his family. I agreed and came down to Sydney with the circus. They had a big mansion at Coogee. They had money and had a maid too. I was the cook and lived in a big room near the kitchen. I enjoyed the work and the tours. They would start from the southern part of New South Wales, go up north, then to Brisbane. They went by train. From Brisbane they would change

---

1   Wirth's Circus was the biggest and most prestigious circus company in Australia, with an international reputation. Founded in 1882 by the Wirth family, it operated as a travelling circus throughout Australia for eighty years, attracting performers from around the world.

into another train. They rented a train and we lived on the train. I travelled in New South Wales and southern Queensland. I used to cook them different kinds of food, roasts, some Chinese food, whatever I knew.

Then the maid began spreading yarns about the food being all rubbish. The boss and his wife and another person became the only ones eating my cooking. The boss told me all about it. Naturally, I wanted to leave, but I didn't see why I should sack myself. So I waited. Since most of the family wasn't coming to eat, I knew something must be going on.

It happened that I liked condensed milk on bread. I know it's not good for you, but to me it was a delicacy. I used to buy it myself. That's what brought about the final showdown. The boss explained it was about something missing from the cupboard, the condensed milk. I told the boss that if I wanted anything I'd buy it, I didn't go to the cupboard and just take it. Then I lost my temper and told the maid off. After that, the boss' elder sister, who was in charge of that sort of thing, paid me off. I told the boss I was happy to leave. I wasn't sorry. I was there for three to four months.

Chinese Youth League

After I left the circus job, I stayed on in Queensland and worked for a friend's restaurant there. Then in 1950 I came down to Sydney for a holiday and stayed on to work in the Mandarin Club restaurant. Some friends from Brisbane had the restaurant and had two others, the Tientsin (天津) and the Peking in Kings Cross. I was living in a hotel over near the old Pyrmont Bridge. I joined the Chinese Youth League (僑青社)[2] in Dixon Street just as they were celebrating one year since the liberation of China and met Arthur Lock (鄭嘉樂), Billy Jong (張岳彪) and Stanley Wai (布德威). The Chinese Seamen's Union shared the same building. Arthur and Billy worked for the union while the Chinese seamen here during the war were working on the building of the Warragamba Dam. I lived at the hotel for quite a very good while and later Arthur Lock joined me there and we shared a room.

Still later, I went to work for Billy Jong, who was making prawn crackers. He was just struggling along. Sometimes he couldn't even pay wages. Meanwhile, a wharfie friend, Albert Lee On, suggested I put my name down to join them. I was still working with my prawn cracker friend, so I got Arthur Lock to go down and see the results of my application. Well, my name was posted. My prawn cracker

---

2   The Chinese Youth League began life as the patriotic Chinese Youth Drama Association in 1939, founded by Fred Wong and others to assist the Chinese war effort through drama and Chinese opera performances. Fred and his protégé Arthur Gar Lock Chang were also actively involved in the trade union movement and leftwing politics, which led to the formation of the Chinese Seamen's Union in 1942 to look after Chinese seamen granted temporary residency in Australia during the Second World War.

friend didn't want me to leave. He said he would match whatever I would get as a wharfie. But he couldn't, of course.

Life as a wharfie

At first you had to work as an extra. When they formed a gang, if you could join, then you'd be in a gang. Later I did join a gang. In the wharfies, they don't call your name, they call your number. There were up to nine thousand numbers when I first went in. Less than ten of them were Chinese.

Sometimes you worked on the wharves, sometimes you had to go down the hatches, sometimes you had to do trucking. When you first went in and had no work to do, they gave you 'appearance money'. But you had to show up. If you didn't wear your number when they called you, you didn't get your 'appearance money'. First-time 'appearance money' was sixty cents a day. But you could live off that in those days. If you could knock off fifteen or twenty pounds in one week, that was good wages when we started in 1950.

Some of the work was heavy and some was light. Sometimes we had to go down to where they carried wheat. That was real coolie's work. You had to be very strong. I knew I couldn't do it physically, so I dodged it by taking days off. Even carrying flour was hard work too. But compared with the Chinese or Japanese or Indian people, the Indian and Chinese work harder. When you're a wharfie, you take your time. You work at your own speed. Now they've got machines. With machines it isn't hard work.

I had a room with a stove down at Woolloomooloo, near the wharves. All I was paying was two pounds two shillings. I cooked my own food. I didn't particularly like wharfie work. It was just a job. For a long time, I was going to leave it. I should have left much earlier. I should have gone in with a friend to run a restaurant for a club. The clubs would subsidise you and it would be your own business. They might give you two hundred or three hundred pounds a week to run it. What you took would be yours. You would just run the kitchen and the dining room. A lot of people made a living that way.

But I didn't, because when you're a wharfie it's more or less like what the Chinese call an iron rice bowl. They couldn't sack you unless you did something wrong. They could only buy you off with the 'golden handshake', pay you off. Besides, being a wharfie wasn't a hard job. Working in a restaurant is hard work. I was trying to get the 'golden handshake' to take me through to sixty-five when you could get the pension. So I stopped when I was sixty. I did a few odd jobs here and there after I left, went back and worked with Billy Jong again. Did a bit of painting.

South Flows the Pearl

Reflections on China and Australia today

Since I retired from the wharfies, I've been back to China several times. Shekki is very crowded and prosperous now compared with before the war, even compared with the period between 1959 and 1964. In fact, there's no comparison with when I was going to school there. There's plenty of everything. In 1959 there were a lot of things you couldn't get. There was only one restaurant serving yum cha, with a special section reserved for Chinese from overseas and Hong Kong residents.

They've got a new policy now. A lot of northern people are going down to Shekki to do business, buying things to take back north. Others are going down to work on road construction and in the clothing trade. Chung Shan has always been more prosperous than the other counties. People called it the home of fish and rice (魚米之鄉).³ Today it's got a lot of industries, especially processing factories. The Hong Kong factories do the cutting and have the clothes made in the villages. There's more living space in the villages. Shekki's a lot cheaper to live in too.

In 1959, the first time I took a bus from Canton to Shekki, it took six to seven hours because we had to cross so many rivers. The buses were very small. When you stood up, you had to bend over. In 1982, the buses were like the coaches in Australia. It cost my wife and myself four Chinese dollars each and took four to five hours.

In 1984, I wasn't feeling too good, so my wife and I took a taxi from Canton to Shekki. It cost just over a hundred Chinese dollars and took about two hours. There was a big queue of cars leaving Canton. We had to wait half an hour before we could cross the bridge to get out onto the main highway to Fatshan (佛山). From Fatshan, we branched off to another road and went straight down to Shekki, not like before when you had to make ferry crossings. We didn't have to cross any rivers at all and they were then building a super highway to Shekki.

We ran into a friend on that trip in 1984 and he took us down to Dai Laam (大嵐) village to have a look. They've got a good concrete bridge across the Shekki River now, not a wooden one like before. The streets were much better too. Dai Laam has electricity now. But they still live a very simple life there. Maybe it has improved, but I think the majority of families are living just as primitively as many years ago. They were still gathering grass for fuel. If I was to go back and live under the same conditions now, I don't think I could stand it.

We had a look at the old family house and the street it's in, Gou Kuk Hong (九曲巷, Lane of Nine Turnings). I didn't go in to see who was there because I couldn't afford to give them the gifts they expect. They expect too much. When I first went back in 1959, I took a lot of clothes and they fought over them. Since then I haven't been in touch with them. The foster father's second wife moved to Hong Kong long ago and I lost contact with her too.

---

3   A Chinese proverb meaning a land of plenty.

12 Return to Australia

Nineteen fifty-nine was the first time I went back. I was that excited, thinking this was the first Chinese socialist country I was going into. I went in from Macao, straight to Chung Shan. It seemed the people were working with heart and soul to make the transition to socialism. If anyone picked up something in the street, he would find the owner and return it. If you were looking for something, somebody would help you. Even a small boy would say, 'Oh, I'll take you there,' or he'd tell you where to go and how to get there.

But today they reckon it's different. People coming back say the individual has become very important. It's 'I' who counts. At one time they used to say '*mong chihn hon* (往前看, look forward)'. You know how they play on words with the same sound. Now they've altered the *chihn* (前) for 'forward' to *chihn* (錢) for 'money'.

The Chinese in Australia are still old fashioned. They still object to intermarriage. They like Chinese to marry Chinese. But they've got no say now. They can't stop it. So they say young people have their own way of thinking.

Today they think differently to the days when they used to go back to China. Before when they made a bit of money they went home. They might take a suitcase with them. All a market gardener knew was to go from the garden to the market and back to the garden. He might come out to Chinatown to buy a few things, some food, a hunk of meat. When he got back to the garden, he would salt the meat down. That would do for the next week when he went to the market again and bought another lot. Vegetables he didn't need to worry about. He only needed rice, oil, fuel and *see you* (豉油, soya sauce). He lived in a shack.

But today the market gardeners are flash. They have houses, fridges. It's all young people now. They're not like the old Chinese market gardeners. They've got machinery to plough the land. They've got pipes all around. They don't carry buckets of water anymore like the old Chinese used to.

I don't think there are Chung Shan gardeners anymore. The Kou Yiu people are still holding on. But they're modern gardeners, not like the old type. Even if they have an old-type market garden, they live in houses like other people, not necessarily new ones, maybe twenty years old. They seldom use organic fertiliser. It's mostly chemical. As for the Australian-born Chinese, they won't do market gardening at all. It's hard work.

Some of the Chinese are now getting their kids to learn tai chi (太極, karate). In the Australian schools they've always got bullies and they stand over the Chinese. So, if you have a fight with them, beat them. If you can beat them, they will leave you alone. That's how it is in the Australian schools.

A lot of Chinese here like their offspring, the ones that are born here, to know something about China. They are trying to create what they call a Chinese identity, because, if you don't teach them, don't let them go to Chinese school or speak Chinese to them, they eventually become yellow-skinned Australians. Their ways, habits and everything is Australian. But they don't look Australian. When it comes to an argument with Australians, it makes no difference. You can be well educated, but you're still a Chinese, and you're still a bastard.

In China they used to think you could pick up gold in the street here, that we were all *gum shan haak* (金山客, travellers from the golden mountain). They thought they could just come here and dig the gold and go home. They didn't realise, if those people wanted gold, they had to dig very hard. They also had to defend themselves from people trying to take the gold off them.

Now they think when they come here they can get a good job. Unless they come from Hong Kong or Singapore where they've already got a trade, they have to rely on cafe work. A skilled cook from Hong Kong can get a job very quickly. Or you can be a waiter or a waitress. The waiters supplement their pay through the tips. Sometimes they can only get jobs in the kitchen. It's mostly men who are the cooks. Very few women do *wok chaan* (鍋鏟) work – they call cooks *wok chaan* (wok stirrers). They might let you do the deep-frying or prepare dainties. You may not enjoy it, but you do it because you're getting paid for it.

Today, a lot of people in China, if they've got an opportunity, want to come here. It's a funny thing. They still think Australia is a golden mountain. It's not a golden mountain.

Postscript

Frank continued to work as a waterside worker in Sydney until he retired. He married Sue Lee Gee but they did not have children. Frank's foster father, George Lee Gee, had retired and was living with Frank in Brisbane in June 1944 when he was knocked down by a taxi and died in hospital. His foster mother Elsie Kwong passed away in 1982 in Charters Towers, Queensland. Frank died in 1995 and is buried in Rookwood Cemetery in Sydney. Sue, who was much younger than Frank, lives in a Sydney nursing home.

13
Wartime

Evelyn Yin Lo (黎鑽好)

The early Chinese wanted their Australian-born children to have a knowledge of the Chinese language and Chinese culture. Those who could afford it sent their sons and sometimes daughters to China for this purpose. As Canton and the Pearl River Delta had already been occupied by the Japanese, Evelyn, aged sixteen, and her younger brother, Cecil (黎滿枝), were sent to Hong Kong in 1939, and she tells in this chapter of her first impressions of Chinese society.

They stayed in the infamous area known as Kowloon (九龍) City. This was a small, densely populated walled area of six and a half acres, over which China was to have retained jurisdiction under the agreement leasing the New Territories to Britain for ninety-nine years, ending in 1997. However, shortly after the agreement was signed, the Chinese officials were unilaterally expelled on the grounds of defence requirements; over time, the precinct became overcrowded and, being left to its own devices, uncontrolled and lawless. The area remained a source of friction in British–Chinese relations until 1987 when both sides agreed to demolish the original city walls and old buildings and transform it into a public park.

With the outbreak of the Second World War in 1939, Evelyn and Cecil returned to Sydney, where they helped their father run a second cafe in Chinatown. As her father's health declined, Evelyn took on more and more responsibility at a young age.

At the end of the war, Evelyn married Don Yin Lo (羅順忠), a former Chinese seaman who joined the US armed forces and served in New Guinea. He narrowly escaped being deported from Australia under the *Wartime Refugees Removal Act 1949*. Evelyn and Don had a big decision to make – whether to remain working in Sydney's restaurant community or take up a business opportunity in California.

Figure 13.1. Evelyn in Hong Kong, 1939. (Yin Lo family)

Hong Kong

In 1939, Dad sent Cecil and myself over to Hong Kong on the understanding we were to learn Chinese. He was very keen for us to know Chinese and be able to speak it properly. We went on the SS *Tanda* and, on the way over, Cecil and I became very friendly with the captain, M.B. Skinner. We arrived at the end of the winter, before the Chinese New Year, and stayed with friends of Dad's in Kowloon City. They had a shop selling sandshoes and other dry goods, while the family, a very large one, lived upstairs.

13 Wartime

In the beginning, I felt a bit homesick and used to cry a lot. One of the women where we were staying would try to comfort me. Kowloon City was a real Chinese city surrounded by a wall. You could go behind the wall and you'd find all sorts of shops and little factories. In fact, you never knew what you'd find. The people we stayed with worried about me going out by myself. Cecil and I used to stay out till quite late. Sometimes it was even difficult to find our way back.

Malcolm Gock Chew and Morgan Wong See were already in Hong Kong, studying Chinese. We grew up and went to Sunday school together. They were staying in the Wing On (永安) Company and took Cecil and myself out to a tea house for yum cha (飲茶).

One of the first things I noticed about Hong Kong was there were no drunken men in the gutters. Chinese didn't get drunk. If they did, they went to bed. There were poor people, but never any drunks. It was a wonderful feeling not to see a drunken man lying in the gutter. Also, in Hong Kong the Chinese always wore shoes. In Australia, people didn't wear shoes. I used to think those people in Sydney who didn't even have shoes were very poor.

I also noticed the refugees who'd been forced out of their homes by the Japanese. I would cry when I saw them sleeping in doorways after the shops had closed. People said they had come down from Shanghai.

The Chinese in Hong Kong called Australia *gum shan* (金山, the golden mountain). This was the traditional name for Australia. They really believed you could pick up gold off the ground in Australia. They didn't know it wasn't as easy as they thought.

Cecil and I went round again and again, looking at the way the little factories made *haam yu* (鹹魚, salted fish) and how they pickled eggs. One workshop was making little round cakes in moulds. You hit the mould with a wooden hammer to release them. We both tried it. We sat on stools and went 'bang, bang, bang' with hammers. Everybody laughed at us. They called me a *gwai paw* (鬼婆, barbarian woman). I knew what they were saying, but I didn't care. I would go into their places and say I just wanted to see what they were doing. They always called us *faahn gwai* (番鬼, foreign devils), but they always invited us to go again.

However, one day I got very annoyed. It was winter weather and I only had European clothes. I went to the market wearing a nice woollen suit. I had nothing else to wear. Now when the Chinese bought a fish in the market there was no paper to wrap it up in. They just tied it with a piece of straw. Well, a woman dangling a fish on a straw called me a *gwai paw* and swung the fish head against my skirt. I became real cranky. I had to go home and change. My nice woollen skirt!

One of the sons of the family we were staying with was Wesley, also from Australia. His brother was Australian too, but their father was Chinese. I knew Wesley when he was going to school up in the New South Wales country town of Aberdeen. He used to come down to Sydney a lot. Then he went off to Hong Kong and got married there. He was very dark for a Chinese and they called him *haak*

Figure 13.2. The Parkee family, c. 1941. Back Row: Edna, Cecil, Basil, Leslie, Lindsay Front Row: Malcolm, Annie, Lai Parkee, Evelyn, Edward (Yin Lo family)

gwai jaai (黑鬼仔, black barbarian boy). I don't know whether he minded. I always called him Wesley.

'Listen, Wesley,' I said. 'I'm getting tired of people calling me a foreign devil. Has your wife got a spare Chinese costume? I'll borrow it off her.' It happened to be Chinese New Year when the shops closed up for three days and you couldn't get anything made. I was only slim in those days. Anyhow, Wesley's wife lent me a dress and I came down in it, complete with Chinese slippers. 'You don't walk like a Chinese,' Wesley said. 'You shut up,' I said. 'I'm trying to be a Chinese. Well, how does a Chinese girl walk different from an Australian?' 'They slouch their feet,' he said. 'Okay,' I said. 'I'll fix it.'

I went back to the market and this time no one dared to slush me. After the New Year I had a Chinese dress made. But when you're born in Australia, your skin's different. They could still tell I didn't belong there. Whenever I appeared in the market, the women would snort 'Huh!' – as if to say, 'What are you doing here?'

I was always trying to have a look at the little snacks the hawkers were selling on trays. I liked the pig's cheek, cut up in little pieces and served on toothpicks. I would have one of them. We didn't eat too much tea because it was such a big family, you hardly got anything to eat. We didn't mind though, because we had the money. One day I was taken to a place belonging to an old lady wearing a two-piece black silk suit. It turned out to be a bigger factory, full of dried fruits that were laid out to dry and later to be put in big vats. There were all kinds of *haam mooey* (鹹梅, salted plums) and pickled fruits. I'd never seen anything like it before. 'What do you want to go back to the golden mountain for?' the old lady said to me. 'You come here, you can sleep on this bed.' She proudly showed me a Western mattress on a Chinese bed. 'Come and live with me,' she said. 'I'll take care of you.'

Any biscuits that came from overseas were the in-thing over there. We'd brought about six tins of Arnott's mixed biscuits with us. They were given to us. Travelling by boat, it was easy to take them. The Hong Kong people called them *gum shan bang* (金山餅, golden mountain biscuits). There were a lot of kids where we lived and I felt sorry for them. They always used to be hanging around, hoping we'd open a tin of biscuits. I used to give them some, but once you do that, they're always waiting. When we weren't home, they'd go and pinch them. I got annoyed with that. I was willing to let them have some any time I was home, but I didn't want them to steal them. Also, their maids were very curious about my silk stockings and what we had in our tin trunks. I was real annoyed because they tried my stockings on and put ladders in them. Then they threw them back. They'd never seen anything like it before.

Shortly after we arrived in Hong Kong, I turned seventeen. The *Tanda* was still in the harbour, so Cecil and I went back to see Captain Skinner. Cecil told him it was my birthday. 'She's very unhappy because she's got no birthday present and she's been crying,' Cecil said. So Captain Skinner said, 'Well, she's not going to miss out on her seventeenth birthday! You come up to my cabin and we'll have a little birthday party.' That's exactly what we did. That night the three of us had a little party. He told us if we ever needed to send anything home, he would take it for us. But he also foresaw the danger of war breaking out with the Japanese. He said he'd told his company to put us on any of their ships if the need arose. 'Never mind about the money,' he told the company. 'You book them on my line.' He said the company promised him they would do so. In the meantime, he was returning to Australia. Actually, the money for our return passages had already come through. But he didn't know that.

The Second World War broke out in September that year and we returned to Australia, again on the *Tanda*, but on a later trip. Captain Skinner planned to take us to visit his wife when he went on furlough. They had no children. But he never had the opportunity. In 1942 his ship was sent to the war zone and hit by the Germans. Practically the whole crew went down. The chief steward was one of those who survived. He got in touch with me two or three years later. I wrote to Mrs Skinner and she sent me a photograph of Captain Skinner.

Chinatown during the war

Sydney's Chinatown today is centred in Dixon Street in Haymarket. This used to be the market area where all the fruit and vegetable agents had their shops. During the war years, however, the best restaurants were in Campbell Street. As you walked up Campbell Street from George Street towards Elizabeth Street, the Capital Theatre was on the right. Further up, the Tivoli Theatre was on the corner of Campbell and Castlereagh Streets. The Shanghai (上海) Restaurant, long since gone, was also on the right between Elizabeth and Mary Streets. The Tientsin (天津) Restaurant was upstairs, across the street on the left-hand side of Campbell Street. If instead you turned right after reaching Elizabeth Street, the House of Five Sons, or Ng Gee Gooey (五子館), faced you across the road. The Nanking (南京) Restaurant was on the left-hand side of Campbell Street, between Pitt and George Streets.

After Cecil and I returned from Hong Kong, Dad took up two shopfronts on the right-hand side of Campbell Street, opposite the side exit of the Tivoli Theatre. Here he started the Canton restaurant, the Kwang Chow Lou (廣州樓). Now all the Tivoli stars started going to the Canton. Dad would make up their favourite dishes for them. He also served regular meals just like any other restaurant. He was the only one doing the cooking. Mum continued to run Ng Gee Gooey in Elizabeth Street, so we had two places going at the same time. We got to know the doorman of the Tivoli well. Some of the entertainers came from overseas, including America and China. Among them were the Kwan brothers and George Wallace. They used to give us tickets to their shows, but we had no time to go.

Our clan cousin, Lai War Hing (黎和興), didn't like this competition at all. The Nanking Restaurant had five or six chefs, they were a big concern. They must have been making thousands. We were only a small family business. There were a lot of drunks in those days and the Nanking would send them up to our place. I don't know what type of people they were. I suppose after they'd had their meal they felt relaxed. They'd put their heads in their plates and go to sleep. I used to hate that. We couldn't get them out. My little sister was only nine then. She used to take their hats and put them outside the shop. Then she'd say, 'There's your hat outside the door. Someone'll pinch it if you don't hurry up and get it.'

We also had customers who were walking out on us. We had to ask them to pay. Dad needed me to keep an eye on things at the Canton now and I couldn't get Sundays off anymore. I had to give up going to church. The church people kept asking me to go back. But I felt my first responsibility was to my parents. Dad didn't want me to work in the restaurant because it was hard work for a girl. He was trying to get another cook from China. So I said to him, 'Listen, Dad, you're not well and we need the money, so I'm going to help. It doesn't matter what you think.' As for Dad's friend, who was arranging for another cook to come, he kept saying, 'The papers are coming through.'

Figure 13.3. Evelyn Parkee and Don Yin Lo outside Central Station, Sydney, 1945. (Yin Lo family)

Social life

Meanwhile, I began to lead a fairly social life with other young Chinese. Billy Jong (張岳彪), Stanley Wai (布德威), Fred Wong (黃家權) and some others set up the Chinese Youth Association. I was the first girl to join them and we used to go for picnics. They wanted me to attract other Chinese girls into the association. Thinking of my own lonely childhood, I thought it was time something was done for young Chinese. There weren't many of us in Sydney then. But the other girls didn't want to join, so that idea fell through. Cecil used to go with me to the association's gatherings because he used to bring me home. Each week two young fellows would cook for us in their club kitchen. We would have a very nice dinner, with fried noodles, spring rolls and duck. Later, the club's name was changed to the Chinese Youth League (僑青社). It's very popular with young Chinese today.

    I went out with Billy Jong long before he or I married someone else. I once went with him to the pictures. He put his hat under his seat and someone kicked it away. He also gave me a big box of chocolates, which I took home to the family.

    Don Yin Lo was one of our regular customers. He was a seaman and his family also came from Tung Koon (東莞) like my father. Don used to ask me to help him address envelopes in English when he wrote to his brother in Hong Kong, and also to help him with his shopping. I would take him to Anthony Horderns, the big department store on the edge of Chinatown.

Don was six years older than me. He told Dad he'd like to marry me. Dad said he thought I was a bit too young, but it was up to me. At that time I wasn't interested in Don. I didn't think it was a good life to be the wife of a soldier or a sailor. You'd get very fond of him and then he'd have to leave. I didn't want to marry someone who would leave me. At the time, I was going out with a group and I was very keen on another chap from Hong Kong. He was tall, dark and handsome. We used to go dancing at the Kuomintang (國民黨) club every Saturday night. Now and then one of the chaps would get a job somewhere else and drop out. That's how this Hong Kong chap went off. Then Don disappeared, and I didn't see him for years. I didn't even know where he went. In any case, I wasn't ready to get married. Besides, Dad needed me in the business.

The man who was supposed to be arranging for another cook to come from China kept taking my father's money, but the cook never arrived. We got some help from some seamen who looked after the upstairs, the private wing, while Cecil and I took care of the downstairs. Dad's health was failing, but he was still able to cook and I became his offsider. All the Hong Kong evacuees were coming in then. Some of the Chinese girls married to British servicemen asked us for jobs. It was a good time for the business.

Looking after Dad

I never did spend much time with my father before, but I did have to when his health failed. I had to more or less run the Canton on my own. Cecil was about sixteen after we came back from Hong Kong. Of course, we didn't run the Canton entirely by ourselves. Dad used to come over when he was able to. I helped do the cooking. Dad had the stockpot ready. He told me exactly what to do. Everybody thinks I'm a good cook. Actually, I just used the stockpot. You see, the flavour's already there. I had about four years' experience under Dad. So I did the cooking and Basil (黎宗枝) made the noodles. That's how we managed to keep the Canton going for a couple of years. I'm even more aware today of how important it is to do the best you can for your parents when they are not well. You don't blame your parents. It's a matter of survival.

In December 1941, the Japanese came into the war. We were still living in Foster Street near the Central Railway Station when a midget Japanese submarine entered and shelled Sydney Harbour. The expected cook never arrived, so Dad had to sell out. That's how he lost the Canton restaurant in the end. I always thought we shouldn't have sold it. Four or five seamen bought it cheap.

We only had the Ng Gee Gooey going after that. But Dad had to let someone else run it and everything was lackadaisy. Dad was sick and tired. Two years later he sold the business very cheaply. I had already taken on a job in a fruit shop in Parramatta and Basil had gone off with the Allied Works Council, doing war

13 Wartime

construction work in Darwin. I was furious when I heard about it. I said to Dad, 'You didn't need to sell that business. I could have run it.'

But Dad was always worried the Central Railway Station would be a target and he moved the family to Burwood, a suburb west of the city. At first we rented the house, then Dad put down the deposit and Cecil and I put our money in and eventually the family bought it. After we moved to Burwood, Dad and Mum just retired. By this time the older boys had jobs and were helping keep the family. Cecil was already working with Australian Wireless Amalgamated. But I was earning more than the boys. I was always lucky. Dad's health was failing fast now and he became a bit bored. He got in with a crowd of people who came from See Yup (四邑) in China. They'd moved down from Darwin.

Mum also made friends with a lady who lived around the corner from us. She was working in a woollen mill in Alexandria. Her name was Lee Tim-tay and her husband was Chin Loong Tong. We called her Yee Paw (姨婆). They came from Toishan (台山) county. Mum wanted to go out to work too, but she wouldn't while Dad wasn't well. She just pottered around the house, took care of Dad, took up gardening and visited sick friends.

The only way Dad could tell which train to take to Burwood was by the two 'o's at the end of the word. The newsagent on the Burwood platform had a little stand with books and papers. Dad used to have a look and buy comics or story books for my young brother. The newsagent became quite friendly with Dad and would offer him his seat. When Dad's train came in, he would say, 'Here you are, Mr Park, your train.' Dad asked him to come up to the house and meet the family. He was very young, maybe about twenty, or a little older. He used to come when he could. He lived over Campsie way and the bus stopped outside our front gate. Probably as he grew older he gave up that job. We lost touch with him after all those years.

I don't think Dad was a very good businessman. He was too soft. Every time he saw the kids, he'd say hello, invite them into the shop and give them dim sims (點心). That was his style. Dad died in October 1945. We buried him in Rookwood Cemetery.

Mum was very sad after Dad's death. Yee Paw urged her to take a job at the woollen mill in Alexandria. We knew Mum was bored at home, so for her own good we decided to let her go. It wasn't for the money. We were keeping her. All the Chinese women working in the mill were older women. Mum reckoned it was good working there. She was placed in the spinning workshop. She started at four o'clock in the afternoon. I would walk her to the railway station going, while Yee Paw would come back with her. You could travel late in the night then. Nobody would molest you. Some days Mum would go with Yee Paw and other days by herself. But Mum wasn't there very long because the mill closed down.

Figure 13.4. Evelyn and Don at their wedding, 10 August, 1946. (Yin Lo family)

Love and marriage

A few months after Dad died, Don Yin Lo returned to Sydney. All this time he'd been serving in the US Air Force in New Guinea. He was in New Guinea for four years. Finally, he contracted cholera and was shipped to the United States for hospitalisation and recuperation. Now he was returned to Australia. We renewed our friendship. Don proposed again and this time I accepted.

Our wedding was a very happy occasion for me. We got married in St Andrew's Cathedral in the heart of the city. There were twelve choir boys. My sister was the only bridesmaid and there was a little flower girl. The reception was held at Miss Bishop's restaurant and about two hundred and ninety guests came.

According to Chinese tradition, the bridegroom's family meets all the expenses. Don paid for everything. In any case, my mother didn't have the money. Before he died, Dad had been hoping that one of us would get married so that he'd have some grandchildren. Our parents expected the boys to marry. So, because I was the second eldest and Basil wasn't married, it was a Chinese tradition that something had to be done to prevent the family wealth, the *foo* (福), from flowing out. My mother didn't even know about this custom, but she always listened to Yee Paw. So to please Mum in the Chinese tradition, I did what she wanted. Don bought a pair of trousers, *foo* (褲), and hung them over the door I had to walk through to leave the house to get married. We took them down afterwards.

13 Wartime

Years later, when my little sister announced she was going down to Melbourne to get married, none of us could go to the wedding. She also married a man whose family came from Tung Koon. I felt sad because I only had one sister and I wanted her to have the same happiness as myself.

While Don was in New Guinea, he had served in the officers' mess. A lot of Australians had their camps next to them. The Americans were eating turkey while the Australians were having bully beef, Don told me. He thought it was a shame to waste such good food, so he used to hand over to the Australians what was left over. He wasn't used to such affluence. Half a pound of butter would go for half a dozen pieces of toast, he said. I'm sorry I didn't keep a very flattering story about Don in the army paper, when he was returned to California for recuperation. But Don said the story was a lot of 'boloney'.

Don now had a very light job. Most of the time he met planes and settled high-ranking officers in their quarters. The drivers would pick Don up. We lived with Mum in Burwood and Don went to work in his uniform every day. He got all his living-out allowances.

The Sydney Chinese used to call Don the Chinese Yank. The new proprietor of the old Ng Gee Gooey restaurant was a friend of Don's. They were short of waiters just then, so whenever Don went in he would be asked to help out. 'No, I can't do it,' Don said the first time he was asked. 'I'll get caught.' 'But one Chinese face isn't any different to another,' Don's friend said. 'Give us a hand.' Then Don took his uniform off and did the waiting. But he only did it because they were shorthanded. Several years later, when my third daughter, Beverly, was a baby, I helped them out for ten days, so the boss could go to the Royal Easter Show. Beverly sat in the kitchen. The *see tou fu* (師頭婦, boss' wife) also had a little girl. We went in at eleven o'clock and finished about three thirty. I did the waiting and business end of the work. The name of the shop was changed to Cheong On Lou (長安樓, House of Eternal Peace).[1]

During the early years of our marriage, I had a lot of support from the family. Our first baby was Diane. My brothers had never experienced a young baby, I being the first to be married. They were very good. Whenever the baby woke up, they would all run. My mother practically looked after the baby for me. She bathed it, taught me what to do. Meanwhile, I did the housework and breastfed Diane. Don and Mum got on very well together. He did everything he could to help in real Chinese fashion. I didn't have rice very much. But Don liked his rice and so did Mum. The two of them would have their breakfast together and she'd push the pram with one foot to keep the baby from crying. I would have my breakfast and do the housework while they minded the baby. It was a sort of fifty-fifty basis. They used to talk for hours. About old times, anything.

Mum would cook the breakfast rice and ask Don what he wanted. As long as there was something to go with the rice, Don didn't care what he had. Like Dad,

---

1 The restaurant was advertised and known by the name Cheong On cafe (長安餐室).

Don liked *haam yu* (salted fish). He'd cook it himself. He would buy anything that he thought was tasty. He liked to steam everything. He wasn't keen on deepfried dishes. Once a month, Don and I would leave the baby with Mum and go dancing at the Kuomintang club. Don was very keen on dancing.

Don was planning after his discharge to go into a delicatessen business with a cousin in California. I was willing and Don prepared all the stencils for our luggage. Then suddenly the army asked Don to go to the Philippines before returning him to the United States. However, they weren't prepared to send me with him. Don said, 'No, either my wife travels with me or I don't go at all.'

But by this time, I no longer wanted to go to America. I knew my mother would miss me and I didn't want to leave Australia. So Don said, 'It doesn't make any difference where I live as long as you're happy. We could stop here.'

The army personnel officer asked me to go in and see him. He wanted to know why I didn't want Don to leave. He said, 'Look, you'll be paid here, you'll be well looked after. We know you've got a family.' I insisted that I didn't want Don to leave Australia. So in the end the officer advised Don to wait and get his discharge.

At the end of 1948, when my second daughter, Margaret, was only six weeks old, a *Sydney Morning Herald* reporter suddenly rang me up. I don't know how she got my number. It was when a lot of Chinese who had married Australian girls were being deported. 'Did you know,' she asked, 'that your husband is another deportee case? He's got to be out of the country by the sixteenth.' 'You've got to be joking! Under what conditions?' I asked. 'Being Chinese,' she said. 'Are you going to sign a paper to try and stop his deportation?' I told her that my husband was an American ex-serviceman, that I would not sign any paper that would endanger his position or his staying in Australia, that I would fight for him to stay.

Don and I went downtown to the US Army headquarters in Grace Building. The army rang up the Immigration Department and we had to go down there. As we walked down the street, trying to get a taxi, I was crying and the tears were running down my face. Don said, 'Will you stop crying! People will think I'm bashing you up.'

The result was Canberra apologised. They said they didn't want to put Don out of the country. The army put up a bond for Don and in the end the money was returned to us.

Evelyn's story continues in Chapter 15

14
The Lineage

Leung Pui (梁社培)

Leung Pui's story in Chapter 9 finished with the Japanese invasion of Hong Kong in December 1941. His father-in-law was still in Australia and responsibility for both his own and his wife's family fell on him. They were sheltering with him in Hong Kong when the British surrendered on Christmas Day in 1941 and they had no alternative but to return to their village of Lung Hooey (隆墟). The Pearl River Delta had already been occupied by the Japanese and conditions were perilous, with survival dependent on communities banding together.

Most villages in south China consisted of one or two surnames or clans. Up until the republican revolution in 1911, social order was maintained by village elders from the gentry who exercised a paternalistic authority. The dominant feature of village life was the overriding influence of the clan, with family and clan loyalty stressed above all other obligations. In the delta as much as half a village's rice fields were owned by the clan and rented out. The income was used to operate the village school, maintain the ancestral temple, carry out ancestral sacrifices, build roads, pay for the militia and dispense charity. During the warlord period that followed the 1911 republican revolution, however, banditry became rampant. The better-off gentry moved to the safety of the cities and power in the villages fell into the hands of warlord and bandit elements.

Leung Pui's wartime experiences reveal the role of human relationships and lineage ties in the functioning of the Pearl River Delta village society. Following the Japanese defeat and surrender in 1945, the postwar liberalisation of Australia's immigration policy allowed Leung Pui the opportunity to come to Australia in 1951 when an uncle in Sydney sponsored him to work in a new restaurant.

Escape from Hong Kong

The problem after the surrender of Hong Kong to the Japanese was the lack of rice while hold-ups were taking place everywhere. Ngoi Fuh (外父) was still in Australia, so my mother-in-law, my own family as well as other relatives were all staying with me in the Wanchai (灣仔) district, near the city. I had rented the whole floor of a single building there. All throughout the Japanese attack, we had seen the Japanese planes coming over and heard the shelling across the harbour from the mainland. Fortunately, we were sheltered by the multi-storey Luk Kwok Hotel (六國飯店) on the waterfront. At night we could even see the shells fired across the harbour. But we worried about the military stores near us. Robberies went on every night.

The attic above our floor was occupied by a friend of mine. He had gone off to Macao a few days before the Japanese launched their attack. But soon after the occupation, he stole back on a small fishing boat and quickly took his wife and brother-in-law to Macao. Before they left, I asked him to let me know through the fisherman taking them of his safe arrival. I had begun to think that we ought to consider leaving Hong Kong too. When I told the other relatives, they said they also wanted to leave. In this case, one fishing boat wouldn't be enough.

The fisherman returned shortly afterwards and said my friend had arrived safely. 'When did we want to go?' 'Could he find an extra boat,' I asked? 'No problem,' he'd get two boats. So we fixed a date for our departure.

No trams or buses were running then. We would have to move our luggage by rickshaw to reach the fishing boats at West Point (西角). The women relatives wanted to take everything they could with them. I insisted they limit themselves to necessities only. Altogether, there were more than twenty of us and the only men were a cousin and myself. All the rest were women and small children. So we divided ourselves into two groups and the price for the boats was fixed at two hundred Hong Kong dollars each. You couldn't even get change for a one-hundred-dollar note then. After paying for the boats, I had two one-hundred-dollar notes left. I hid them under my collar and secured them with my tie. I didn't know how much the women and children might have, so I carried some loose cash in my pockets.

We had to hire nine rickshaws to carry our luggage. Almost every one of us walked the whole distance, about ten kilometres. Fortunately, I had an acquaintance who lived in the building where my uncle's boarding house was. I told him I was worried we might be robbed on the way to West Point. He worked for the Lou Shree Wong (老鼠王), the sanitation department rat trappers. They were the street scavengers and wore a yellow uniform. To my surprise, he said he'd send two of his *fo ki* (伙計, workers) with us. He did, and they accompanied us all the way to the jetty. Normally you had to pay an extortion charge to standover men before being allowed to board a boat but nobody obstructed us. I found out later that besides catching rats, the scavengers picked up the corpses as well as people beaten up by thugs and left for dead. The lives of such people depended on the scavengers. That was why they were so widely respected.

It was still in the early days after the surrender. The ferry services between Hong Kong and Kowloon on the mainland hadn't been restored. After we boarded our two little boats, they quietly moved along the coastline and then stole out to sea. The Japanese were not in a position to keep a watch everywhere then. We just slipped away. There was no wind that day, so we moved very slowly. We were also rather scared. Finally, we reached Tai-O (大澳) on Lantau Island (大嶼山), still in the territory of Hong Kong, where our boats had come from. They were prawn fishing junks with one sail each. But there was no wind and we couldn't sail at night. So we anchored in Tai-O and spent the night on board the boats.

The boatmen were extremely hospitable. They cooked us a meal of steamed fish roe and dried king prawns, which I'll never forget. Even today, it would be impossible to obtain what they served us. To them it was ordinary fare. That's what they ate all the time. But to us, it was absolute luxury.

The next morning we set sail again. We hadn't gone far when a motor vessel intercepted us. It was operated by Formosans working under the Japanese. They robbed the women of some jewellery and let us go. But they didn't search me. We started up again after that misfortune, the wind was with us now, so we moved swiftly. But the faster we went, the more the boats tipped to one side. We began to take on water and the women and children started screaming. The boatmen insisted there was nothing to fear. We were almost in sight of Macao when a junk with three sails caught up with us. Bang! A shot was fired, ordering us to stop.

I would still recognise that man today, sitting there and firing at us. He wore a pair of dark glasses. 'Who are you? Where are you going?' he asked. Hearing that we were refugees from Hong Kong returning to our village, he said, 'In that case, you only need pay one hundred dollars each and we'll let you pass.'

It was a hold-up. I told him we'd just had all our money taken by the Japanese. I purposely said Japanese. He didn't believe me and started lowering a small boat. I said he could come and see for himself. We had nothing of any value, we were only refugees. The small boat came alongside and two armed men climbed on board our boats. I could see they were inexperienced and nervous, so I kept on talking. I insisted we had nothing valuable left. They asked whereabouts the Japanese had searched us. When I said it was close by, their faces paled. They shouted back to their own boat that we didn't have anything of value. Just then a wisp of smoke appeared on the horizon. They probably thought it was a Japanese ship, so their leader ordered them back.

Macao

We arrived in Macao soon afterwards. By this time I'd become quite jittery myself. Here we were surrounded by strange people, clamouring to carry our luggage. Who were they? Communications between Hong Kong and Macao had been cut off before we left. For all I knew, the Japanese might have taken Macao. I said we didn't need anybody to carry our luggage. We'd been robbed at sea.

Finally, a Chinese in a Western suit came up and said he understood we'd been robbed. He showed me his identity card, describing him as a plain-clothes policeman. He wanted to know exactly where the robbery had taken place – was it inside Macao territory? I described the whereabouts of the hold-up and then asked if he could help us to find and move our luggage to suitable lodgings. This he did.

While we were waiting at the waterfront, the children were scampering around in excitement. I warned them to keep together and stay with the luggage. As I did so, I patted one of them on the shoulder and felt banknotes sewn into his clothes. I relaxed then because I realised we did have some money left, after all.

We found out at the lodging house that trucks were still running between Macao and Shekki (石岐). They still had gasoline in Macao. But each traveller crossing the border from Macao was required to show both urine and stool test certificates. To avoid further trouble, we split into parties of five and travelled separately. That's how we got to Shekki and finally reached our village of Lung Hooey.

Smuggling

Food was always a problem during the war. Except for those who cultivated their own land, the rest never had enough to eat. My family never had enough to eat. We ate rice sweepings and sweet potatoes. When there was a shortage of sweet potatoes the price was high. If you had a crop, you had to sell it before it was ripe to avoid losses from stealing. The more you grew, the less you reaped. Only when sweet potatoes were cheap, would nobody steal them. Nowadays of course, nobody eats sweet potatoes in the village anymore. They all eat good rice. But during the Japanese occupation, families depending on remittances from Lung Du (隆都) men in Australia faced a very difficult situation. Previously it wasn't considered elegant for the women of such families to work in the fields, so they had rented out their rice fields. But now the standover men kept the rents. The families had no income at all and starved. It was better across the river in districts like Leung Du (良都). There the women had saved their remittances and worked in the family-owned fields themselves.

Since there wasn't anything I could do in the village, I decided to take my chances and joined a smuggling group. We carried goods between occupied and free China. To do so, you had to find a spot where you could slip across the lines unnoticed. People coming to Shekki from Hong Kong and Macao were bringing with them imported goods like toothpaste and soap, which were in demand in free China. On the return trip we brought back vegetable oil and grain products. We had to use two currencies – puppet government banknotes, and Central Bank of China notes in five-dollar and ten-dollar denominations. The Japanese also had their own

14 The Lineage

Figure 14.1. Leung Pui's father-in-law (centre front row) and his family, Shekki, 1952–3 (Leung Pui)

military currency. Added to this, the notes we used in free China couldn't be used in the occupied areas and vice versa. Instead of taking banknotes, we took goods for barter. We took in old clothes and consumer goods and brought out beans, peanuts and vegetable oil.

We had to cross the West River (西江) wherever we could slip through. It was always risky. We would travel by back streams to reach Hok Shan (鶴山) and Sun Wooey (新會) counties near the mouth of the West River. The Japanese patrolled this area in motorboats and they shot to kill. Lots of people were killed.

I went across twice and they were terrifying experiences. At high tide the river was very wide and at low tide very narrow. We would get into a sampan and pay so much for each person to be ferried across. As soon as we got on the sampan, each of us was given an oar and told to paddle for our lives. We couldn't afford to waste one minute. The local people had a lookout post at the top of a hill, which signalled when no Japanese boats were in sight. If there was no signal, it wasn't safe to cross. When you finally got across in a low tide, wading through the mud was even worse. You could lose your life at any time. There was no protection. On top, you had the Japanese and their puppet officials. At the village level, you had the local bullies or standover men. We called them the *dai tin yee* (大天二).

In Chinese dominoes, *tin* (天, sky) is the highest card with a value of twelve points. *Dei* (地, earth) is the lowest with a value of only two points. The rascals were the big *tin* oppressing the smallest people, that's how you arrived at the term *dai tin yee* – the big sky overriding the number two, or *yee* (二).

Family ties

Although some trade still went on in Shekki, it wasn't as prosperous as before. The people in power patronised the restaurants and shops. But the schools still operated. My children went to the village school. The same people as before ran the schools and in our village, the villagers supported the school.

The principal of the Chung Shan (中山) Middle School was a good friend of mine and he still held his job. One day he looked me up and asked if I would go with him to a place called Kim Mou (乾霧) at the mouth of the delta, Mo Dou Mun (磨刀門), in fact, a polder field area. It was criss-crossed by streams and was an old pirate lair. The school owned rice fields down there and badly needed the revenue. They hadn't received any funds for a long time. My friend wanted to go and talk to the leading *dai tin yee* there. This man, who had a fierce reputation, was collecting all the rent and wasn't passing it on. He was known to be very powerful.

'How on earth had the principal thought of me?' I asked. I wasn't even a graduate of his school. I had no arms. I didn't pose any threat. I could do nothing. But the principal said it was precisely because I wasn't belligerent or a threat in any way that he'd asked me to go. He explained that the two of us could never match the ferocity of this man. We were not trying to match force with force and that was exactly why the two of us would be just the right mix to offset him.

So we took a little sampan down there. It was freezing cold and I was shivering all the way. To my surprise, the *dai tin yee* received us very politely. He showed us round the dykes, told us which fields had yielded crops and which hadn't. Of course, we didn't know how much of what he said was true. But in the end, he did pay over some of the rent he'd collected.

I found out after we got there that everyone down there was surnamed Leung (梁). There were ten thousand people down there, all of them Leungs. That was why the principal had asked me to go. I was a Leung. It just goes to show how deep the lineage tie is in China. The Leungs down there were members of the same Leung clan in my own village. The principal himself wasn't a Leung. He wasn't even from Lung Du. But it's so much easier for people of the same lineage to communicate with each other. That's why our mission was successful. While we were being shown around, I ran into two people I knew. I knew they weren't Leungs, but they did come from Lung Du. They quickly took me aside and asked me not to reveal their identity. Of course, I had no intention of doing so. They explained they couldn't make a living in Lung Du, so they'd gone down there, claimed to be clansmen and

Figure 14.2. Leung Pui after arriving in Australia in 1952. (Leung Pui)

asked for help. They were allowed to farm there. That's how important the clan relationship is.

Return to Hong Kong

In 1945, after the war ended, I went back to Hong Kong. A friend and I set up a business in an office in the central district. By then Chinese seamen were arriving on boats from Australia. They brought a lot of goods with them – Australian woollen yarn, woollen blankets and surplus army goods. Hong Kong's trade hadn't been restored and there was a great shortage of supplies. We bought up the seamen's goods and resold.

Our next step was to set up a shirt-making factory. One of us would do the cutting, while the other went out shopping for orders. This wasn't as easy as selling the seamen's goods. We lost everything in the end. Again I went back to the village for a while. But even when I returned later, it was still difficult to make a living in Hong Kong.

However, the manager of the Kwong War Chong (廣和昌) company in Sydney, another uncle on my mother's side, now wrote and urged me to come to Australia. He was starting a new restaurant, the Sun Sai Gai (新世紀, New World), near Martin Place in Sydney, and needed an assistant. So under my uncle's sponsorship, I was given a temporary visa. That's how I finally arrived in the golden mountain.

Sydney

I stayed at the dormitory in the upstairs of the Kwong War Chong company in Dixon Street, not far from the place where my dad used to work. This was in a shop in Kimber Lane, just off Little Hay Street in Haymarket. It's still a tomato repacking business! It was only after coming to Australia that I realised how true every word of my father's was, and what a lonely life he must have led here.

But more bad luck was in store for me. Not long after my arrival, the owner of the building housing the Sun Sai Gai sold it. The restaurant was forced to close. I was named an illegal migrant and ordered by the Department of Immigration to leave the country. 'We'll go to Canberra and talk to the department,' suggested Billy Liu.[1]

We were received by the secretary of the department, who listened to my case. I said I objected to being described as an 'illegal migrant'. I hadn't done anything illegal. I had simply lost my job suddenly through no fault of my own. Billy Liu pointed out that there were supposed to be 50,000 illegal migrants in Australia and nothing was being done about them. He asked why the department was picking on me. I had arrived in Australia legally.

Fortunately, at the last minute, I was given a three months' extension to my visa. This gave me time to find another sponsor, the manager of the Lean Sun Low (聯新樓) cafe. So from then on I worked in the Lean Sun Low. Ultimately, the restrictions on Chinese were relaxed, I was allowed to stay and have lived here ever since. I have mostly worked as a waiter.

---

1 William J. Liu, OBE (1893–1983). Born in Sydney of Chinese-English parentage, Billy Liu was a leading Chinese businessman and community leader for more than six decades. Two of the many issues on which he advocated to governments on behalf of the Chinese community were seeking permanent residency for Chinese nationals stranded in Australia on temporary visas after the Second World War and agitating for a review of the Australian government's immigration policy.

Since my retirement, I have visited Chung Shan a number of times. There have been a great deal of changes there in the past century. Although Shekki has prospered and extended its boundary across the Shekki River to the district of Lung Du, it is no longer the county centre, but a section of Chung Shan city. In fact, Chung Shan is now a city or municipality, not a county. Its economy is booming, to the extent that the just over a million population has to be supplemented with skilled labour from other areas. Instead of the old junk ferry service, hydrofoils now connect Chung Shan with Hong Kong daily. The journey takes only two and a half hours. A modern highway from Canton, now called Guangzhou (廣州) city, passes through Shekki to Macao.

At one time in Chung Shan, it was considered a calamity to have three daughters. It cost a fortune to raise and arrange marriages for them. Even until recently, one of the most treasured items in a young woman's dowry was a sewing machine. Nobody wants one now. Today, with three daughters, a father can stop working. Every village has its little workshops and every young woman has a job, doing processing work for export. The girls can earn at least a hundred *yuan* (圓) a month. There are jobs for the older women too, snipping cotton ends and so on. Naturally, wages are lower and life is simpler than in Hong Kong or Macao, but the cost of living is much cheaper and there is far more space in the villages.

During the land reform in the 1950s, lots of mistakes were made. My father never bought any rice fields, so our family wasn't affected. But the families of many Chinese in Australia suffered. This came after undergoing a lifetime of exploitation abroad to purchase the fields. The work teams didn't realise that nine out of ten landowners in Chung Shan were hard-working returnees who, by living frugally, had saved enough money to buy a few *mow* (畝) of land while they were abroad, so how could they be labelled 'landlords'? It's been admitted since that this was a mistake. But those people who suffered still love their home villages. Because they suffered, they don't want others to suffer. So when their villages promote new ventures, they gladly support them.

Postscript

It was not possible to locate any of Leung Pui's family members prior to publication. Not discussed in Leung Pui's story was the tragedy that befell his wife and son. In 1974, some family members suffered a severe medical episode that caused the death of his wife Lum Yook Wun (林玉雲) and son Kit Yee Leung. Leung Pui survived. A coronial inquiry determined it was the result of lead arsenate poisoning after using a highly toxic insecticide in their backyard vegetable garden. Incidents such as this led to regulatory changes in respect of insecticides and herbicides in the state of New South Wales. Leung Pui passed away on 27 May 1996 and is buried at Rookwood Cemetery in Sydney.

15
Postwar

Evelyn Yin Lo (黎鑽好)

In the immediate postwar years, the total number of Chinese in Australia reached its lowest point, falling below 10,000. The White Australia policy and the inability for many to bring out their Chinese wives and families had its inevitable effect. The establishment of the People's Republic of China in 1949 also dramatically reduced the rates of Chinese immigration. Many of the remaining Chinese who had come to Australia in the late 1800s and early 1900s were elderly and often found themselves alone and with little financial resources.

Although Evelyn Yin Lo's parents had a limited knowledge of English, the children received a basic education in Australian schools and grew up in two cultures. Evelyn's first social role was that of child interpreter for the Chinese who frequented her parents' cafe. She tells how she contended with Chinese traditions and Australian values. This early experience prepared her for the postwar period, during which she became a battler and a forerunner of today's Australian Chinese lifestyle. Her own children acclaimed her as the backbone of the family.

The postwar years were not easy for people in Evelyn's situation. Evelyn tells of the struggles she and Don had, working long hours at whatever they could turn their hands to in order to provide for their growing family. To survive, the Chinese community had to look beyond their own confines and seek employment in hotels and clubs, suburban restaurants, factories and offices.

Mixed business

When Don came out of the air force, he had a lot of money. We didn't think of investing it then. We should have. That's when you should invest. But in those days

Figure 15.1. The Yin Lo General Store at 318 Harris St, Pyrmont, Sydney. (Yin Lo family)

we didn't worry about investments. We were living with Mum. We had the first two kids and we were happy. Don wanted to have a bit of a break after army life. For a few years after our marriage, we continued to live with the family at Burwood and Don worked in factories. But in 1952, when Diane was five, Don and I decided to go into business ourselves. A Chinese friend asked if we would like to take over his mixed business in Harris Street, in Pyrmont, next to the city. I thought he was pretty genuine, so I bought the goodwill, and Don gave up his factory job to join me.

The original owner of the mixed business lived at the back of the shop and I had to pay the rent to her. Her place was closed off from ours. We used the front of the shop for the business, while she lived in the back. Her husband worked for the wool stores nearby.

We sold morning teas to the wool stores opposite, as well as sandwiches and groceries. Early in the morning, the orders would come in for morning teas and lunches. There was only Don and I, so the man who brought the orders used to help get them out. We usually gave him his lunch. He was friendly and we treated him as part of the family. We would let him have anything he wanted. We really couldn't afford another hand.

In a mixed business, you've got to be there all the time. We opened at half past seven in the morning and stayed open till six o'clock at night. We lived on the premises. Don used to cook the dinner. He was pretty good at it. A friend of his stayed with us and both of them cooked. I used to do the washing and tidy up.

A lot of European migrants lived in the Pyrmont area and mostly all the women worked. They would order their groceries, book them up and then not pay. They were always one step ahead of us. They'd no sooner pay for one bill than they'd get another lot of groceries. I lost a lot of money that way, I'd say a thousand pounds. I just couldn't collect the money. Before the shop opened in the morning, I used to pretend I was going for a walk, creep out and catch them before they got out of bed. They had the money, but they used to drink it all up. Besides, I could never turn a sob story down. They had children and I had children. In the end, I got real mad with them. We never got our money back. Don said, 'I told you not to give them credit, Ev. They never pay.'

It was very cruel. I used to worry myself sick. So since the business wasn't paying, Don had to get in a factory again, just to bring in some money to keep the family. Mum was wonderful. When we were staying with the family, Mum looked after Diane and taught me what to do. My second daughter, Margaret, stayed with my mother till she went to school. I was carrying my third daughter, Beverly, when we had the mixed business. We didn't have enough money and Margaret had skin trouble. Mum used to take her for me to a specialist. Mum would bring Margaret to see us every Friday and my brother Basil (黎宗枝) would take them home.

I didn't speak to the original owner of the shop for a long time. Then we got to talking. She was a diabetic and had two daughters who were working. I very quickly realised the tenancy was still in her name, although I was supposed to have bought it. When I told her this, she said she didn't care as long as she had a place to live. But later on she decided to move out. She asked the landlord to put the tenancy in my name, but they wouldn't unless I bought the shop. I couldn't afford to and the landlord wouldn't sign it over.

I don't think anyone ever noticed I was pregnant at the time. When Beverly was born, my sister came and ran the shop for a week or two. She was doing a typing job in Chinatown. Anyhow, we took the man who sold us the goodwill to court. We were paying out about one hundred pounds each time the solicitor went to court – that is, every couple of months. The case dragged on for about a year. In the end I decided I'd have to speak for myself. When I appeared before the judge, he asked, 'Madam, where is your solicitor?' I told him straight out I didn't have the money for one. The business wasn't doing so well. Money was scarce, very hard to get. 'I advise you to talk to one of the clerks outside. He will get you a public solicitor,' the judge said. I got one in the end, but it didn't do any good. We were fighting against United Distilleries, the big wine people, which was the landlord. What poor working person would have a chance against United Distilleries! I always remember the judge felt so sorry for me.

So we lost our first business because we made a boo-boo. We had to get out. We rented a house from a Chinese friend in Alexandria. Eventually we bought it and it's been our home ever since. It was only an old house, but at least it was a home. It was fairly close to the Chinese Temple in Waterloo. I was always busy though, and never went there. My dad used to go to the See Yup Temple (四邑關聖帝廟) at Glebe Point to pray for good luck, probably because our family had more contacts with people from See Yup (四邑). The Waterloo temple was set up by people from Kou Yiu (高要) county, a long way from Tung Koon (東莞). The Kou Yiu people in Sydney have been very successful market gardeners. They own a building in Chinatown and have their own club.

After this disaster, Don mostly worked in a factory as a machinist and the two of us did restaurant work together, with Don coming on after his daytime job. He did the cooking and we helped each other. We made a good team, but this didn't give Don the chance to speak a lot of English and he didn't have any time to learn. Don would always say, 'Let my wife explain.' That's how it went all the time. We were very close and I always helped him. I did all his paperwork. I should have pushed him to learn to do it himself. But now he's gone and I can't do anything about it.

Our next venture was a partnership with my brother Basil in a little fish shop in John Street, also in Pyrmont. We did that for a couple of years, while we were living in Alexandria. Then the big enterprises started their own canteens and business slackened. So we left the shop to Basil. Towards the end of our stay in the John Street business in 1962 our fourth daughter, Wendy, arrived.

Job hunting

Whenever Don needed to apply for a job, I'd go with him. He didn't know the street names, but we had a truck. I'd sit with him and direct him. Once when he was really desperate for a job, we found an ad in the paper for a place that was making soap. We went down and they were boiling up bones. 'Oh, Ev,' Don said, 'I couldn't work there. I can't stand the smell even before I get inside.' 'You've got to take it,' I said. 'It's all right for you,' Don said. 'This is not just one of those casual jobs. I'd have to work here for years and I can't even go in the door.' So I directed him the way home.

Another time, Don got the sack because he produced more than the others. He was working as an assembler at Ti-Technical, at Marrickville. He got put off because he was making too many screws or too many something. You wouldn't believe he got put off because he worked too hard. They used to give him bonuses. But the other fellows couldn't keep up with him. They said, 'Don, you'll have to cut out making so many.' Don said, 'What am I supposed to do? I'm just working like normal.' They told him to go to the toilet and have a cigarette. Don came home and

Figure 15.2. A dance at the Trocadero, Sydney, including (left to right) Don & Evelyn Yin Lo, Lindsay Parkee and Edna Wah, and (at far right) Cecil Parkee. (Yin Lo family)

asked me, 'How many cigarettes can you smoke, Ev?' I said, 'I don't know. You've got to be joking.'

He finally came home one day and told me he'd got the sack. I was going to go out to the factory and demand an explanation, I felt that sick. But Don said, 'No, don't do that.' He didn't want the fellows to know his wife was helping him. So I rang the boss and asked, 'Why did my husband get the sack?' I demanded a reference explaining why Don was put off. The boss said, 'Oh, we'll give him a nice reference.' I said, 'But that's not the point. What did he get put off for?' 'Well,' said the boss, 'he was overdoing it.' I wouldn't have believed it otherwise. He cut down as much as he could and still made a hundred more than the others. And he got put off for that!

Don got another job. There was plenty at that time. Let's face it. We needed the money. That was when I was pregnant with my fourth daughter, Wendy. I used to know how to get a job by looking at the advertisements in the paper every morning. But I still don't know how people can tell lies to get a job when they're out of work. We didn't know how to tell lies, we didn't know anything. Finally, friends got Don a job as an assembler with Pongrass, making marine boats and furniture. He worked there for close to twenty years. They gave him a gold watch.

Don and I always shared the work. When his friends saw him putting the clothes out on the line one day, one of them said, 'Fancy that! Helping her!' They couldn't understand it. That was just the way Don was. He was a good sewer, too. He used to hand sew my dresses for me. Not his shirts, though he didn't mind sewing on his own buttons. When he put on a shirt that missed a button, he'd get very cranky. But if a button came off, he'd sew it back on again. All you had to say was, 'There's the button, put it on, Don,' and he'd do it.

Fish and chip shop

After we left Basil, a Chinese couple we knew in Harris Street offered us their fish and chip shop just up the street from our old mixed business for a low rental. The husband wasn't well and they didn't want to run the business anymore. It was only a small shop. They were from Tientsin, had no children. So I took it on. I managed the shop in the mornings till about half past one when we closed it. There wasn't much business after then, until about four o'clock. After his daytime job, Don would mind the shop in the evenings. I had to leave about half past three or four o'clock to go home to Alexandria and cook the kiddies' tea. They went to school during the day.

By now the Chinese were allowed to bring out their wives from Hong Kong and China, but without a knowledge of English, they had problems. Our little fish shop was next to the Cecil Kwoks. Cecil was from Chung Shan (中山) and he worked in the Wing On (永安) Company in Haymarket. His wife was from China and she couldn't eat Australian food. When she had a baby, he had to cook for her. But while she was in hospital, he had to stay home and take care of the other children. I helped out by taking her *faahn* (飯, rice) and other dishes, to the King George Hospital. That's the maternity hospital in Newtown. Instead of going home directly, I'd go by way of Newtown.

My fifth daughter, Cheryle, was born in 1964 while we had the fish shop in Harris Street. I rang Mum the day Cheryle was due to arrive and said, 'I think I'll be going to the hospital this afternoon.' 'That's all right,' she said. She came down to the shop and took Wendy home with her. Took care of her while I was in the hospital and after. Mum would look after her while Don was in the fish shop in the evenings. She'd take Cheryle back to Burwood with her and sometimes she'd stop in Alexandria. She never worried. Instead of telling my brothers what to cook, she'd cook for them. She'd come down to Alexandria when she got fed up cooking for the boys. Don would say, 'Tell them you're not coming home for tea. If they can't cook, let them starve.'

We left the fish business in Harris Street after the husband died. Beverly was four then and I had time on my hands. So I went to work for a fish and chip shop in Erskineville, the suburb next to Alexandria, from eleven in the morning till half past one. I took Beverly up with me. The boss used to go and buy the fish while I got the batter ready. I'd make up the batter and help him serve. Beverly used to sit outside with a book and look at the people passing by. I'd give her a little bag of chips and an apron to keep her from getting grubby.

Family life

Like my father, Don was very strict about observing cemetery day. He told our girls, 'You go to the cemetery first, and after that you can go wherever you want.' Dad never said that, but Don did. He always said we must go and pay our respects. Of course, by this time, the girls had a grandfather up in Rookwood. When I was young, girls didn't count and were supposed to stay at home. Although Don and I had all daughters, he insisted on their going. He always watched the date on the Chinese calendar. He wasn't pleased if anyone didn't go. Even on Sunday, they had to forfeit Sunday school, unless there was some special occasion.

By then everybody had cars. Don would drive us up to meet with the other Tung Koon people at Rookwood. We would all be given a share of roast pork by the Tung Koon society. If you were Tung Koon *yan* (東莞人, your family was from Tung Koon), then you were entitled to a share. In fact, there was a bit of fighting over the pork. There would be complaints that someone was taking too much. Some people even took plastic bags to take the pork away. I think some just came to get their share. Don used to get mad about this. He didn't care whether we got any pork or not. Don's attitude was, if you had money you should buy it yourself. But after the pork was chopped up, there would be lots of *jue gwut* (豬骨, pork bones) and they made very tasty congee. I didn't see why it should go to all the others.

We didn't eat much up there. We mostly ate some of the pork and then came home and had a good lunch. Don used to take along a *jam baan* (碪板, chopping block) and two choppers in the station wagon. He'd chop up all our pork and then he'd say to his friends or anyone around, '*Na, sik la* (你吃啦, there you go, eat).'

The Hakka (客家) people usually went to the cemetery a week earlier than the Tung Koon people. My sister-in-law, Drene, wife of my younger brother, Ted, makes it to the cemetery a week before us. She's Hakka. Drene and Ted are tennis players. The Chinese Tennis Club is more than fifty years old and was started by Drene's brother. Drene used to be the social secretary.

Whenever he could, Don would go to Chinatown to meet with other Chinese, mostly *haang suen jay* (航船仔, seamen). If they came from Tung Koon, he'd bring them home and cook his head off. He'd get so involved with talking. Other times the seamen would invite us down to their ships and we'd take some food down with us too.

Don had a lot of friends who belonged to the Gee Gong Tong (致公堂, Chinese Masonic Society), so he joined. My dad used to be a member. I would say to Don, 'What's the good of it to you? They only come to collect their money. "You haven't paid your dues", that's what they say.' I don't know how much they collected a year. But all Don would say to them was, 'You always come to get my dues, but when there's something on, you never tell me.'

Don liked to be connected with the Chinese. That's why he went with the Chinese at the Chinese Youth League (僑青社). They didn't demand anything, he told me. He could go in there and they made him feel welcome all the time. He never joined. He wasn't political.

Another place Don liked to go to in Chinatown was the Kwong War Chong (廣和昌) company. He used to buy a lot of Chinese herbs there. They were importers and exporters and sold all the Chinese goods. The company was set up by the Lee (李) family from Chung Shan. When I was a child, they rented the upstairs for accommodation. The old Chinese from China, the men especially, didn't care as long as they got somewhere to sleep. They'd rent a place upstairs in Kwong War Chong. That building is as old as Dixon Street itself. It was what you called a *gum shan jong* (金山莊, golden mountain shop). Besides being a general store, they'd loan you money, help you find a job, receive your mail, send money back to China for you.

Sailing club

When Wendy was six and Cheryle four, I took over a club job from a friend of Don's, who wanted to move on to another club with more prospects. I was ambitious. It was a nice family size and wouldn't cost too much to start. We didn't have to pay anything to get in, just had to be recommended. I thought of all the possibilities and agreed to take it on without Don consenting. It meant I had to work six and a half days, but Don had to work seven days because he had another job. The club didn't pay that well during the day. It was the night work that counted.

The club gave us an eighteen-month contract. They paid for the gas and electricity and any profits were ours. But it was a heavy responsibility. You had to run it as a business. There were also restrictions. For example, we had to make toasted sandwiches. These sandwiches were a bit of a headache. It was four sandwiches to a plate for a dollar. In other words, a cheap meal. But you could only put three on the toaster at a time. You had to wait a long time for the fourth, while the others were getting cold. Not only that. Someone had to watch them. And if you're trying to cook Chinese food, you can't. Most would be burned. We always got about three dozen loaves of bread, mostly at weekends. The members wanted toasted sandwiches, so we had to make them. We had fish cocktails and prawn cutlets too, all for a dollar.

I worked in the club during weeknights on my own and Don would join me when there were parties. Diane and Beverly had their own jobs and Don cooked tea for the family on weekdays. During the day, Don was working at Pongrass in the machine shop. He'd come over to the club after he finished there. On busy nights we'd finish about one o'clock, tidy up and wash the floor before we got out. During the weekends, the girls did the waitressing. That was our busy period. So they were working six and a half days too, before they were married. They had to give up their weekends when there was sunshine and they liked to go to the beaches too. The girls didn't mind working at the club, but it was a lot of work for them. Don used

15 Postwar

Figure 15.3. Evelyn in 1945. (Yin Lo family)

to give them a bit of pocket money. They saved it all up and bought little luxuries when they had the time. Then someone broke into the house and took a good few of the luxuries, so they mostly went down the drain.

Sailing was a big thing then. It still is. We belonged to the eighteen footers. I'd arrive to find the members waiting at the door of the restaurant for us to open. I'd say, 'If you let me in, you might get something to eat.'

They had television then, although we could only seat thirty people at a time. The men at the club used to bet on the boats, just like at the races. The year we were there was one of the best. A lot of people came over from sailing clubs in New Zealand and they thought I was Maori. I was a broad Chinese, though I wasn't as broad as I am now. They used to put their arms round me and say, 'Oh Ev, you're one of us.' It didn't make any difference whether I was or not. They always made you feel like one of them. So I'd say, 'Oh yes, sure.' The stewards were a very friendly lot. They would have a break between three and four and they used to come in, asking, 'You made that cake yet, Ev?'

Don never ate out much. He liked to cook everything himself. His friends would take him out but he'd bring them home. He rarely ate out. Even if we had a family outing, he'd go because it was family, but he'd still come home and cook his rice. If he was hungry, he might make something for himself at the club. I was always glad to get home. I used to say to Don, 'Cook me a curried prawn or curried chicken,' and I'd bring it home with me. You couldn't eat there much at all.

While we were in the sailing club, our eldest daughter, Diane, decided to join the Women's Royal Australian Naval Service. She was twenty-one and had never been away from home, but she thought she'd try to be independent. She had to leave home and wear a uniform. She served in naval hospitals. Don didn't want her to go, the girls being protected at home and all that. He cried when she left. She was away for four years. It wasn't easy for her either, because she was too close to the family. Then she married Terence Young, an Australian-born Chinese. He's an accountant and comes from a very old Australian Chinese family in Glen Innes in New South Wales. They have a hobby farm at Cowra, with horses, chickens and ducks, a beautiful background. But I'm city born. I don't like country life. I can only go for a little while.

We enjoyed working in the club, but it was killing us. One night we had to work up to two o'clock in the morning cleaning up. We never had time to spend a weekend with the family. So when the contract was finally up we decided to leave. The club people cried when we left. Anyhow, financially we managed to catch up a bit after that boo-boo we made when we went into a mixed business twenty years earlier.

Full-time work

After we left the sailing club, Cheryle was old enough to go to school and I began to work full-time. I used to go up the street to get the rolls and that for the kiddies' lunches. The corner shop lady had no children and had taken a liking to Wendy. She got out little cradles and dolls and dressed them all up and gave them to Wendy. She asked me what I was doing. She wanted someone to make up lunches and do the morning tea orders. So I took on the job from half past eight till ten thirty. Then I went to town to another job. This was in the snack bar of the New Market Hotel in Campbell Street in town. Don didn't like it. He worried about me working at that hotel. He said, 'They swear there and there're so many drunks.'

Actually, the people there were very polite. I worked in the hotel's little kitchen for about fourteen months. The original owner used to tell me what she wanted and I'd make it. When the fellows came in, they'd say, 'What've you got on, Ev?' They'd open the lid and say, 'Aw, gee, that looks nice, we'll have so many.'

I gave up this job after new people turned up. The new lady was mean. She came from the country and she expected you to work for nothing. She was only twenty-six or twenty-seven, a real nice-looking blonde, beautiful figure. She used to entertain the drinkers, drink and talk with them. Never did any work. She used to put out all the food that was left over and ask me to sell it. Instead of giving the customers half a chicken, she'd cut it down to a quarter. 'Don't give them so much for their money,' she said. I said to her, 'Look, Mrs What's-a-name, we had the business going real well. If you cut down now and give them less, you're going to lose a lot of customers. They're all regulars. I know them by name.' Oh no, she wouldn't listen to me. She'd make a pot of stew with the leftovers. I'd just as soon throw it in the garbage tin. I said, 'You can't do those sorts of things. If you can't eat the stuff yourself, you don't want to sell it.'

As for her husband, he didn't know nothing about cooking. All he knows about is the bar. One day, he looked strange, so I said, 'What's wrong with you?' 'She won't get up, Ev,' he said. 'I don't know what to do.' So I said, 'Don't worry about it, I'll take over.' I ended up cooking all the chickens she was supposed to cook for whatever menu was on for the day. It was very cheap, a dollar or so a plate.

With the old owner I used to finish at three o'clock to get home before the kids. I had a system, I'd have all the washing up finished by then. But the new woman would say, 'Do this, and this, and that.' Then she'd reckon I was taking too long. She came from the country where everybody bogs in and helps. But that didn't help me. One day, a friend of hers must have said something to her. When it came to half past one, she said, 'You can knock off, me friend'll do it.' I thought to myself, 'Good on you!' The next day she said, 'I think you'd better go back and do it, Ev.' Then she whispered to me, 'My friend took too long.' But it was her friend! She gave me back the job. I said, 'I don't want it.' She offered me more money to stay on, but I said, 'Look, I'm not going to work for you.' It ended up they sold out.

I got myself another sandwich job in Alexandria, from half past eight till half past one. That was all I wanted then. I stayed in this sandwich job because the money was coming in. I needed the money. But I had to follow the lady around until she got the money to pay me. Finally, I said to myself, 'I'm not going to put up with this any longer.'

I began looking in the *Sydney Morning Herald* for another job. Very soon I spotted an advertisement for a tea lady at a factory in Rockdale, which meant travelling from home. I went down to find out more and apply. It was an agency. They said they'd let me know in the afternoon by half past four. When I got home, I looked in the paper again and found another job, also for a tea lady, right in Alexandria, almost around the corner. It was a factory making plastic tubing. So I rang up. I didn't want to waste my time, so I said to the girl on the telephone, 'Do you take Chinese?' She said, 'Look, we take all sorts here. It's quite an international centre.'

The man at Rockdale never rang back. But early the next morning, the man in charge at the Alexandria factory rang and asked me to go round for an interview. 'Look,' he said, 'the job's for twenty-two and a half hours a week, and we're only offering twenty-nine dollars fifty.' Well, I was making sandwiches and I was only getting twenty-five dollars. I wasn't even getting paid regularly. This job was almost five dollars more. I thought I'd go there for the time being and have another look round. 'I'll take it,' I said. The man asked me if I could start the same day, or even on Thursday or Friday. 'No, I'm sorry,' I said. 'I'm making sandwiches. I don't like to leave people in the lurch. Let me finish this week out. Friday's the day I finish.' 'Fair enough,' he said. I went back and told the sandwich lady. 'I've got another job. I've got to go,' I said. Of course, she was disappointed. She had to find somebody else and I could do everything.

I went into the factory the following Monday. It was very international indeed. The people who worked there were very mixed, from all sorts of countries and nationalities.

Tea lady

My job was to make morning teas and lunches and afternoon teas. I had a break in between. I used to start at a quarter past nine, make the tea at ten o'clock for the office, then I'd make all the lunches and knock off at twelve thirty. I didn't have a rest during the break. I did the family shopping.

It wasn't easy getting started. The girls treated me awful. They used to talk about their sex lives in front of me. I wasn't used to their garbage talk. The boss gave me five dollars to start off buying things, which wasn't enough. Then the staff didn't pay me for what they ate until the end of the week. Where would I get the money to pay for the ham and rolls? I was only charging ten cents a sandwich, but they were too lousy to pay even that.

Since I'd only just started there, I didn't like to say anything. So I told the fellow who made the daily deliveries that I was being compelled to run a credit system. 'I have to pay out my money, and I don't get it back until they pay me,' I said. 'I tell you what,' he said. 'I'll give you the bill at the end of the week. We'll do it that way.'

That's what we did after that. But I had to make all the arrangements. I didn't go to the boss about it. The girls were always trying to diddle me out of money, even ten cents! When I told them how much they owed me, their answer would be, 'I didn't have that.' I had to make up the books every day to show them. I'd say, 'There, that's what you had on Wednesday.' Oh yes, they'd admit. They spilled tea, burned the tables with cigarettes. It was very hard for me, but I decided to stick it out until I could get something better. One day one of the girls asked me, 'Don't you ever

15 Postwar

Figure 15.4. Evelyn and mother, Annie Parkee. (Yin Lo family)

get mad, Ev?' 'Of course I get mad,' I said. 'Well, you never show it,' she said. 'You'll never see it,' I told her.

In the end, by being patient and trying to think of ways to vary their teas and lunches, I mastered those girls. But it was so very hard for me at first. It turned out to be the perfect job, made for me. I only had to work for twenty-two and a half hours a week, which suited me. After that, whenever I had to take a day off, the girls used to make tea for everybody and wash the dishes too. When I left for my holidays, they would say they wished I wouldn't take my four weeks off.

Mum

During my childhood, I didn't have much chance to get to know my mother. She was always busy in the restaurant. She never stopped working, not even for one day. Just the same, she was a good loving mother to us all. I don't think Mum had much freedom. She had nine children and accepted things as they were. Chinese women of her generation didn't ask for many favours. They didn't have many friends. They visited relatives and attended community functions. Otherwise, they were more family-oriented.

It was a great shock to us when Mum was killed in a motor car accident on 8 March 1973. She went out shopping that morning in Burwood and rang us up in a very happy mood. But soon afterwards, the hospital rang to say they were sorry they could not save her.

We found a docket in her purse for six dollars. We were very curious, so we paid the six dollars and got the lay-by out. It was a little baby blanket for my coming second grandchild. Mum must have seen the blankets and put one on lay-by for the coming baby. She was always so thoughtful with the children. She didn't live to see the second one.

Evelyn's story concludes in Chapter 17

16
Pioneers in Western Australia

John Fong (鄺寶贊)

Perth businessman John Fong (1925–2008) was one of the best informed about the first Chinese migrants to Western Australia. With the exception of a few seamen who jumped ship, most were indentured labourers recruited through European agents in Singapore by the colonial government in 1847 to fill the labour shortage. This continued intermittently until the early 1890s. While recruited in Singapore, these early labourers originally came from the coastal areas of Fukien (福建) and Kwangtung (廣東) provinces, including Hainan Island. They were mostly sent to remote pastoral stations in the north-west and to small towns to work as station hands, land clearers, carpenters, cooks and domestic servants. Private recruitment also took place, particularly for the pearling industry, and continued up until the outbreak of the Second World War.

After gold was found in the Kimberley in 1886 and in Coolgardie and Kalgoorlie in the 1890s, a new stream of Chinese came from Darwin and the east coast areas, as well as from China and south Asia. Almost all were from the Pearl River Delta area.

John Fong was born in Broome in north-western Australia in 1925, the centre of the world pearling industry at the turn of the century. In 1928, he and his siblings were taken to Toishan (台山) by their father to be immersed in the world of their extended family. Toishan is one of the four counties, commonly known as See Yup (四邑), in the south-west of the Pearl River Delta. Its people are said to be the first Chinese to have had contact with the West.

Because Toishan's rocky soil is the poorest in the whole delta, it was unable to feed its people. Traditionally they had to turn to the sea and to trade to eke out a living, and are well known for their daring spirit. When gold was discovered in California in 1848, there were already hundreds of Chinese merchants in San Francisco. The news spread quickly and a rush of Chinese gold diggers began from See Yup, half of them from Toishan. But as the gold became difficult to reach, shipping agents in Hong Kong redirected the See Yup diggers to the colony of Victoria in Australia.

Having returned to Broome in the late 1930s, John Fong was attending school and helping in his uncle's store when the town was bombed by the Japanese in 1942. When he turned eighteen, he enlisted in the army and served in Bougainville and the Solomon Islands. In the 1950s, he commenced managing a shop in Perth's Chinatown district. He shared a close rapport with the old Chinese indentured labourers and market gardeners in Western Australia, many of whom he helped in the postwar years either to return to China or to negotiate Australia's social welfare system.

Early life

The Chinese came to Western Australia for economic reasons, to earn a living the best way they could, mostly in the labour force. It was the same story in the Philippines and Malaya. They moved from famine and disaster to try to find better conditions. They had to be in very difficult circumstances to leave their homes. Also, lacking a knowledge of English, it was very hard to establish themselves.

My dad came to Australia before the turn of the century, from Sunning (新寧) county in Kwangtung province. Now the name's changed to Toishan. Dad's name was Louey Fong Kong, but through misunderstanding of Chinese names, it became Fong Kee in English. He had a clothing shop in Broome, doing tailoring and selling clothes. Broome was a bit like Darwin. Most of the shops were owned by Chinese, and quite a few were run by Fongs (鄺), and they were all around Carnarvon Street, which you might call Chinatown. Then, apart from the Chinese business community, you had the pearling people on the luggers.

I was born in Broome in 1925, but my mother was born in Darwin. Her name was Mary Chong Hay. Her family was there for a long time. I don't know how they got there because we didn't talk about it in the olden days. Her brothers, Percy and Tommy Chong Hay, were working in the shearing sheds.

When I was three, my parents divorced and my mother went to Perth and later remarried to an Australian man. Dad took all the children back to his home village of Shek Joong (嶺背石冲) – Shek (石) for stone and Joong (冲) for valley. That's how I was fortunate enough to spend a few years in Toishan. Next to our village there was Nam Hung (嶺背南坑, South Village), Jook Hung (嶺背竹坑, Bamboo Village) and Buck Hung (嶺背北坑, North Village).

Figure 16.1. A family believed to be the Fong Kee family, Broome, 1928. (State Library of Western Australia, Image: Number: Image Call Number: 27078P)

Toishan

Some of the time I went to the village school, but it was a long distance from our home. Also, we moved around a lot, living in the village and Toishan city. In recent years, the villagers who went overseas to Sydney and Melbourne, San Francisco, to California and New York, have sent money back to build a modern high school for the whole area, so as to give the kids there a better education. There were of course the odd ones in the olden days who got the opportunity of an education. We had a clan cousin, a Fong, who was sent to the Philippines as a diplomat by the Manchu emperor.

I can't remember how the family journeyed to Toishan from Broome but I can tell you how I left. Actually, Toishan has its own seaport, Kong Hoy (江海), along the southern Chinese coast, but we had to go by river boat to the city of Kong Moon (江門) in Sun Wooey (新會) county. From Kong Moon we caught a ferry boat to Hong Kong. From Hong Kong, we travelled by sea to Broome.

When Dad took the family to Toishan, he'd been away for thirty-four years. Consequently, he no longer understood the local situation. The business ventures he backed failed and he lost a lot of money. He only managed to return to Australia just before the outbreak of the Second World War. But he went to Darwin this time instead of Broome and worked as a gardener.

Broome

I came back earlier, when I was thirteen, with my uncle, Fong Henley (鄺榮修). He also had a tailoring business in Broome, called Fong Ly. I think he learned the trade in Hong Kong. When my uncle first came to Australia, he went to Darwin too and did various jobs there. He even went prospecting for gold. So you see, our family became spread out. After I returned to Broome, I went to school for a few years and helped in my uncle's shop after school. There were still quite a few Fongs in Broome then. The Fong Sam family is still a big family there. Fong Kan has a bakery shop there too.

When I go back to Broome now though, I only know a few of the Fong cousins there. The old Broome families have moved away as the years progressed, and newcomers have taken their place. There are quite a few West Australians who are part Aboriginal and part Chinese too. But there aren't many Chinese left today in Wyndham and Derby, the two other north-western towns. The Ah Chees are still a big family in Derby. They have garages and run taxis and have a bakehouse. Then in Wyndham there's Gee Hong Ying's family, the Ah Gees. Lee (李) Tong's family, the Lees, are related to the two old Lees I helped send back to China in 1975.

As a whole, the bulk of the people in Broome came from Asia. They didn't try to learn English, particularly in the pearling industry. Even some of the Australians working with the Malays spoke to them in Malay. The main divers were Japanese, brought out as indentured labourers. There were a few Chinese divers, but the Chinese mostly worked as crew members.[1] They were all indentured labourers and came from Singapore. They didn't earn much money. At one time they were earning between ten and fifteen pounds a year. Through his business, my uncle knew them all.

The Europeans preferred to stay down south where they had much better, what you call pickings. They had land rights for farms and all that. There wasn't much business opportunity for the Chinese down south. Apart from a few gardeners and laundrymen, they could only run very small businesses, like fruit shops. The Europeans got the best pickings down south. That's why Chinese businessmen were attracted to the coastal towns in the north-west where they did very well.

The Chinese involvement in the pearling industry was in trading, not the diving part. They did very well. I had a couple of uncles who managed to get a pearl buyer's licence. They bought some property in Hong Kong, there was a boom and they became millionaires. Although they were Fongs, they traded under the name of Wing Lee and Hong Hing. One would buy the pearls, sometimes travelling as far as Thursday Island in the east, and to Onslow and Shark Bay in the south-west. They bought the pearls from the masters of the luggers. The divers had no part in the pearl

---

1   Begun in the 1850s in Shark Bay, the pearling industry originally relied on Aboriginal skin divers. But as the industry extended northwards and into deeper waters, Chinese were brought in to replace them. Although Asians were excluded from owning pearling vessels by legislation, John had two uncles, Tom and Joe Fong, who managed to get in early and obtain pearling licences.

sales. My uncles sold the pearls in Hong Kong, in Paris, and other world centres. It wasn't easy to get into the pearling business if you didn't know it. But the Fong family was involved in the jewellery trade in China, in Canton and in Shanghai.

There were also three Wong brothers in the pearling industry. George was a licensed buyer, Philip was a trained jeweller and Peter an accountant. Their families had businesses in Broome and later moved to Perth.

Broome has two seasons, the 'wet' between November and March and the 'dry' from April to October. Much of the town is built on tidal flats, with a forty-eight-foot drop by the shore as the tide goes out, a tidal wave sort of thing.

When I returned to Broome from Toishan, the main diet was beef and mutton. The ships came once a month with vegetables, chiefly potatoes and cabbages and other root vegetables. There wasn't much refrigeration. You couldn't grow vegetables because of the water. It was brackish, due to the corrosion of the galvanised iron pipes and had a high salt content. The hot climate was another problem. Some of the old Chinese who came down to Perth in later years had trouble with their digestive functions. The doctors said it was caused by the water supply, especially in the case of those working on the pearl luggers.

I knew a lot of the Chinese who came out as indentured labourers in the early days. They worked on sheep stations as cooks, did land clearing and other farm work. They're all dead now. Jimmy O'Yick was cooking around the stations and fossicking too, even before the mineral booms. He'd be more than a hundred now, if he hadn't died. Charlie Kim was another one. He used to bring in bags and bags of minerals. He couldn't claim any of course, being Chinese. The Chinese had no mining rights. But he wanted to find out what they were. He had a lot of Australian friends. They told him what the minerals were, but he couldn't do anything about it.

There was one old Chinese who did a little mining, Tommy Lee in Roebourne, a little town in the Pilbara area. In the end, old age caught up with him. He was married to a Japanese lady from Broome. They finally moved to Perth, had a home there, adopted a couple of part-Aboriginal girls and left their estate to them.

Quite a few Chinese married Aboriginal or part-Aboriginal women. I had a cousin who was married to a Chinese woman. They got divorced and then he married a part-Aboriginal woman whose first husband was a Japanese diver. Between them they had about twenty children and about thirty-six-odd grandchildren. One of the children married an Australian, another a German and so on. I saw a family photograph and looked at all the faces and joked they were the United Nations. They're the real Australians.

Second World War

When the Second World War broke out a couple of Chinese in the pearling industry were called up into the Australian Army. They were Yap Ching and Lo Ping. They were very skilled in using the ropes on the luggers. They were then transferred from

Figure 16.2. John Fong in Australian military uniform, 1943. (Poon family)

the Australian Army to the American Army as 'specialists'. Did a lot of camouflage work. When the war ended, they were told to go back to the pearling industry.

I was in Broome in 1942 during the two Japanese bombings of the pearling town, following the bombing of Darwin. The authorities arranged for the evacuation of women and children and public servants. But except for one or two Chinese families, there wasn't much provision made for the Chinese community.

I couldn't say it was discrimination, but mistakes were made. Maybe there wasn't enough space.

We couldn't retreat into the desert. With no water there, we wouldn't be able to survive, not like the Aborigines. We had to find our own way. In the end we paid a construction group, Bell Brothers, to take us out on their trucks to Port Hedland. They were up there building airports and taking out their equipment. From Port Hedland we got down to the railway at Meekatharra and eventually got a train down south.

After that, I worked in Sydney Fong's shop in Geraldton for a few months. He was a cousin, also from Toishan. When I turned eighteen in 1943, I was called up into the army and trained for the infantry. Charlie Wong from Perth was with me for a few months. Chummy Fong, one of Sydney Fong's sons, was in the army too.

Before we went overseas, however, I was talked into going into an ambulance unit. Apparently, the Papua Infantry Battalion (PIB) scouts couldn't distinguish between a Chinese and a Japanese. A Chinese doctor in the army was chased because the PIB thought he was Japanese. I served three and a half years in the army, in Bougainville and in the Solomon Islands.

Postwar

After I was demobilised, I spent three years in Carnarvon. I ended up as a catering officer for the Australian Whaling Commission. The Australian government built a whaling station there in 1949. I had some knowledge of cooking, being in the services and all that. Some of my friends did catering and my family had a lot of catering experience. I was up there for nearly three years, until 1952.

You know the old saying, 'after you get tired of the bush, you go to Sydney'. So next I went over to Sydney and got a job with my cousin Joyce's husband Albie Quay, who was a fruit and vegetable agent in Haymarket. That's where I met and married my wife, Winnie Quan Mane (關明).

Perth

Winnie and I settled in Perth in November 1954. There used to be an old Chinese character in Perth by the name of Choong Kim (锺啓镇). He came from Sun Wooey county, next to Toishan. Sun Wooey is also one of the four counties known as See Yup and its county seat is Kong Moon, where you catch the ferry boat to Hong Kong.

Well, Choong Kim used to operate a Chinese business in James Street called Hop Hing (合興). There was no official Chinese representative in Perth in the olden days. But between Choong Kim and the Chung Wah (中華) Association, they took care of all the needs of the old gardeners. They were running around to find out what they wanted.

Figure 16.3. The Hop Hing & Co. and Chung Wah Association Buildings in James Street, Perth, c. 1930. (Chung Wah Association, Perth)

When I first came down to Perth in my young days, Choong Kim used to cart me around with him. He supplied all the old boys with Chinese groceries, as well as helped them fill out forms and solve all sorts of problems. Whenever we went out to their gardens, the old chaps would cut him some prize vegetables in season.

I used to go round all the market gardens in Perth. Through Choong Kim I got to know every one of them. The bulk of them had accounts with his grocery. But Choong Kim was a very generous bloke. Some of the gardeners managed to go back to China for a trip while still owing him money, when Choong Kim himself couldn't afford to make a trip. Of course, there was the Chinese consulate in Perth in the olden days to help people. Choong Kim did a lot of work for the Chinese community. In the end he had to mortgage his property to the bank, but he lived a very happy life. He was eighty-two when he died in 1948, just a few years after I returned from the services.

A Mrs Chiew (趙太) bought Hop Hing and then she resold it. By the time Winnie and I arrived in Perth from Sydney, the Wong brothers from Broome had bought the business. Philip, the jeweller, now talked me into buying it. I wasn't very keen because my Chinese isn't that fluent. But Philip said there was no other

Chinese capable of running it. The shop was importing and exporting with China. It ended up I had a very difficult time. But the old Chinese continued to come in and ask for help with their problems. All sorts of problems.[2]

The Lee brothers

The two Lee brothers I mentioned before were related to Lee Tong up in Wyndham. Lee Ackmen and younger brother Lee Acumen Chong, that's their English names. The younger one came straight from China. The older one came via Portland, Oregon. He was a timber cutter in the United States before he came to Western Australia. They were from Toishan too.

Eventually, the Lee brothers got their own market garden in Mosman Park. Then they moved to York where they must have lived for thirty or forty years, just doing gardening into well over their eighties and near nineties. By that time some of the other Chinese in Northam and York were helping them take in their crops of cauliflowers and lettuce and all that to Perth; like the Kwong Lee family who were all clan cousins from Toishan. They also dealt with Australian families there like the Sims.

The two brothers weren't naturalised and they fell into difficult financial circumstances in their old age. Some friends and I tried to get the land for them. The shire was willing to let them have the title. But one of the brothers was bankrupted during the war and he didn't want to get into a partnership which might mean they would lose the land. So for years they were paying the rates just like tenants. They didn't have the pension because they kept working until they were over ninety. Finally, with the help of a friend in the public service, the two brothers were given the old age pension. They were well known in the district. The younger one liked beer. When he got a bit over the mark, the police would just take him back to their garden to sleep it off.

Well, in 1974 I made a trip to China when it was just opening up to the world again. At the end of the trip I went back to Toishan to see the old villagers of my young days. When I came back to Western Australia and told the Lee brothers about my trip, they became very keen to return to China.

I was then a trustee of the Chung Wah Association, so I wrote to the Chinese embassy in Canberra and asked if they could help. It happened the Chinese had a vessel loading wheat in Albany at the time, with some business representatives on board. The embassy contacted them to go and see the two Lee brothers. A friend and I took the business representatives up to York to meet the Lees. Passages were then arranged through the Chung Wah Association. The association and others also donated money towards the brothers' trip.

---

2 Traditionally, Chinese import agencies also operated as community centres. They served as meeting places, provided postal and banking services, accommodation, job placements, translation and other kinds of assistance.

The Lees had made trips back to China during their younger days and still had families there. One had a son who had migrated to the United States. After they finally arrived back in their home village, their grandchildren cared for them. The older one was well over a hundred by then and the younger not far behind, ninety-nine or a hundred. That's how they went home after a lifetime of toil in Western Australia.

Reflections

We could learn a lot from the experience of the poor old Chinese and all they had to put up with, if we put more perspective into the problems of the present day.

You take opium. Two hundred years ago when Cathay was said to be a sleeping giant, Napoleon Bonaparte said let him sleep. Well, whoever made the decision to use opium to make China sleep, that's what happened through the last couple of hundred years or more.[3]

When I was in the services during the war, I went with a mate to visit his sister in Bunbury, south of Perth, and right there in her garden were straight opium poppies. She said jokingly, 'Oh, Chinese poppies!' So I said, 'Chinese poppies be blowed. They're English poppies!' After all, the opium habit was introduced into China by the British East India Company. That's how the Golden Triangle started. They would take a shipload of opium to China and take away a shipload of gold and silver and other things. So the country got poor.

Another time, a friend mentioned to me that his grandfather used to run a little boat bringing Chinese miners to Australia. He would sail this little old boat back and forth. What puzzled my friend was why his grandfather always went to Burma every time he went back to Hong Kong and China to fetch more miners. I jokingly said to him, 'All these years and you can't work it out. I can guess. Your grandfather had two gold mines, one in Australia and one in Burma in the Golden Triangle, yellow gold and black gold!'

The way I looked at it, with the Chinese and their diggings here, the grandfather was already getting some of their gold. By going to Burma he was getting the rest of the gold anyhow. But it's hard to sort these problems out. My friend still insisted that the logbook never mentioned what business his grandfather was in.

---

3   During the nineteenth century opium was freely available and provided substantial revenue for the colonial governments. In *The New Gold Mountain*, C.F. Yong outlines the struggle against the use of the drug dating from the 1880s. The federal government finally legislated against opium in 1905 following a widespread campaign by the Chinese communities with Australian support.

Postscript

John Fong and Winnifred continued to operate the Hop Hing store in James Street until 1973, when they sold the business to a group of Chinese. They took a short break before opening a new Chinese grocery store in Applecross, a suburb between Perth and Fremantle, in 1975, which closed in 1982 when they retired. John had for a long time been a de facto social worker among the elderly male Chinese community, helping them negotiate the Australian social welfare system or managing their affairs after they died. They retained the business name of Hop Hing until 2002. It was registered for one hundred years. John's wife Winnifred was originally from Sydney's Quan Mane family and was the sister of Kathleen and Doreen Quan Mane, who served in the Women's Army Auxiliary Corps during the Second World War. John died in 2008 and Winnie a year later in 2009.

17
Don and the Family

Evelyn Yin Lo (黎鑽妤)

The long-held desire of Don Yin Lo (羅順忠), Evelyn's husband, to visit his family in Hong Kong never eventuated. Marriage, a growing family to look after and long years of hard work saw to it that he and Evelyn remained in Australia. When his opportunity finally came, ill health intervened and it was too late. So, he asked Evelyn to go for him. In 1984, Evelyn set off for Hong Kong to meet Don's niece and nephew and their families for the first time. On the way over, she worried they might not approve of her Australian ideas and ways. Her only previous visit to Hong Kong was in 1939 when she stayed in the Walled City of Kowloon (九龍) and was called a barbarian woman. To her surprise, however, she found she felt as though she had known Don's family all her life. Evelyn reflects on this time and the delight she had in seeing her daughters mature into successful young women.

Singapore

Don often spoke of making a visit back home. He was very homesick. For a long time, we didn't have the money and he didn't want to leave the family. He always thought the children were still babies. We couldn't all go and we couldn't leave them by themselves. Later, when we had opportunities, someone had to stay home. So Don never went anywhere.

In 1980 Wendy made up her mind to go to Singapore for six weeks. It was an overseas trip. She was twenty-one and very adventurous. She's got more go in her than the other girls, always had. But Wendy suffers with asthma and Don said, 'She can't go by herself. You go with her and when you come back, I'll go.'

He never said 'We'll go.' Then Cheryle would be left at home and he thought one of us would have to stay. 'How can I?' I thought. I've got family. Don was still working then. Then Wendy walked in. 'Why don't you come, Mum?' she asked. 'I have the money to pay your fare.' She had the money to pay her own fare as well as mine and her own pocket money too. She's a saver, like her father was. Diane and her were the only two that had the money. Don said, 'I'll give you some pocket money.' Well, I had some money myself. I had enough to spend. Don always told me to keep the money I made working for myself. 'It's your money, you work hard for it, you keep it,' he would say. He used to give me all the housekeeping money. The next morning, I said to Don, 'Did you mean what you said about me going?' 'I said it, didn't I? I don't say things I don't mean,' Don replied.

'I'll make the arrangements,' Wendy said. She's very organised that way. She knows what she's doing. She took a course in travel. It didn't do her any good, but she uses it. She talks things over with the travel agent and books the cheaper fares.

When the time came we went, and we stayed with the mother of my son-in-law, Peter. Don stayed home to look after Cheryle. The boss made the girls do my work. He couldn't get anybody else, anyhow.

Planning the Hong Kong trip

After we returned, I was going to book Don for Hong Kong. He already had his passport fixed up.

When I asked how he and Cheryle had managed, she said, 'Oh, me and Dad had a good time.' Actually, he'd say to her: 'You coming home for tea or something?' And he'd have the tea ready for her. But she'd say, 'I won't be home today, Dad. I'm going out with a friend.' That's how they got on. But he was used to eating by himself and doing his own washing. He used to be quite good at looking after himself. He was more worried when someone like Margaret or the other families turned up and he'd be wanting to feed them.

'When are you going to Hong Kong?' I asked. 'Oh, one day,' he said. He was never game to tell me that he didn't like to go by himself. He was a bit afraid because he couldn't speak English well. The trouble with his luggage, I would have fixed up all that. He was really within himself. If he had me standing by, he'd feel more confident. But he never told me that.

I took him to the doctor for a check-up. I said to the doctor, 'How is he? I want to take him back to Hong Kong.' As a matter of fact, I nearly bought his ticket. But the doctor said, 'Don't take him yet. Give him another month, Ev.' The doctor was more worried about me. My blood pressure was up. 'You're the patient, not him,' the doctor said. He sent us both down to the Sydney Hospital for x-rays, which didn't show too good on my leg. A breakage when I was a kid had deteriorated. That was when my knee started to play up. 'I want you here every morning to check your blood pressure,' the doctor said.

17 Don and the Family

Not long after, Don couldn't get up one Sunday morning. I called an ambulance. The hospital said he'd taken a light stroke. He had no feeling in his left leg at all. Luckily, he could still eat with his right hand and he was still able to talk. But he had difficulty swallowing. He stayed in the hospital for ten days and then I took him home.

The boss let me have time off to take Don to therapy three times a week. He told the drivers to give me a car whenever I needed one. The factory still paid me, even if I wasn't there. For the next one and a half years no person could have done what Don did in the time he had. He didn't want anyone to help him. He was very determined. He never asked a favour.

Beverly and her family were away in Christmas Island during 1981 and 1982 and Don looked forward so much to their return. He opened up a lot about New Guinea during the war in his last days. Before this he'd kept it all to himself. He told me, 'You don't know how lonely you can get when you go to a strange country. I was in that place so long, I even planted flowers. When the planes came over, you knew you could be bombed straightaway and that would be the end of your life. You never knew when your time would be up.'

His last request was that I should go to Hong Kong to meet his family. He died on 20 February 1982.

Distant relations

After Don's death, his nephew in Hong Kong rang to say how sorry the family there were. At first I thought it was a local call. A voice spoke in Chinese and I answered in Chinese. Then I heard him say, 'Oh, Auntie speaks Chinese!' I felt so happy to hear his voice. Don always used to write to his elder brother in Hong Kong and send over photographs of our children. After Don's parents died, his elder brother took the place as head of the family. The brother in turn sent us photos of his children. Don would talk about taking me over there and showing me places I'd never seen before.

By now only a niece and a nephew and their families remained, and I had never met any of them. From then on, the niece's daughter, my grandniece, kept writing and asking when I was going to visit them. She was the only one who could write in English then. All of them can now, having attended English schools. So in 1984, I decided to go over and meet them.

On the plane over, I thought they must be real scared of what to expect. After all, I'm a bit of a mixture, Australian in thinking, Chinese in looks. People never know how to take me. Also, I'm very family-oriented.

Don and I used to go up to Mum's place once a week after we moved out of Burwood. That's how we used to see each other. My family seemed to be the noisy ones. If we didn't go, they'd say it was too quiet. My sisters-in-law would go with their children, but it was never the same when we were up there. We made it a bit more lively. Don would get us up there in the truck about eleven o'clock, and we'd come home after ten the same night.

We always spent Christmas with Mum. Leslie (黎湛枝) used to make the plum pudding. We all took to cooking, after my father. Leslie went to classes to learn. He used to make a great big plum pudding, enough for twenty-odd people. At one time, we had thirty-seven people, in and out all the time. When we celebrated with Mum and Dad, we would have roast chickens, turkey and we always bought a ham. Plum pudding. It was more of an Australian meal. We ourselves decided to have that, a sort of a mixture. But for the evening meal, we generally had Chinese food and leftovers.

Cecil's (黎滿枝) the only one left up in Burwood. Now they all come down to my place and stop all day. On Boxing Day all the families have a picnic at Chinaman's Beach because it's nice and quiet there. Chinaman's Beach within Sydney Harbour is in the suburb of Mosman. It was named after the Chinese market gardeners in the surrounding area in the early days.

Meeting Don's family

As it turned out, both my family and Don's family have always been very close as families. So I noticed no difference. I was astounded. I felt as if they had known me all their lives.

I stayed with the niece. She and her husband, Mr and Mrs Tam (譚), lived in a low-cost government flat in Homantin (何文田) district in Kowloon, the mainland part of Hong Kong. The nephew was only two years older than my eldest daughter, Diane, and the niece four years older. Until I got there, I hadn't realised that our kids and Don's brother's children were around the same age.

My niece made me feel at home straight away. She sat me down and she could never do enough for me. I found it extraordinary how adapted they were to the conditions in Hong Kong. Every evening after tea we would sit on the lounge bed. The table would be pushed away and folded up, put out on the balcony, together with the fold-up chairs, while all the beds were set up, and the TV switched on.

They lived on the twenty-third storey. The building had two lifts. There was running water, gas and all that. They dried their clothes on bamboo poles extended from the balcony. They really only had one large lounge room. There was a little kitchen and an alcove with space enough for a wardrobe and a double bed, where my niece and her husband slept.

Their five children slept in the lounge room. It had two double bunkers, two chairs and an extension table. There was a fishpond on a stand, a dividing shelf which supported the television and stereo and little cupboards underneath with drawers, where they kept their underwear and children's things. The double bunkers had curtains. While I was there, they let me have one of the lower bunks. One of the kids slept above me. The double bunkers took care of four. Another kid slept on the sofa bed and there were two extra fold-up beds. There was a stand-up shower and toilet together, a gas heater for hot water which you switched on.

17 Don and the Family

Everything went according to a timetable. My niece went to work too, you see. Twenty to seven, she got up and put on the washing machine. It was going all the flaming time. There was a power machine in the lounge from the days when the niece used to do machining at home. One of her jobs was cleaning offices and the other cooking for some Chinese navy men. She'd be back at a quarter to eleven, fixed my lunch, then off again from three to half past six. Mr Tam cooked the tea. He started his taxi at three in the morning.

The kids got their own breakfast. Sometimes they went and bought something at the rows of market stalls downstairs and ate it there. They would go down about ten in the morning. The schools had morning and afternoon shifts. If they thought I might like something they saw, they'd bring their breakfast home to eat. Usually, they ate congee when they stayed outside. Sometimes they bought *bao* (包, stuffed buns) and things like that.

Both Mr Tam and the nephew were taxi drivers. Generally, the nephew had his one day off a week on Mondays. He was living in a single men's dormitory elsewhere, paying twenty-five dollars monthly rent. He always came on his day off with a big box of *saai bang* (西餅, Western-style cakes).

It was really great down in the market. You could get fresh chicken soup, *chaah siu* (叉燒, barbequed pork), vegetables, fresh fish and everything else there. Sometimes my niece would prepare a meal like I used to. She'd go down and shop if she knew what she wanted. Sometimes she couldn't be bothered. She'd say, 'Take Auntie downstairs and see what she wants.'

The niece told me her brother originally wanted to become a teacher. But other members of the extended family ran into trouble and he felt obliged to help them. Also, Mr Tam hurt his back when the children were small, so the nephew helped them with the food. That's why he became a taxi driver.

The niece has three girls and two boys. The oldest, a young man of twenty-four then, was a jeweller. The next, my grandniece, worked for an import-export firm in nearby Yaumati (油麻地) district and walked to and from work. During the weekends, when the races were on, she worked at the Jockey Club. She was learning to operate a computer when I was there. The third, also a daughter, had just started working in a large bank over on the Hong Kong island side. The two youngest, a boy and a girl, were still in school. So you see, job opportunities over there are just as good as over here. They brought out an album and showed me all the photos Don had sent over. I was amazed. I had put theirs away in a box.

The eldest grandniece and her fiancé, a journalist, took me out with them. He was born in Hong Kong but he had a sister married to a Chinese in America. His mother had joined them. I was hoping the grandniece could come to Australia for a holiday, but she has since married the journalist and they have gone to America too.

The nephew spoke just like Don. They had the same voices, they were so alike. While we were standing on top of a bridge overlooking Hong Kong, he suddenly said to me, 'I'll show you places you've never seen before!' I could have sworn it was Don speaking. He used the same words Don had used to me.

'You know,' my nephew said, 'you might have been my mother.' I said, 'I'm quite aware of that.' In fact, because we had no son, Don and I had seriously considered adopting the nephew and bringing him over to Australia. Then Don thought the nephew might be better off in Hong Kong. He had a good job and was earning good money. If he couldn't speak English, he wouldn't be able to drive a taxi here. He wouldn't be able to get a proper job. He'd have to go into the restaurant business.

The family noticed that I sometimes went into the big hotels and ordered a cup of tea. I longed for a decent Australian cuppa. So my grandniece started sending me teabags. She often came home with samples of tea from the place where she worked. Her mother, the niece, was always collecting bits of materials in a box. All the clothes her children grew out of, she put into the box too. Whenever the nephew went up to Canton to see his wife and child, he had to lug a great big bag for the mainland relatives. They wanted to help other members of the extended family who weren't doing as well as them.

Overseas visitors to mainland China were allowed to pay for refrigerators in certain Hong Kong shops and then take delivery, duty free, inside China. My nephew wanted a fridge in Canton so his baby could have ice cream. This privilege didn't apply to Hong Kong residents. He took me to a shop where he picked out the kind he wanted and I took the receipt to Canton to take delivery there.

My nephew didn't have time to take me to see Tung Koon (東莞) where my dad came from. But he helped me join a non-profit seamen's tour of the mainland. It cost about eight hundred Australian dollars in and out of China by plane, train, boat and bus. Because we returned a day early, we got a refund.

That year was China's thirty-fifth anniversary and all the tourists in Beijing were invited to a banquet in the Great Hall of the People (人民大會堂). I had my photo taken there sitting with six hundred people. It was the best meal we had in Beijing. The chefs walked down the aisles to our tables, holding the roast ducks in one hand. Then they took them away to chop them up and brought them back with pancakes. The duck was beautifully cooked. You couldn't get anything better in China than that.

I was disappointed in the *bao* (steamed buns), though. I thought they were barbecued pork buns like we have in Australia. I was thinking we could take them with us on the bus for a snack. But they were only dough. They tasted like a bread roll without butter. No wonder no one was eating them.

In all, we went to seven places, including Hangchow (杭州), Wusih (無錫) and Shanghai. Hangchow was where all the beautiful gardens were. The West Lake (西湖) there was lovely. But Guangzhou (廣州), or Canton, was the place with really good food. We couldn't stop eating when we got back there.

There's one thing in Hong Kong that really makes you mad, though. People there look down on you if you speak English. I went with my niece to the Immigration Department to find out what papers I needed to sign for her to come to Australia. I talked to an older man in his forties and he was very gruff. I think he thought I was showing off by speaking a bit of English. I had to explain that I couldn't speak fluent Chinese because I wasn't born there. After that, he relaxed a bit and said, 'Oh, go around the corner.' Later, when my niece rang him up, he threw the phone down. Then I said, 'Give it to me.' I called back and got a very polite reception. It was, 'No, madam, no, no, we do it like this.' All because my voice was Australian. I thought if I were to go down there once more, he'd give me a slap in the face again.

Before I left Hong Kong, I got in touch with an old friend, who'd stayed with us for a short time when he was a young student in Sydney. Now he's a barrister and solicitor with seventy people working under him. From Australia he had gone on to England for his training. He wanted to take me around Hong Kong, but I didn't want to see the big department stores. I told him I wanted most of all to find the old place where I had lived in 1939, and the old pickle factory where the lady in a two-piece black silk suit had a kapok mattress.

I didn't let him know till the last week because he always wants to take me out. When my niece heard me, she said, 'Don't take Auntie there. It's not safe. Once you go past those walls, you'll see beggars and thieves. You don't know what will happen.' The Australians called it the Walled City. But my niece called it a den of thieves. He took me to see the outside of it. It was dreadful. I didn't even recognise it. The walls were half knocked down. I couldn't believe this was where I used to live. We couldn't recognise that part where the pickle factory was. But at least I made it back to there.

Raising children

I'm very proud of my daughters. I'm a dreamer too and I think they've achieved what I've always hoped for. They've always been obedient daughters. Although they didn't always agree with their father, they respected him. I respected him because he was the man of the house. I didn't believe in everything he said, but I went along with him because he was their father and he wanted it that way.

Don liked the girls to be properly dressed. He wanted them to come home, not to be out all night gallivanting. When they grew up, the three elder girls went out together and they came home together. They used to go to the Kuomintang (國民黨) club dances, down in Thomas Street. One year Diane took part in the Miss Dragon Pageant. Let's face it, Don was only a working man. The others had more backing. But she came third, which I reckon wasn't too bad.

Among the Chinese there were always more boys than girls. My girls would go with a party of others, so there'd be five or six of them together. The trouble was, one boy might like one particular girl, so the next time they would go to where he was, because they were all together. My second daughter, Margaret, got fed up with this, so she went and sat far apart, pretending the girls didn't know each other. It ended up the girls had more partners that way. When one of the boys wanted to take her home, Margaret would say, 'I have to ask my sister.' Then all the girls would get in the car and go home with her. Another girl would say they were all cousins, to avoid becoming attached to anyone.

I used to think my daughters weren't very outgoing. They just went to Randwick Girls' High School. One day they came home from school and said, 'Mum, we're going to go to work.' Yes, they started out working with Woolworths in Bondi Junction, Thursday nights and Saturday mornings. As far as education was concerned, it was up to the girls themselves, and they did look after themselves. I didn't know anything about education. I only knew we had to go and learn things at school. The only one who didn't like school was Beverly. Now she's making up for it by doing a mature-age university course. When I went to Japan to visit my sister-in-law, Kasue, I found that Japanese women are supposed to do what their husbands tell them. I didn't like that.

I didn't like school when I was a kid. But then, I think my mother and father needed me at home to help. They had waitresses working for them, but they were very unreliable in those days. Some days they wouldn't turn up and I had to help Dad and Mum. I used to do everything, cook and take the food out to the customers and collect the money at the same time. Everybody laughs at the way I used to do things. The main thing is, we got results. It doesn't matter how you go about it as long as you get results. That's what I think.

I think the Chinese coming from overseas to Australia now spoil their children. The young ones complain they're having a hard time. They never think how their grandparents survived and didn't do the things they wanted to do. It's only through hard work that we got to the position we're in today. We battled through, but we could take a lot more because we went through a lot more. I think the younger generation are getting it the easiest of the lot!

St Vincent's Hospital

A few years ago, because of my hypertension, my doctor sent me to the Diabetes and Heart Centre at St Vincent's Hospital for a check-up. My blood pressure is always high when I go to those doctors, but when I go to my acupuncturist, she says it's low. I've found out since that acupuncture brings the blood pressure down.

The first time I went to St Vincent's, the specialist said, 'Can you cook Chinese?' He wondered why I laughed. I asked if he was looking for a Chinese cook. 'No,' he said, 'but we're short of a Chinese cook to help out sometimes in the kitchen here.' We went on to talk about Chinese food, and then he said, 'What did you come in for, anyhow?' 'Here's a letter from my doctor,' I said. 'You're a diabetic,' he said. 'Good! We'll take you.' That's how I started going over to St Vincent's sometimes to give them a hand.

17 Don and the Family

Chinese food

Australians didn't go for Chinese food like they do now. Although the restaurants made dim sims (點心) in the old days, there was no variety. They hadn't got the chefs. A lot of the chefs today are not the real thing. But the ones down in Dixon Street are. Many of the Chinese restaurants are now enticing Hong Kong chefs to come out under guarantee. They bring the husbands over first. Then they offer to bring their families over and provide accommodation, and after a while, cheaper wages. The bosses make big money out of them. When the chefs see somebody working for more money and put in for more themselves, the bosses say, 'Well, you've signed a contract, you can't get out.' Some do stick to the contracts because they're under threat of deportation. Besides, too many people are coming over, so that breaks the line. But some have made their money and some are lucky enough to get out of their contracts.

Helping others

I'm a Pisces. I always feel sorry for the underdog. I believe we're not here to gain what we can. We're here to try and help each other. What I enjoy most is helping other people. I get more satisfaction out of that than anything. Some people want money for everything they do for you. If they're going to do you a favour, they first ask how much it's worth, how much it's going to cost them, and that's bad.

Before I retired, I used to help a friend out. They have five girls and I've known them since they were babies. Took them to the clinics and hospitals. Whenever that family had trouble, when they couldn't get the message through, they'd sing out 'Lai Parkee (黎柏)' – that's me. I used to help this friend on Friday and Saturday nights in a club with only a little kitchen. Then the club was renovated to seat five hundred. He did the Chinese cooking, but he had to put in a couple of chefs to do the Australian cooking. Then another chap began working there. This man didn't know a thing. He just watched and he learned English. My friend was too busy. This chap persuaded my friend to go in with him into a partnership and move to a still bigger club. It was supposed to be a half-share business but the other chap is getting seventy-five per cent. He takes trips to Hong Kong while my friend has to take care of the business. He outsmarted my friend. That's what makes me cross. So I told the other fellow off. He can't stand a bar of me. My friend told me I'm about the only one who treats him fairly.

Chinese cliques

The trouble with the Chinese community is it's too divided. When my son-in-law, Peter, came here to study at university, he wanted to get into the Chinese community and make something of it. But he was from Singapore and the Singapore, Malaysian and Hong Kong Chinese didn't get on well together. Peter was civic-minded. He wanted to teach karate and physical fitness. But they wouldn't talk to him.

With the Chinese community here, it used to be one side was communist and the other nationalist. The beaut was the communist part of it. Just because you were friendly with someone, people would say, 'Oh, you're a commo!' The nationalists were more standoffish. But if you try to get in with the Chinese today and you're not in a clique, they don't know you. It's not a friendly atmosphere. Things are supposed to be changed, but in their hearts they're still nationalists.

That's the reason I've been going to the Senior Citizens' Club at Alexandria for the past several years, sometimes three times a week. It's not so much for the lunch as for the company. I'm the only Chinese member. Yet they treat me as one of their own. I don't think they ever feel I'm different. I went on the committee for one year, but I've got too much on my plate now. My doctor told me not to get too involved, so I help them voluntarily when they need it. When I first went up there, I didn't know anybody. But my children grew up with theirs. They were all neighbours. When I got there, they all said, 'How're you going, Ev?' They made me welcome.

Postscript

Evelyn and Don had a family of five girls, all of whom have gone on to have productive careers in Sydney. After Don passed away in 1982, Evelyn continued to live in her house in the Sydney suburb of Alexandria. She died in 2008 at the age of eighty-six and is buried along with Don in Rookwood Cemetery.

Evelyn's older brother Basil Parkee (黎宗枝) was well known in the Sydney Chinese community, serving as president of the Chinese tennis club for many years. Her younger brother Cecil Parkee had a sideline as a ventriloquist and magician, and later in life as an actor in such films as *Far East* and *We of the Never Never*, and the television series *Cyclone Tracy*, *Harp in the South* and *Poor Man's Orange*.

Figure 1. Yin Lo family 1969. Back row: Margaret, Beverly (Saulan), Evelyn, Don, Diane. Front row: Cheryle, Wendy. (Yin Lo family)

Figure 2. Evelyn (centre front row) in Hong Kong with Don's relations, 1993. (Yin Lo family)

Figure 3. Yin Lo family, Christmas 1996. Back row: Cheryle, Beverly (Saulan), Diane, Margaret. Front row: Wendy, Evelyn. (Yin Lo family)

Figure 4. Albert Lee On (second left) with siblings Fred (far left), Jessie and Moody. (J and M Wing collection, courtesy S. Canning)

Figure 5. Evelyn and Don Yin Lo in the 1970s. (Yin Lo family)

Figure 6. Frank Lee Gee in late 1970s with Mavis Yen on far right and Mavis' sisters Sheila Jitts, far left, and Edna Kepert. (Yen family)

Figure 7. Doris Fong Lim pictured with her mother and prominent Darwin businesswoman Lorna Lim. (Lim family)

Figure 8. Elizabeth Lee with her daughters at her 90th birthday party in 2004. (Lee family)

Figure 9. Harry Gock Ming with one of his grandsons. (Gock Ming family)

Figure 10. Hoy Lee pictured in April 1998. (Googan family)

Figure 11. Winnie and John Fong with their grandchildren. (Poon family)

Figure 12. Photograph of Leung Pui on his gravestone at Rookwood Cemetery. (Richard Horsburgh)

Figure 13. Mavis Yen, c. 1990s. (Yen family)

Figure 14. Peter Wong, 2020. (Richard Horsburgh)

Figure 15. Thelma and Leslie Chang, c. 1980s. (Ken Chang)

18
Gold Rush Heritage

Hoy Lee (黄沛均)

Born in Stuart Town, Hoy Lee's (1911–2006) story is a blend of Chinese traditions and Australian landscape. All his life he got on well with European Australians because he played cricket and tennis with them, even when his parents would have preferred his help in the family store. He tells of the close relations shared by the early Chinese and European Australians.

Originally known as Ironbarks, Stuart Town is located in Wellington Shire in central-west New South Wales. Situated between the larger townships of Wellington to the north and Orange to the south, it is not far from Ophir, where Australia's first official discovery of gold was made by Edward Hargraves on 12 February 1851. During the gold rush days, the coach horses were changed at Ironbarks on the route from Orange to Wellington.

White settlers first appeared in this area at the beginning of the nineteenth century to engage in sheep farming and wheat growing. Even before the announcement of the discovery of gold near Ophir, alluvial gold was being picked up in and about Ironbarks. Then followed a rich find in 1856 at Stoney Creek (later renamed Farnham, some six kilometres from Ironbarks) and a rush began. The Europeans were greatly outnumbered by the Chinese, many of whom were buried at Farnham, their bodies later exhumed and the bones returned to China.

By 1858, however, there was a shift to Ironbarks, Mookerawa and Burrandong, with richer finds there. An estimated two thousand diggers spread over the area at the height of the rush. The Chinese concentrated along the Mookerawa Creek (mookerawa being an Aboriginal word for the ironbark tree, or eucalyptus sideroxylon). Just ten kilometres from Ironbarks, the Mookerawa settlement became a boom town, with wine bars and shops, a big Chinese store and a Chinaman's hut and vegetable garden on almost every river flat.

Remains of the Chinese alluvial diggings and ovens can still be found in the area.

Ironbarks became central to all the local diggings and a new township grew up there. The diggers brought their wives and families with them and the first school was opened in Ironbarks in 1858. In 1880, the railway from Orange was extended to Ironbarks and Wellington. In 1889, Ironbarks was renamed Stuart Town.

Hoy Lee reveals a deep-seated affection for Stuart Town and the various communities making up the diverse population of this region: the European Australians; the Eurasian descendants of the original Chinese diggers; the later Chinese arrivals like his father; and the Aboriginal population. During the Second World War, Hoy Lee went to Sydney to work, staying on to join a Chinese seafood importing firm. Sydney's Chinatown opened a totally new world to him. He came to admire the way the Chinese helped each other, but was saddened by the loss of Chinese language and culture by the younger generations. Hoy Lee had a lifetime of memories that he had much pleasure in sharing.

My parents

The Chinese came out to look for gold; that's why they called Australia *gum shan* (金山, golden mountain). They came out here with the idea of making money and sending it back to China, or going back to China to die in their old age. A lot had wives and families in China and they would send money home to support them. Others married Australian women.

By the time my father arrived in Australia the gold rush had ceased. He was brought out to work for Fong Lee (芳利) & Co. in Wellington in the 1880s. The fellow who started Fong Lee was a clansman, a Wong (黃).[1] He brought out quite a few clansmen including my father and his three brothers. My father's name was Wong War Lai (黃華禮) (pronounced Wah Lay). He came to Wellington in 1888. By Chinese reckoning he was twenty but he may only have been eighteen.

Wellington is situated at the junction of the Macquarie and Bell Rivers. There are river flats in Wellington and there were a lot of Chinese gardens there. There were three mixed businesses like Fong Lee and three selling fruit and vegetables. That was the extent of Chinese businesses other than the gardens. Fong Lee had a staff of eight or nine and they lived in the same building. They all came from Baak

---

1   The Fong Lee & Co. department store was established by Sydney merchant Hong Wong and managed by clansman Kum Sing Lee in the 1880s. In 1896 family member Wong (William) Suey Ling took over the management until his death in 1936. Born in Melbourne in 1877, he expanded the clientele to reach well beyond the Chinese community and became respected throughout the wider district for his generosity and community spirit.

Shek (白石) village in Jaang Sheng (增城) county. The business dealt in grocery and ironmongery and drapery, mainly for Australians, though they would have a few Chinese gardener customers too. My father was made the cook. He said he had to get up at four in the morning to cook breakfast for seven o'clock. After finishing in the kitchen, he had to weigh up potatoes and help get things ready for the next day. So he never got to bed till ten or eleven o'clock.

My father worked for quite a number of years and when he had saved up enough money he got married by proxy. Then he returned to China and brought out my mother in January 1903. My mother, Lum Dai Wong (馮林弟),[2] was from Jaang Sheng's neighbouring county of Tung Koon (東莞). I don't know what village she was from.[3] She had bound feet. When they got here, they settled in Stuart Town, twenty-two miles south of Wellington, where Pop set up his own general store, Yee Lee (義利) & Co.[4] I guess he thought it was better to work for himself than someone else. When I was growing up there were two other general stores there, but we were the only Chinese shop.

Stuart Town used to be an old gold mining centre. Chinese diggers concentrated there along the Mookerawa Creek and you could see the remains of their mining operations, ovens and races. There was one particular race along the Mookerawa Creek that you could see for years until it was flooded by the waters of the Burrendong Dam. It was built like a canal, from higher up the creek, so they could run the water round the side of the hill to wash the dirt and gravel into the cradles where they wanted to sluice for gold.

I was born on 18 June 1911 and the midwife was Mrs Sarah Dong (董). My brother was six years older and my sister a few years older than me. I was the youngest and we were all born in Stuart Town. Sarah Dong (nee Driscoll) was an Australian lady married to a Eurasian, Jack Dong, but she was a midwife. Because my mother had bound feet, she had to put up with a lot of hardship for the sake of us children, and we being the only Chinese family there, she did not have an opportunity to learn English. Sarah Dong used to try and help my mother, but my mother couldn't speak English, so they couldn't talk to each other. My father would have an uncle or a brother or someone working for him. They'd be busy all day and wouldn't have time to talk with my mother. That's why my mother had a very

---

2   The third character used on her gravestone is 娣. The character used on the letters from her father and family members is 弟.

3   A recently discovered family letter from China written in the early 1900s shows Hoy's mother's village was Fung Cyun (馮村), within the same township of Sun Tong (新塘) as Hoy's father's village of Baak Shek.

4   Australian businesses usually went by the name of the proprietor, while the names of Chinese enterprises were carefully chosen as omens of good luck. Sometimes this resulted in Chinese men becoming known by their business name. Hoy Lee's family have a copy of the passenger list for Hoy's father's arrival in Sydney with his wife in 1903 which records their names as Mr and Mrs Yee Lee. This indicates that by then Hoy's father was already known by his business name, the Yee Lee & Co. store having been in operation from 1892.

lonely life. Now looking back, I realise that I was pretty unkind to my mother in the sense that I always wanted to run out and play. It was the Eurasian women who befriended her. They would try and bid her the time of day, make a few signs, but no way could they converse. I could speak a little bit of Chinese to her when I was young. If there was a word I did not know I would say it in English. She couldn't understand but she would somehow realise what I was talking about.

Stuart Town only had about three or four hundred people and about one hundred of those were children. There was no doctor, no dentist, no hospital, no ice boxes, no nothing in Stuart Town. There was no ambulance. If you needed to go to hospital, you went to Wellington. You might get someone to take you. We didn't even have electricity or mains water. No modern sewerage. We had a big hole dug down the back. It was only many years after when they wanted to do alluvial dredging on the Macquarie River out from Wellington that they had to bring the electricity up from Lithgow through Stuart Town. So they decided they could give it to us too.

But we were one of the first towns to get automatic telephones. The government wanted to try it out, so they used Stuart Town because they had a postwoman there and there were about twenty phones on the line. We had one in the shop. I had a mate. It was after I'd grown up. He was Australian, round about twenty, and he worked for us in the shop. One day he heard my father speaking to someone in Wellington on the telephone in Chinese. He walked up to me and he said, 'How the heck can you speak Chinese on an English telephone?'

My father's name was really Wong Wah Lai but the Australians called him Tom Lee and the family surname became Lee. But he thought the surname was Tom as Chinese surnames come first. So my brother was registered as Tom Lee and I became Tom Hoy. Our sister was Louie Lee (黃來弟). But our surname in Chinese is really Wong. It was only after my father passed away that I adopted the surname of Lee by deed poll. My father could read and write Chinese but he didn't know much English. He kept the accounts for the shop in Chinese and he wrote the names of the customers in Chinese the way he thought they should be written. Just their first names, Bill or Jack.

As I said, my mother had bound feet, she was not able to do anything. So my father had a pretty hard life too. He had to open the shop at half past seven in the morning. In those days in a country town you sold anything and everything – groceries, vegetables, some hardware or a bit of drapery. Transport was very bad and anyone who lived in the area bought things locally. There were no cars. If you wanted anything you got it at the local shop or they would get things in for you. Later on, when cars were more common, people would travel to Wellington for shopping. When you live at the shop it never really closes. After it was closed at night, anyone wanting something would see a light in the house and knock on the back door. You really did not have any free time.

My father did all the cooking, because he used to be the cook at Fong Lee in Wellington. Being Chinese, he cooked us a hot breakfast. Either rice porridge or

Figure 18.1. The town of Ironbarks, c. 1880s. (Mitchell Library, State Library of NSW)

rice. We had no lunch but we had a cooked tea. You wouldn't get your tea till after he'd closed the shop though. In the summer months, the butcher could only kill two sheep. There was no refrigeration. If he killed a bullock, he'd have no chance of selling his meat. The population was too small. So we used to have mutton or something like that. My father would have to cook a Chinese meal, so he would open a tin of corned beef and cook it with whatever vegetables were available. If you wanted pig's trotters, well, you opened a tin of pig's trotters. You had everything in tins. He cooked on an open fireplace inside the house. There was a fire down below and two bars of steel across the top. You put your pot on the two bars.

Beliefs

All my mother's ideas were what she learned as a child in China. There were two churches in Stuart Town, Church of England and Catholic. We children went to

Figure 18.2. Wong Wah Lay Family, 1927. Standing (left to right): Hoy Lee, Louie Lee, Tommy Lee. Seated (left to right): Wong Wah Lay, Lum Dai with baby Norman, Pearl Lee. (Googan family)

the Church of England and Sunday school but my parents did not believe in that. My mother used to worship the moon. Because she couldn't speak English, all her thoughts were Chinese you see. When I was going to Sunday school as a child, I asked her about it. She told me that the moon governs the tide, the tide governs the seasons and the seasons govern your crops. So if you haven't got a good season, you starve. Therefore, you worship the moon to govern all those things. If you have anything left, then you have your festival to the moon, you give to the moon. That is why I do not argue with anyone about it today. She always prayed to the spirits on the first and fifteenth of each lunar month. My father used to drink some rice wine every night. He would pour it into a bowl and the first thing he'd do, he'd put his chopsticks in and splash some wine on the floor. That was drink for the spirits to bring good luck. He always done that and waited before he drank himself.

Because the other kids had a Christmas celebration, we had one too, but not to the same extent. We got our stockings and something from Santa Claus. Then my mother used to celebrate Chinese New Year and that. We didn't celebrate that much. My mother always used to pray to the spirits. We would have a big dinner the night before. We'd have a fowl and mandarins and oranges as well as rice wine. She did it in the China fashion. On New Year's Day we had vegetarian food. We were given lucky money. But my mother always celebrated the moon festival (中秋節), the fifteenth day of the eighth lunar month. She would make offerings to the moon then. You couldn't get moon cakes in Stuart Town. You'd never have moon cakes unless someone came from Sydney or sent them to us.

Home cooking

In those days you could not even buy ground rice. My mother used to grind the rice herself. With bound feet, she wasn't able to get around and do much, but she could sit and turn the millstone. I think whenever she was in the mood, she would make rice flour dim sims (點心) for us. We had a stone mill from China. I've still got it. After my mother and father passed away, my brother brought it down to Sydney. His daughter took it to Shepparton where her husband had a restaurant. But after her mother-in-law died, Joyce said she had no use for it and brought it back. It's lying out in the yard now.

My mother used to make *chaah siu bao* (叉燒包, barbecued pork buns) for us too. My father would make the *chaah siu* (叉燒, barbecued pork) and my mother would go over to the baker's shop and ask for a piece of dough from the bread making. She never made her own dough. We didn't celebrate the boat race festival (端午節), but we would have sticky rice puddings which you're supposed to have then. My mother always looked after that type of thing. Lots of times it might not have been on the day of the occasion, just when we had the stuff to do it.

You couldn't buy beef every day, so Pop had a lot of fowls and ducks running down the yard. You'd kill your own duck, then you would roast it. Your pot wasn't big enough to cook your chicken or roast the duck, or to make *chaah siu*, so he built a round brick oven in the yard. The oven was covered with mud on the outside. There was a little hole at the bottom to drag the ashes out where you put a brick. When you fired the oven, you put a brick in to keep it hot and threw ashes over it. He hung the meat down from a bar of steel.

In order to stop it from burning he placed a camp oven with water in the bottom of the oven, on top of the coals, to catch the fat. To keep the heat in he would throw a big tin dish with a wet bag over it over the top of the oven. He knew about how long it would take to cook. The dripping from the *chaah siu* would fall into the camp oven which had water in it, so it wouldn't burn. The Eurasians used to like to come up and have Chinese meals with us.

Cars

When we had visitors from Wellington, because they had a motor car or hired a car, Pop would catch a fowl and he'd have it on the table in two hours. There was always boiling water all the time. If you got the boiling water on, you'd catch a chook, kill it in twenty minutes. He used to prepare a quick meal.

We never had a car until after I started working. We had a bicycle to use in the shop before that, but I don't remember having my own bike when I was little. My first ride in a motor car was when I was seven or eight and my sister a couple of years older. Some Chinese in Dubbo hired a motor car and came down to visit us. We wanted to have a ride, so on their return trip they took my sister and me with them for about a mile down the road then they dropped us off and we had to walk back.

School

We three children went to the primary school in Stuart Town, which had about fifty or sixty students and two teachers. There was a Catholic school too with about thirty or forty because there was a Catholic church. The priest came out from Wellington. The other church was Church of England, which had a minister, where we went to Sunday school every now and again. When you finished sixth class, you went into the seventh class and you sat there all day doing nothing. You got your qualifier's certificate when you were about thirteen. After that the teacher wasn't bothered with you. He'd give you something to do, just kept you there till it come Christmas time. He couldn't care. He was only paid to teach. End of the year you were fourteen and you left. There were two teachers, a man and a girl. I suppose they were good teachers, but it was up to you, whether you wanted to learn or not. When I was fourteen and a half, I left school too. It was the same with my brother and sister. We never went to high school. The high school was at Wellington, twenty-two miles away, so we couldn't go. There'd be a train at six o'clock in the morning and a train back at eight o'clock at night. Today they run buses in for the schoolchildren.

Stuart Town was a small place when I was at school. When I was a little kid we never went anywhere. We would only go to Wellington once a year and that was to go to the Wellington Show.

My parents reckoned I was a *faahn gwai jai* (番鬼仔, foreign devil or barbarian kid) when I was growing up. I got on well with Australians all my life. I used to be running off, playing all the time with English kiddies, just coming home for meals and other things. As I grew older, I wanted to play cricket and tennis when I think my father thought I should stay at home and do some work in the shop.

Local business

In those small towns like Stuart Town, people had to buy everything locally. You had to give credit to a certain degree. A lot of local people were seasonal workers and when the shearers were away we would always give credit to the families. The

Fong Lee store in Wellington had customers who were wheat farmers or wool farmers and they would only get an annual cheque so they'd have to carry them.

We were the only Chinese shop. There used to be about two other general stores that done the same kind of business. But we relied on the Eurasians and part-Aboriginal people. I don't know why. Maybe we being Chinese treated them a bit more sociably and politely and the Australians maybe looked down on them. We did not get such a big percentage of the Australian trade. Pop used to order Chinese groceries from a Jaang Sheng business in Sydney for our own use every month. Soy sauce we would get in an earthenware container, probably imported from China. The Eurasians would buy some of this off us too. They bought a lot of bean vermicelli, dried shrimps and fermented bean curd. They used to eat the preserved bean curd with bread and butter, made sandwiches with it. This was their culture, because they were Eurasians. They'd learned from their elders.

The Eurasians were descendants of the Chinese gold diggers and Australian women. Now there's many generations of them. You see, the Chinese miners were at Mookerawa and that's where the Eurasians were born, so the majority lived in that area and then they spread out. We grew up with them. The part-Aboriginal people lived at a small settlement called Farnham, a few miles from Mookerawa.

The main Chinese Australian families were Lee, Cohen, Davis and Dong. There was Sarah and Jack Dong, and the brother Fred Dong. There were a whole string of Cohens in the early days, eight or nine or ten kids. There were four Lang boys. Their father was a shearer. The Foxhalls had seven or eight kids. They would come home for Christmas. We'd have a cricket match, with a keg of beer. In Stuart Town they did whatever work their parents did. Quite a few joined the army. If it hadn't been for the war, I wouldn't have left Stuart Town either. The others never intended to leave. Nowadays the grandchildren hardly ever come back.

The Chinese shops around where we were didn't just deal with Jaang Sheng businesses in Sydney. For groceries, we would buy from companies like John Bardsley & Co. and D. Mitchell & Co. and the same with drapery. They would have representatives come round and take your orders.

The only other foreigners in Stuart Town were two Indian hawkers with a horse and cart. One of them used to go to Sydney occasionally to places like Nock & Kirby and buy odds and ends, same with clothing and that sort of thing, which they'd put in their shop or go round hawking.

Employment

You take a little place like Stuart Town. I can only remember two Chinese that were market gardeners because the soil there is not really suitable for market gardening. Probably the gold days had run out and they just lived there, so they grew a few vegetables. So a lot of the people were seasonal workers. They'd go away shearing. The husband would be away for a few weeks in the hot weather from October to

February. Even in Wellington, there were a lot of wheat farmers. When the shearing season stopped they would do a bit of rabbiting or bush work.

Rabbiting was a fairly good industry. In those days there was no such thing as myxomatosis. Rabbit skins were a pretty good price. When there was no really good work, the locals would get their rabbit traps out. There was always someone buying rabbits at the railway station. They would put them on the train and take them into Orange or Wellington and freeze them. Then they'd sell them on the Sydney market. The locals skinned the rabbits first and sold the carcasses. The skins were always sold because in the winter months when there would be no shearing or other farm work, the rabbit skins would be at their top price. They would have their winter coats on and be better value than in the summer. We didn't deal in rabbits, but we sold rabbit traps or strychnine or quince jam which was used to poison the rabbits.

I think the Eurasians had to battle pretty hard to get a living, but at least they worked hard and they survived. In those early days there were no such thing as the dole. You had to go and work, and work for a low wage. People with land wanted to clear the land. Trees would have to be ringbarked and then every twelve months saplings would grow, they would have to do sucker cutting. It was all seasonal work, casual farm labour. There was no such thing as permanent jobs. I don't think many landholders ever had permanent hands to do work. Everything was done on casual labour and wages were very, very low. Even when there was the dole in the Depression, the dole in those days was very cheap.

When I came to Sydney to work at Hardman & Halls at Newtown in 1942, there were fellows I used to play sport with who couldn't come down with me because they had jobs, ringbarking or sucker cutting. They had to work five and a half days a week. They had to work half a day Saturday, then catch their horses and ride home. They'd get home at three or four o'clock. They would have to ride back out again to their jobs on Sunday afternoon, take their food out to be on the job at daybreak on Monday morning. They camped on the station. They'd come home on Saturday and go back out on Sunday. They'd have to take bread that was baked on Friday to last them until they came back the next week. The stations only gave them what they called meat. So much a week plus their meat. Probably the meat was only what they didn't want off the sheep that were killed. A landowner didn't want to kill too many sheep. In those days, food wasn't that plentiful.

Race relations

All my life I've had pretty good relationships with Australians because I played sport, cricket and tennis, and went out with them on the weekends. They invited me to their parties. We didn't have many parties ourselves. But being Chinese, I would imagine my parents might have found it a little hard because there was a bit of racial thing in those days. There was some racial feeling among the children. We were all of course 'Ching Chong Chinaman'. Where there's kids, they always look down on you. We had our fights. They called you things, but you sort of turned a deaf ear to them, to a certain extent. We got used to it, see.

Fortunately, after I grew up, I worked in Stuart Town for quite a number of years, in our own business. During the war I was walking down the street in Orange, not Stuart Town. A bloke there had a couple of beers in him. He wouldn't have said anything if he wasn't drunk. He looked at me and he said, 'I have me doubts about you.' He didn't know whether I was a Chinaman or a Jap. But he wouldn't have said that if he were sober.

This is my belief. You get a little kid that cannot speak and doesn't know black from white. That child would be friendly. It's only when the kiddie gets older that his mother will say, 'If you play up a blackfellow or a Chinaman will get you.' I got nieces, they're over sixty now, but I knew them before they were born. They used to get a few ding dong bats, all this type of jive kids used to call them. See, that went right through the generations.

I would say the Eurasians were tolerated. We called them *sap jat dim* (十一點).[5] They were more Australian in outlook. They went to church and took part in the local activities. They were born in the area and in those small country towns, you knew everyone. If you were a neighbour from childhood, you were accepted. There were a lot of intermarriages, not arranged. Not many Eurasians married Chinese. Even in my time the Eurasian women I knew were older than me. Their families are all intermarried with white Australians now. In a lot of the country towns, when there're four or five generations, well, if you want to fight with one, you'd probably take on the whole crowd. One would be married to someone who's related to someone else.

Most of the Chinese that I knew in my childhood were in gardening. In those days because you were Chinese you weren't able to work in any trade or occupation, you weren't wanted, you couldn't get in. They had to work for each other. It's only in the latter years have the Chinese, in my experience anyhow, been given a free hand in their occupations.

Roy Stewart Lee

Roy Lee was born in Stuart Town of a Eurasian mother and a Chinese father. Although he was a brilliant student, came top of Orange High School, he suffered discrimination because of his colour. He joined the Anglican church and from Sydney University he went on to gain a PhD at Oxford. He and his family eventually settled in England, where he held a number of church positions, including vicar of the University Church in Oxford for fourteen years.[6]

---

5   This would appear to be a phrase used in Australia. It could be translated as eleven point or eleven o'clock, i.e. not the full dozen.

I didn't know Roy Lee himself. By the time I grew up a little bit, he was going to high school in Orange and from there he left Stuart Town for Sydney. But I knew his mother and his stepsisters. His mother was Mary Dong and her mother was Australian. There were six girls and three boys in the Dong family. Mary Dong married a Chinese, Ma Kwei Gee, and he adopted the name of Lee. They had two sons, Roy Lee, and I forget the name of the younger brother. Well, Ma Kwei Gee went back to China and did not return. So Mary Dong gave her house in Stuart Town to her brother, Jack Dong, who was married to Sarah Dong, the midwife, and moved to Mookerawa to live with her sister, who was married to Higgy Cohen. My father always called that house Ma Kwei Gee's house. Later on, Mary Dong remarried Higgy Cohen's brother, Tommy Cohen, and they had three girls. I remember meeting Tommy Cohen. During the First World War he came home from the army on leave and my uncle, Wong Wah Hum (黃華欽), took a lot of his photos. I was only six or seven at the time. But after he went back to the army he was killed in action.[7] The Cohens were Eurasians too. Their father's name was Kwong, I think. My father used to call him Fook Gong Kwong. He must have come from some place called Fook Gong. They anglicised it to Cohen.

Depression

Even before the Depression you had a lot of people who were called tramps. They would carry their swags and walk from place to place. They'd go to a station and beg for a meal and for something to do. They didn't have money. One fellow I can remember used to walk the roads chasing food. He walked through Stuart Town every November on his way down to Orange. He reckoned he'd get two weeks cherry picking there and that'd be enough to last him for the rest of the year. Because he would beg his food. It was only when he wanted something he couldn't beg that he would buy it. He'd go from station to station, farmstead to farmstead, and beg and that'd see him through. I think a lot of people lost their lives and no one would know about it. These men would camp under a bridge, then there'd probably be an argument. Someone would get knocked off, they'd get rid of the body and no one would know. No records.

Things were pretty hard in those days. Gold was very scarce. A Welshman told me he carried his swag off the goldfields and it wasn't unusual they wouldn't have any tea to drink. So when you made your pot of tea, you dried your tea leaves and used them again. Many of the poor women had to go and catch a few rabbits and then get some vegetables to try and make a stew. There were no handouts. People

---

6   The Rev. Roy Stuart Lee was vicar of the University Church of St Mary the Virgin in Oxford from 1947 to 1961.
7   In November 2020 the Australian government announced that the remains of Private Thomas Cohen had been identified. He had been killed in France in September 1918 shortly before the end of the war and buried in an 'unknown soldier' grave.

had no luxuries. They were lucky to get bread and dripping, bread and syrup, just the bare necessities. Even before the Depression days, I think there were a lot of families that had more mealtimes than meals. There was no work and there was nothing to be given out.

The dole started in about 1929 when the Depression began. Not for Chinese, because they couldn't get the dole. During the Depression, a lot of young Australians came from Sydney to Stuart Town to live because it was an old gold mining area. They would get the dole each fortnight and in between they'd do a bit of fossicking. They said they could not get the dole and live at home. The government would not give you the dole if you lived at home with your parents. You had to leave home. At Stuart Town they could fossick for gold and get a little bit of extra money to help them with their dole. Like everyone else, I also went fossicking when I was young and foolish, but I never found any gold.

The police administered the dole in those days. There was one police sergeant and one constable at Stuart Town. If someone went to the police station to get the dole, he would get a coupon from the policeman. He would bring that down to the shop and sign a voucher to say he had received such and such goods. Then we would send the account to an office in Sydney for payment. But the dole vouchers were issued by the policemen. You see, in a little country town like Stuart Town there's no other government offices.

A lot of young people used to 'jump the rattler'. They would travel by train. Because at first you could get the dole any day of the week at police stations, they might get the dole today at Orange, then jump on the train and come to Stuart Town, get off and go to the police station and get the dole. Then they'd get on the train again and go to Wellington. They'd get the dole two or three or four times a week. After the government realised that they only used to give them the dole once every two weeks.

Then the government cut the dole out and gave relief work. A single man would get two weeks' work in eight, and a married man probably two weeks in four. I think in Stuart Town we done fairly well because there was the dole and unemployment relief work. I don't know if any Chinese got the dole. But sometime after that my brother got the pension for a few of the elderly Chinese in the gardens in Wellington. He was a Justice of the Peace and they could talk to him. They weren't game to ask anyone else. He used to do a lot of that work. Some didn't apply because they came to Australia with someone else's paperwork. I asked one man I knew why he wasn't retired as he was about seventy. He said he'll never be able to get to retiring age of sixty-five as his paperwork says he was only about forty years old!

Returned soldiers

Some of the blokes around Stuart Town were returned soldiers from World War One. Their nerves were gone. Take a bloke on the dole and he'd only get two weeks'

Figure 18.3. The Yee Lee General Store (Richard Horsburgh)

work in eight. That meant he only got four pound a week, he only got eight pounds for eight weeks. He had to live within that. They liked to drink and he wanted a drink badly. So he'd go into the shop and get a tin of salmon, which cost a shilling on credit. He'd take it somewhere and sell it for sixpence to go and buy a beer. When they needed a drink badly, they'd do anything.

One fellow, Kelly, he came down and wanted a tin of salmon. He'd been in the bush, was sort of rough and ready. I'd say to him, 'No, you can't have a tin of salmon because your credit is getting behind.' Then he'd say, 'But I'm hungry.' So I'd say, 'All right, if you want a tin of salmon, I'll open it for you. I'll put the billy on, give you some bread and butter and you can have a meal here out in the kitchen.' Then he would say, 'But I'm not hungry yet. I want it when I go home.' He wanted to sell it, so I wouldn't give it to him.

Then one day he came in and asked for ten shillings. He'd been arrested for being drunk. He said there was a ten-shilling bail on him. He wanted to pay his bail. But the policeman let him out, see. He was much older than me, a returned digger. I gave him the ten shillings and he never came back again. Then another bloke told me Kelly only had five shillings bail on him. So I waited till I caught him outside and I tackled him. I said, 'You come and borrow ten bob off me for bail. You only had five bob bail on you and you told me ten bob. You were telling me a lie. Don't ever come back to me again.'

There were five or six of them who used to come and pay their accounts when they got their relief money. They always paid their accounts. We had to stop up till the mail train came in at eight o'clock in the evening. They went to Wellington either to do road construction, work on the railway line, or bridge building, and got paid in the afternoon. But they had to wait for the evening train to come back. If you didn't wait for the train, you shut up at six o'clock when you were supposed to, they'd be at the pub the next morning drinking all their money. So we had to keep the shop open and they'd come and square their accounts. Kelly was the last bloke to get served. He said to me, 'Come outside, I'd like to see you.'

I went out and we stood there. Kelly dug into his bag and picked out a package of grapes. He said, 'Now you're cranky with me because I told you a lie. If I had told you the truth, that I only had five shillings bail and wanted another five shillings for beer, you wouldn't have given it to me.' Then he said, 'What could I do? I had to tell a lie. Here's a few grapes, will you forget it?' So I said, 'All right,' and I shook hands with him. He paid me back, see. They were honest blokes, but their nerves were gone from the war.

Dad's brothers

My father was the first of his brothers to come to Australia. Then because he had gone to the golden mountain, the others wanted to come too. Three others came, also to work in Fong Lee in Wellington. One was Wong Wah Gee (黃華智). Later he left Fong Lee and went to Cobar to trade. He didn't know what name to call his business, so having worked for Fong Lee, he called his shop Fong War Lee (芳華利). He and his wife had two daughters and a son, my cousins. The son set up a food shop in Blackheath in the Blue Mountains. But Wong Wah Gee passed while he was visiting his son in 1930. The wife and the two daughters had his body embalmed and took it back to China. They sold the business before they went. They buried my uncle in China, but the Japanese came and knocked the graves down and used the headstones to make footpaths. As a result, I don't think my cousins now know where their father was buried.

It wasn't till 1988 that I found out by accident that one of the sisters, Ivy Low, now in her late eighties, lives at Woy Woy and I go up and see her. She returned from China after the war but went to New Zealand before coming back to Australia, where her son Ken Low is now a medical doctor.

Years later, in the 1950s, I was being treated for TB at a hospital in Wentworth Falls in the mountains and I got talking just by accident to a chap who said he once embalmed a Chinaman. That was my uncle!

Another brother was Wong Wah Shu (黃華樹). He retired from Wellington and went back to China, where he passed away. Then there was Wong Wah Hum. He was single. He may have had a China wife, I don't know. He passed away in Wellington.

There was still another brother, Wong Wah Yee (黃華義), but he was older than my father, and he came out later.[8] He used to work for his brothers and he didn't work hard. He saved all his money and he went back to China quite a few times. I remember him telling my father when they caught up at Chinese New Year about his trips. He'd go steerage, you know, the cheapest way.

My parents never went back to China again. I think my father was too busy trying to make a living. I don't know what was in the back of his mind. Although they had to work hard, we were fairly comfortable. But still money was pretty tight, so we never travelled much, didn't go anywhere, just lived in the one area.

Wellington

Wellington had a fairly big Chinese population because it had the rich river flats and a lot of Chinese had gardens there. Property was pretty cheap in the early days and they actually bought the land. They used to employ a lot of Chinese casual labour. Now I realise that those Chinese in Wellington, Dubbo and further out all came from the same part of China as my parents, from Jaang Sheng and Tung Koon, because the gardens were owned by people from those counties and they knew one another. Some of the wives came from China. There were the Ah Yooks, the Mow Fungs, the Loo Siks and so on. I don't think the women had bound feet. My mother was about the only one. There could have been ten or more gardens, which meant there was a lot of seasonal work in the different towns. The men would get enough work around Wellington and Dubbo. Dubbo had river flats too. There were no flats in Stuart Town.

Near the river in Wellington there was a place where the gardeners would stop, where they could get a bed and cook. They called it *daah lan gung* (打攬工, doing labouring).[9] My father used to point it out to me. He'd say, 'that's a *daah lan gung* place'. When they grew tobacco, there'd be the cutting of the tobacco, so they'd have to have labour. They grew good tobacco in the Wellington area as well as all sorts of vegetables, mostly catering for local businesses in Wellington, Dubbo and Orange. Nowadays, with modern cultivation, they concentrate on one particular thing. They

---

8   NAA: ST84/1, 1917/211/71-80. A Statutory Declaration within this National Archives file shows that in fact Wong Wah Yee was the first brother to arrive in Australia, arriving in 1879. Other family records show that he established the Yee Lee general store in Stuart Town with Hoy's father Wong Wah Lai in 1891. Four years later Wah Yee sold his share to Wah Lai and returned to China. He came back to Australia and worked for many years in Sydney as well as with his brothers in Stuart Town, Cobar and Wellington.

9   This phrase refer to 'seasonal workers who do hard work'. It has not been possible to verify the middle Chinese character; it could also be 打纜工.

still grow a lot of beans and tomatoes that they sell to Edgells for processing.[10] In the early days you could get labour to do weeding and harvest the crops but now you use machinery. Years ago, Wellington had an Aboriginal mission fairly close to the gardens. The Chinese could get the Aboriginal people to come. But today the Aboriginal people won't do seasonal work.

There was one family in Wellington, the Coons, with about eight children. They had all the family picking the beans and there were quite a few other Chinese families around with four or five children. But they still had to employ labour. They employed Chinese labour if it was available, but as the years grew on, the Chinese got too old or retired, or went back to China. But now there's not too many Chinese gardeners even around Dubbo or Wellington. The children are working in jobs where you haven't got to do manual labour. In the early days they didn't have the education for that. They are no longer interested in gardening. A lot of the families that used to be in gardening have drifted away.

I wouldn't say the people in gardening have entirely disappeared. In the early days land was fairly cheap. The Chinese did not throw their money around. If there was any adjoining property for sale, they would buy it. Therefore, they would have too much land. Someone told me that later one of the children of the Coon family I knew worked in a bank in Wellington, but because their parents had land, they can still put in a crop. They work the land on the weekend. They make some extra money.

Another case, George Coon, retired from his grocery business in Coolah and went back to China. But the Japanese came, they took his money and he was broke. So he and his family of about seven children had to come back. His brother-in-law offered the use of some land at Wellington. The family went there and grew beans against the advice of the other gardeners in Wellington. Because the gardeners in Wellington usually grow their beans about Chinese New Year and harvest for the Easter market. The previous year the Sydney market was very low and the gardeners in Wellington decided it wasn't worth putting in beans. He had about seven children, the kids picked the beans, he got a good price and they have never looked back. Some of the Chinese gardeners ended up with big houses in town.

When my brother and I were running the shop at Stuart Town, we used to visit Wellington and pull up and have a chat with Tommy Coon and his wife, who ran a roadside stall. Any vegetables that they grew themselves they would give to us. They had to buy in other vegetables to run the stall and those you had to pay for. The Chinese gardeners in Wellington used to tell us to be sure and call because they couldn't sell everything and there was a bit of waste. We used to go to quite a few of the gardens. A lot of them were related to us. They were all from Jaang Sheng and Tung Koon.

Besides gardening, there were about three big Chinese general shops like Fong Lee that sold groceries, drapery, ironmongery and all that, see. Then there were

---

10 The Edgell canning company was established by the Edgell family in Bathurst, NSW, in 1926 and expanded to a second cannery in Cowra in 1943.

Figure 18.4. Wong Wah Lay & Lum Dai, 1927. (Googan family)

probably another three who sold fruit and vegetables. That seemed to be the main industry for the Chinese other than the gardens.

Funeral traditions

Because there were so many Chinese working in the gardens at Wellington, occasionally one would pass away. A Christian burial service would first be held in a local church. Then there would be a Chinese service at the Chinese section in Wellington cemetery. This service would take place after the body was put in the grave but before it was filled in. A local man, Ah Yook, handled this because he knew what to do. Actually, Ah Yook was married to a Wong from Jaang Sheng, related to the Wongs in Fong Lee & Co. The Chinese in Wellington would roast a pig. Ah Yook had an oven on the side of the riverbank. They would also have a boiled fowl. These offerings were made to the spirit of the deceased. After that, they would cut up the roast pork and everyone would eat some. If there was any surplus they would take it home. A lot of English people used to go to the ceremony at the cemetery. It was like a wake. They burned incense and gave everyone there two pennies to buy some candy to take away the taste of bitterness. Firecrackers would be let off. A bowl of rice would be left with a bowl where they put some wine. There's a portion of the Wellington cemetery where the Chinese are buried. In the early days, the Chinese used to dig up the graves and send the bones of their clansmen back to China. But they had to stop after the Japanese arrived.

The Jaang Sheng and Tung Koon people have got a property in Dixon Street.[11] They combined to buy it and manage it together. It was from there in the early days they used to get the remains of the bones of the Chinese to send back to China. It's next door to the old Lean Sun Low (联新楼) building. They would dig up all the remains of the Chinese people and put them into boxes and send them to Hong Kong. From Hong Kong they were transferred to the villages. That's all they did until the war. I didn't see them do it, but I did know someone who did that. My brother-in-law was sent to China during his schooling days and he had a good knowledge of Chinese and Chinese culture. He took a lot of interest in that property in Dixon Street and I used to hear talk about what was going on.

Deaths in the family

My father worked in the Stuart Town business until he died in 1936. He was in his seventies. After he passed away, my mother wanted to go back to China. She told my brother Tommy that she wanted me to go back with her. He was married with children but I was not married then so it would have been easier for me. She might not have wanted me to stay there, but she wanted me to take her home so that she could stay there. My brother could take care of the shop and I could go with her. But the Japanese attacked China and it was too late. She couldn't go then.

After my father's death, my brother and I ran the shop together. He was already married and had two girls and a boy. My sister Louie had married a Chinese man named Peter Googan (劉顯材) and moved to Sydney.[12] Although he was born in

---

11   The Luen Fook Tong (聯福堂), a society for Jaang Sheng people, and the Goon Yee Tong (公義堂), a society for Tung Koon people, were formed in the second half of the nineteenth century. In 1899 members from both societies formed a third association, Loong Yee Tong (聯義堂). In 1916, the joint association purchased land in Dixon Street and built three three-storey adjoining buildings at 50, 52 and 54 Dixon Street.

Australia, he could speak good Chinese because he went to China as a child. They later ran the Eastern restaurant in Dixon Street for a number of years. During the war my brother continued to run the shop in Stuart Town while I came down to Sydney in 1942 and worked in the defence industry for an English munitions firm, Hardman & Hall, in Newtown. I boarded with a Chinese family in Liverpool. The lady had come from Wellington but had married a fellow named Percy Nom Chong from Braidwood. The Nom Chongs were a large family in Braidwood from early days and that's where Quong Tart (梅光達) came from too.

My mother died at the end of the war in 1945. She and my father are buried in the Chinese section of the cemetery in Wellington. After her death my brother decided he would sell the business in Stuart Town and move to Sydney. His wife had already passed away many years before at a fairly young age. Two of their three children had married and gone away, leaving one daughter at home. His daughter stayed with him till she married and went to Dubbo. In Sydney, my brother worked for the railways doing clerical work. But he had a stroke in the 1950s and passed away in his late fifties.

My sister has passed away too. She had four daughters and three sons. Two of the sons died. One of the daughters married an Australian and lives in Perth. The others all married Chinese. I'm the only one left now.

Wu Hop Trading Company

After the war, a second cousin of mine, Les Ling (黃吳蘇), suggested that I work for a new Chinese firm, Wu Hop (五合). He was their auditor. Les was the eldest son of William Suey Ling (黃瑞麟), who ran Fong Lee at Wellington at one time. Wu Hop wanted someone who could speak Chinese and do bookkeeping. I'd done a postal course in Sydney in bookkeeping with the Metropolitan Business College. Apart from working for our family business, Wu Hop was the first and only Chinese firm I ever worked for. It was all right. They paid me better than the munitions firm. I was there for nineteen and a half years, until I retired.

You see, lots of merchant seamen from Hainan Island were working on boats and caught in Australia when Hainan was occupied by the Japanese. They were allowed to stay. After the war they became cooks and opened restaurants. Chinese meals were then becoming popular and frozen prawns were in demand. But there was a monopoly of the prawn trade and supplies were uncertain. A man named A.J. Arena ran the prawn business, dealing in local Australian prawns. If you weren't a regular customer, sometimes he wouldn't sell to you. Meanwhile China started to export frozen prawns, so some of these ex-Hainanese seamen decided to

---

12   Victor Peter Googan, who owned and operated the Eastern restaurant in Dixon Street next door to the Lean Sun Low cafe. The Eastern was the first Dixon Street cafe to cater for a broader Australian clientele and to obtain a liquor licence.

set up the Wu Hop Trading Company and import their own supplies to keep their restaurants open. They got the aid of a few other Chinese who knew a bit more about doing business in China.

It became a pretty big company because in those days there weren't many people selling frozen prawns. Of course, the Chinese here wanted to buy with Chinese firms. So Wu Hop served a wide range of customers, not only in Sydney, but in the country towns. You take Dubbo. It's one of the biggest towns in New South Wales. It started off with one Chinese restaurant, now there're seven or eight. Today there's hardly a cooked prawn that is peeled, cooked and processed in Australia. Labour is too expensive. All the prawns served in Chinese restaurants are either from India or Singapore or somewhere like that. Wu Hop imported all sorts of things including frogs' legs and tinned cashews, both from India.

The country Chinese customers of Wu Hop would come down to Sydney every now and again. When they were here, they would come into the shop and ask how much they owed. I'd tell them and they'd go away and come back later with cash. I don't think they went to a bank. They would have gone down to Dixon Street to one of their clan associations who were holding money for them.

Years ago, hardly anyone went to Chinese restaurants. It's only since the war that whenever a Chinaman comes to Sydney from Hong Kong, he opens up a Chinese restaurant. One of the first Chinese cafes in Dixon Street before or around the wartime was Lean Sun Low. You could get a meal on a Sunday for one shilling and sixpence. Then there was the Tiensin (天津) and the Shanghai (上海) up in Campbell Street and below there was the Hong Kong and the Canton. My uncle even had a restaurant up in Kings Cross called Wong Lee, which made the best spring rolls.

Marriage

I didn't get married till late in life and I married an Australian girl, Freda Mitchell. I took up Chinese cooking then because she liked Chinese food. We had actually met way back when I was living in Stuart Town. We had wanted to marry before the war, but her parents were against it. My parents wouldn't agree either as they thought I should marry a Chinese girl. Well after the war, I decided if I never got married then, I never would, so I put the question to Freda again. She took me on and we got married in 1960. We went back to Stuart Town for a real church wedding.

Freda's family ran the post office in Farnham for fifty-five years. All women. First her grandmother, then her mother, then Freda ran it until we got married. Freda's sister did it after her till the post office closed in 1970. Freda passed away in 1972 and is buried in Stuart Town.

Speaking Chinese

After I joined Wu Hop my Chinese improved a lot. When I came to Sydney my Chinese was very bad and when I wanted to converse with someone in Chinese I didn't know all the words. The Chinese then in Sydney were either Australian-born or Chinese that had come out before 1900. They would help me a lot because I could not speak Chinese.

But one of the drivers in Wu Hop was Hong Kong-born. He was a student and he used to laugh at me because my Chinese was no good. One day one of the restaurant owners rang up and wanted to add something to their order. He picked up the phone and the bloke told him what he wanted. 'So right,' he said, 'the bloke wants a pound of *ha mai* (蝦米, dried shrimps)'. We didn't sell them so we had to go over the street to buy some. When the driver delivered the order, the chap didn't want it. The fellow said because I couldn't speak Chinese, he tried to speak to me in English. He wanted a pound of 'halmonds' (almonds). But he was speaking to a Chinaman. After that when I was talking on the phone this driver would be sitting back laughing. Then I'd say, 'I'm buggered if that fellow wanted *ha mai* or *hung yun* (杏仁, almonds).' He stopped laughing then because he didn't want his mates to know he'd made a mistake.

None of my brother's children speak Chinese. They've lost all touch. My niece at Dubbo goes for a holiday somewhere every year. But now her husband says it's embarrassing to go to Hong Kong because the people there speak to him in Chinese and he cannot reply. Just the other day I was talking to a bloke about going to Hong Kong for a holiday. He too said being Chinese, the people there would speak to him in Chinese and he had to look up and say he couldn't speak. My own Chinese is still not very good. The last time I was in Hong Kong I rang up a cousin there, I think on my father's side, and asked him to come to the YMCA to see me. He had to ask me to ring someone else and tell him the address in English so that person could tell him in Chinese. Anyhow he turned up. We could converse slowly in Chinese. He tried to tell me how he was related to me but I couldn't follow him. I couldn't tell the difference between maternal uncle and paternal uncle. I got tangled up.

China

I was sixty-eight and not yet retired when I made my first trip out of Australia to China in 1978. A friend and I joined a tour arranged by the Chinese Youth League (僑青社). We were taken to communes, places of interest and beauty spots. But only what they wanted to show you. I found different Chinese at different places and we had trouble conversing with one another. Some couldn't speak Cantonese and some couldn't speak Mandarin and some could only speak this and that.

When we had a spare day in Canton, I thought I'd like to go and see where my father came from. I didn't know where it was and asked the Chinese lady who was guiding our group to help me get permission. She said she would take me and my friend at least to the area so I could see what it was like, since I didn't know anyone there. But she would have to find someone who knew that part of the country. She hired a cab and off we went. It took a little over an hour to get there. She must have contacted the local authorities because we went straight to their offices where we were invited in for a cup of tea. One of the local officials said he would show us the actual village. He got the taxi driver to take us down and wait for our return. We spent a couple of hours walking around, looking at all the shops and other facilities. Before we left, he said we should come back when the lychees (荔枝) were ripe, have a feed of lychees and *see mew mai* (細苗米, finely polished white rice).

My impression at the time was how fortunate I was that my father had migrated to Australia. The kids around the area were very poorly dressed in 1978, their clothes were ragged, they were dirty and all that. Maybe our family did not have much money but we did have plenty to eat.

However, ten years later I went back a second time and everything had changed. This time I went with my niece, Joyce, and her husband, Archie. Things had improved immensely. I learned more on my second trip than I did on all the touring I had made previously. We went on our own straight to Jaang Sheng and Tung Koon. The difference was we were with our own people. What happened was Archie contacted a cousin in Hong Kong, a high school principal, who got in touch with his people in Tung Koon, so they were expecting us. His cousin and two brothers had built a new three-storey house in Tung Koon. When we were there, they still didn't have sewerage or running water and that's why the cousin's wife wouldn't go there with him, but Archie himself has been there since and it's all installed now.

Success in Australia

After I moved down to Sydney I used to visit one of Roy Lee's sisters, Lily Cohen. She was a few years older than me. She came down to Sydney when she was about fifteen or sixteen and married an Australian bloke. We'd kept in touch because all the Cohens still lived in Stuart Town. I used to visit her on Melbourne Cup days. We'd have lunch and listen to the Melbourne Cup race together. Then a few years ago I met her granddaughter. She was going to Peking with a trade delegation and wanted to ask me a few questions about China. After her return I heard she'd gone off to Oxford. She'd been awarded a Rhodes scholarship. I felt so proud. Why? Because her grandparents were friends of mine. We all came from Stuart Town!

Figure 18.5. Hoy Lee and Freda Lee, 1960s. (Googan family)

Postscript

Following his interview with Mavis Yen, Hoy Lee was interviewed a number of times in the 1990s by historians who were fascinated by his memories of the Chinese communities in Stuart Town and the nearby larger centre of Wellington. Hoy was gregarious and photogenic; he performed as an extra in film and television shows in his later years, notably in the 1997 film *Oscar and Lucinda* starring Cate Blanchett. In 1997, Stuart Town celebrated the 140th anniversary of the Stuart Town Public School and the 100th anniversary of the Stuart Town Catholic School. Ninety-four-year-old Chinese Australian Amy Moore and eighty-seven-year-old Hoy Lee were invited to open the ceremony. Hoy Lee died in 2006 and is buried at Rookwood Cemetery in Sydney.

19
'We Grew Up in the Bush'
Albert Lee On

Albert Lee On (1916–unknown), also known later as Albert Leong/Leon, grew up in the north Queensland outback. Both his maternal grandfather, Sam Ah Bow (c. 1853–1932), and his father, Sam Lee On (c. 1855–c. 1939), landed in Darwin in the 1870s and crossed the Queensland border intending to head to the Palmer River goldfields, but settled instead in outback Queensland. His grandfather married an Aboriginal woman, Opal Maginmarm (c. 1866–1941), from Brunette Downs. Albert's grandfather, father and brothers all worked on the large sheep and cattle stations in northern Queensland, a world away from the rice fields of their ancestors. Even today, this is an exceptionally isolated part of Australia, being more than 1,000 kilometres from the nearest coastal cities of Cairns and Townsville, 2,000 kilometres from the state capital of Brisbane and 1,500 kilometres from Darwin, the capital of the Northern Territory.

On his birth certificate, Albert is registered as Ben Kong Lee On, born on 28 February 1916 at Louie Creek, Lawn Hill station, the son of Sam Lee On, a cook, and Lorna Ah Bow. Albert's father was absent from home for long periods working as a station cook, while his mother raised the children.

In the 1920s, his father bought a house in the Queensland–Northern Territory border town of Camooweal so that the younger children could go to school. The town only had about a hundred residents and they were the only Chinese family. Albert's older brothers were already working by then and together the family saved enough money to buy a roadside eatery business in Camooweal, which the father operated while the children attended the local bush school. They had no education in Chinese.

In order to escape his father's old-fashioned ways and the third-class citizenship conferred on Chinese at that time, Albert left home at age nineteen with a drover on a cattle run to South Australia, before working in Adelaide, Melbourne, Hobart and finally Sydney. The warmth extended to him by the Chinese communities in his travels led him to develop a lifelong interest in China. After the Second World War, he became a waterside worker in Sydney. Albert tells his story from an Australian perspective.

My family

I don't know much about my maternal grandfather. When the old Chinese used to talk to us, they said he came from around Canton. He was one of those who stayed on in the Gulf area after the gold rushes. My sister's grandkids were trying to trace our family. That's how I got a copy of Grandfather's marriage certificate. His name was Sam Ah Bow from Tai Po Kong (大埔港) in China. His father was Det Fung, a Chinese doctor. He became a cook at Lawn Hill station, which is between Camooweal and Burketown. Subsequently, he rented and cultivated a big garden at Lawn Hill.

At Lawn Hill he met and married an Aboriginal woman, Opal Maginmarm, who was also employed there. The date on my grandparents' wedding certificate was 5 May 1898 but they must have been together for a long time before that as my mother was nearly ten then and she had older sisters. According to their marriage certificate, Opal was born at Brunette Downs in the Northern Territory, the daughter of Cooloondoonowal, a hunter, and mother Budjagwe. Ah Bow and Opal had four daughters, who were among the earliest Chinese Aboriginal women in north Queensland. The third, Lorna, married my father Sam Lee On.

My father came to Australia from Hong Kong when he was eighteen years old. After landing in Darwin, he and two brothers walked to Daly Waters and Brunette Downs in the Northern Territory up to the Nicholson River, that's still Northern Territory. Then they crossed into Queensland to reach Normanton, Croydon and finally the Palmer River. The two brothers found it hard and returned home to China but my father decided to stay here. He became a cook and worked on stations. My father was a lot older than my mother. In fact, he was as old as my mum's father. She was probably about fifteen years old when they got married in 1905 although the wedding certificate says she was seventeen. When I was born in 1916, he was sixty-one years old and my mother was only twenty-seven. By then they already had three boys, Willie (nine), Johnny (seven) and Moody (five). I had an older sister too, Jessie, but they forgot to put her down on my birth certificate.

We stayed at my maternal grandfather's garden till we were little kids. Dad used to work on stations, cooking and gardening. Chinese those days could do anything, they could build houses, go cooking, do gardening. As we grew older, he realised that we had to go to school. So he brought us to a place called Camooweal,

19 'We Grew Up in the Bush'

Figure 19.1. Sam Lee On pictured about the time he returned to China in 1938. (J and M Wing collection, courtesy S. Canning)

near Mount Isa. It's a border town, nine miles from the Northern Territory and 139 miles from Mount Isa.

Ben Kong, that's my Christian names, because we all got Chinese names. Albert was only given to me. I never changed it. I was born in a leap year on 28 February. My mother told me I was born a couple of hours after midnight, so it should have been the 29th, actually leap year. But they didn't know too much about dates those days.

My birth certificate shows the nurse in attendance was registered as Oh Boo. That's my grandmother, Opal. They didn't bother with doctors those days, cause, you know, they could deliver. The only one that was born in a hospital was my last brother. We lived in the bush and we never had any doctors. Most people didn't. Just a midwife.

My grandfather and Opal had four daughters. The two eldest daughters got sent back to China. My mother was going to be sent back, but she didn't want to go to China. So she fled up in the hills, they got hills up in Lawn Hill. She stayed up there until her father went away to China. He came back but he left the two girls there. They never ever came back. We don't know what happened to them. My mother and another young sister stayed here.

We call her Aunt Dolly. She married a chap from Darwin, Ah Kup. He was a Chinese from China but for a Chinese he understood English very well. He used to do all the interpreting in court in Darwin. He had an interest in law – they all said he was a bit of a bush lawyer. They had four or five girls and they were living in Grandfather's garden when he died in about 1930. Well, there was a Chinese chap with a big shop in Cloncurry. He wanted to get married to one of the daughters, so he wrote to Ah Kup saying he could come and stay in his place. They passed through Camooweal just before I went droving. They lived at this fellow's place and of course the girls grew up but they had nothing to do with him. So this fellow sued Ah Kup for their board and keep and so forth. But Ah Kup had kept all the letters this Chinese chap sent to him, telling him he could stay there. This chap took him to court, but Ah Kup popped it over.

My mother died in 1928. She'd had polio. We didn't know what she had. Like, polio was unheard of in those days. After that she couldn't walk, but she kept on having children. I don't know what happened. Four died. I don't know if they had polio. She had my last brother and the next day she died. I don't think she was forty.

My older sister Jessie had to look after the baby. She was only fourteen. It was difficult. She didn't know the first thing to do. Anyway, she reared him up. She used to get advice from different older women around the town. We only had goat milk. The ladies at the town told her not to give the goat milk, it was too strong, to break it down. Anyway, she had to rear him up from a baby. It robbed her of her youth. Years later when my brother went to boarding school, he was about eight or ten, she married a half-Aboriginal, half-Chinese chap from Darwin. It was before the Second World War. He joined the army and became a boxer. He was a good fighter. If only he wasn't such a larrikin, he might have become a champion. Jessie had more connection with Chinese than we did. She was closer to my father. My father used to tell her things. She'd often say to me, 'Oh, the trouble with you boys, you wouldn't listen to Dad.'

My father used to work around stations, like he cooked and did gardening. So we never had much contact with him. Because he's working all the time. He'd be away for months. Then later on, my other two brothers went to work on the stations too. They saved up enough money to buy a shop at Camooweal. Then my father decided to give up working and we bought this little old house. You see, the two brothers kept on working on the stations. They were cooks. In those days Australians didn't like cooking. My father taught all of us how to cook and all

19 'We Grew Up in the Bush'

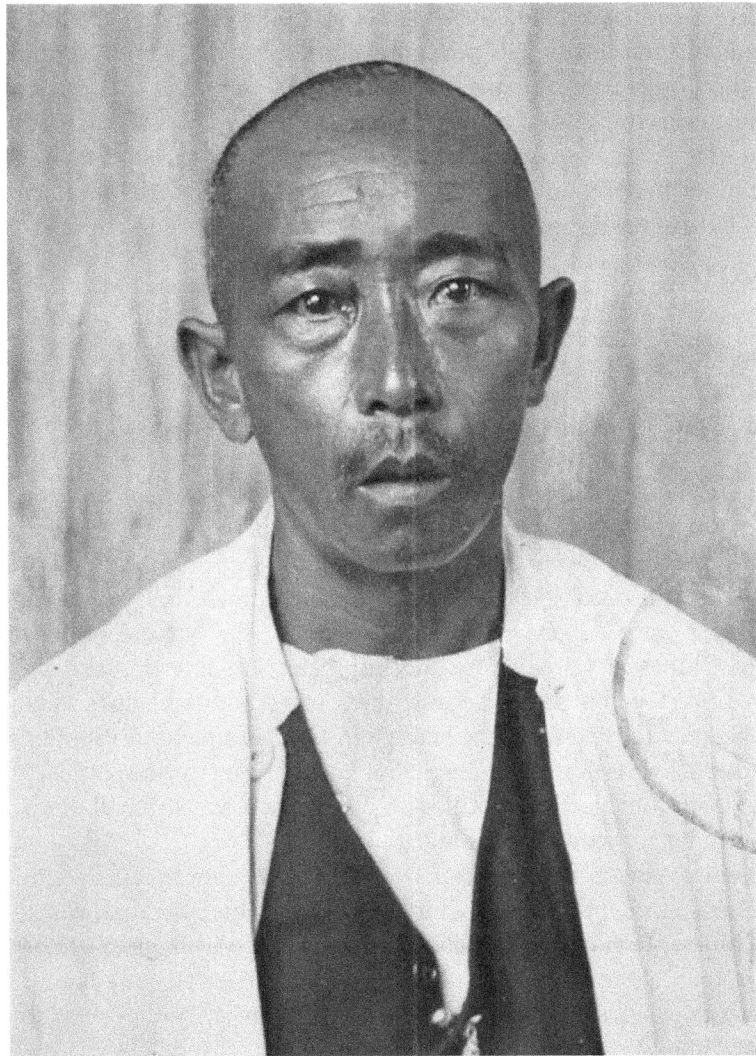

Figure 19.2. Sam Ah Bow, c. 1904. (National Archives of Australia: J2482, 1904/220)

about gardening. I'm no good cook, but in those days there wasn't much to cooking Australian style – just roast meat and things like that. It was good wages for those times. It wasn't worth good wages now. But those days it was very hard to get work and cooks were needed. The one thing Australians could never take on is cooking – they couldn't cook. So we were very lucky.

My first two brothers went out to the stations and did some cooking. Then my third brother, as soon as he grew up, he went cooking too, in the mines. He was a good cook. He used to get tips from other people, he wanted to become a chef. So we had three brothers keeping the shop going. In the old days the Chinese lived a close family turnout. Everybody put in the money. It was Depression time. We had the shop then, but we didn't make much money.

We sold everything. We had a grocer's shop, a restaurant, a baker's shop. Most of the trade we done was passing trade. People used to go through and they needed bread. A lot of people wanted something to eat. They could always come to our place. My father cooked any time of the day. He always had something to cook. We lived on the place so we were there, a twenty-four-hour service.

Camooweal

We were the only Chinese family there. About a hundred people lived in Camooweal. Later on they had a church. But they had a school with thirty to forty children. Only one teacher. That's all there was. There was only three outsiders at the school, the rest of them were Anglo-Saxons. There was my brother, my sister and myself from Chinese parents. And there was a couple of Aboriginal kids. Being a small town, you didn't feel that racial thing so much, but you could still feel it there. There wasn't many European migrants in the outback in those days, it was mostly Chinese, a few Chinese. Most of them were English, Irish and Scottish people. We didn't fight in school because the young Aboriginal bloke and myself, we were the biggest. They wasn't game enough to say anything to us. Not to this young Aboriginal bloke. I couldn't fight much, but I could beat any one of those chaps. We never had that problem in this local school because it was so small. Probably if we had been in a bigger school, it would happen.

My youngest brother went to a private boarding school years later in Charters Towers. He said he suffered being Chinese. He felt it there because, you know, they pick on Chinese. They called him 'chow', 'Ching Chong Chinaman', all that. He was my last brother. None of us others could go. But between all my family working, and my sister was working too then, as a cook on a station, so they sent him because they wanted to give one of us a good education.

We used to always have Chinese dishes in the night. It was always Chinese style. Just bloody old chop suey (雜碎) and all this quick Chinese fare. It was made up. My father used to make it up. The Chinese used to make things up, you know. They chopped everything up. When we were going to school, we used to just come and have a quick lunch – sandwiches, Australian. Even at breakfast we used to have porridge and stuff, English style. But we were disadvantaged because you couldn't have much variety at meals. We used to have our own goats, our own fowls, ducks, pigs, we had a bit of land.

When we went to Townsville we used to stay at a Chinese shop called Hook Lee Jeng. They always had a room somewhere for us. They used to put us out in the back shed. They had blankets and we'd just eat there. We used to eat some good Chinese food there. A lot of people would be there. We'd go out to a big table and they put the rice in a corner. We paid no rent. They would be speaking there and I wouldn't know what they was talking about. All I knew is I used to enjoy their food. There was another shop, it had the same name as ours, Lee On. We used to deal with them too, get fruit and things like that from Townsville. They would send it to us by train. We used to sell fruit, anything, to the districts.

We weren't the only business people in Camooweal. There were a couple of other stores. But you know what Chinese are like, they've got plenty of initiative. We could speak Chinese a little bit when we was children. My father always kept on talking to us in Chinese, but the trouble is we didn't have contact with him till later, when we got the shop and we were fairly big then. He was still working in the shop, doing the baking and I was doing the baking. We were the local baker – we made good bread, better bread than they make here in Sydney. Anyway, we had this shop and as we grew up we took it in turns to run it. Then my turn came.

Leaving home

But my father was a very old-fashioned Chinese. My three brothers and my sister could put up with him, but I couldn't. He was too dominating in the old Chinese way. We weren't living in China, we were living in Australia. I couldn't put up with the old Chinese way. So after I grew up I got a job on a station. There was a chap there they called an engineer. He wasn't an engineer at all, but he used to fix the bore up and so forth and he had a little car. I was his offsider. I had to cook for him while he was out but when we came back to the station we ate at the station. We might go away for a week. We took rations and I used to do the cooking and help him. I used to cook corned beef. They killed the whole cattle and they had their own butcher shop. There was no refrigerator those days. Everything had to be corned meat, because otherwise it'd go bad. Fresh meat you had to eat as quick as possible.

I hated the outback life. Living in the back country and being Chinese you were always regarded as a third-class citizen. Though we wasn't downtrodden, it was the Aboriginals who were downtrodden. They were classed as nothing, they wasn't even on the census. But there's one thing I hated to be classed as, so when I was about eleven or twelve I said to myself, 'I'm going to do something about this.' I resented being a third-class citizen. I didn't know what to do but I knew I had to get away, because there was nothing there.

I was thinking about it. I used to read books about development in China. I didn't know anything about China. In fact, when I went to China in 1977, they asked me about my history. I said, 'Well, when we grew up we never knew much about China. I used to read about it. But all I used to read about was wars, famines and floods. Now that I've come here, I can see the difference. Things are not as good as in Australia, but you don't have the problems like you had fifty years ago with people dying in the street and prostitutes everywhere.'

Adelaide

The thing was that I couldn't stand my father and I couldn't stand being a third-class citizen. So I worked it out that I'd work a couple of years on the station and save up. Then I got a job cooking. They used to have big cattle runs, Northern Territory into Queensland and into South Australia. Well, I got a job cooking with a drover.[1] With the six months there, good money at the time, and what I saved up, I said, 'Albert, no more Northern Territory for you. I'm going.' And I wasn't going to come back. I was nineteen then.

Anyway, after I went droving I ended up in Adelaide where I had to wait for my cheque to be cleared. I stayed in the Salvation Army People's Palace for a week. Country people always would stay at the People's Palace (they don't have it now) because it was a safe place, there's no drunks. With hotels or boarding houses, you don't know. I didn't like Adelaide, it's got something about it, so after a week I decided to go to Melbourne.

Melbourne

I had a few quid at the time. I got a cheap room in Melbourne and then I met someone. We got talking and I said I didn't know what I was going to do. He suggested I go on the dole. The dole was ten shillings at the time. It cost me six shillings at this place I was staying, you could wash there, of course it was cheap in those days. So I went and got the dole – that paid for my rent. In Melbourne in those days they used to have what they called labour positions, places where you can get jobs. You'd have to pay five shillings to get a job and you'd go along. Well, I thought the best way for me to find out about Melbourne was to take a job. Sometimes it'd last a week, after I got sick of the place. Because I had money, see. I didn't spend it. I just kept it. From the droving and what I saved up.

I was twenty. I was in Melbourne and I was full of adventure. I liked Melbourne because it was a different atmosphere to Adelaide. I got to know people. They were more friendly. So then I met another chap. I think he was Maltese. He used the same restaurant as I did. We got friendly. He was working, making brooms. He would take me to different places, we'd meet, have a cup of tea and through him I got to know more people in Melbourne. I used to take a job on sometimes. I thought I'd better go and take this job while it's going. I stayed in Melbourne for about two years doing that.

I used to go to the Salvation Army turnouts. All the stiffs used to go. I got to know the Salvation Army people and they used to have music and entertain big. I met some Chinese there. They asked if I would like to go to a job in a garden in

---

1 'Drover' is an Australian term for a stockman who moves livestock, usually sheep or cattle, 'on the hoof' over long distances.

Hobart. I was twenty-one then. So I said, 'I'll go over there, see what it's like.' I only knew a little bit about gardening.

Hobart

They paid me fares to Hobart and everything, cut it out of me wages later. An old Chinese chap and myself got there. This fellow was about forty or fifty. Him and I went there and then this fellow said, 'No good send you, might as well work in the shop here.' They knew that I could speak English and they wanted people to work in the shop too. So instead of going to the garden, I ended up in the shop. I worked there for six months.

I know it wasn't too much they paid me, but I was eating there, I lived there. We used to work six days a week. Get up early in the morning, get things ready. At a certain hour I would go out with a chap on a horse and cart to deliver orders to people that used to come. Hobart was good. I had a good job there. But it was getting cold. I remember I had Anzac Day there. I was there Christmas Day 1937 and I left Hobart in May 1938 to come to Sydney.

Sydney

I don't know what made me come to Sydney. But years ago, in 1926 or 1927 when I was a little child, I came down with some Chinese from Darwin. My mother didn't want me to come. An old Chinese chap came down from Darwin, his name was Wing. He had a young boy with him, Charlie Wing. He said he'd take me. I just wanted to see Sydney. We stayed with the Lum Yews. They were relatives of this boy and they had a shop in Coogee. We stayed about two months and they sent me to school at Kensington for a while, while Charlie went to a school at Coogee. Then my brother, Willie, came down and took us home. That was why I always wanted to come back.

Anyway, in Sydney I did the same thing I did in Melbourne. I worked at different jobs. I paid five shillings to get a job. I didn't work for Chinese till later on when I got a job in the vegetable market. I worked for a fellow called Herbie Chee. He had a forestall there, an agency. We had to start at three o'clock in the morning, getting everything prepared. He used to go around and do the buying. He had a garden himself. I worked there for a long time with him. We used to finish about eleven o'clock. I didn't go out at night because I used to get up early. But I could have a good sleep in the afternoon. I used to go out in the weekend because we didn't work on Sunday. Saturday we worked. All the Chinese mostly came in horse and cart. Only the wealthy used to have motor cars.

There was a fellow there by the name of Wong. He had a son and two daughters. He used to have a Chinese restaurant near the market. The two girls would bring those little trolleys to the market. Little kids. You know what Chinese are like.

You'd have to work extra hard to keep the thing going. They were one of the few Chinese shops. People used to make a lot of money in the market. They had that old pak-ah-pu (白鴿票, lottery) going. All the people around the markets used to buy tickets. They used to draw it twice a day. Local Aussie women used to turn up. Australian people all used to go because there was not many lotteries in those days. It was based on the lotto. You had to buy so many numbers. They used to put the result around certain places. It wasn't legal, the Chinese just ran it themselves. Nobody took no notice of them. I remember Herbie Chee's father once won the pak-ah-pu. He shouted me out to everything.

There used to be a Chinese church up at Campbell Street. Most of the Australian-born Chinese used to go there. We would all get around together. I never went to church before, but I went there for company. We used to play tennis together. That's where I knew the Parkees. I was a bit sweet on Evelyn at the time. I never took her out and later she told me she married a Chinese seaman. I was closer in age and friendlier with Basil Parkee (黎宗枝). Cecil Parkee (黎滿枝) comes to my place nowadays at Arncliffe sometimes and the Parkees often come at New Year's Eve for a party.

I also used to go to the Chinese Youth League (僑青社). The Chinese who went to church didn't because they couldn't speak Chinese. They didn't fit in because everything was done in Chinese at the Youth League. But I went even though I couldn't speak the language and that's where I met Fred Wong (黃家權), Arthur Lock (鄭嘉樂), Frank Lee Gee (李植良), Billy Jong (張岳彪), Stanley Wai (布德威) and others. Frank, Arthur and I were also among the original members of the Australia China Friendship Society.

The war was on in China and the Youth League was doing a tremendous job rallying the war effort. They were collecting funds for Madame Sun Yat-sen (孫逸仙) for medical supplies for the 8th Route Army. Mr Lai War Hing (黎和興) of the Nanking (南京) cafe, he was a very patriotic Chinese. He donated a lot of money. So did that bloke with the restaurant in the market, the one with the kids who used to go early in the morning. A lot of the Chinese donated money. When I was in Hobart someone came down from Melbourne. They had a big meeting – all the Chinese were there, all bachelors mostly. They go for the restaurants too. I suppose they did it in a bigger way in Sydney, to help the war effort.

The Chinese seamen who were here during the war took an active part in the Youth League but when the war was finished they moved into Chinese restaurants. They owned restaurants everywhere. They became wealthy because Chinese food became popular. We used to have a bit of a dance in the Youth League or something on. A lot of the Chinese that worked in restaurants had Australian girlfriends. They used to come along. We couldn't get too many Chinese ladies down. It's only in Sydney that I mixed with Chinese. There was no Chinese up there in Mount Isa. These Chinese that used to go to church, they never mixed up with Chinese.

19 'We Grew Up in the Bush'

Figure 19.3. A Chinese Seamen's Union gathering in the early 1950s. Albert Lee On is kneeling at front on the far left. (Douglas Chang)

But I was always interested in China. When I was in Melbourne I ended up in the library. I was reading all these books about China and I picked up *Red Star Over China* by Edgar Snow. I didn't know anything about the communists, I didn't know what was going on in China, but I was attracted to this book. From there on, I always said, this is the way that China's got to emancipate itself. The only way China would become unified was under Mao's plan because everything was warlords then. That book sort of influenced my life. That's what kept me closer to the Chinese than most Australian-born Chinese boys. So I used to go to the Youth League during the war period. I used to go there and then I used to meet a few Australians. I met a chap there. His mother was Australian but he could speak Chinese because he went to China. He never mixed with Australians that much. He was like me, he hung around Chinese. He worked for the trade union covering people who worked in restaurants. Whenever there was any court case on, he used to do the interpreting.

Dad's return to China

Just before the war started when I was down in Sydney, in about 1938, my father decided to go back to China. He wanted to take my youngest brother, he had everything arranged. But my two older brothers wouldn't let him because the war was on in China. They stood there and they wouldn't let him take Fred. My youngest brother wanted to go – he wanted to travel, to go and see what it was like. He was crook on my eldest brother for years for not letting him go. He didn't realise that the war was on. I think what happened is, my father, being a pretty thrifty sort of a bloke, and the fact that my brothers were working on stations, they saved a bit with the shop and my father had some money there. I knew he used to send money back to China, but I don't know how much. So he went alone. Six months later we received a letter from a relative. It was written in English. He said he was our half-brother and that our father had died. My brother just read the letter and threw it away, instead of keeping it. So we put it that our father was married before he came to Australia.

Working with my brothers

During the war the government put a road from Mount Isa to Darwin and from Alice Springs to Darwin. It came under what they called civil construction engineering. They needed cooks, so my brothers were called up into the civil construction corps. I left the markets before the war when a Chinese mate of mine got me a job in a steel factory at Mascot, Hatfield – we were making refrigerators and things like that. But it was a protected industry. I was called up to go into the army but they wouldn't let me go so I stayed there till the end of the war.

Although I was a bit of a rebel, when my father went to China, he said to my youngest brother Freddy, 'When you grow up you get in touch with Albert, he knows his way around Sydney.' So after the war, Fred came down to Sydney. He was down here a week and I got him a job where I was working at the factory. Plenty of work, you know. He worked there for a long time, in the electricity department. But he didn't like the city, he liked the bush. He went back after many years here. He ended up working on the bulldozer on road repairs. He got this dust in him. They didn't wear masks or anything. So the last years of his working life he worked in the Queensland Railways. He was pretty conscientious. They sent him to schools and he became an examiner. But he was always affected by the dust. He's retired now, but he has to use a mask to breathe. He bought himself some land at Cloncurry, outside of Mount Isa. He built himself a little house and he grew things. I often think, if anything happens to him, I'll catch an aeroplane and go straight up.

Six months after Freddy came down, another brother under me, Arthur, he got sick of the bush and decided to come down. The same Chinese mate who got me my job got him a job the next day. You know Chinese. He said, 'It's not good him hanging around. You might as well get him a job right away.'

Not long afterwards I got onto the wharves. I think I was the first Chinese that was taken on the wharves. I was pretty active in the Waterside Workers Union and got a few other Chinese down there. I got Frank Lee Gee a job there. There wasn't many. They didn't seem to like it very much. I worked there for twenty-seven years. They wanted some of us to retire when we got up to sixty. So they paid me out a lump sum equal to about eighty per cent of four-and-a-half years' pay for early retirement to take me up to the official age of sixty-five. That's when I got my birth certificate to show my age. I invested me money and after that a chap I knew got me a casual job two days a week in the meat works at Homebush. Then I got bad gout so I ended up on the invalid pension when I was sixty-two. I'm eighty now.

Forced marriages

You know what those old Chinese used to do? In those days they didn't tell anybody. When they had a daughter, they used to sell her. There was an old Chinese chap up there in Camooweal and my father was a bloody gambler. They used to gamble down in his garden. We had our shop not far from the garden. They used to have a gamble every now and then. He wanted my sister to marry him to pay off the debt, but my sister wouldn't do it, because she'd been born in Australia, been to school. She said, 'Oh blow him, I'm not going to marry him.'

Later on, another Chinese chap came along and he was married to an Aborigine. He had a young daughter and he must have done the same thing, got into debt and so the old man married this other girl. She was not so young as my sister. She didn't know as much as my sister did. This other girl never went to school. So she ended up marrying him.

Years later I met her. I used to go up on holiday. She was a lot older then. I used to have a few drinks with her. She told me straight out – she said, 'My father sold me like a cattle.' But the man treated her very well.

Family today

As the war ended there was plenty of work around. My three older brothers ended up working in the mines for thirty years. Willie was a rigger. Moody became the chef there. All his family got apprenticed to the mines. His daughters got really good jobs in the mines' offices. They never went to the stations like we had to.

Aunt Dolly is now living in a nursing home in Mount Isa and my sister, Jessica, is living in Katherine with her daughter. Her husband died years ago. The daughter has a job in Katherine working for the air force. She cooks there. She's got two daughters working around there and their Australian husbands are working there too. My second brother's daughter lives in Darwin. Her husband was a plumber in Mount Isa but after the cyclone in 1974 they went to Darwin because he could see he could make plenty of money.

Trip to Hong Kong and China

After I retired, I went on a trip to Hong Kong and China in 1977. A mate of mine and I joined a Chinese group of about twenty-five. All the others were wealthy, my mate and I were the only poor ones. Well, we had some money. The first night in

Hong Kong a friend of my mate picked us up with a motor car and took us to all the nightclubs. He introduced us to all the fellows, everybody seemed to know him. There were all these young girls hanging around and of course he's buying them drinks. I thought that's like Australians, you go out together and you all shout in turns. We only stayed half an hour, then he took us to another place and the same thing happened. I wanted to shout. 'No,' he said. 'It's all right,' my mate said. 'Don't worry about it, he'll fix it up.' So we were going to all these flash joints. When the young girls found out we were from Australia, they thought we were all millionaires!

After we did all the good places we went down to the dens, Wanchai (灣仔) or something. All this dancing was going on. Girls were coming over. We went round different places and they all wanted us to enjoy their company. Anyway, we got back to the Holiday Inn, where we were staying, about three o'clock in the morning. That was the big night. Later on, my mate and I took all his family out. When we came back to Hong Kong we met them again. I had an attack of gout but he took us around in the motor car. He took us right up where they have the cable car. He took us everywhere.

When we went into Canton, you could buy a lot of things in Hong Kong you couldn't get there. So my mate said, 'Look, I'm buying all this stuff and putting it in your name.' We got to Canton and I saw he had my Chinese name all written in Chinese. The customs fellow said, 'Is that your turnout over there?' I said, 'Oh, yeah, that's right.' I didn't know it was mine or not. He had all these Chinese delicacies, you know. I'll never forget it. And we had all these turnouts in my name! They all brought some themselves, but they wasn't allowed to bring so much.

We stayed at the hotel in Canton for four days. A lot of them went to the village for about three days, while we others stayed at the hotel. But they left all their things in my room. I couldn't get around.

In Shanghai, my mate said, 'Look, a friend wants to get a bicycle and he can't get one in the shop because it's only for overseas visitors. You can get one.' 'All right,' I said, 'I'll get one'. His friend wasn't even allowed in the shop. So we went up there, he told me which bicycle, I paid for the bicycle and took it out. My mate's friend was waiting outside, so I gave it to him. He wanted this bicycle because it was better than a bicycle they made in China.

Everywhere I went, I kept the name of the hotel I was staying at in my notebook. In a store in another place, the friend with us had to go off and do something else. Well, my mate, he couldn't speak Mandarin. We got on a taxi and the driver couldn't speak Cantonese. So when he said, 'Where are we going?' I said, 'Oh, I got the turnout here,' and I showed him my notebook. He took us straight there.

Postscript

Albert remained in contact with his extended family in Queensland and the Northern Territory. While attending a family reunion at Mount Isa in 2000, he learned of the origins of his maternal grandfather, Sam Ah Bow. A relative informed him that Ah Bow's name was actually Chu Kum Bow. His surname was Chu, and in the familiar Chinese custom of saying a given name he was known as Ah Bow. Australian officials then misinterpreted Ah Bow to be his surname. Albert had always believed Ah Bow had come from Tai Po Kong near Canton in China. At the reunion someone said he was born in Tai Po Kong, an important market town in the New Territories of Hong Kong, the name of which was later changed to Tai Po Market (大埔墟), but that is conjecture only and the location of the ancestral village is still unknown. A memorial plaque for Sam Ah Bow and his wife Opal has been placed by family members at Adels Grove, near Lawn Hill station in Queensland.

Like Hoy Lee, Albert Lee On was a favourite interview subject during the 1990s for oral historians, particularly for his political activities after the Second World War. Albert had friends in the Communist Party of Australia and was active in the Chinese Seamen's Union, which used the Chinese Youth League offices in Dixon Street, Haymarket, as its headquarters. Albert never married. In the early 1960s he moved into a house in the Sydney suburb of Arncliffe with a cousin and his wife. When interviewed, Albert had with him a family history that his brother Moody had written; however, no copies were made and its whereabouts is unknown. At the date of publication only limited contact has been made with members of Albert's extended family. They have confirmed that Albert passed away on 14 October 2008 and that his ashes were scattered in Botany Bay.

Figure 19.4. Albert Lee On in the 1970s. (J and M Wing collection, courtesy S. Canning)

20
From a Chinese Garden

Peter Wong (黃寶榮)

Before Hong Kong was ceded to Britain in 1842, Macao was the chief port for Western trade with China. In 1557, the Portuguese were permitted by the Ming dynasty (明朝, 1368–1644) to settle on an island that became Macao at the southern end of Heung Shan (香山, Chung Shan 中山) county, some sixty-five kilometres west of Hong Kong. Three centuries later, they took possession of two offshore islands – Taipa (氹仔) in 1851 and Coloane (路環) in 1864.

Coloane is where Peter Wong, born in 1937, spent his childhood amid the horrors of starvation and persecution under a brutal Japanese occupation during the Second World War. In 1951, the postwar relaxation of restrictions against the entry of Chinese to Australia enabled fourteen-year-old Peter to join his sixty-six-year-old market gardener grandfather, Jack Wong (黃章澤), in Manly Vale on Sydney's northern beaches. While attending school, Peter worked in the gardens, first at Manly Vale then near Penrith in Sydney's far west, which was then part of the farm belt that supplied much of the city's fresh food. From school he joined the Australian and then the growing Chinese restaurant industries. He tells how he witnessed the dismantling of the White Australia policy, became acculturated into Australian society and married an Australian woman. During the 1970s, he and his wife Marie defied the still lingering Cold War atmosphere and sent all their three children to Macao to learn Chinese. Peter took an active role in reviving the role of the Chinese Youth League (僑青社) when the Whitlam government renewed relations with mainland China following the election of the Australian Labor Party to federal government in 1972.

Japanese occupation

My family has lived in Macao for generations. My great-grandfather moved to Macao from Sun Wooey (新會) county. He must have been a merchant because the family owned a house in Macao and when anybody owns something they must be doing business. But I think we came to live on the island of Coloane, which is part of Macao, because of my grandmother. I have a granduncle, my grandmother's younger brother, and a lot of relatives there. They are really natives of Coloane.

I was still very young when the Japanese invaded Kwangtung (廣東) province during the late 1930s. Although Macao was not actually occupied, the condition of the people was just as bad. We could see the Japanese in action across the river. There was a lot of starvation. During the cold winters we would get up in the morning and see people dying in the streets and begging for food. We didn't have enough to eat ourselves. We couldn't help too much. Coloane is only a small area. You couldn't drive a car up its narrow streets. Every morning a truck would come down and we could see the corpses being dragged and chucked onto the truck. People were so hungry they even practised cannibalism.[1]

My father was working in a department store in Hong Kong but he had to come back to Macao. Although we had a shop in Coloane selling groceries, we really depended on our grandfather who was a market gardener in Australia. After Hong Kong was occupied by the Japanese, we had no more communication with Grandfather. Most Chinese overseas sent money to support their families and they got no more support either. So we were in a terrible state. We had a family of eleven people, eight brothers and sisters, Father and Mother and Grandmother.

My eldest brother, Chong (黃祥), was fourteen. He had to go to Macao to work for an uncle and auntie. They had a shop selling rice and groceries. He was given the cooking to do, but he didn't know how to cook. They didn't pay him a big wage. But when you're young, you say 'might as well go and learn something'. Later he moved to another uncle's shop which made banners and pennants of congratulation. The characters were sewn on to the banners. He learned how to brush characters from our uncle there. He'd only been to primary school then. But he still does a lot of calligraphy in Sydney today.

With no more communication with Grandfather, we were in a terrible state. At times we were starving. Although we had the shop for a few years, we finally had to close it down. We lived on different things. We ate mustard cress boiled with sweet potatoes. When we had a little bit of rice, we boiled a big pot of gruel with very little rice. Then we added a spoonful of shrimp paste, which we made ourselves, to make it a bit salty and drank it. After the war, my mother told me she would never eat shrimp paste again. She said, 'I had that too much and I hate it when I see it.'

---

1   Instances of cannibalism have been documented in a number of sources: see Geoffrey C. Gunn (ed.), *Wartime Macau: Under the Japanese Shadow* (Hong Kong: Hong Kong University Press, 2016).

Tam Gong temple

We went through this situation for quite some time with no relief. The funny thing is that the local Tam Gong Miu (譚公廟), the Tam Gong (譚公) temple, actually saved our family. My father was well known in Coloane. He was always willing to help others and the local people had a great deal of respect for him. At the time, Coloane was more like a fishing village, but not now of course. There were lots of fishermen coming back with their boats and catches. It used to be a very busy place. My mother was always very kind to the fishermen. They called her their foster mother. We used to sell their fish and do anything we could for them, but they didn't come all the time. Once the fishing season is finished, then you are stuck with no income. We tried other things as well. We sold firewood. People gathered grass in the hills to use for cooking fuel.

Well, something happened to the couple taking care of the temple. Suddenly, one morning, their bodies were discovered on the rocks near the water at one end of Coloane just where the temple was situated. They had been murdered. Later on, the murderer was caught. But now the temple was left with no one to look after it. The neighbourhood residents wanted to find somebody reliable and trustworthy to take care of the temple and they appointed my father. You see, the fishing people were still very superstitious. But this helped us because there was always somebody coming to the temple to *bai shen* (拜神, pray to the spirits), they would buy *heung* (香, incense) and *laap juk* (蠟燭, candles) to burn. They would also pay a fee for the *heung you* (香油, fragrant oil). This was like a donation and you called it *heung you*. You always put a bit of oil into the burner so as to keep the light going. When anyone paid the donation, then you hit a gong and beat a drum and called out in order to wake up the deity – Tam Gong of course.

Now in the temple there was a set of sixty-four sticks called *chim* (簽). Sometimes when you went to the temple you might want to make a request. Perhaps you wanted to ask about your house or whatever you wished for. So you shook the jar of sticks until one fell out. When I was six, seven and eight I also worked in the temple. Each bamboo stick represented an ancient story printed on paper. As we ran short, I had to print more copies. We had a wooden block carved with characters. I would ink the block, then scrape it and then print copies. So during the day I would read these stories over and over again. I actually memorised all the sixty-four stories. I knew which were the better messages. I could say, 'Oh, this is a good one.'

The stories were all about ancient times, but they would reflect what you might want to hear, though it wasn't always true. But it eased the person's conscience, gave some relief if the deity was actually consulted. Well, this earned the temple some income. As long as we looked after the temple, kept it operating, then we could keep the rest of the income for ourselves.

Figure 20.1. Peter Wong's parents in old age. (Peter Wong)

The eighth day of the fourth month in the lunar calendar is the Tam Gong festival (譚公誕). This is a very busy period. Everyone came to the temple to *bai shen*. You could earn a lot of money then. But, of course, at other times nobody came. Anyhow, this helped us through the difficult war years. Whenever I go back to Macao, I also go to the temple to *bai shen*.

During the festival they always put on Cantonese operas, called *Shen Gong Hei* (神功戲), Cantonese or Guang Zhou operas (粵劇團) about deities. We used to watch them and I enjoyed it all. I think it was the neighbourhood people who took care of that. They weren't related to each other, they mostly came from other parts of China. There were a lot of people from Chung Shan county and from See Yup (四邑), and other places too. It was mixed like in Hong Kong.

My father never had the opportunity to come to Australia when he was young, but he and my mother visited us in the late 1980s. My mother passed away in 1994, while my father died in 1998. When I went there earlier to celebrate his ninetieth birthday, I went to the Tam Gong Miu again. It hasn't changed much. There is a replica of a dragon boat inside, made from the rib of a whale with small carvings attached. It's still there. My father always reminded us that this temple kept our family alive during the war. We have a saying in Chinese, *yup uk giu yun, yup miu bai shen* (入屋叫人，入廟拜神), meaning when you enter a house, greet those present and when you enter a temple, pay your respects to the deities.

I donated some money for the *heung you* and my sister bought some incense and candles to burn. Whenever I come across any temple I always do that. I'm not very superstitious-minded but that's my upbringing. Like my elder daughter, Li-Lin (黃麗蓮), when she was going to Chinese primary school in Macao, she became used to asking everyone else to start eating before she herself began a meal. She still says '*daai ga sek faahn* (大家吃飯, everyone eat, please)'. It's part of the tradition of showing respect for your elders and taking care of the upbringing of the young.

Travelling to Australia

When the war ended in 1945, we began to receive news from Grandfather again. He was in Sydney and was very anxious about us. He started to send us all his savings. At that time his wages were very low, even though he was in a partnership with others. They had four or five partners in the garden. Two had families with them and three like my grandfather were by themselves. Grandfather's name was Cheung Jaap (章澤), or Jack Wong. Well, he kept sending letters back and he suggested that one of us grandchildren should go to Australia. My eldest brother, Chong, was the one that should go because he was the eldest. He said, 'Oh, that's good,' so we went through all the paperwork for him to go to Australia, to go to school. But there must have been some obstacles in the way. Things couldn't be arranged for a couple of years, and by the time his papers were released, he was too old to be a student. So then it was suggested I might fit into the age category. So I was the one to come. Actually, Chong came three months later on a different paper to work in the same market garden as my grandfather.

I was on the boat for fourteen days from Hong Kong. I came on a new boat called *Taiyuen*. We travelled by the lowest class, *dai chong* (底艙, third class), below deck. It was much cheaper. That was the way people mostly came. The two old boats called *Changte* and *Taiping* were too slow. I came to Hong Kong and stayed in the Wing Shun Yuen (永順源) hostel, a *gum shan jong* (金山莊), because Chinese went

Figure 20.2. Peter Wong's grandfather Jack Wong. (Peter Wong)

through a *gum shan jong* to go abroad. It was run by the Kwong War Chong (廣和昌) company, operated by people from Lung Du (隆都) district in Chung Shan county. At that time my grandfather had a lot to do with Kwong War Chong. The old people never put their money in a bank. Grandfather put his money in Kwong War Chong. They got a little book. They didn't speak English, so when they took money out, they just wrote it in the book. My father and mother came to Hong Kong to farewell me. We all felt very sad. But I was only young, you don't know what you are doing. I just carried a bed roll, a suitcase and off I went.

There were a few kids who also stayed at the hostel. Once on board we started playing around. We didn't know what was in front of us. Some old Chinese who were returning to Australia advised us to go below deck and have a rest. I didn't know what they meant. Then all of a sudden the swell began to churn things up and we all felt sick. I had a terrible time. From the time I left Hong Kong I stayed down below on my bunk. There were sixteen double bunks all in one place, thirty-two people. I was on a top bunk. I stayed there till we reached Sandakan. I was very sick for a few days. The boat was rocking. When I looked on one side I saw all water. On the other side it was all sky. It wasn't a bit funny. I couldn't eat and when I got up to go to the toilet, I had to grope my way upstairs somewhere. I felt dizzy and was really in a bad state. I couldn't get up to go to the dining room either. One of the stewards was very kind. He brought us some rice porridge and came down to try and feed us. Quite a few of us were sick, but not all. Some old-timers were pretty good. They told me fewer and fewer people were turning up in the dining room. When we reached Sandakan, we all came up on deck again. Looking at the sunshine and feeling the fresh breeze you really felt good. After that it was more peaceful but just before we reached Sydney it was rough once more and we were sick again. We arrived in Sydney on 3 September 1951.

We berthed at the wharf where I waited with my luggage for my grandfather. I had never seen my grandfather. I had no idea what he looked like. He was away from home between twenty and thirty years. For one thing the fare for a trip back to China cost a lot of money, there's no one really could afford it. When I came to Australia, Grandfather had to borrow money for my fare. Nowadays you can work for two weeks and you can get a plane and go home with that wage, but then you've got very little money, you could never get enough to go home. The other thing was Grandfather was sending money home to support us. Not even my eldest brother had seen my grandfather. We sent some photos of myself to him and I was given one of his photos, but probably not a recent one. Anyway, I was waiting on the wharf and suddenly I saw a gentleman, quite tall, well-built and a bit grey. But when I looked at my photo I could see no resemblance to my grandfather. Then he spoke to me. He had one of my photos. He came up and said, 'I'm not your grandfather, I'm your grandfather's friend. I've come to meet you first. He'll be coming very soon.'

He introduced himself to me as Cho Baak (曹伯, elder uncle Cho). So I thought, 'Gee, my grandfather won't look too bad, he's big-built and looks very strong.' But a little later my grandfather arrived and his back was stooping and he was walking slowly. I felt so sorry to see him. You see, he'd been working in the garden and they didn't have water pipes. Now they have pipes, you just turn on the water. The water system for irrigation is very good now. But at that time Grandfather had to carry two drums of water on a carrying pole to water the garden. That's why his back was bent. He didn't walk very conveniently either. Grandfather also introduced me to another uncle who spoke good English. He was born in Australia and went back to China for his education and returned to Australia. 'This is Bew Sook (表叔, external younger uncle),' my grandfather said.

Then we all got into a truck they had brought to take me and my luggage to the garden. That's more than forty years ago.

Market gardening

All the partners in the Kwong On (廣安) market garden were from Sun Wooey county. It was located at Manly Vale near a creek. Much later on a school was built on the site.[2] The property there used to be relatively cheap, but now it's very expensive. The garden was well known for its celery. That's how they made good money to buy a much bigger garden later on. They had a little hothouse. It was only about four by fifteen feet in area. They used galvanised iron all around to make it high on one side and covered it with glass. During the daytime the sun could shine through the glass. At night they put chaff bags over it to keep the frost out and the warmth inside. There was no other heating except manure.

They had to use a lot of manure. I went to the market with them. There were a lot of horse-drawn carts there and they had a lot of this manure which we had to buy. We would get a truck in and shovel all the manure onto the truck. Sometimes they used the manure on the ground too. But the horse manure was so hot, it burned you. We had to wear gumboots. I don't think anybody does that now. There was a place in the market where we always went to get the manure. They had it already packed, with dry hay in it.

At that time there was some opportunity to make money because they always got into the early season, like with the celery. Celery is very hard to grow just after the winter and mostly came from South Australia. The transport wasn't that good then. If the local product came out at the right time, then you got good money. So they grew this celery. During the winter they put a lot of horse manure in the little hothouse. Horse manure is very warm and helped the little seedlings to come out. Once they came out they transferred the seedlings to the fields to grow. When they reached a certain height, the gardeners cut up chaff bags into strips and used them to help the celery grow upright and make it look whiter. People liked to eat that celery, so every year they had a good season of celery.

The garden had its own store in the market in the city, where the Entertainment Centre is now. You brought in your produce in the morning and stacked it along one side of the store. The customers, like green grocers' shops, came in the mornings and they bought it wholesale to take away and retail. Two persons always drove the truck to the market. They looked after the store.

When I first arrived, I had to look after my grandfather because he was getting on in age. He was sixty-six then. The place we lived in was a tin shed and sometimes

---

2   Jack Wong's garden was at the corner of Campbell Parade and Quirk Road, Manly Vale. Rented from 1941 by five partners including Jack Wong, Harry Ah Cann (蔣全福) and Ah Kin (趙權), the garden was named Kwong On, meaning 'big and peaceful'.

it leaked. We had a room, just big enough for Grandfather to have a bed and my bed opposite him, then another bed, but no furniture. We lived very primitively. There was no shower and no running water. Every night I got a big basin of water for Grandfather to have a sponge bath.

The gardeners got up as soon as it was light. They always had something to eat before they went out, some bread. We didn't have a fridge. Everyone had an ice chest. Every morning the iceman delivered a block of ice which you put on the top of the chest. You kept the meat or whatever, milk, underneath. By the time the ice melted, that's the end of the day. We didn't have a water closet. Instead, the sanitary people came and took your toilet can away and left an empty one.

School

There were about five kids in the garden, all going to school. We could not enter a public school, the reason being that we were not entitled to this facility, because our grandfathers were not naturalised citizens. There were very stringent regulations, although our grandfathers were paying tax just like everybody else. I was told then that you needed to be in Australia for fifteen years before you could apply for permanent residence, not naturalisation. So a lot of people who were married had to stay here like single people for fifteen years before they could return home to see their families. That's how they could never see their first child. You would miss seeing that child growing up. The next sister or brother would be fifteen or sixteen years younger than the first child. That's why you mostly saw single persons, you didn't see any girls around of Chinese origin.

Since I couldn't go to a public school, I had to go to a Catholic school. So I went to the Christian Brothers College in Manly. We used to enter sports in different houses. When we competed with other schools, we had a war cry to urge our teams along. I still remember it, 'Who are, who are, who are we? We're the boys from CBC' (that's the Christian Brothers College, you see), and then you spell it, 'M-A-N-L-Y, Manly'. We had to learn it and sing out to our team.

After school duties

In the garden we boys mainly helped after school to pack the vegetables to go to market the next morning. At that time the gardeners might be still cutting the vegetables. We used wooden cases. Now they have cardboard boxes. It's different. We had to place the lettuces, for example, inside, then nail the wooden cases together and stack the boxes one on top of the other. The tomatoes had to be graded into small, large, first and second grade. They went into long wooden cases and had to be nailed down also. If the gardeners were cutting spinach, we had to tie it up in bundles. During the weekend we helped rotary hoe the ground, because sometimes when you harvested a plot, you had to plough up the soil again. We'd go around and do that type of individual job.

Actually, we were treated very well. We weren't forced to do anything. We had a little plot for the kids to manage. We were told, 'If you grow something, you can sell it and get some pocket money,' just to encourage us to do something in the garden. So we grew marrows, you don't see them now, not the zucchini, but the white ones. They were very nice and used to sell well. We just picked them when they were young and sold them. The truck went to the market every morning. When it came back, someone would say, 'oh, that's yours.' So we got some pocket money.

Naturally, we couldn't just come home from school and sit there. Because we had a bit of Chinese teaching, you know, you got to listen to your elders, we had to do our share as well. After all, we were helped to come to Australia. The way we looked at it, we could learn something. Whether it was gardening or not, we didn't know how we would finish up, but we had to do some work in the garden. The gardeners never placed any restrictions on us. They didn't tell us we had to stay and work in the garden. They themselves had shares in the Sun Sai Gai (新世紀, New World) restaurant in the city at 17 Castlereagh Street down near Martin Place. So during holidays, like on a Saturday, we would go to the Sun Sai Gai restaurant to work for one day, peeling prawns. Cooked prawns used to be sold in big boxes, with the shell and everything else still there. It wasn't like nowadays when you can buy a block of cooked and peeled prawns. So the restaurants needed people to peel the prawns. We used to make ten shillings a day. Then we had money to go to picture shows, buy new shoes and everything. We just spent it after we left.

Penrith

In 1953 they sold the garden to some people from Kou Yiu (高要) county.[3] The partnership bought a dairy farm of seven or eight acres, one railway stop before Penrith.[4] Actually, there were a lot of dairy farms up there. Two months before we moved, we had to sink a well and put up some housing. The Bew Sook I met at the wharf when I arrived was Harry Ah Cann, the one who spoke very good English. He was really surnamed Cheung (蔣), but in Australia the given name was always taken as the surname. People will tell you that all the time. Well, Harry not only spoke good English, he was also mechanically minded. He knew how to build houses. We had to build six or seven rooms, just a wooden frame with a roof like a

---

3   The garden lease was bought by Soo Sut Dak. The Department of Education bought the land in 1962 and built Manly Vale High School (now Mackellar Girls Campus secondary school), which opened in 1968.
4   The new Kwong On market garden was located on McCarthy's Lane, Cranebrook, near the historic Cranebrook Farm. The garden area now forms part of the Penrith Whitewater Stadium built for the 2000 Olympic Games.

triangle. He mapped it all out, worked out all the details. We built it ourselves, with all of us taking part.

We also had to sink a well. The dairy farm itself was shaped like two hills, with a creek down the middle. We sank the well near the creek so we didn't have to dig too far to reach water. There were a lot of rocks there. We used those big cylindrical rounds of cement to make a wall. We put one down first. Then we dug in the middle and it sank. When one round sank a level, we put another one on top and then we went on digging. We had to use three or four of these cement cylinders until we thought the water was coming out strong enough for us to use. Then we stopped. After that we had to put in a generator to pump the water out. I think a technician installed it and when we wanted to use it we pressed a button. All this had to be done before we could move. The Manly Vale garden was kept operational until then. You see, instead of using the rotary hoe, we were going to use a tractor.

After we moved up to Penrith, we still didn't have a water closet. We dug our own big hole and chucked everything in. Now of course in Australia we are learning from high tech that instead of pumping the nightsoil out to the sea and polluting the sea, it would be more useful to put it in the ground. But I don't think it would have been allowed then. Now they say we are wasting all that we flush out. The fertiliser we are using has side effects which are killing the river system. The Darling River is now in big trouble because of all the algae coming out, killing all the marine life.

When we first moved to Penrith and before we converted the dairy farm into a market garden, we had a funny but interesting experience. Forty or fifty cows and a milking machine in a shed came with the farm. The next morning, we heard the cows moo-mooing and they came to the gate. By evening it seemed they were in some pain. Then somebody realised they needed to be milked. So we went over to a neighbouring dairy farm and asked if they could help us milk the cows and keep the milk. Our neighbours did so and later on they were auctioned off.

After we built the house in Penrith, installed the pump, had running water, everything set to grow things, we found out the soil was very hard. During the dry summer it was hard like a rock. But when it rained it was so soft you would go down knee deep. It was terrible. Things weren't growing well at all. They grew a lot of cauliflower, cabbages, beetroot, carrots, celery as well as other vegetables. But later they grew pumpkins, potatoes and other things. One person always looked after the seeds. He knew when to grow what. You had seasonal things. In winter certain things grew better, in summer you grew other things. We grew tomatoes as well. The main thing is tomatoes have seasons, celery has seasons, and then cauliflower is a winter vegetable. They also grew some Chinese mustard cress, bok choy (白菜) and that kind of thing. At that time in Australia there wasn't a great variety of Chinese vegetables. You didn't even see much Chinese spinach. The garden sold a lot of celery and mostly Australian vegetables.

New school

At first in Penrith we kids tried to go to another private school, because normally we wouldn't be allowed to attend a public school. But there was no boys' private school, only a girls' private school. So we had to go for a test. I don't know whether it was an IQ test or just a normal test. After that we were admitted to the public school. I attended fourth and fifth classes in CBC in Manly. You see, whether you pass or not in Australia, you go up, even if you fail in the test. They just let you go up because you are that age. I didn't do very well the first two years because I had to catch up in English. In CBC the teacher felt that we couldn't catch up in the normal class, so every afternoon we had to go to the third-year class where the boys taught us elementary English, even simple words and things like that. Sometimes they taught us the wrong thing, they had us say it again and again. I didn't know why they were laughing, but I think they were making fun of us. Well, anyway, that's normal.

In Penrith I was put in the sixth class, because I was in the fifth class for a year in CBC. I was doing quite well then. I caught up a little bit. Actually, I came first in the class. So I went to the first and second years of high school in Penrith as well. Maybe the school standard was not as good as in Manly. I don't know why I did so well.

We did have some fights in school because they called you names. Mostly they sang out, 'Ching Chong Chinaman', all that kind of thing, they used abusive language. So sometimes it ended up in a brawl. It just comes out, you react, that's how it is. Normally everyone treated us very well, but there's always a few nasty instances like that.

On my own

I stayed in the garden until 1956. My grandfather was preparing to go home and went back to Macao that year. So I moved out of the garden and had my third year of high school in the Paddington Boys' High School. The boys were real rough, they were called the 'Paddo Boys'. Everybody knew about them. They were very good in sport. The teacher encouraged me to go on, but I looked at my own situation. I had to look after myself. I was seventeen or eighteen. I had to become independent. I was boarding with a lady, Auntie Ho (何), in Surry Hills. A couple of other boys were staying there too.

Actually, a lot of things were happening in my life then. While I was still in Penrith I used to come down to Sydney during the weekends. I worked in a restaurant in town as a waiter. The Taiping (太平), it's no longer there. You don't need to know too much English to be a waiter. It's very simple. You just ask the customer what he would like, and then you lay the table with a spoon and a fork, not very elaborate. The meals were very simple, not like today. Chicken chow mein, omelettes, chop suey, all that type of thing – Australianised Chinese dishes. They were mainly Australian customers. But still the restaurant had a busy time. I think the US sailors are the ones that brought the Australian people to the Chinese restaurants. They helped the business develop during the war. So I worked in the Taiping in the weekends, and because I liked table tennis, I used to go up to the Chinese Youth League, they had a table there.

I had another brother, the second, not the eldest. He came a year after me and worked in the Sun Sai Gai restaurant. It's no longer there. Because my brother was a bit of a rebel, he had some quarrels with the people he was working with. He was not very happy with the managers and he joined the union. You see, inside the premises of the Chinese Youth League there was the Chinese Workers Association.[5] It had been set up to help the contract labourers. In Chinese we call contract labour the 'pig' (豬仔) trade. I had a couple of friends who contracted to work for this restaurant. The restaurant paid them lousy wages and treated them badly, but they could not get out of their contracts. Well, there was an Australian organisation called the Hotel and Restaurant Clubs Union which looked after the restaurant workers. So my brother went from the Chinese Workers' Association to the Australian union to fight for his welfare. I made a very good friend at the Youth League, Voy Sang Lee (李會生), he was one of the 'pigs' working for the restaurants and he fought his way out too.

The Chinese Youth League

All the single young Chinese in Sydney, once they finished work, they had nowhere to go for recreation. If you went to a picture show, and you didn't know English, then you wouldn't enjoy it. There were no Chinese films. So we all ended up going to the Chinese Youth League to play table tennis, play chess, sing, have picnics, go swimming, all sorts of outdoor activities. That's how I met all these people. I kept up my Chinese because my brother used to subscribe to some health magazines. He liked bodybuilding. He sent to Hong Kong for them, and we did a bit of bodybuilding ourselves, just for fun. But I always liked sport. I played soccer as well. I was a good table tennis player, at that time anyway. The Youth League provided us with very good outlets.

Besides the Chinese Workers Association, the Seamen's Union was also there. The Seamen's Union played a big part in helping those seamen who were stranded in Australia after the war to settle down or repatriate. The Youth League supported the New China. I was told they were the first to hoist a five-starred red flag after the founding of New China. They had a lot of literature from China there and I started to read it. One of the magazines, *Chinese Youth*, explained what a youth

---

5 As Cold War tensions escalated, many members of the Chinese Seamen's Union, the Chinese Workers' Association and the Chinese Youth League who were politically active and were either members of the Communist Party or considered to be communist sympathisers came under the notice of the Australian Security Intelligence Organisation (ASIO) in the late 1940s and 1950s.

should be doing. I found it very valuable as well as interesting and learned a lot from it, although my chief interests at that time were sport and cultural activities. Actually, the people who went to the Youth League at that time fostered the hope that China would become a strong country. I don't think they had political struggle in mind. You see, Chinese overseas had to put up with a lot of discrimination, you were looked down on, insulted, so when New China came into being, we just hoped we would not be kicked around again. After all, China was subjected to foreign invasion for one hundred years, there were always civil wars whenever there was a transfer of dynasty, it was always fighting. I think the last fifty years has been the only peaceful time in China.

So that's how I got involved in the Youth League. Jack Young was working for the Australian restaurant workers' union and he recruited a lot of members from the Chinese restaurants. He was Australian-born but he could speak Chinese. The restaurant union had a dance group and various cultural activities that we could join. That's how I met my wife, Marie. She worked in a restaurant and she won the first May Day Queen contest. In 1959 she went on a youth delegation from Australia to a festival in Vienna.[6] They were invited to visit China on their way to Vienna. We got married in 1962, that's a long time ago. Intermarriage is common now, but even in my time it was not easy, though it was easier then. My family in Macao was against it and Marie's family also advised against it. Nowadays it's nothing. But we understood each other. Marie has feeling for China. It was a big thing for her to let our children go to Macao to learn Chinese.

Work

I left Paddington High School after I finished third year – intermediate certificate, they called it. There were two more years to go. Now it's six, but it was five years of high school then. I thought I had better get a job. Of course I had no skill. Well, Harry Pang (馮海星) was the secretary of the Youth League. He always liked to help young people. He was an old seaman and he was working as a chef in an Australian chain of restaurants called Cahills.[7] They no longer exist. I was seventeen, going on eighteen, and Harry said, 'Come to work at Cahill, I'll help you.' I said, 'I don't even know how to grill a steak.' But he said, 'It's not that hard. You come and work for me and I'll teach

---

6   The World Festival of Youth and Students commencing in 1947 was a Soviet-sponsored international sporting and cultural festival initially held every two years in Soviet-bloc European countries. While it became a vehicle for Soviet anti-imperialist propaganda, the festivals were very well attended with over 100 countries represented. Australia sent delegations to most festivals generally organised by left-aligned unions and organisations.
7   Established by Theresa and her brother Reg Cahill, beginning with the Italian Coffee Shop in 1933, at its peak the Cahill chain operated twenty-five ethnically themed restaurants in the greater Sydney area. Tudor Hall was decorated in a mock English Tudor style.

you. You work for me as a grill cook.' So I said, 'All right.' That's how I started working in a place called Tudor Hall in Martin Place. It's no longer there either.

I worked there for Harry and he taught me how to do things. From Tudor Hall I was transferred to another Cahill restaurant, a fast-food service and they needed someone to cook Chinese. They put on a few dishes like sweet and sour pork, omelettes, curries and things like that, very simple. I worked there for some time, then I was transferred to still another Cahill restaurant. I finished up working in about four of their restaurants.

Then I fell ill. Actually, I went for a TB test and one of the x-rays showed some marks. The doctors said they didn't really know what I had, whether or not I had any TB, but to make sure they sent me to Juliana Hospital in Pymble. It's also closed down now. But TB is already eradicated in Australia. I stayed there for three months. The government paid for everything. They didn't find much wrong, so I was discharged and went back to stay in Surry Hills with Auntie Ho.

Now I went to work in the Nanking (南京) Restaurant as a waiter, because the Nanking was one of the biggest restaurants in Chinatown. I worked there for a few months. In 1958 a friend of mine introduced me to work for the United Services Club in Sutherland as a caterer. I'm not a chef, but I like cooking. I got my training from my friends and actual work experience. So I was managing and doing catering in the club. I would do the buying and preparations. I did that for nearly ten years. It was a great experience for me. I gained broad contacts with Australian people in different walks of life, because I like socialising. Although I got free beer in the club I didn't drink that much. But I liked talking to people. I talked to policemen, banking staff, butchers, all types of people. I learned a lot of things in the club.

Visit to Macao

By 1970 I wanted to make a trip back to Macao to see my parents and the family. But I had no paper stating what my status was. However, the secretary of the club approached the Labor Member for Sutherland, Les Johnson, a good friend of his, on my behalf. Through the good offices of Mr Johnson, the Immigration Department said they would issue me with a certificate of identity with a re-entry permit to Australia. So I got ready to go and went off for a few months.

I didn't see my grandfather again. He went back in 1956 and died a few years later. My youngest brother was working in a department store in Hong Kong and he came home too. He said he wanted to go to China to have a look. I wanted to go too but my certificate of identity stated that I was not to visit North Korea, North Vietnam and China. I'd heard so much about China, I wanted to go. I decided to go with him. We went to Beijing and to Wu Xi (無錫) to see another brother there and of course to Canton. Probably that's the reason why my application for naturalisation wasn't approved till after the Whitlam Labor government was elected in 1972 and Al Grassby became Minister for Immigration.

Figure 20.3. Peter Wong with his father in Macau, 1970. (Peter Wong)

Business opportunities

I took a few months off work after I returned. Then I started working again with my brother and my friend Voy Sang Lee in the Balmain Leagues Club. I was there for a year and a half, cheffing and everything. But now I'm in the seafood trade.

My brother and I joined the Wu Hop (五合) seafood distribution people in 1973. I stayed with them till 1981 when a friend asked me to do something similar. So in 1981 we formed a company called Wing Shing (永盛). Wing Shing only lasted a few months because a Hong Kong company wanted to join us so as to develop their markets here and we set up the Wah Loong (華隆) Trading Company. That went on for five or six years. Wah Loong is still operating. But we couldn't resolve the differences between the Hong Kong and the Australian interests. Three of us were Australian. Because two of us were bound by contract not to engage in the same type of work for at least six months, the other partner started up Wing Yick (永益) Trading, where I am now.

Educating our children

During the 1970s, Marie and I sent our three children to Macao to learn Chinese. Of course we missed them. But if we wanted them to learn the Chinese language, the best way was to have contact with the people speaking that language and, besides, my mother and sister were looking after them. They not only learned the language, but some Chinese traditions. Their daily contacts with the people and other students helped them to understand the culture as well. You wouldn't know Li-Lin, my elder daughter, is Chinese. But she speaks Chinese like a Chinese and her English is just like an Australian.

Li-Lin went when she was between six and seven and came back when she was between twelve and thirteen. She completed primary school there. Until she had her own two children, she was teaching in a primary school in the Fairfield area where there are a lot of migrant children from Vietnam, Cambodia and Indochina. They spoke Chinese and when they first enrolled and found out she knew Chinese they clung to her. She became an asset to the school and used to translate the notices to parents into Chinese.

Melinda (黃美蓮) and Andrew (黃學勇) were in Macao for three and four years. Melinda is also a teacher now. She teaches art. Andrew is a student. After they returned, they retained their speaking ability because they participated in the Youth League activities. But Li-Lin can still read Chinese. While they were in Macao they also learned music, dancing and singing. Li-Lin learned to play the *pipa* (琵琶, Chinese lute). Melinda learned the *yueh chin* (月琴, moon shaped Chinese lute), while Andrew learned to play the *lau yip kum* (柳葉琴, willow leaf shaped Chinese lute). The two younger ones didn't take their music studies as seriously as Li-Lin, but they can still play. Melinda and Andrew also speak English like Australians and Chinese like Chinese. Here, as well as over there, people say, '*Ni goh gwai jai do sik gong jung man ge* (你個鬼仔都知道講中文, this barbarian boy knows how to speak Chinese)' and '*Ni goh gwai mooi gong jung man ge* (你個鬼妹講中文的, this

Figure 20.4. Peter and Marie Wong outside the family home in Coloane, 1996 (Peter Wong)

barbarian girl speaks Chinese)'! You shouldn't take it as an offence. It's just a way of speaking. It is discriminating in a sense, but now people take it more light-heartedly.

Multiculturalism

When I came back from Macao in 1970, the Youth League had already started a Chinese class with four volunteer teachers. More and more people enrolled until we couldn't accommodate them all. So the school moved out and became the Sydney Chinese School in the premises of the Cleveland Street High School on Saturdays. Today the school is over twenty years old, has eight hundred students, Saturday morning and afternoon sessions and between thirty and forty teachers.

The Youth League has played a big part in familiarising our members with Australian society. We had a lot of seamen and later on we had people working in restaurants. So we had a lot to do with the Seamen's Union and the Waterside Workers' Union, helping them to find jobs after the war, to repatriate and settle in Australia, all that type of thing.

Then the contract workers in the restaurants, all young single people, needed something to do after work. The hotel and club restaurant union helped us organise social dances and picnics for them. These social functions enabled our members to meet different kinds of Australian people. But because of our connections with the unions we became branded as leaning to the left, and if you showed any feeling for New China then you were pro-this and pro-that. Even now, with freedom of speech, all that type of thing, there's still a fear, you may get your name in a black book. Mind you, people of different professions and different ethnic backgrounds have contributed a lot to Australian society.

Now of course, with the normalisation of diplomatic relations, everybody is friendly to China, it's a different situation altogether. The Youth League is just one of the organisations in the Chinese community. We have already existed for fifty-six years and are still going. That means we are doing something worthwhile. But the world is changing. We have more older people as well as younger ones. We need to keep evolving in a new direction in order to serve our membership better.

The Italians and Yugoslavs were here when they introduced the term New Australian. The Chinese were another class, but the people from Europe were New Australians. We don't use that term anymore. But even after the new *Migration Act* (in 1958 this Act abolished the dictation test), the barrier was still there for people from Asia. Apart from naturalisation, you still found it very difficult. When I travelled by public transport, even some ladies on a bus or trains moved away from you. Maybe it was because of the White Australia policy. It was very strong at that time. I know that people from Italy and Yugoslavia were called all sorts of names. But when Mr Whitlam was elected he actually did away with that discrimination. The whole country has changed so much. After ethnic-origin people went into parliament to voice their opinion, that had a lot to do with it too. Recently we have people of Chinese origin going onto local councils, into parliament and at different levels of government. All this helps multiculturalism to flourish. It seems this is the way more or less in harmony, there is not so much conflict as in other countries.

I think we are really doing well in Australia. When I first came to Australia in 1951 there was a lot of industrial unrest. It's not funny, this concept of 'you come from Europe, you from Asia', all that type of thing. I think the community was divided because of that policy. Mr Whitlam did a great job when he legislated against discrimination of people for their ethnic background. Migrants from different countries will remember him as the one who dismantled the barriers dividing the people.

A lot of people in the Youth League know a bit of history, of the suffering in the Sino–Japanese War, the Taiping rebellion (太平天國), the Opium War (鴉片戰爭). That's why the Youth League hoisted the first flag to celebrate the birth of the New China. The simple reason is that we shared a passion for the Chinese nation. I think anybody has a feeling for his origin. I have lived in Australia for so long, I have a feeling for Australia too. When you're there, that's your roots. So where I come from, I have roots there as well.

Postscript

At the time of publication, Peter Wong is aged in his eighties and living in Sydney with his wife, Marie. His three married children are also settled in Sydney. Peter has always been an active member of the Chinese community in Sydney. He was a key organiser in reviving membership of the Chinese Youth League during the 1970s after interest in it had fallen during the late 1950s and 1960s Cold War era. He was president from 1975 to 1986 and maintains his connection with the League to this day.

21
The Northern Territory Story

Doris Fong Lim and Norman Yeend

The circumstances surrounding Chinese immigration to Australia's Northern Territory were materially different to other Australian states. Initially, Chinese numbers were far in excess of the local European population and their labour was crucial to the construction of many significant infrastructure projects. The Territory was then annexed to and administered by the colony of South Australia. The main settlement was established in 1869 and named Palmerston, although the port was always known as Port Darwin in honour of the famous British naturalist Charles Darwin (the town officially became Darwin in 1911). In 1874, the colonial government decided to recruit cheap Chinese labourers in Singapore and the first party of 176 arrived in Palmerston on two-year contracts. They were immediately dispatched to work on the overland telegraph line and to the various mining companies.

After their contracts expired, nearly all elected to stay. Their headmen, usually businessmen, had set up stores and small businesses, and were even operating mines of their own. No restrictions were placed on Chinese arrivals and, as more followed from Hong Kong and China, by 1879 the Chinese population soared to some three thousand. Some diversified into servicing the mining settlements, from gardeners and butchers to tailors and engine drivers. Pine Creek was one hundred miles south of Palmerston and became the biggest centre of Chinese at the time, boasting a large temple, vegetable gardens and sizeable stores.

At first the Chinese businesses concentrated in the mining settlements, but with the increase in numbers they set up stores in Darwin, competing with the port's European traders and storekeepers. Chinese merchants put up substantial buildings in the original ramshackle Chinatown area there, and by 1885 over one hundred Chinese had become naturalised. The Chinese labourers were in no position to bring their families from China; however, the merchants were able to do so.

The European business community became actively anti-Chinese when in 1885 the South Australian government decided to allow the contractors for the Palmerston–Pine Creek railway to use cheaper Asian labour, mainly Chinese. In 1886, the Goldfields Amendment Act followed, excluding Chinese in the Territory from any new goldfield discovered by a European for two years. The result was an exodus of Chinese miners for Queensland.

During the railway's construction, the number of Chinese in the Territory continued to rise from 3,237 in 1886 to 6,122 in 1888, while the European population was between one and two thousand. Chinese immigration to the Northern Territory finally ended in 1888 when South Australia raised its restriction from ten tons to five hundred tons for each arrival and revoked its previous exemption for the Northern Territory. By 1910, the population was more evenly balanced.

With no new arrivals, the Chinese merchants moved their operations from the settlements to Darwin. Chinese merchants often brought their families with them and so more families developed; however, socially the Chinese kept to themselves.

Doris Fong Lim (1929–2002) was the fifth of nine children born to George and Lorna Fong Lim. Her grandparents had come out to seek gold at Pine Creek and her parents ended up as storekeepers at Katherine. They later established a successful general store in Darwin after the Second World War and her father became the licensee of the popular Victoria Hotel. The Fong Lim family became an integral part of Darwin's multicultural community. Doris and her husband Norman Yeend tell how they married in Darwin in 1952 and broke the ban on mixed marriages, on the Chinese as well as on the Australian side.

Due to the limitations of the interviews with Doris and Norman Yeend, Mavis Yen wrote this chapter in a different style to provide a more complete telling of their story.

Grandparents

'I can't remember much about the gold mining towns, but I can remember a fair bit of the hardships we went through,' said third-generation Australian Doris Fong Lim.

Both of Doris' grandfathers arrived in the Northern Territory in the 1880s. Her paternal grandfather, Fong Ding, joined the rush to Pine Creek after arriving from Hoy Ping (開平) county. Hoy Ping is one of the four counties in the Pearl River Delta collectively known as See Yup (四邑). Diggers from See Yup were in the forefront of the Chinese gold rushes, both to California and Australia. Fong Ding

Figure 21.1. Doris' Maternal Grandfather, Lowe Dep Chit, and grandmother, Lie See, with Jack & Harry Lowe. (Library & Archives NT, https://hdl.handle.net/10070/737037)

married a Darwin girl and they settled in Brock's Creek, a sizeable gold mining township. Doris' father, George Fong Fook Lim, was born at Fountain Head, a nearby mining settlement, in 1902.

Originally the Territory government had hoped the first Chinese labourers would stay and cultivate the land, but their interest was in the gold. 'They came for the gold,' said Doris. Her family very early on opted to service the mining communities with storekeeping and other essential jobs.

Doris' maternal grandfather, Low Dep Chit, came from Shanghai. From working on the railway, he went into market gardening, in Pine Creek, and ultimately in Darwin he had a big garden now occupied by a golf course. 'He was a big man,' Doris says. 'He was ninety and he was out there chopping wood and just dropped dead.'

One of Low Dep Chit's daughters, Lorna Low Sue Gee, was born in the township of Yam Creek in 1904. She married Doris' father, (George) Fong Fook Lim, at Pine Creek in 1921.

The flight of the miners to Queensland, their departure for home and the lack of new arrivals, prompted the goldfield merchants to shift their operations to Port Darwin from the late 1880s. A few hundred older miners remained in the mining settlements up to and throughout the First World War, but failing health finally forced them to withdraw. By the time of federation in 1901, the ratio of Chinese to Europeans in the Territory was down to three to one, but by then Chinese merchants in Port Darwin had become a powerful commercial force. The 1920s saw Darwin, instead of Pine Creek, as the centre of the remaining Chinese, the descendants of the former merchants.

Doris recalls the families of both her grandfathers were at the settlement of Emungulan along the railway, doing market gardening and storekeeping for the mining communities further away from Pine Creek.

George and Lorna

During the 1920s her parents shifted from Emungulan to Katherine, to become one of the founding families there. She grew up in Katherine, where her parents had a general store and a bakery. They also did some market gardening and peanut farming. The children had no opportunity in Katherine to learn to read and write Chinese, but Doris became a bilingual speaker. At home the family spoke the See Yup dialect. Doris learned English after she went to school. Lorna taught Doris and her sisters to cook both Chinese and Australian food. But in Katherine they had to contend with drought, floods and a fluctuating market. So, in 1938, the family moved to Darwin.

Although the Chinese merchants now dominated Darwin's trade, they still operated from within Chinatown. On social occasions they mixed with the European community but otherwise kept to themselves. After moving to Darwin, the Fong Lim family defied this tradition by setting up a general store in the heart of the European community in Smith Street, apart from the Chinese businesses which were located in Cavenagh Street. The work was hard, but the whole family, who lived above the shop, helped and they prospered. 'He was a hard worker,' said Doris of her father.

When Darwin was bombed by the Japanese in 1942 and the civilian population dispersed, Doris' family had to begin all over again. They evacuated to Alice Springs where they set up a cafe and a tailoring business.

At the end of the war, a considerable number of the evacuated Chinese families returned to Darwin to find their Chinatown homes had been destroyed. But with their old isolation broken down by their wartime experiences, they threw themselves into rebuilding the whole of Darwin. They not only reestablished their former businesses, but went on to set up new ones. The young people joined the public services, they entered every profession. Doris' father, George Fong Lim, launched into the hotel industry and became one of Darwin's leading merchants.[1] In 1966, the late Harry Chan became the first Chinese mayor of Darwin. In 1983,

---

1   George Lim became the first Chinese in the Northern Territory to own a licensed business when he bought the Hotel Victoria in 1946. He operated it for the next twenty years. They also owned a large general store, Lorna Lim & Sons. Both the hotel and store were in Smith Street, Darwin.

Figure 21.2. Lorna and George Lim with their children, 1927. (Library & Archives NT, https://hdl.handle.net/10070/732161)

Doris' younger brother, the late Alec Fong Lim, was elected Lord Mayor of the city of Darwin.

Marriage and family

'We were actually the first Australian Chinese couple to openly get married in Darwin in 1952,' says Doris' husband, Norman Yeend. 'There had been some couples before who whizzed off to Sydney or somewhere to marry and most didn't come back. My family accepted it quite well. But Doris' family didn't. When I told the fellows I worked with I was going up to tell Doris' father we were going to get married, they were placing bets on how far I'd get before he shot me. So I went up and tackled him on it, but I admit I was dead scared. He was a hard man! He guarded his daughters very jealously.'[2]

'He ruled us like an iron rod,' Doris said, 'but he was fair'.

---

2   Norman had a sideline as the leader of a popular dance band in Darwin, besides being a prominent sportsman, and perhaps this had something to do with George Lim's initial view of him.

Figure 21.3. Left to right: Gerald, Richard, Alec & Arthur Lim, c. 1940. (Lim family)

'He told me he was going to cast her out,' said Norm. 'She'd no longer be able to share with the family. But you know, that was the way it went. They wouldn't come to the wedding on principle.'

'It was only principle,' Doris laughed.

'It only took two or three weeks,' Norm went on. 'Then they put on a party for us at their house, and no one could have had better in-laws than I had. It would have been pretty horrible to have been married and not to have had any contact with Doris' family at all. You see, it was because of the old ladies.'

'The old ladies were all on our side,' said Doris

'The funny part was the old ladies liked me,' said Norm. 'And they were quite okay. They gave Doris wedding presents on the sly.'

'Oh, they all liked him,' said Doris. 'Everybody did. We had two lovely grandmas. We used to love them, particularly our mother's mother. She was only about four foot ten.'

'I think the only reason why they didn't approve was because of the older generation,' said Norm. 'I gathered that in the eyes of the old people, if a Chinese boy or girl married an Australian or anybody other than Chinese, they would think that their sons or daughters hadn't brought up their children in the right way. So, in Doris' father's eyes, he felt it would be a stigma against him for Doris to marry me.

'I was in Darwin with the army, as a public servant. I was in the finance branch at the time and when we got married, the colonel withdrew my membership of the officers' mess. I've still got his letter. He says, "Dear Norm. I was very surprised

Figure 21.4. Left to right: Lily, Eileen, Mary, Isabel & Doris Lim, c. 1940. (Lim family)

to learn of your recent marriage … such a matter is entirely your own concern but you must admit this is rather unusual." It might have been unusual for him because he was a bloody old bachelor. "During your previous service here you have been accorded the privileges of the officers' mess although your status doesn't really merit it. I think it might be advisable, to save embarrassment, if you refrain from exercising these privileges." The thing was, I couldn't tell Doris, so I went without lunch for about twelve months. I wasn't going to tell anyone I couldn't get any lunch. Doris was working at their shop and they all thought I was having lunch at the officers' mess. But on the civilian side, my boss in Adelaide accepted it very well. He wrote and said he didn't care if I married so long as I did my job and wished me luck. That feeling was still around in 1952, but it wasn't from then on. Because after we got married, there were a number of other mixed marriages. In Doris' own family two of her sisters and a brother married Australians.'

What did her father do about it? 'Nothing,' said Doris. 'There's nothing you can do. They're all intermarrying now.'

'You see,' said Norm, 'towards the end of the last century and well into this century, Territorians were developing an important part of the country virtually from nothing. I'm talking about the general development of a whole city which had to change its location over time. Darwin wasn't always where it is now. It required a lot of hard work, just to grow vegetables or anything else. It was the hard work that the Chinese people did, the descendants of those out there from the gold mining, like Doris' father and mother. Those Chinese worked very hard and it caused some

Figure 21.5. Norm and Doris Yeend, c. 1955. (Lim family)

jealousy because they produced and made money and were good businessmen. The Australian element, they were all right to go up there as administrators, sit in offices with the fan overhead. But there weren't too many of them willing or capable of getting out to do the hard manual work. Of course, there were a few Australians who worked enormously hard, particularly out on the stations.'

'The Australians were generally not known to be hard workers, not really,' smiled Doris.

'I think,' said Norm, 'it's generally accepted, that if it hadn't been for the Chinese element, the Northern Territory would never have been developed as it is today.'

Postscript

Doris and Norm were living in Canberra when interviewed. Norm worked for the Australian Commonwealth Department of Defence, mostly in the finance area. Initially living and working in Darwin, Norm was the paymaster for Australian servicemen assigned to the Commonwealth Infantry Brigade stationed in Malaysia during the Indonesian Confrontation in the early 1960s. They also spent time in Port Moresby, Singapore and Adelaide as Norm was transferred. When Doris passed away in Canberra in 2002, Norm returned to live in Darwin, where their children reside. At the time of publication, Norm was still alive and living with one of his daughters.

Doris mentioned that her younger brother, Alex, was Lord Mayor of Darwin in the 1980s and it is interesting to note that Alex's daughter, Katrina, continued the family's commitment to civic duty by serving as Mayor from 2012 to 2017.

22
'I Was the Lucky One'

Elizabeth Lee (李)

In 1911, administration of the Northern Territory was taken over by the Commonwealth government and the name of the principal town, Palmerston, was changed to Darwin. From then on, Chinese were excluded from government employment and Chinese merchants from tendering for government contracts, a policy that continued up until the Second World War. Nevertheless, the Chinese continued to dominate Darwin's trade.

Darwin's first Chinese general store, Wing Cheong Sing (永昌成), was set up by Elizabeth Lee's (1914–2010) grandfather, Chin Wah Leung, and a brother, Chin Mee Leung, in the 1880s. The two brothers came from Toishan (台山) county in the Pearl River Delta and their combined tailoring and grocery business was well established by the 1880s.

Chin Wah Leung had three wives. The second was the mother of Elizabeth's father and all her children were born in Darwin. In those early days, Chinese in business who could afford it sent at least the eldest son to China for a Chinese education. However, Elizabeth's father, Chin Loong Dep, a first-generation Australian, sent all of his four daughters to school in Canton, the cultural centre of south China. It was while attending an elite boarding school there that Elizabeth met her future husband, Tom Lee, also a Darwin boy. After her marriage in 1932, Elizabeth's father moved to Broome in Western Australia to establish a successful tailoring business and became a prominent citizen there.

Theirs was not a totally arranged marriage. The choice was hers and the union turned out to be a very happy one indeed. Following the bombing raids over Darwin by the Japanese air force during 1942 and 1943, Elizabeth and her family were evacuated to Sydney, where they remained. Not all family relations were harmonious, however. Elizabeth's mother-in-law clung to her traditional beliefs and, being a second-generation Australian, Elizabeth upset the traditional daughter-in-law relationship. The result was that they frequently clashed.

Through her personal and family story, Elizabeth gives an example of the Australianisation of the Chinese in Australia that has been taking place over more than a century.

Family business

Because I'm old, I like travelling. I go by myself or with my friends and family. I'm at home everywhere. About six years ago I went to Beijing, Nanking, Shanghai, Sian (西安). I didn't go back to Toishan. I've got no one there now. My father's people are out here for six generations. If I did go back, if I went to *heung ha* (鄉下, the village) you have to give people money, you know, because you're a *gum shan haak* (金山客, visitor from the golden mountain). Even a dollar, you have to give it to them.

When I went to Honolulu, I went to see the warships sunk by the Japanese. There were people translating Mandarin and Japanese and I was very surprised. They said they studied to be tourist guides. My son's children in Brisbane are studying Japanese. 'Why don't you study Chinese?' I asked them. They said, 'Because Japanese people are coming to Queensland for business.' So I said, 'When you grow up there might be Chinese business.'

Wing Cheong Sing[1] was started by my grandfather, Chin Wah Leung, who came to Darwin with his brother. They were merchants. They came to do business. None of our family ever went to dig gold. All business. They did tailoring and had a grocer's shop. There are a lot of Chins in Darwin. Most of them come from Toishan county. Not quite cousins. We are the generations coming down from our forefathers. We speak the See Yup (四邑) dialect.

There used to be a photo of my grandfather and his brother, all dressed up in real nice costumes, hanging up right in the middle of the store. Anyone come in, one look, they will see these two brothers sitting down there, like real big shots. Why did they come to Australia? They got the money, they came here looking for more money. If you've got no money, you can't open a business. They had education and all. If they hadn't got the education, they wouldn't be able to wear all these nice clothes. In the early years, the government gave a party for all the big businesspeople. They were included.[2]

My grandfather had three wives. My grandmother came out here and had all her children in Australia. I don't know much about my grandmother. She was the second wife, but she was my father's mother. My father was born in Darwin. My

---

1 The Wing Cheong Sing store was located in Bennett Street, Darwin.
2 The reception of Chinese merchants by the governor of South Australia at the government residence in Darwin in 1905.

22 'I Was the Lucky One'

Figure 22.1. Chinese Merchants at a Government House Reception in 1905. Wing Cheong Sing (Chin Mee Leung) is in the second row, first on the left. (Library & Archive NT: https://hdl.handle.net/10070/732242)

grandmother had three daughters and two sons in Darwin, the other one I don't know. She died in her eighties in Macao. She went back to live in Macao because her number four daughter-in-law lived there. It was a better life in Macao than in the village.

In those days they had children on their own. All the children were just born at home by themselves. Might be friends helped. Some of them didn't have anyone to help them. Like now, we believe in Panadol, any little thing wrong with you, well, take Panadol. You don't have a proper doctor.

Childhood experiences in China

When I was five I went to China. I came back to Australia when I was ten and went to a convent school in Darwin for one year. I don't think I went to school from five to ten. My father was known as one of the Wing Cheong Sing sons. But there were four sons, too many, you know how it is, and the business was run by one of them. So, in 1928 my father pulled out and went to Broome to start his own business.[3] He was named Chin Loong Dep but he called his business C.L. Dep and he was well known. Even now in Broome a downtown traffic garden island is named after him. I went over there because my parents were there. I was still young.

When I turned fourteen, Mum became sick and I was given the task of accompanying my mother to China for medical treatment. So I only had three years' Australian education. There wasn't any plane then. We went by boat to Singapore, on the *Centaur*. From Singapore we got another boat to Hong Kong and we stayed in one of these Chinese hostels. I don't know what you call it, hostel or hotel. They called it a *gum shan jong* (金山莊, Chinese import-export businesses set up to trade with the golden mountains of California and Australia, which also provided accommodation).

Sadly, Mum died in Hong Kong. After she died, I went back to the village. Our village was not what they call a dump. It was all brick buildings. Most of the villagers had returned from Australia, many from Darwin and even from Alice Springs. But coming from Australia after so many years, you go back to the village, you can't stand the way they live.

My father was a very good father. He had four girls. There was my older twin sister, myself and two younger ones. He sent all my sisters to Canton. They all had a good education and went through college. When I went back, I had to learn from what the Australians call the ABC. But I was the only one he brought back to Australia. The other three were left behind. I was the lucky one.

When I was seventeen years old I was going to boarding school at Pui Ching (培正) Academy (an elite girls' school started by Christian missionaries). It was a very good school but terrible for me. I was with little kids because of the language and my lack of schooling. They were very good mannered, they called me *je je* (姐姐, elder sister), but you get very embarrassed to be among the little ones, you know. One of my sisters became a teacher. My twin got married. I also got married, when I was eighteen, to a boy from Darwin.

One day he came to the college with his mother to visit his sister's daughter. She was in the same class with me and I happened to be there. Somehow, we started talking and I asked him what he came back to China for. It turned out he came back to get married. He was asked to get married to any girl in Darwin. There were families there with a few daughters. He could pick whichever one he wanted. But he said he would never marry a Darwin girl because none of them were good-looking. But I was pretty good-looking.

His mother asked me if I had a boyfriend. In those days, you were never allowed to have a boyfriend. Actually, I had a boyfriend, an American boyfriend, and we went boating together. On the other side of Pui Ching there was a boys' college, they were all students from America, Chinese Americans. I said, 'no'. Then

---

3   C.L. Dep Tailor and Mercer operated successfully in Broome for many years, and included a popular gambling room at the rear.

she asked did I go to see pictures. Well, I went to the pictures every week. You were only allowed to go out once a month. But I sneaked out. My father sent me money. One pound was a lot of money in those days. I had money enough to pay other girls to buy their monthly passes. Not everyone had money to spend, you know. I forget how much I paid. I used to walk from Tung Shan (東山) where our school was, to Sai Kuan (西關) in the west, and to Nam Kuan (南關) in the south to see pictures, and then walk back.

Anyway, his mother said, 'His name is Tom, you can be friends with him.' So we got together and somehow we were writing to each other when I went back to *heung ha* (the village) and he to Hong Kong. Our parents knew each other well, we grew up in the same street. But little did he know that I was a Darwin girl. He didn't want to marry a Darwin girl but he had to because his mother was pushing him. His mother forced him to get married to me. He couldn't help it.

Then he wrote and asked would I like to marry him. Of course I married him because I wanted to get away. I was fed up with China. So I got married into the Lee family in Hong Kong in 1932. He didn't know I was a Darwin girl and I didn't know he was eight years older than me. But it was all right. We learned to be happy. We were said to be a handsome couple.

The Lees are from Hoy Ping (開平) county, also in See Yup.[4] I'm from Toishan county. Our Chin family was never poor. In the very olden days they used to have slaves. You bought the man and wife and the children. For generations they had to work for you. It was very cruel. In those olden days you could buy a title with money. But our family earned a title, for something they did. It was sent down officially. That was why our family was addressed differently to the village people, because we got a title. I just heard a little bit of this and a little bit of that. Myself, I'm just an ordinary person.

Married life in Darwin

We came back to Darwin and stayed for a while. My husband was working for his brother-in-law, C.P. Chong, in his shop. Then I became pregnant. I went to Katherine to his brother's place and had my eldest daughter there. I didn't go to hospital. There were Australian midwives there. I still remember Sister Green. I had a girl, Eulalie. My husband chose that name. You see, we came back to Australia on the same boat as Eulalie Wong from the Wong family in Brisbane. She was blind and he promised her he would name his first daughter Eulalie.

Anyway, eighteen months after I came back from Katherine to Darwin with my baby, I had twin daughters. My father-in-law, Lee Yuen, was staying with us.

---

4 Tom Lee's parents were Youin Gon Lee and Mow Tam (Margaret) Lee, who migrated to Australia around 1900.

Figure 22.2. Elizabeth & Tommy Lee on Thursday Island. (Lee family)

He was so good to me. He helped me so much, he cooked and washed and helped me to iron.

Mother-in-law

My mother-in-law was not cruel or anything, but she was very sarcastic. She never told you straight. She moaned behind you and she talked in different directions. But that didn't hurt me. I didn't care. She used to say things to me and I used to answer her back. She said I was *dai daam* (大膽, impudent), that I *ding kui* (頂她, defied her). She used to go mad at me. She would say, '*haak dou hai baak* (黑都是白, black is still white)'. She meant no matter what, she was right.

I was married to her second son so they all called me Yee Sou (二嫂, second sister-in-law). All her friends called me Yee Sou. She had two daughters. One of her daughters was one year younger than me. She stayed with her now and again, but they didn't get on. Nobody could stand her except me. Because I didn't care.

Anyway, when we were in Broome my mother-in-law used to stay with me, and when we were in Darwin she stayed with me. When we were in Sydney she stayed with me. She had other daughters-in-law and other sons. They all got space for her, but me, with one bedroom, with four beds like a dormitory, I only had that much room.

I'm the type, I don't worry too much and I don't take notice of anything. Come in one ear, go out the other ear. A lot of my friends call me *faahn gwai na* (番鬼奶, foreign devil woman) because I don't care about nothing. But in the end, the last few years, my mother-in-law was very good to me. The whole of Sydney knew about me because she went out and told people.

Chinese–Australian relations

In the early days, a lot of Australian people ill-treated the Chinese people. It was very, very bad. When the Chinese walked down the streets they always wore trousers, but the Australians called them pyjamas and stripped the clothes off their backs. These Australians hated the Chinese. The Chinese used to have pigtails. When my father was young, he had a pigtail. The Australian boys in Darwin would tie their pigtails together, you know, they were so cruel. That's why the Chinese people hated Australians. But since the Second World War, we are all good friends, even in Darwin, because the young generation go to school, they mix with their schoolmates, they go to each other's houses and all that, see? But in the olden days the Chinese suffered a lot. Most of these Australian boys were not well educated. They'd be lucky if they finished primary school. They just knocked around, they didn't care. That's why the Chinese people were known for holding a chopper. Because if you wanted to fight, all right, a chopper. That's how it all begins. They treated the Aborigines badly too. Even in the 1930s they wanted to kill the Aborigines, they gave them flour and tea and sugar and poisoned it.

When the Chinese went to the gold mines and all that, there weren't enough Chinese girls around and boys were boys, they wanted girls, so they took up with Aborigine girls. There are lots of Chinese Aborigine children, in Darwin and elsewhere. They gave them Chinese names. There's Loos, Chings, Youngs and Lees and what not. Some of their fathers took them back to China and they married Chinese there. They even went to cultivate the rice fields. I was in Alice Springs in 1933 when my husband went there to work as a tailor, and I knew a girl there. Her father had a garden. He sent her home to Chung Shan (中山) to be educated and she spoke the real *heung ha* (village) Chung Shan dialect (中山話).

Religion

None of my children are Christians. I believe in God, we all believe in God, but we're not Christians. They've married into Christian families, but they are still not baptised. We don't go to church. We go for a wedding or a funeral. My second twin daughter's husband's family are all Catholic but she's not. My youngest daughter married a Catholic. But none of my children are Catholics. I had a friend the same age as me. One of her parents was Catholic, the other Church of England. The father or mother didn't agree to baptise her in one of the churches. So because she wasn't baptised, she couldn't marry in church, supposed to be illegitimate, not legally married, you don't have a paper. She wasn't allowed to say she got married in the Registry Office. Then she got to know a Presbyterian minister. He told her, if you believe in God, that's it. Never mind what church.

One of my sons didn't get married till he was forty and I didn't know if he was going to get married. So when I went to Malaysia to visit my eldest daughter, she said, 'Let's go and see a fortune teller and find out when you're going to have a daughter-in-law.' We were in Kuala Lumpur. We just went to one of these street people, fortunetellers, they are everywhere. She told him I had two sons but no daughter-in-law. So this man said to me, 'Oh, you will have a daughter-in-law. End of this year if your son is not married you will never have a daughter-in-law.'

Well, 18 December he got married. If you want a fortune teller, they will tell you anything. Whether it's true or not, they tell you, but it was true. It's very cheap, *gei ho ji* (幾毫子, a few ten-cent pieces) or something like that.

Jobs, war and Sydney

Because of the Depression, my husband never had any job. He went anywhere just to find a place to make money. At first we went and stayed in Broome and he worked for my father. We had three children then. My father liked Australian food. So I used to cook him Australian stuff. The dish he liked best was steak and eggs. He also liked stew, with everything in his plate, just one hot dish. My children grew up eating stew, vegetables and plenty of gravy, with their rice. People say to me, at your age how do you look so young? I say it's rice. Which is true. All Chinese people eat rice. I still get down on the ground playing marbles with my great-grandchildren, even now. I still climb trees. I've got three mango trees, but there's no more mangoes these last two years. Two years ago, I climbed trees to get the mangoes down. My daughter-in-law said, 'Mum, when I get to your age, I hope to be as strong and as active as you are.' So I said, 'You've got to eat a lot of rice.'

We returned to Darwin when things there started to improve again. But we were bombed out and had to move to Sydney. In Sydney my husband first worked in a government clothing factory. After the war he worked for the telegraph office in the general post office. We did not return to Darwin. But I never had a hard time. My father had money and always supported me. During the war he sent me material, cloth and needles, even chewing gum. He sent little packets of chewing gum to the kids by post. We had six children then and one man working for five pounds a week. My father told me of all his children I was the one that he really loved. I suppose it was because they brought me back and I was living with him all the time. He loved all the others, but I was always there. He died in Broome in his eighties, but I couldn't tell you how old he was. We were separated for so long. I knew he loved me and I loved him and he wouldn't want me to grieve over him. When my young sister rang up and said Dad died in his sleep, I said, 'Oh well, God bless him.'

Family

After my husband died in 1976 that was hard too. For nine months I lived on my own. I used to look up at the ceiling and cry, because we were married for over forty years. He died of a heart attack.

Before he died, he said, 'Mum, you got a house over your head, you got a car and you got three meals a day and enough money to keep you a lifetime. But never, never should you ask the children for money.' That's what he said to me. I will never ask my children for money. That's how the Chinese people always think of their children.

But I'm used to it now. I like to get out of the house. Anytime friends ring to ask me to play mahjong (麻將) I say yes. They don't have to ask me first. They get three and then they ask me 'cause I've got nothing else to do. I've also had girl students staying with me. The young people are all very good. The one with me now, she wants to stay as long as I will have her.

Now I like travelling. Money is no good to me if I don't spend it. I feel at home everywhere. I feel at home in Malaysia, in China, Hong Kong, Thailand, in London, in Edinburgh, in New York, Boston, Sacramento, in Milan. I've been to all those places. I go by myself. I go with family and friends.

Of all the difficulties and heartbreaks I went through, the hardest was when my son Richard had to undergo five major operations for a duodenal ulcer when he was sixteen. He was vomiting blood by the bucketful. He was so sick we had him transferred from Canterbury Hospital to St Vincent's because a friend knew a top surgeon there. If we had waited one more hour he would have died. He was

Figure 22.3. Elizabeth Lee and her children prior to their evacuation from Darwin, c. 1942 (Lee family)

in hospital for three months. After he recovered, my husband said, 'God's will gave him back.' He's only got one-eighth of his stomach left. Today Richard is working as a conductor in Italy, having started off as a violinist.

I can't complain about my children, they are so good to me. Even my grandchildren are so affectionate. I've got five daughters, and all married Chinese. I've got four in Sydney and Eulalie in Perth. One son in Brisbane and one son in Italy. He went to Milan to study the violin. My eldest daughter, Eulalie, she married a chartered accountant and went to Malaysia. They sent two small boys to a boarding school near Campbelltown. They were very homesick. When they would come to visit me, they would put their arms around me and say 'Oh Po Po (婆婆), it's nice to come home'. My daughters told me the boys got too upset when I visited them so one of my daughters took over looking after them. When they were up to high school, Eulalie moved them to Perth so they could all be together. Now they've grown up. One got married and he's got two beautiful sons. The younger one is in Russia. He got a job there and he's got a Latvian girlfriend.

My youngest daughter is married to a Hong Kong boy. The twins married Chinese boys from Suva, Fiji. They're both retired now. I'm a great-grandmother to four, two in Perth and two in Sydney. I see them at least three times a year, on Mother's Day, my birthday and Christmas. All my daughters' mothers-in-law thank me for my daughters, which the Chinese never, never do. When the mother-in-law of the youngest was dying of cancer, the hospital said it couldn't do any more. Instead of putting her in a hospice, my daughter brought her home to die in her new home, only about two years old. The mother-in-law asked why she was so good to her, and my daughter said, 'Because of what my mother did for my grandmother.'

Actually, I didn't bring my mother-in-law home. She was in the hospital for three months and died there. But I took her lunch, I took her dinner, I washed her. I did all her laundry. That's why God is so good to me, that I live to this age and see all my great-grandchildren and I have had a very happy life.

Younger generation

Now Darwin is Australian, Chinese, Malays all equal, no difference. I think everything was beginning to change just before the world war started. Some of these young people were educated in the south. They knew English, they knew the law and customs and all that and so they joined the union. That's how they started to get their jobs. Even before the war some of them were working on the wharves.

Chinese are different now, very Westernised in lots of ways. In the early days, See Yup were not allowed to marry Hakka (客家). Now they get married just the same. This young generation don't care what nationality, what *yup* (邑, See Yup dialect for county) they belong to, as long as they are happy. In my days you got a scolding for standing outside the door.

I think after the war when these young kids went to college or to university, they all mixed. My children used to bring their friends back to the house. Even then my mother-in-law said it's all right to go out and have fun, but don't marry a white boy. She said that. Anyway, all her great-grandchildren are intermarried now.

My grandsons married Australian girls and my granddaughters married Australian boys. They all had big weddings.

You can't stop it. My son married a Pommy. She came and asked me would I mind if she married my son. I said go ahead with my blessing. I didn't mind. We have no chance of going back to China. Even if you pay me to go back to live there, I wouldn't like to, because we are here too long. These days these young people make friends for years and years before they get married. They might come to my house or my children might go to their house and then families become friends.

My mother-in-law was still very old Chinese. She believed in *bai shen* (拜神, praying to deities and spirits). When she was with us, we had to keep the Chinese festivals. Now we don't have Chinese New Year. We only have Christmas. All those young people want is a big Christmas dinner. Australian style!

Postscript

After the Second World War, Elizabeth and Tom Lee lived in suburban Sydney. They raised a large family of five girls and three boys before Tom passed away in 1976. Tom's brother was Charles Lee (李貴方, 1913–1996), the first member of the Australian diplomatic corps with Chinese heritage. Elizabeth continued living in Sydney until she passed away in 2010. Both Elizabeth's and Tom's ashes are interred at Rookwood Cemetery, Sydney.

Conclusion

According to the law of the unity of opposites, the situation is changing all the time. Depending on how you go about it, a bad situation can be transformed into a good one and likewise a positive into a negative one.

In 1901, the Commonwealth *Immigration Restriction Act* introduced a dictation test of fifty words in any European language directed at excluding undesirable immigrants, particularly Chinese. In 1903, the *Nationality Act* cancelled the naturalisation of non-Europeans. Also cancelled that same year was the clause in the Act permitting the entry of the wives and dependants of already domiciled non-Europeans. Instead, Certificates of Exemption from the Dictation Test for limited periods were issued to enable the already domiciled to make return trips overseas. These certificates were also issued to import-export merchants and their assistants, and to students. During the 1930s, this concession was extended to local traders, substitutes for local traders, and their assistants, also to chefs and cafe workers, thus enabling sons to join their fathers' small businesses or gardens. However, wives and dependants were excluded; the wives of import-export merchants of good standing were allowed to visit Australia for six-month periods only. Consequently, with the continuing return of the older Chinese, the Chinese population in Australia fell from 30,000 in 1901 to 12,000 in 1947.

However, by the end of the Second World War, Australians began to see the Chinese in a new light. A growing number of church leaders, intellectuals and individual politicians began demanding changes to the immigration laws.

One of the earliest reforms was the lifting in 1947 of the 1903 ban on wives and dependants. It also became easier for students and business assistants, chefs and cafe workers to enter the country. However, the White Australia policy was still in place. Australia had embarked on a massive postwar migration program and the *Wartime Refugees Removal Act 1949* was introduced to hasten the departure of non-Europeans who wished to stay.

Nevertheless, during the 1950s the postwar liberalisation of the immigration policy continued. By 1957, naturalisation was granted to non-Europeans with fifteen years' residence. Ten years later, in 1966, this was reduced to five years. In 1958, a new *Migration Act* replaced the *Immigration Restriction Act 1901*, abolishing the dictation test, resulting in a small but steady flow of Chinese migrants from mainly Hong Kong, Singapore and Malaysia.

The liberalisation continued. Distinguished and highly qualified non-Europeans were to be admitted for permanent residence. This concession was later extended to professionals and semi-professionals. Admittance was granted to Eurasians and the non-European spouses of Australian citizens. This meant that Australian-born Chinese could marry Chinese women in Hong Kong and China and bring them to Australia. As a result of these reforms, in 1971 the Chinese population reached 26,000, as against 23,568 in 1961, ten years earlier.

Then suddenly, towards the end of 1972, landmark decisions by the government thoroughly changed the nature of Chinese immigration. Non-discriminatory immigration was introduced and the policy of multiculturalism was adopted. At the same time, Australia recognised the People's Republic of China. Now the small flow of Chinese migrants from Hong Kong, Singapore and Malaysia increased. With China opening its markets to the world in the 1980s, Australia and China began exploring trade and investment possibilities. Chinese business migrants and entrepreneurs began arriving from Hong Kong and Taiwan, as well as highly trained specialists from China. By 1986, the Chinese population of Australia registered 200,000. In 1991, it stood at 350,000, with Chinese the third most spoken language. By 1996, when census returns placed the Chinese population at around 450,000, the philosophy of the old immigration policy had begun withering on the vine.

Mavis Gock Yen

Epilogue

When Mavis Yen penned her conclusion in the mid-to-late 1990s, she wrote with a sense of optimism for the future of Australian–Chinese relations. She couched her conclusion against the gradual loosening of restrictions on Chinese people to enter Australia due to her personal history. When Mavis returned to Australia as an eighteen-year-old in 1935 after ten years living with her family in China, she disembarked in Sydney and produced her Australian travel documentation. It was a copy of her birth certificate with a photo of herself as a nine-year-old attached and her finger and palm prints on the back. It was somewhat of an epiphany for her. 'I was born here,' she thought. 'They fingerprinted me, a little nine-year-old girl, like a criminal!' That moment was one of many that inspired her to write this book.

Mavis was also reflecting on the vast opportunities opening up to the younger generation of Chinese Australians. Speaking to her interviewees, she learned about the world opening up to their children and grandchildren. They were teachers, lawyers, doctors, bankers, finance specialists, health and community workers, celebrity chefs and cookbook writers rather than restaurant workers, artists and fashion moguls. They were free to love and marry whom they chose and they were creating families of their own. They were buying houses and moving out into the sprawling Australian suburbs. They were an intrinsic part of mainstream Australian society in a way that many of her interviewees and their parents and grandparents could hardly imagine.

The renewal of diplomatic relations in the early 1970s not only brought about closer political and economic ties but heralded a concerted bipartisan effort over the following twenty years, pursued by successive governments, to create a deeper understanding of China, its people and culture. The gradual opening of the Chinese economy to the world at that time was seen as a sign of hope and was supported by Western capitalist nations. The efforts of the Chinese government to lift its people out of poverty were applauded and there was genuine optimism that China would fully embrace the emerging post-Cold War world order.

Sadly, for a wide range of reasons, that hope and optimism for the future of Australian–Chinese relations had diminished by the time this book was being prepared for publication. This would have greatly disappointed Mavis. She would have worried about the base level of current debate about China in the media and in government circles that harks back to the jingoistic days of the *Bulletin* from the 1880s and 1890s. Not because she was blind to the flaws of China – after all, she had lived in China from 1946 to 1981 and rode the ups and downs of failed economic policies, the madness of the Cultural Revolution (文化大革命) and the cruelties of an authoritarian regime – but because she thought there had to be a better way.

Mavis was more interested in the shared common humanity, the desire of people, both in Australia and in China, to work and provide for their families and communities. Her interviewees had endured the 'Ching Chong Chinaman' days and she did not want a return to ingrained racism. Her hope in writing this book was to inspire greater mutual understanding. Still, she would have been buoyed by the fact that in 2018 there were 526,040 Australian residents born in China, up from 387,420 five years previously.[1] The 2016 census found that Australia was home to more than 1.2 million people of Chinese ancestry.[2] The Australian lifestyle clearly has increasing appeal in China, with approximately three-fifths of Australian residents born in China arriving here since 2006. The relatively young median age of Chinese-born residents (thirty-three years) would have heartened Mavis with the hope that they, as well as all Australians with Chinese heritage, would continue to invest their talents and abilities in the future of a tolerant and welcoming Australia.

Richard Horsburgh

---

1 Australian Bureau of Statistics Media release, 'ABS reveals insights into Australia's Chinese population on Chinese New Year', 16 February 2018, https://tinyurl.com/ebxsxvww
2 See Australian Bureau of Statistics 2016 Census QuickStats Country of Birth, https://tinyurl.com/y3xufcf3

Acknowledgements

South Flows the Pearl is a tribute to the foresight, ingenuity and dedication of Mavis Gock Yen, who recorded the lives of twelve Australian Chinese families in the late 1980s and early 1990s. As she said at the time during the interviews, 'I want to show the Chinese people [in Australia] as they really are'. Coming from the same community background as her interviewees and having a similar lived experience, this is truly a book written from the perspective of an 'insider'.

South Flows the Pearl could so easily have been lost for all time. Fortunately, many enthusiastic and dedicated people have worked tirelessly and enthusiastically to see this book published. Firstly, we would like to thank the families of all the interviewees. As the interviews were conducted by Mavis Yen some twenty-five to thirty-five years ago, and all the participants with the exception of two have passed away, it was with a mixture of detective work and a dose of good fortune that we were able to track down family members spread all across Australia. None of them were aware that the interviews had taken place so we were pleasantly surprised that they all contributed so willingly to the project and were very kind and cooperative in supplying us with family photos and providing extra information about their families.

We acknowledge and thank the Heritage Council of NSW and the Royal Australian Historical Society for their funding and encouragement by means of the 2020 Small Grants Program to see this work published. Without that financial support this book would not have been the quality product that it is.

To Sydney University Press, many thanks for believing in this work and recognising its historical value. This quality production is a tribute to their dedication and professionalism.

The Chinese Australian Historical Society sponsored our grant application and we would like to thank its members for their support and encouragement.

Many people who work in the field of Chinese Australian history have provided great assistance throughout, be they academics, staff of various libraries and museums, and the many dedicated researchers in this field both at the community level. There are too many to mention by name but we would like to thank Dr Kate Bagnall and Dr Sophie Couchman on the professional side for their initial encouragement and all the interested community supporters.

We had a dedicated project team who worked closely with us. Dr Sophie Loy-Wilson, Senior Lecturer in Australian History at Sydney University, has not only written the book's introduction but was instrumental in engaging the support of the Sydney University Press. Her introduction reflects on Mavis Yen's achievement and provides a contemporary perspective on the individual stories and takes into account the advances in scholarship in Chinese Australian history in the intervening years. Dr Michael Williams, Adjunct Professor with the Australia-China Institute for Arts and Culture at Western Sydney University, has been a public champion of the book from day one and provided invaluable editorial guidance. Dr Cheryle Yin Lo, Co-founder and Director of Cultural ConneXions, gave all-round assistance and encouragement. Cheryle's mother's story plays a prominent part in the book. We were honoured that the Former Dean of Arts, Hong Kong University, Kam Louie agreed to write such a heartfelt foreword.

Finally, thanks to our son James, who has put up with his parents' obsession over the last decade but has always been supportive.

Bibliography

Published works consulted by Mavis Gock Yen (郭美華)

Allen, M.T. Chinese Religious Traditions and Practice in Sydney NSW in the 20th Century. Unpublished honours thesis, University of Sydney, 1981.
Atkinson, Anne. *The Bicentennial Dictionary of Western Australians Volume Five, Asian Immigrants to Western Australia 1829–1901.* (Perth: University of Western Australia Press, 1988).
Bolton, G.C. *A Thousand Miles Away* (Brisbane: Jacaranda Press, 1963).
Braga, J.M. 'The "Tamao" of the Portuguese Pioneers', *Tien Hsia Monthly* 8(5): 420–32.
Char Tin-Yuke. *The Sandalwood Mountains* (Honolulu: University of Hawai'i Press, 1975).
Char Tin-Yuke. *The Bamboo Path.* (Honolulu: Hawai'i Chinese History Centre, 1977).
Chinn, Thomas W., H. Mark Lai and Philip P. Choy. *A History of the Chinese in California: A Syllabus* (Ann Arbor, MI: Chinese Historical Society of America, 1969).
Choi, C.Y. *Chinese Migration and Settlement in Australia* (Sydney: Sydney University Press, 1974).
Chung Kun Ai. *My Seventy-Nine Years in Hawaii* (Hong Kong: Cosmorama Pictorial Publisher, 1960).
Chungshan Wen Hsien (*Chungshan Gazetteer*) (Chungshan, 1946).
Gockchin, P. *The Origin and Development of the Wing On Spirit* (Hong Kong, 1960).
Heungshan Yuen Gee (*Heungshan County Gazetteer*) (Shekki, 1874).
Hodge, Brian. *Frontiers of Gold* (Penshurst, NSW: Cambaroora Star Publications, 1979).
Horsfall, David. *March to Big Gold Mountain* (Ascot Vale, VIC: Red Rooster Press, 1985).
Jones, T. *The Chinese in the Northern Territory* (Darwin: NTU Press, 1990).
Jupp, James. *The Australian People* (North Ryde, NSW: Angus & Robertson, 1988).
Krone, Rev. Mr Rudolph. 'A Notice of the Sanon District', *Journal of the Hong Kong Branch of the Royal Asiatic Society,* 1967.
Lo Hsiang-lin et al. *Hong Kong and Its External Communications before 1842* (Hong Kong: Institute of Chinese Culture, 1963).
May, Cathie. *Topsawyers: The Chinese in Cairns, 1870–1920* (Townsville: James Cook University, 1984).
Lary, Diana. *Warlord Soldiers: Chinese Common Soldiers, 1911–1937* (Cambridge: Cambridge University Press, 1985).
Morse, H.B. *The Trade and Administration of China* (New York: Russell & Russell, New York, 1908).
Morse, H.B. and MacNair, H.F. *Far Eastern International Relations* (New York: Houghton Mifflin Company, 1931).

Palfreeman, A.C. *The Administration of the White Australian Policy* (Melbourne: Melbourne University Press, 1967).
Pott, Francis L.K. *A Short History of Shanghai; Being an Account of the Growth and Development of the International Settlement, Shanghai* (Shanghai: Kelly & Walsh, 1928).
Sincere Company. *Twenty-Fifth Anniversary Commemorative Book of the Sincere Company, Hong Kong* (Hong Kong, 1925).
Wing On Co. Ltd. *Twenty-Fifth Anniversary Commemorative Book of the Wing On Co. Ltd., Hong Kong* (Hong Kong, 1932).
Wai Jane Char and Tin Yuke Char. *Chinese Historic Sites and Pioneer Families of Rural Oahu* (Honolulu: Chinese History Center of Hawai'i, 1988).
Wang Sing-wu. *The Organization of Chinese Emigration 1848–1888, with Special Reference to Chinese Emigration to Australia* (San Francisco: Chinese Materials Center, Inc., 1978).
Yarwood, A.T. *Attitudes to Non-European Immigration* (Stanmore, NSW: Cassell Australia Limited, 1968).
Yarwood, A.T. *Asian Migration to Australia: The Background to Exclusion, 1896–1923* (Melbourne: Melbourne University Press, 1967).
Yen Ching-Hwang. *Coolies and Mandarins: China's Protection of Overseas Chinese during the Late Ch'ing Period* (Singapore: Singapore University Press, 1985).
Yong, C.F. *The New Gold Mountain* (Richmond, SA: Raphael Arts, 1977).
Zhong Shan Wen Shi (Cultural History of Chung Shan). Chinese People's Political Consultative Conference, Kwangtung, Selection No. 13, 1987.

Glossary

Villages and Locations

English	Chinese	Pin Yin
An Yuan	安遠	An Yuan
Baak Shek	白石	Bai Shi
Bubbling Well Road	南京西路	Nan Jing Xi Lu
Buck Hung	嶺背北坑	Ling Bei Bei Keng
Chai Ky Lok	茶奇落（槎橋）	Cha Qi Luo
Chau Bin	曹邊	Cao Bian
Chekiang	浙江	Zhe Jiang
Chekiang Road	浙江路	Zhe Jiang Lu
Cheung Gock	象角	Xiang Jiao
Chongqing	重慶	Chong Qing
Chuk Sau Yuen	竹秀園	Zhu Xiu Yuan
Chung Shan	中山	Zhong Shan
Coloane	路環	Lu Huang
Dai Fun	大汾	Da Fen
Dai Laam	大嵐	Da Lan
Dai Ma Loo	大馬路	Da Ma Lu
Dixwell Road	溧陽路	Li Yang Lu
Dong Shan	東山	Dong Shan
Doo Tow	渡頭	Du Tou
Dou Mun	斗門	Dou Men
En Ping	恩平	En Ping
Fa County	花縣（花都）	Hua Xian
Fatshan	佛山	Fo Shan
Foong Lock Lee	豐樂里	Feng Le Li

South Flows the Pearl

English	Chinese	Pin Yin
Fukien	福建	Fu Jian
Fung Cyun	馮村	Feng Cun
Gou Kuk Hong	九曲巷	Jiu Qu Xiang
Guangzhou	廣州	Guang Zhou
Haam Yu Laan	鹹魚欄	Xian Yu Lan
Haang Mei	恆美	Heng Mei
Hah Ki	下岐	Xia Qi
Hainan Island	海南島	Hai Nan Dao
Hangchow	杭州	Hang Zhou
Henan	河南	He Nan
Heung Chow	香洲	Xiang Zhou
Heung Shan	香山	Xiang Shan
Hei Fung Waan	起鳳環	Qi Feng Huan
Hok Shan	鶴山	He Shan
Hongkew	虹橋	Hong Qiao
Hoy Ping	開平	Kai Ping
Huangpu Park	黃埔公園	Huang Pu Gong Yuan
Jaang Sheng	增城	Zeng Cheng
Jook Hung	嶺背竹坑	Ling Bei Zhu Keng
Ki Shan	岐山	Qi Shan
Kiang Si	江西	Jiang Xi
Kiangsu	江蘇	Jiang Su
Kim Mou	乾霧	Qian Wu
KiuKiang Road	九江路	Jiu Jiang Lu
Kong Hoy	江海	Jiang Hai
Kong Moon	江門	Jiang Men
Kou Ming	高明	Gao Ming
Kou Yiu	高要	Gao Yao
Kowloon	九龍	Jiu Long
Kukong	曲江	Qu Jiang
Kwangsi	廣西	Guang Xi
Kwangtung	廣東	Guang Dong
Kwei Chow	貴州	Gui Zhou

Glossary

English	Chinese	Pin Yin
Kweilin	桂林	Gui Lin
Lantau	大嶼山	Da Yu Shan
Leung Du	良都	Liang Du
Ling Ding Island	內伶仃島	Nei Ling Ding Dao
Ling Ding Shan	伶仃山	Ling Ding Shan
Lung Du	隆都	Long Du
Lung Hooey	隆墟	Long Xu
Lung Ngan Sy Chung	龍眼樹涌（樹涌）	Long Yan Shu Chong
Maan Geng Sha	萬頃沙	Wan Qing Sha
Meiling Pass	梅嶺關	Mei Ling Guan
Mo Dou Mun	磨刀門	Mo Dao Men
Nam Hong	南雄	Nan Xiong
Nam Hung	嶺背南坑	Ling Bei Nan Keng
Nam Kuan	南關	Nan Guan
Nam Mun Gai See	南門街市	Nan Men Jie Shi
Nam Yung	南雄	Nan Xiong
Nanking (Road)	南京	Nan Jing
Nanking Road	南京路	Nan Jing Lu
Nanling ranges	南嶺山脈	Nan Ling Shan Mai
North Szechuen Road	四川北路	Si Chuan Bei Lu
Saah Kai	沙溪	Sha Xi
Saam Kwok Jetty	三角碼頭	San Jiao Ma Tou
Saam Nam	三南（龍南縣、定南縣、全南縣）	San Nan
Sahp Baat Gaan	十八間	Shi Ba Jian
Sai Kuan	西關	Xi Guan
Sai See Gaai	西市街	Xi Shi Jie
Salted Fish Lane	鹹魚欄	Xian Yu Lan
Sandalwood Islands	檀香山	Tan Xiang Shan
Sau Mei Yuen	秀美園	Xiu Mei Yuan
See Yup	四邑	Si Yi
Sha Chung	沙涌	Sha Chong
Shameen	沙面	Sha Mian

English	Chinese	Pin Yin
Shanghai North Railway Station	上海北站	Shang Hai Bei Zhan
Shek Joong	嶺背石冲	Ling Bei Shi Chong
Shekki	石岐	Shi Qi
Sheung Tong	上塘	Shang Tang
Shiu Heng	肇慶	Zhao Qing
Shiukwan	韶關	Shao Guan
Shun Tak	順德	Shun De
Sian	西安	Xi An
Sin Feng	信豐	Xin Feng
Soochow Creek	蘇州河	Su Zhou He
Sun Tong	新塘	Xin Tang
Sun Wen Central	孫文中路	Sun Wen Zhong Lu
Sun Wen East Street	孫文东路	Sun Wen Dong Lu
Sun Wen West street	孫文西路	Sun Wen Xi Lu
Sun Wooey	新會	Xin Hui
Sunning	新寧	Xin Ning
Szechuen	四川	Si Chuan
Tai Po Kong	大埔港	Da Pu Gang
Tai Po Market	大埔墟	Da Pu Xu
Tai-O	大澳	Da Ao
Taipa	氹仔	Dang Zai
Taiwan	台灣	Tai Wan
Tit Sehng	鐵城	Tie Cheng
Toishan	台山	Tai Shan
Tong Ka	唐家	Tang Jia
Tung Koon	東莞	Dong Guan
Tung Shan	東山	Dong Shan
Um Tong	安堂	An Tang
Wanchai	灣仔	Wan Zai
West Lake	西湖	Xi Hu
West Point	西角	Xi Jiao
West River	西江	Xi Jiang

Glossary

English	Chinese	Pin Yin
Whangpoo Park	黃浦公園	Huang Pu Gong Yuan
Whangpoo River	黃浦江	Huang Pu Jiang
Woosung Road	吳淞路	Wu Song Lu
Wu Xi	無錫	Wu Xi
Wuhan	武漢	Wu Han
Wusih	無錫	Wu Xi
Yangtze River	揚子江	Yang Zi Jiang
Yaumati	油麻地	You Ma Di
Yenan	延安	Yan An
Yit Loi Gaai	悅來街	Yue Lai Jie
Zhongshan	中山	Zhong Shan

Temples and Associations

English	Chinese	Pin Yin
A-Ma-Gau	媽祖閣	Ma Zu Ge
Chee tong	祠堂	Ci Tang
Chinese Youth League	僑青社	Qiao Qing She
Chung Shan Society	中山同鄉會	Zhong Shan Tong Xiang Hui
Chung Wah	中華	Zhong Hua
Gee Gong Tong	致公堂	Zhi Gong Tang
Goon Yee Tong	公義堂	Gong Yi Tang
Gum shan jong	金山莊	Jin Shan Zhuang
Heaven and Earth Society	天地會	Tian Di Hui
Heung Shan Society	香山同鄉會	Xiang Shan Tong Xiang Hui
Hok Goong	學宮（內有儒學、孔廟，合稱學宮）	Xue Gong
Hong Shing Temple, Sydney	洪聖宮/要明廟/要明洪福堂	Hong Sheng Gong
Hung League	洪門	Hong Men

English	Chinese	Pin Yin
Kong Chew Society	岡山同鄉會	Gang Shan Tong Xiang Hui
Kuomintang	國民黨	Guo Min Dang
Lai Gee Wooey	黎子會	Li Zi Hui
Luen Fook Tong	聯福堂	Lian Fu Tang
Loong Yee Tong	聯義堂	Lian Yi Tang
Ma Ga Chee	馬家祠	Ma Jia Ci
Ma Ga Dai Chee	馬家大祠	Ma Jia Da Ci
Ma Kok Miu	媽閣廟	Ma Ge Miao
On Yick Lee	安益利	An Yi Li
See Yup Society	四邑會館	Si Yi Hui Guan
See Yup Temple (Melbourne)	四邑關帝廟	Si Yi Guan Di Miao
See Yup Temple (Sydney)	四邑關聖帝廟	Si Yi Guan Sheng Di Miao
Tam Gong Miu	譚公廟	Tan Gong Miao
War Gook Miu	禾穀廟	He Gu Miao
Wing Lock Tong	永樂堂	Yong Le Tang

People and Names

English	Chinese	Pin Yin
Ah Baak	阿伯	A Bo
Ah Goong	阿公	A Gong
Ah Je	阿姐	A Jie
Ah Kin	趙權	Zhao Quan
Ah Mung/Ah Ming	阿明	A Ming
Ah Paw	阿婆	A Po
Ah Sook	阿叔	A Shu
Ah Yeh	阿爺	A Ye
Andrew (Wong)	黃學勇	Huang Xue Yong
Ayee	阿姨	A Yi
Arthur Lock	鄭嘉樂	Zheng Jia Le

Glossary

English	Chinese	Pin Yin
Baak	伯	Bo
Baak Moo	伯母	Bo Mu
Baak Sooey Goong	百歲公	Bai Sui Gong
Basil (Parkee)	黎宗枝	Li Zong Zhi
Bew Sook	表叔	Biao Shu
Billy Jong	張岳彪	Zhang Yue Biao
Cecil (Parkee)	黎滿枝	Li Man Zhi
Chang	張	Zhang
Chang Hsueh-liang	張學良	Zhang Xue Liang
Chang Tso-Lin	張作霖	Zhang Zuo Lin
Charles Lee	李貴方	Li Gui Fang
Chen	陳	Chen
Chen Chai-tong	陳濟棠	Chen Ji Tang
Chen Danyan	陳丹燕	Chen Dan Yan
Chen Geng Meng	陳炯明	Chen Jiong Ming
Cheung	蔣	Jiang
Cheung Jaap	章澤	Zhang Ze
Chiang	蔣	Jiang
Chiang Kai-Shek	蔣介石	Jiang Jie Shi
Cho Baak	曹伯	Cao Bo
Chong (Wong)	黃祥	Huang Xiang
Choong Kim	锺啓镇	Zhong Qi Zhen
Daisy Kwok	郭婉瑩	Guo Wan Ying
Don Yin Lo	羅順忠	Luo Shun Zhong
Dong	董	Dong
Evelyn Yin Lo	黎鑽好	Li Zuan Hao
Fong	鄺	Kuang
Fong Henley	鄺榮修	Kuang Rong Xiu
Frank Lee Gee	李植良	Li Zhi Liang
Fred Wong	黃家權	Huang Jia Quan
Gock	郭	Guo
Gock Bew	郭標	Guo Biao
Gock Chin	郭泉	Guo Quan

English	Chinese	Pin Yin
Gock Kway Fong	郭桂芳	Guo Gui Fang
Gock Lock	郭樂	Guo Le
Gock Lum Song	郭琳爽	Guo Lin Shuang
Gock Ming	郭明	Guo Ming
Gock Pui Heen	郭沛勛	Guo Pei Xun
Gock Quay	郭葵	Guo Kui
Gock Son	郭順	Guo Shun
Goong	公	Gong
Gwoo Moo	姑母	Gu Mu
Harry Ah Cann	蔣全福	Jiang Quan Fu
Harry Gock Ming	郭桂芳	Guo Gui Fang
Harry Pang	馮海星	Feng Hai Xing
Henry (Parkee)	黎鑑枝	Li Jian Zhi
Ho	何	He
Homantin	何文田	He Wen Tian
Hoon Mun	煥文	Huan Wen
Hoy	(郭)海	(Guo) Hai
Hoy Lee	黃沛均	Huang Pei Jun
Hoy Poy	靄培	Ai Pei
Jack Wong	黃章澤	Huang Zhang Ze
Jarng So Hing	湛素興	Zhan Su Xing
Je je	姐姐	Jie Jie
Jee Jeng	致政	Zhi Zheng
John Fong	鄺寶贊	Kuang Bao Zan
Joong Jau	宗周	Zong Zhou
Kou Fuh	舅父	Jiu Fu
Kuang Hsu	光緒	Guang Xu
Kway Fong	桂芳	Gui Fang
Kwong	鄺	Kuang
Kwong Sue Duk	鄺仕德	Kuang Shi De
Lai	黎	Li
Lai Park Sun	黎柏燊	Li Bo Shen
Lai Parkee	黎柏	Li Bo

Glossary

English	Chinese	Pin Yin
Lai War Hing	黎和興	Li He Xing
Lam Tim Yuk	林添玉	Lin Tian Yu
Lee	李	Li
Lee Goon Ick	李觀益	Li Guan Yi
Lee Sing	李成	Li Cheng
Les Ling	黃吳蘇	Huang Wu Su
Leslie (Parkee)	黎湛枝	Li Zhan Zhi
Leong Cheong	梁創	Liang Chuang
Leung	梁	Liang
Leung Gum Seui	梁金水	Liang Jin Shui
Leung Pui	梁社培	Liang She Pei
Leung Seui	梁水	Liang Shui
Li-Lin (Wong)	黃麗蓮	Huang Li Lian
Lindsay Parkee	黎金枝	Li Jin Zhi
Lo	劉	Liu
Lo faahn	老番	Lao Fan
Lo gee	撈主（父親）	Lao Zhu
Louey	雷	Lei
Louey Joong	侶翁	Lü Weng
Louie Lee	黃來弟	Huang Lai Di
Lum	林	Lin
Lum Dai Wong	馮林弟	Feng Lin Di
Lum Song	琳爽	Lin Shuang
Lum Yook Wun	林玉雲	Lin Yu Yun
Ma	馬	Ma
Ma Joe Sing	馬祖星	Ma Zu Xing
Ma Sin Saang	馬先生	Ma Xian Sheng
Ma Ying Biu	馬應彪	Ma Ying Biao
Mao Tse-tung	毛澤東	Mao Ze Dong
Mao Zedong	毛澤東	Mao Ze Dong
Melinda (Wong)	黃美蓮	Huang Mei Lian
Mrs Chiew	趙太	Zhao Tai
Ngoi Fuh	外父（岳父）	Wai Fu

English	Chinese	Pin Yin
Ou Yeung Mun Hing	歐陽民慶	Ou Yang Min Qing
Pang	彭	Peng
Pang Yoong Kwun	彭容坤	Peng Rong Kun
Peter Googan	劉顯材	Liu Xian Cai
Peter Wong	黃寶榮	Huang Bao Rong
Po Po	婆婆	Po Po
Pui	培	Pei
Quan Mane	關明	Guan Ming
Quong Tart	梅光達	Mei Guang Da
Saam Baak	三伯	San Bo
Saam Baak Moo	三伯母	San Bo Mu
Saam Gor	三哥	San Ge
Sek	(郭)錫	(Guo) Xi
Siu Gim Hee	蕭金喜	Xiao Jin Xi
Stanley Wai	布德威	Bu De Wei
Sook	叔	Shu
Sue Yung Lee	李瑞榮	Li Rui Rong
Sun	孫	Sun
Sun Chuan Fang	孫傳芳	Sun Chuan Fang
Sun Yat-sen	孫逸仙	Sun Yi Xian
Tam	譚	Tan
Tang Shao-Yi	唐紹儀	Tang Shao Yi
Tsai	蔡	Cai
Tsai Ting-Kai	蔡廷鍇	Cai Ting Kai
Voy Sang Lee	李會生	Li Hui Sheng
William Suey Ling	黃瑞麟	Huang Rui Lin
Wong	黃	Huang
Wong Wah Gee	黃華智	Huang Hua Zhi
Wong Wah Hum	黃華欽	Huang Hua Qin
Wong Wah Lay	黃華禮	Huang Hua Li
Wong Wah Shu	黃華樹	Huang Hua Shu
Wong Wah Yee	黃華義	Huang Hua Yi
Yang Fu-sheng	楊虎城	Yang Hu Cheng

Glossary

English	Chinese	Pin Yin
Yee Paw	姨婆	Yi Po
Yee Sou	二嫂	Er Sao
Yu	余	Yu
Yu Han-mou	余漢謀	Yu Han Mou
Yuan Shih-Kai	袁世凱	Yuan Shi Kai
Yuen	阮	Ruan
Yuen Hoy Poy	阮靄培	Ruan Ai Pei

Businesses and Organisations

English	Chinese	Pin Yin
Beijing Second Foreign Languages Institute	北京第二外國語學院	Bei Jing Di Er Wai Guo Yu Xue Yuan
Cantonese or Guang Zhou operas	粵劇團	Yue Ju Tuan
Cheong On Lou	長安樓	Chang An Lou
Cheong On Cafe	長安餐室	Chang An Can Shi
Chinese Indusrial Cooperatives	中國工業合作協會	Zhong Guo Gong Ye He Zuo Xie Hui
Dai Dong	大東旅社	Da Dong Lü She
Great Eastern Hotel	大東旅社	Da Dong Lü She
Fong Lee	芳利	Fang Li
Fong War Lee	芳華利	Fang Hua Li
Great Hall of the People	人民大會堂	Ren Min Da Hui Tang
Hop Hing	合興	He Xing
Jun Kwong	真光	Zhen Guang
Kwang Chow Lou	廣州樓	Guang Zhou Lou
Kwong On	廣安	Guang An
Kwong War Chong	廣和昌	Guang He Chang
Kwong War Fong	廣和芳	Guang He Fang
Kwong War Hong	廣和祥	Guang He Xiang
Lean Sun Low	聯新樓	Lian Xin Lou
Luk Kwok Hotel	六國飯店	Liu Guo Fan Dian

English	Chinese	Pin Yin
May Seven Cadre School	五七幹校	Wu Qi Gan Xiao
Nanjing (University)	南京	Nan Jing
Nanking (Restaurant)	南京	Nan Jing
National Peasant Movement Institute	廣州農民運動講習所	Guang Zhou Nong Min Yun Dong Jiang Xi Suo
Ng Gee Gooey	五子館	Wu Zi Guan
People's Hospital	人民醫院	Ren Min Yi Yuan
Sang On Tiy & Co.	生安泰公司	Sheng An Tai Gong Si
Shanghai (restaurant)	上海	Shang Hai
Shanghai Wing On Company	上海永安公司	Shang Hai Yong An Gong Si
Sincere	先施	Xian Shi
Sincere Company	先施公司	Xian Shi Gong Si
Sun Sai Gai	新世紀	Xin Shi Ji
Sun Sun Company	新新公司	Xin Xin Gong Si
Taiping	太平	Tai Ping
The Sun Company	大新公司	Da Xin Gong Si
Tientsin (restaurant)	天津	Tian Jin
Wah Loong	華隆	Hua Long
Wing Cheong Sing	永昌成	Yong Chang Cheng
Wing Hing	永興	Yong Xing
Wing On	永安	Yong An
Wing On & Co.	永安果欄	Yong An Guo Lan
Wing On (fruit)	永安果欄	Yong An Guo Lan
Wing Sang	永生	Yong Sheng
Wing Shing	永盛	Yong Sheng
Wing Shun Yuen	永順源	Yong Shun Yuan
Wing Yick	永益	Yong Yi
Wu Hop	五合	Wu He
Xinhua News Agency	新華通訊社	Xin Hua Tong Xun She
Yee Lee	義利	Yi Li
Yee Sing	日昇	Ri Sheng

Glossary

History

English	Chinese	Pin Yin
Beiyang	北洋	Bei Yang
Beiyang government	北洋政府	Bei Yang Zheng Fu
Beiyang warlords	北洋軍閥	Bei Yang Jun Fa
Ching dynasty	清朝	Qing Chao
Eastern Chou	東周	Dong Zhou
Hakka War	土客械鬥	Tu Ke Jie Dou
Ming dynasty	明朝	Ming Chao
Opium War	鴉片戰爭	Ya Pian Zhan Zheng
Sian Incident	西安事變	Xi An Shi Bian
Southern Sung dynasty	南宋	Nan Song
Sung	宋	Song
Sung dynasty	宋朝	Song Chao
Taiping rebellion	太平天國	Tai Ping Tian Guo
Tang dynasty	唐朝	Tang Chao
Cultural Revolution	文化大革命	Wen Hua Da Ge Ming
Yuan dynasty	元朝	Yuan Chao

Miscellaneous

English	Chinese	Pin Yin
Bai shen	拜神	Bai Shen
Bao	包	Bao
Bin gwei la	變鬼啦	Bian Gui La
Boat race festival	端午節	Duan Wu Jie
Bok choy	白菜	Bai Cai
Bok hop guns	駁殼槍	Bo Ke Qiang
Cha	茶	Cha
Cha lou	茶樓	Cha Lou
Cha wooey	茶會	Cha Hui
Chaah siu	叉燒	Cha Shao

English	Chinese	Pin Yin
Chaah siu bao	叉燒包	Cha Shao Bao
Chaan Lou	餐樓	Can Lou
Chai	柴	Chai
Cheong	槍	Qiang
Cheong saam	長衫/旗袍	Chang Shan
Chihn	前	Qian
Chihn	錢	Qian
Chim	簽	Qian
Ching	清	Qing
Ching dang	清黨	Qing Dang
Ching Ming	清明	Qing Ming
Chung Shan dialect	中山話	Zhong Shan Hua
Chop suey	雜碎	Za Sui
Choy gee	財主	Cai Zhu
Choy gee lo	財主佬	Cai Zhu Lao
Da foo tou	大褲頭	Da Ku Tou
Daah min	打麵	Da Mian
Daah lan gung	打攬工/打纜工	Da Lan Gong
Daai ga sek faahn	大家吃飯	Da Jia Chi Fan
Dai chong	底艙	Di Cang
Dai daam	大膽	Da Dan
Dai tin yee	大天二	Da Tian Er
Dei	地	Di
Dim sims	點心	Dian Xin
Din Ma	癲馬	Dian Ma
Ding kui	頂她	Ding Ta
Faahn	飯	Fan
Faahn gwai	番鬼	Fan Gui
Faahn gwai jai	番鬼仔	Fan Gui Zai
Faahn gwai na	番鬼奶	Fan Gui Nai
Faai yun	廢人	Fei Ren
Faan gwai gern	番鬼仔	Fan Gui Zai
Faar kei gwai	花旗鬼	Hua Qi Gui

Glossary

English	Chinese	Pin Yin
Fan kwai mui	番鬼妹	Fan Gui Mei
Fan tan	番攤	Fan Tan
Fo ki	伙計	Huo Ji
Foo	福	Fu
Foo	褲	Ku
Fung shui	風水	Feng Shui
Gay tou	雞頭	Ji Tou
Gei ho ji	幾毫子	Ji Hao Zi
Gompooyie	金背	Jin Bei
Gong de m'wooey gong, paaa nei meia	講都不會講，怕你什麼	Jiang Dou Bu Hui Jiang, Pa Ni Shen Me
Gou keui deih	告他們	Gao Ta Men
Gum shan	金山	Jin Shan
Gum shan bang	金山餅	Jin Shan Bing
Gum Shan Haak	金山客	Jin Shan Ke
Gwai	鬼	Gui
Gwai Jay	鬼仔	Gui Zai
Gwai paw	鬼婆	Gui Po
Gwei Mei	桂味	Gui Wei
Gwoon choy lo	棺材佬	Guan Cai Lao
Ha mai	蝦米	Xia Mi
Haak dou hai baak	黑都是白	Hei Dou Shi Bai
Haak gwai jaai	黑鬼仔	Hei Gui Zai
Haak Yip Chee	黑葉枝	Hei Ye Zhi
Haam mooey	鹹梅	Xian Mei
Haam yu	鹹魚	Xian Yu
Haang suen jay	航船仔	Hang Chuan Zai
Hak ka	客家	Ke Jia
Hakka	客家	Ke Jia
Hei faan	開飯	Kai Fan
Heung	香	Xiang
Heung ha	鄉下	Xiang Xia
Heung you	香油	Xiang You

English	Chinese	Pin Yin
Hia puen	吃飯	Chi Fan
Hoi	開	Kai
Home of fish and rice	魚米之鄉	Yu Mi Zhi Xiang
Hung	洪	Hong
Hung yun	杏仁	Xing Ren
Jam baan	碪板	Zhen Ban
Jau	酒	Jiu
Jau Lau	酒樓	Jiu Lou
Jau mai pou	酒米舖	Jiu Mi Pu
Jin hou	戰壕	Zhan Hao
Joong	冲	Chong
Jouh mooi yan	做媒人	Zuo Mei Ren
Jue gwut	豬骨	Zhu Gu
Ki Kong Dou	歧港渡	Qi Gang Du
Kway Fong loi	桂芳來	Gui Fang Lai
Laap juk	蠟燭	La Zhu
Lap Cheong	臘腸	La Chang
Lau yip kum	柳葉琴	Liu Ye Qin
Lingnan	嶺南	Ling Nan
Lishee	利是/紅包	Li Shi
Lo ba	老闆	Lao Ban
Lo baak seng	老百姓	Lao Bai Xing
Load	擔	Dan
Loi lek bat ming	來歷不明	Lai Li Bu Ming
Long March	長征	Chang Zheng
Lou Shree Wong	老鼠王	Lao Shu Wang
Luk Fook Ting	六福亭	Liu Fu Ting
Lung ngans	龍眼	Long Yan
Lychee	荔枝	Li Zhi
Mahjong	麻將	Ma Jiang
Mid-autumn festival	中秋節	Zhong Qiu Jie
Ming	明	Ming
Miu jok goong	廟祝工	Miao Zhu Gong

Glossary

English	Chinese	Pin Yin
Mong Chihn hon	往前看	Wang Qian Kan
Moon festival	中秋節	Zhong Qiu Jie
Mou chihn	沒錢	Mei Qian
Mow	畝	Mu
M'sai bei chihn	不用給錢	Bu Yong Gei Qian
Na, sik la	你吃啦	Ni Chi La
Nakayama (Japanese)	中山（日文）	Zhong Shan
Ngou ye	過夜	Guo Ye
Ni goh gwai jai do sik gong jung man ge	你個鬼仔都知道講中文	Ni Ge Gui Zai Dou Zhi Dao Jiang Zhong Wen
Ni goh gwai mooi gong jung man ge	你個鬼妹講中文的	Ni Ge Gui Mei Jiang Zhong Wen De
Nor Mai Chee	糯米枝	Nuo Mi Zhi
Pa shan	爬山	Pa Shan
Pai gau	牌九	Pei Jiu
Pak-ah-pu	白鴿票	Bai Ge Piao
Pig (trade)	豬仔	Zhu Zai
Pipa	琵琶	Pi Pa
Piu, to, yin, t'sui	嫖賭煙醉	Piao Du Yan Zui
Pui Ching	培正	Pei Zheng
Putt to bu	疋頭部	Pi Tou Bu
Saai Bang	西餅	Xi Bing
Saam Yuet Hoong	三月紅	San Yue Hong
Saar ngan	沙眼	Sha Yan
Sap Jat Dim	十一點	Shi Yi Dian
See mew mai	細苗米	Xi Miao Mi
See tou fu	師頭婦	Shi Tou Fu
See you	豉油	Chi You
Seng Chun ge	姓Chun的	Xing Chun De
Seng Lai ge	姓黎的	Xing Li De
Shaang-Ki-Lung	省歧隆	Sheng Qi Long
Shanghai Princess	上海的金枝玉葉	Shang Hai De Jin Zhi Yu Ye
Shek	石	Shi
Shen Gong Hei	神功戲	Shen Gong Xi

English	Chinese	Pin Yin
Shiu jau	燒酒	Shao Jiu
Siu aap	燒鴨	Shao Ya
Siu maai	燒賣	Shao Mai
Tai chi	太極	Tai Ji
Tai jee jay	太子仔	Tai Zi Zai
Tam Gong	譚公	Tan Gong
Tam Gong festival	譚公誕	Tan Gong Dan
Teng Ka	蜑家	Dan Jia
Three Character Classic	三字經	San Zi Jing
Tin	田	Tian
Tin	天	Tian
Tin gau	天九	Tian Jiu
Tiy Sang	泰生	Tai Sheng
Tong	唐	Tang
Tong Shan	唐山	Tang Shan
Tung Koon yan	東莞人	Dong Guan Ren
Wai Chee	淮枝	Huai Zhi
Watch tower	碉樓	Diao Lou
Wok chaan	鍋鏟	Guo Chan
Wun sihk, hai ma	覓食，是嗎	Mi Shi, Shi Ma
Wun tun	雲吞/餛飩	Yun Tun
Yee	二	Er
Yee shong	衣裳	Yi Shang
Yin cheong	煙槍	Yan Qiang
Yin fa	煙花	Yan Hua
Yin toong	煙斗	Yan Dou
Yuan	圓	Yuan
Yueh chin	月琴	Yue Qin
Yukh faan	吃飯	Chi Fan
Yum cha	飲茶	Yin Cha
Yup	邑	Yi
Yup uk giu yun, Yup miu bai shen	入屋叫人，入廟拜神	Ru Wu Jiao Ren, Ru Miao Bai Shen

Index

Aboriginal people 185, 246, 247, 281, 289, 297, 300, 302, 303, 309, 349
Adelaide 304
Ah Chee family 246
Ah Gee family 246
alcohol 209, 212, 239, 251, 278, 283, 286, 310, 327
Alice Springs, NT 336, 350
Amoy dialect 137, 155
ancestor worship 21, 51, 60–61, 77, 90, 150
Anzac Day 111, 305
Atherton, QLD 77–84, 197
Atkinson, Peter 198
Australia China Friendship Society 306
Australian Labor Party 198, 313
Australian Security Intelligence Organisation (ASIO) 325

Baak Shek village 274
Babinda, QLD 81
banana trade 45
bandits 121, 139, 145, 147, 154, 159, 163, 184, 219
Bendigo, VIC 39, 40–42, 41, 50, 97, 99
Blackheath, NSW 287
bound feet *see* foot binding
Bourke, NSW 187
Brisbane, QLD 67, 201, 206
Broome, WA 97, 243, 244, 246–249, 343, 349, 350
Brunette Downs, NT 297

cabinet-making 111, 159
Cairns, QLD 196–201

California 99, 148, 244, 245, 334, 346
Camooweal, QLD 297, 302
Canada 88, 100, 158
Canton 46, 87, 88, 92, 124, 160, 167
Canton uprising 167, 172
Carnarvon, WA 97, 118, 249
carpenters *see* furniture industry; *see also* cabinet-making
cattle stations *see* pastoral stations
cemetery day 60, 235
Certificate of Exemption from the Dictation Test (CEDT) 12, 72, 107, 116, 129, 135, 184, 193
Chai Ky Lok village 99, 107, 151
Chan, Harry 336
Chang Hsueh-Liang 176
Chang, Leslie 39–50, 127, 128
Charters Towers, QLD 103, 302
Chau Bin village 50
Chen Chai-tong 166, 168, 174
Chen Geng Meng 47
Cheung Gock village 100, 111, 159
Chiang Kai-shek 48, 93, 128, 129, 139, 146, 160, 165, 168, 173, 175, 176
childbirth 115, 234, 275, 299, 300, 345, 347
Chin family 347
Chinatowns 2
  Atherton 78–80, 83
  Bendigo 42
  Broome 244
  Darwin 333, 336
  Perth 97
  Sydney 52–57, 212, 235, 274
Chinese Communist Party 91, 165
Chinese Masonic Society *see* Gee Gong Tong

381

Chinese New Year 56, 90, 151, 210, 278, 289, 354
Chinese Presbyterian Church 51, 54
Chinese Seamen's Union 202, 311, 325
Chinese Tennis Club 235
Chinese Workers Association 325
Chinese Youth League 51, 202, 213, 235, 294, 306, 311, 313, 325–326, 330, 332
Ching dynasty 47, 87, 87, 121, 146, 155, 160
ching ming *see* cemetery day
Choong Kim 249
Christianity 54–55, 80, 104, 105, 111, 129, 277, 290, 306, 321, 350
Christmas 109, 258, 278, 281, 354
Chuk Sau Yuen village 98, 100, 103, 105, 114, 121, 133, 145–164
Chung Shan county 47, 61, 67, 68, 69, 70, 78, 83, 88, 98, 100, 135, 136, 141, 145, 147, 186, 227, 350; *see also* Heung Shan county
Chung Shan dialect 180
Chung Wah Association 249, 251
clan 219, 224, 353
clothing 88, 137, 139, 141, 152, 209, 210, 349; *see also* tailoring
Cobar, NSW 287
Cohen family 281, 284, 295
Commonwealth Restriction Act 135
Communist Party of Australia 198, 311
commuter labourers 135–137, 142
Confucianism 74, 76, 126, 128, 135, 138, 139, 161
conscription 166, 178, 308
Cooktown, QLD 77
Coolgardie, WA 100, 243
Coon family 289
Cultural Revolution 141, 191

Dai Laam village 88, 90, 204
Darwin, NT 245, 300, 308, 309, 333, 336–339, 343–354
Davis family 281
department stores 45, 46, 48, 69, 105, 117, 120, 128, 131, 143, 179, 274; *see also* Sincere Company, Wing On department store
deportation 218, 226, 263
Derby, WA 118, 246
dictation test 13, 135, 331, 355; *see also* Certificate of Exemption from the Dictation Test (CEDT)
discrimination *see* racism
Donald, W.H. 176
Dong family 281

Doo Tow village 103, 154
Dou Mun district 163
dragon boat festival 151
droving 304
Dubbo, NSW 288, 289, 293

Echuca, VIC 41
education 67, 80, 138, 207, 229, 245, 302, 329, 343, 346; *see also* school
Emungulan, NT 40
English language 57, 71, 80, 104, 196, 232, 244, 246, 275, 294, 300, 324, 329, 336
Eurasian Australians 276, 281, 282, 283

factory work 230, 232, 239–241, 308
federation (of Australia) 135, 335
Fiji 45
Fitzgerald, Shirley 5
Fong Henley 246
Fong, John 243–253
Fong Lee & Co. department store 274, 291
Fong family 118
Fong Lim, Alec 337
Fong Lim, Doris 334–340
Fong Lim, George 336
Fong Lim, Katrina 341
Fong Ly 246
food 71, 80, 88, 91, 108, 121, 149, 168, 170, 180, 186, 201, 209, 210, 217, 222, 234, 235, 247, 260, 263, 276, 279, 281, 301, 302, 314, 324, 350; *see also* restaurants
foot binding 90, 99, 131, 149, 152, 275, 276, 279, 288
Foxhall family 281
Fremantle, WA 118
Fukien province 137, 243
funeral traditions 290
fung shui 152, 160
Fung Cyun village 275
furniture industry 52, 67, 70

gambling 40, 44, 56, 79, 114, 162, 184, 309; *see also* pak-ah-pu (lottery)
Gee Gong Tong 57, 78, 84, 235
George Lai (Parkee) 52
Geraldton, WA 97, 118, 249
Giese, Diana 4
Glen Innes, NSW 238
Gock Bew, George 105, 122, 183
Gock Chew, Harry 43
Gock Chew Gum 157, 184

Index

Gock Chin, Philip 103, 105, 121, 180
Gock Hoy 149
Gock Hoy Buck 102
Gock Hoy Gei 103, 149, 159
Gock Kway Fong *see* Gock Ming, Harry
Gock Lock, James 45, 103, 105, 120, 154, 180, 180
Gock Lum Song 121, 180
Gock Ming, Harry 12, 97–116, 117–133, 145–164, 179–191
Gock Ming, William viii, 97, 102, 190
Gock Son, Alan 122, 126, 127, 128
Gock Son, William 121, 122, 180
Gock Yea 104, 125, 127, 158
Gock Yen, Mavis *see* Ming, Mavis
gold rushes 39, 57, 77, 97, 99, 105, 129, 243, 273, 275, 281, 297, 334
Googan, Victor Peter 291
Goon Yee Tong society 291
Grassby, Al 327
Great Hall of the People, Beijing 260
gum shan (golden mountain) 274, 287, 344, 346

Haang Mei village 99, 122, 147, 148, 154, 156
Hainan Island 243, 292
Hakka people 90, 235, 353
Hardoon, Silas Aaron 46, 48
Hawai'i 68
Heaven and Earth Society 57
Herberton, QLD 80
Heung Chow township 93, 167, 177
Heung Shan county 43, 45, 87, 98, 121, 128, 136, 141, 147; *see also* Chung Shan county
Hill End, NSW 44
Hobart, TAS 305
Hong Kong 45, 46, 69, 72, 87, 88, 105, 117, 120–121, 124, 144, 146, 194, 207–212, 220–221, 225, 294, 309
Hoy Ping county 40, 334, 347
Hoy Poy family 111, 159
Hung League 57

immigration papers 102, 116, 260; *see also* Certificate of Exemption from the Dictation Test (CEDT)
Immigration Restriction Act 1901 98
immigration restrictions 72, 75, 77, 135, 321, 327, 331, 334; *see also* deportation, legislation
indentured labourers 243, 246, 247
Indian Australians 281
Irish Australians 39, 41, 50

Ironbarks, NSW *see* Stuart Town, NSW
Italian Australians 70, 77, 81

Jaang Sheng county 47, 52, 275, 288, 289, 291
Japan 48, 55, 57, 114, 122, 125, 144, 147, 165, 189, 214, 219, 313, 336, 344; *see also* Sino–Japanese War
Japanese Australians 97, 246, 247
Jenkins, Mabel 97, 104
Jun Kwong Company 45, 144

Kalgoorlie, WA 100, 243
Katherine, NT 309, 334, 336, 347
Kiang Si provence 150, 168
Kimberley region, WA 243
Kou Yiu county 232, 322
Kuomintang 48, 78, 91, 131, 139, 165, 172
Kuranda, QLD 199
Kwangsi province 160, 165
Kwangtung province 87, 150, 160, 166, 178, 243
Kweilin 142
Kwong Lee family 251
Kwong Sue Duk 9, 77, 79
Kwong War Chong company 236

Lai War Hing 42, 43, 47, 57
land reform 227
Lang family 281
Lang, Jack 186
laundries 70
Lawn Hill Station, QLD 297, 311
Lee family 281, 347
Lee, Elizabeth 343–354
Lee family 251
Lee Gee, Frank 12, 77–85, 87–95, 165–178, 193–206, 308
Lee, Hoy 9, 273–296
Lee, Jessie 141
Lee On, Albert 202, 297–311
Lee, Roy Stuart 283
Lee Sing 67–76
legislation 67, 77, 97, 135, 334; *see also* immigration restrictions
Leung Du district 145, 222
Leung Pui 135–144, 219–227
Ling Tin Island 146
literacy 142
Liu, William J. 226
Loong Yee Tong society 291
lotteries *see* pak-ah-pu (lottery)
Luen Fook Tong society 291

Lum clan 159
Lum Jack Hing 56
Lung Du dialect 137, 155, 159
Lung Du district 68, 69, 72, 88, 91, 100, 136–141, 145, 155; see also Dai Laam village
Lung Hooey village 136, 222
Lung Ngan Sy Chung village 103, 157

Ma Ying Biu 105, 154
Macao 69, 74, 87, 90, 93, 141, 161, 163, 177, 221, 313–317, 327, 329, 345
Macgregor, Paul 5
Malay Australians 97, 246
Malaya 244, 350
Mao Tse-tung 170, 172, 307
Mao Yee Chut 160
market gardens 40, 44, 51, 61, 70, 137, 142, 184, 187, 205, 250, 251, 274, 281, 283, 288, 289, 313, 320; see also Wing Sang company
markets 103, 137; see also Wing Sang company
marriage 71, 103, 104, 126, 136, 142, 156, 158, 216–218, 227, 281, 283, 293, 298, 309, 326, 334, 337–340, 346–354, 354
Masons see Gee Gong Tong
May Thirtieth Movement 124, 139
Melbourne, VIC 43, 101, 104, 104, 304
military service 50, 166–178, 189, 216, 217–218, 230, 238, 244, 247, 253, 281, 284, 285, 300
Ming dynasty 87, 99, 151
Ming, Mavis vii–xii, 1–9, 10, 13–15, 17, 113, 127, 176, 357
mining 39, 44, 247, 333, 335; see also gold rushes
Mirriwinni, QLD 83
Moon family 163
moon festival 151, 279
Moree, NSW 184
Mossman, QLD 84, 197
Mount Isa, QLD 274, 276, 281, 289
multiculturalism 6–9, 13, 331, 356
Muswellbrook, NSW 163

Nam Hong village 168
Nam Yung village 150
Nanking 48, 130, 139
Nationalist Party see Kuomintang; see also Muswellbrook, NSW
New South Wales 39, 100
new year see Chinese New Year
New Zealand 138, 275, 276, 287
Newcastle, NSW 140, 141, 188
Ngoi Fuh 141

Nom Chong family 292
Northern Territory 189, 308, 309, 333–340, 343–354

opera 316
Ophir, NSW 273
opium 79, 146, 175, 181, 184, 187, 252
opium wars 87, 117, 124, 160, 331
Orange, NSW 273, 283, 283
Ou Yeung Mun Hing 43

pak-ah-pu (lottery) 81, 162, 306
Palmer River, QLD 297
Palmerston, NT see Darwin, NT
Pang clan 159
Pang Gin Ping 161
Parkee, Basil 44, 52, 306
Parkee, Cecil 53, 207, 213, 306
Parkee family 53
pastoral stations 297, 298, 300, 303
Pawngilly, QLD 83
Pearl River Delta viii, 4, 7, 14–15, 37, 87, 98, 105, 138, 219
pearling 243, 244, 246, 247
Perth, WA 97, 100, 103, 108–116, 159, 249–253
Philippines 70, 194, 244, 245
pigtail see queue (pigtail)
Pine Creek, NT 333
police 102, 111, 123, 187, 285
poll tax 102

Quan Mane family 54
Quan Mane, Winnie 249, 253
Queensland 67, 69, 100, 102, 297–311, 334
queue (pigtail) 136
Quong Tart 292

racism 4, 59, 74, 85, 108, 111, 120, 127, 131, 205, 247, 249, 281, 282, 283, 302, 324, 326, 331, 338, 343, 349
remittances 50, 71, 136, 138, 139, 145, 222, 245, 274, 308, 314
republican revolution (1911) 81, 88, 121, 122, 135, 136, 141, 145, 147, 155, 160
restaurants 52, 53, 56, 59, 62, 70, 75, 201, 206, 212, 214, 217, 236, 238, 292, 292, 306, 322, 324, 326, 326, 330; see also food
rice farming 42, 47, 72, 87, 90, 222, 227
Rolls, Eric 5
Rookwood Cemetery 15, 60, 149, 215, 227, 235, 296, 354

Index

Saah Kai village 136
Salvation Army 44, 60, 304
Sandalwood Islands *see* Hawai'i
Sang On Tiy & Co. 105
Sau Mei Yuen village 158
school 57, 81, 83, 88, 90, 91, 111, 126–131, 135, 138–141, 144, 163, 245, 246, 280, 302, 321, 324, 329, 336, 343, 345, 346, 349
secret societies 57; *see also* Hung League
See Yup dialect 83, 100, 118, 336, 344
See Yup district 40, 42, 70, 118, 243, 334, 353
Sha Chung village 99, 105, 120, 148, 154, 156
Shaang-Ki-Lung dialect 138; *see also* Lung Du dialect
Shameen village 160
Shanghai 46–48, 115, 117, 121–133, 179–183
Shanghai Wing On Company *see* Wing On & Co.
shearing 244, 281
Shek Joong village 244
Shekki 69, 72, 74, 83, 88, 91–93, 99, 121, 131, 136, 137, 140–141, 145, 161–164, 167, 204, 224, 227
Sheung Tong village 99, 101, 151
shopkeeping 230–231, 244, 253, 336
Shun Tak county 158
Sian Incident 176
Sincere Company 45, 105, 122, 128, 154
Singapore 97, 119, 243, 255
Sino–Japanese War 48, 62, 165–178, 181, 194, 291, 306, 307, 331
smuggling 222
South Australia 304, 333–334
sport 273, 280, 281, 282, 300, 306, 321, 325; *see also* Chinese Tennis Club
Stuart Town, NSW 10, 16, 273–296
sugar cane 70, 77, 80, 102, 200
Sun Company 45, 179, 187
Sun Sun Company 128
Sun Wooey county 40, 151, 245, 249, 314, 320
Sun Yat-sen 88, 91, 98, 139, 141, 147, 160, 165, 172
Sung dynasty 39, 44–46, 56, 59, 74, 83, 99, 150
swimming 80, 113
Sydney Chinese School 330
Sydney, NSW 39, 42, 212–218, 226–227, 229–242, 249, 305
   Alexandria 215, 232, 234, 239
   Arncliffe 311
   Ashfield 62
   Botany 61
   Burwood 215, 217, 230, 242
   Chinaman's Beach 258
   Coogee 305
   Double Bay 50
   Erskineville 234
   Flemington 52
   Glebe 232
   Haymarket 74, 135, 137, 184, 212, 249, 311
   Lidcombe 149
   Manly, Manly Vale 159, 190, 320, 324
   Newtown 282, 292
   Paddington 324, 326
   Paddy's Market 51
   Penrith 322–324
   Pyrmont 230, 232, 234
   Redfern 189
   Rocks, The 51
   Surry Hills 43, 51, 53, 58, 324
   Ultimo 52, 74, 104
   Waterloo 71, 232
   Woolloomooloo 203

Tai Po Kong district 298, 311
tailoring 244, 246, 343; *see also* clothing
Taiping rebellion 331
Taiwan 137
Tam Gong temple 315
Tamworth, NSW 43–45, 52, 187
Tasmania 305
taxi drivers 259
tea 40, 93, 111, 137, 260, 284
Teng Ka people 90
Tenterfield, NSW 102
Tit Sehng *see* Shekki
Tiy Sang 105
tobacco 44, 52
Toishan county 39, 83, 243, 343, 344, 347
Tong Ka district 90, 93, 141
Tong Shan county 137
Townsville, QLD 95, 201, 302
treaty ports 117
Tsai Ting-kai 48, 62, 173
Tung Koon county 52, 55, 61, 100, 184, 187, 213, 235, 260, 275, 288, 289, 291

unions 198, 202, 307, 308, 325, 325, 330, 353
University of Sydney 39, 42, 43, 44, 47, 189, 283

Victoria 39, 100, 244; *see also* Bendigo, VIC

Wah Loong Trading Company 329

Wang Gungwu 2
warlords 46, 122, 125, 130, 146, 165, 176, 219, 307
waterside workers 308
Wellington, NSW 273, 280, 288, 289
Western Australia 67, 97, 100, 111, 118, 243–253; *see also* Carnarvon, WA, Perth, WA
W.G. Pan Kee & Co. 184
whaling 249
White Australia policy 1, 6–13, 43, 51, 229, 313, 331
Whitlam, Gough 313, 327, 331
Williams, Michael 5
Wing Cheong Sing general store 343, 345
Wing Hing & Co. 97, 100, 103, 108, 109–116, 118, 159
Wing On department store 125, 128, 179–182
Wing On & Co. 40, 43, 45, 46, 48, 103, 105, 105, 107, 120, 121, 122, 145, 160, 179–183, 209
Wing On Savings Bank 125, 147, 161, 180
Wing Sang company 68, 70, 74, 103, 105, 105
Wing Yick Trading company 329
Wirth's Circus 201
Wong clan 274, 291, 347
Wong, Fred 202
Wong, Peter 313–332
Wong See family 54
Wong Wah Lai 276
Wong (William) Suey Ling 274
World War I 50, 81, 83, 112, 284, 285, 335
World War II 48, 50, 70, 74, 84, 125, 189, 207–217, 219–225, 244, 247, 281, 292, 306, 313–317, 325, 336
Wu Hop Trading Company 292, 329
Wyndham, WA 246, 251

Yang Fu-sheng 176
Yee Hing Company 57
Yeend, Norman 334–340
Yen, Mavis *see* Ming, Mavis
Yeung, Louey Ga 41
Yin Lo, Don 15, 207, 213–218, 229–238, 255–261
Yin Lo, Evelyn 51–65, 207–218, 229–242, 255, 264, 306
Yin, Louey *see* Yeung, Louey Ga
Yu Han-mou 175
Yuan dynasty 150
Yuan Shih-Kai government 141
Yuen clan 159
yum cha 94, 164, 174, 176, 184

Zhongshan 145; *see also* Shekki

www.ingramcontent.com/pod-product-compliance
Lightning Source LLC
Chambersburg PA
CBHW080611230426
43664CB00019B/2860